CONFLICT RESOLUTION QUARTERLY

Conflict Resolution Quarterly (ISSN 1536-5581) is published quarterly by Wiley Subscription Services, Inc., a Wiley company, at Jossey-Bass and the Association for Conflict Resolution. A subscription is included as a benefit of membership. For information about becoming a member of the Association for Conflict Resolution, please contact ACR's membership department at (202) 464-9700, or visit www.ACRnet.org.

Conflict Resolution Quarterly is indexed in PsycINFO, Sociological Abstracts, the National Child Support Enforcement Clearinghouse, and the International Bibliography of the Social Sciences.

TO ORDER subscriptions or single issues, please refer to the Ordering Information page at the back of this issue.

EDITORIAL CORRESPONDENCE: see the Information for Contributors pages at the back of this issue.

www.josseybass.com

CONTENTS

This special double issue of *Conflict Resolution Quarterly (CRQ),* "Conflict Resolution in the Field: Assessing the Past, Charting the Future," will be a resource to our field at a time when we are experiencing some profound changes, as Terry Amsler notes in the Final Comments section. It is always wise for a field to take stock of what it has accomplished, but it is essential to do so when questions of efficacy require cogent answers to continue to receive support for current and future efforts. Our field is in such a moment, and our future is colored by our ability to honestly portray the progress of our past.

The focus of this issue is twofold: (1) to report and critique existing field research in seven practice areas and (2) to suggest future directions for research, policy, and practice in each area. Respected scholars have provided review articles and commentaries in the areas of family, court, community, workplace, environmental, restorative justice, and conflict resolution education arenas. In each review article, a strong organizing principle was the emphasis on structural elements in the field that have an impact on the outcomes of conflict resolution practice. Review articles report comprehensive results from methodologically rigorous evaluations, with efforts to include unpublished sources such as dissertations, grant reports, and private organizations' evaluations. Due to space constraints, the review authors do not integrate the valuable research done in nonfield settings. To scholars and practitioners who are ably informed by this body of work, we certainly acknowledge its value and foundation as professionals use theory to inform practice.

It is tempting to summarize across a body of work as diverse and complex as that reported here. But any conclusion is too much of a gloss to be helpful. I encourage readers to carefully consider the conclusions offered in each practice area. My own assessment of this information is positive: the field of conflict resolution has proven itself in most areas. Still, we have not yet completely confirmed the true potential of our field to accomplish interpersonal and social change. There is much more to do.

I would like to acknowledge several people who made this issue possible. First and foremost is Lisa B. Bingham. This volume would not have happened without her vision and encouragement. Lisa proposed the original idea for the issue and provided generous financial support from her Hewlett funding at the Indiana Conflict Resolution Institute (ICRI). She acted as cocreator at every stage of development. My sincere thanks also go to Terry Amsler and the William and Flora Hewlett Foundation for approving the financial support for this issue offered by ICRI. Accomplishing a special double issue requires flexibility and support from both the journal owners and publishers, the Association for Conflict Resolution (ACR) and Jossey-Bass. Special personal thanks go to David Famiano, journals editor for *CRQ* at Jossey-Bass; Dawn Walker, production editor for *CRQ* at Jossey-Bass; and David Hart and Sangita Sigdyal at ACR. And finally, I appreciate and applaud all of the review authors and commentary writers in this issue. Their patience, productivity, and passion for honest critique in their areas of expertise is a model for scholars, and certainly for the editors who work with them.

TRICIA S. JONES
Editor-in-Chief

Family Mediation Research: Is There Empirical Support for the Field?

JOAN B. KELLY

When family mediation emerged on a national level twenty-five years ago, divorce mediation was promoted as less expensive and time-consuming, more humane and satisfying to participants than litigation, resulting in better compliance with agreements and reduced relitigation. It was expected to enhance problem-solving skills among the disputants, promote cooperation and communication regarding children, and result in better adjustment of adults and their children to the divorce and be more empowering of the participants than traditional adversarial processes.

Research was initiated in public and private sectors to assess these claims and to respond to the strident challenges and opposition to divorce mediation that quickly emerged. Lawyers were openly skeptical that the process was more fair and less costly. Women's advocates, who questioned women's ability to negotiate equitable arrangements with men, made policy pronouncements advising women against participating in mediation. Ironically, these claims were made in the absence of empirical studies assessing the fairness and impact of adversarial divorce processes on participants, including those with a history of domestic violence.

Early research focused on the basic questions of settlement rates, client satisfaction, time and cost efficiencies, comparison of outcomes, compliance, and, to a lesser extent, impacts on parental conflict, communication, cooperation, and psychological adjustment (see Beck and Sales, 2000; Emery, 1994; Kelly, 1996). This first-generation research, conducted in the United States, Canada, England, and Australia, constitutes the largest body of empirical research among any of the mediation sectors. Variations in research populations, methodologies, measures, and dispute settings have been the norm, making it problematic to generalize about family mediation or rely on a single study. Many research publications failed to provide basic descriptors, such as the nature of the population served, number of sessions and hours of service, the model (if any) mediators used, and whether premediation screening was used. Legal rules and cultural contexts of the jurisdictions that might affect outcomes were rarely described. Despite these problems, convergence on many questions has emerged over two decades, indicating that some major findings regarding family mediation are robust and replicable across settings.

This article summarizes a selected group of family mediation studies published over the past twenty years, with a focus on four custody mediation programs in the public sector, two studies of public and private sector comprehensive divorce mediation, and three court-connected programs for mediation of child protection or dependency disputes. Studies selected for inclusion had adequate sample sizes, objective measures, appropriate statistical analyses, and, when available, comparison groups and longitudinal designs. The primary structural elements described in the family mediation research have variously included the timing of intervention, whether it is voluntary, who pays, the level of self-determination, and the training of neutrals. The criteria used to determine the success most often have been settlement rates, satisfaction of participants, efficiencies in time and cost, and, to a lesser extent, evidence of changes in relationships and durability of settlement. Because most mediation in the custody and divorce family sector occurs between male and female parties without lawyers present, the issue of who can mediate has been an important one, and the nature of the disputes, domestic violence, and characteristics of the parties is described as available. It should be noted that all group or gender differences were statistically significant.

Custody Mediation in the Public Sector

Research on child custody mediation in the public sector has been concentrated primarily in California, Virginia, Canada, and several multiple jurisdictional studies.

Custody Mediation Research in the California Courts

California legislation mandated mediation for all separating parents with custody and visiting disputes, effective 1981. The Statewide Family Court Services, now the Center for Families, Children and the Courts (CFCC), initiated in 1991 a series of interlocking studies that provide a unique uniform statistical database consisting of representative and longitudinal data from nine data collections involving over eighteen thousand contested child custody cases that used mediation. Because mediation was mandatory, there was no litigation comparison group. These snapshot studies have described the population, services provided, case complexity, the usefulness of mediation for contested child disputes, and the participants' feedback about their experiences.[1]

Structural Elements of the Statewide Program. Custody mediation is an early intervention for disputing parents, who are required to schedule a mediation appointment within several weeks of filing a motion or petition. Attendance at one mediation session is mandated, and services must be provided free of charge. Subsequent legislation provided for separate sessions, opt-outs for parents, and special assessment for families where domestic violence was alleged or had occurred. When domestic violence was raised as an issue, in 57 percent of cases, parents attended separate mediation sessions (Center for Families, Children and Courts, 2002).

Parents can return to custody mediation following judicial settlement conferences and following divorce or final orders. Parents can opt to use private fee-for-service custody mediation, or settle through private ordering, but the majority of disputing parents use family court services. In 1996, 84,550 mediation cases were seen, and 26 percent of these were seeking a modification of existing orders (Center for Families, Children and Courts, Report 12, 2000).

Currently, in thirty-four of California's fifty-eight counties (C. Depner, personal communication, Dec. 8, 2003), mediators are authorized to make recommendations to the court for custody and visitation when parents are at impasse, whereas in the remaining counties, mediation is confidential. Thus, in "recommending" counties, mediation incorporates an evaluative component that most likely shapes the style of mediation offered. The extent of self-determination varies according to whether parents are able to reach partial or full agreement in mediation, must rely on either mediator recommendation or other more formal evaluative processes to have the issues resolved, or when allegations of child abuse or violence require temporary orders.

California statute provides that court mediators have a master's degree in family counseling or behavioral sciences. The number of mediators with extensive or formal mediation training is unclear, although all staff attend an annual three-day conference for mediators and family court judges. Mediators are salaried by the state, with the exception of those in rural counties with small populations, who serve on a contractual basis.

Participants in mediation have a right to counsel, but attorneys are rarely included in the mediation itself. In 53 percent of court family mediation cases, at least one parent is not represented, a trend that has increased over the years and is related in part to the lower socioeconomic status and higher unemployment rates of mediation participants, compared to statewide means (Center for Families, Children and Courts, 2000). The court custody mediation population is quite diverse: 48 percent white, 29 percent Hispanic, 8 percent African American, 4 percent Asian/Pacific Islander, 2 percent Native American, and 5 percent other. In contrast, 80 percent of custody mediators identify themselves as non-Hispanic white (Center for Families, Children and Courts, 2001). Despite efforts to hire bilingual mediators and recruit interpreters (one county had forty-seven languages represented among parents), language and cultural barriers remain a challenge.

The large numbers of parents reporting domestic violence present additional challenges. In the CFCC snapshot study, interparental violence was reported by at least one parent in 76 percent of the twenty-five hundred mothers and fathers. Sixteen percent of mothers and 8 percent of fathers reported violence during the prior six months. In 47 percent of mediated cases, at least one parent reported on the (independent) survey that violence had ever occurred, but neither parent raised domestic violence as an issue before or during the session.

Outcomes of Custody Mediations in California Courts. In California, custody mediation research reports on outcomes such as settlement rates, satisfaction, and changes in participant relationships.

• *Settlement rates.* In a two-week period of 1991, the snapshot study of 1,388 families in 1,388 mediation sessions (comprising 82 percent of all mediations during that period) reported that 55 percent of the families reached agreement. Among the 45 percent who did not reach agreement, more than one-quarter were scheduled for further mediation, but the number of those who settled in later mediations was unknown. The context for this settlement rate is that 48 percent characterized their interparental conflict as high, and more than half raised at least one serious issue (for example, child neglect or abuse or substance abuse). The most common issues raised were domestic violence (in 29 percent of cases), substance abuse (25 percent), and maligning (21 percent) or harassing (19 percent) the other parent. More than half of disputants were or had previously been protected by domestic violence restraining orders, and one-third reported serious concerns about a child's emotional well-being. On a level-of-difficulty scale (from 1 to 10), 2,812 mediators in the 1999 CFCC snapshot study rated 23 percent of their cases as a 9 or higher and 39 percent as an 8 or higher. Cases were rated higher in difficulty when one (32 percent) or both (26 percent) parents raised multiple serious issues, and at least half of difficult cases (rated 8–10) did not reach agreement in one mediation session (Center for Families, Children and Courts, 2003a). CFCC has recently decided that a single settlement rate statistic is no longer useful because of variations in case complexity, different services available in various courts, and legislative mandates requiring special assessments in domestic violence cases.

• *Satisfaction of participants.* The majority of over sixty-seven hundred mothers and fathers in the 1991 and 1993 snapshot studies reported substantial satisfaction on sixteen aspects of the mediation process and the outcomes (Statewide Office of Family Court Services, 1992; Center for Families, Children and Courts, 1993a). More than 90 percent of clients said the mediator explained mediation procedures clearly, treated them with respect, listened to their concerns, and tried to keep them focused on their children's interests. Seven in ten clients said the mediator helped them to see more ways to work together as parents. However, 13 percent of mothers and fathers complained that they felt pressured by the mediator to go along with things they did not want, and up to 17 percent felt rushed by the mediator. The percentage of dissatisfied clients is consistent with other studies. Overall, 86 percent of parents said they would recommend mediation to a friend. Gender differences appeared on four of sixteen indicators of client satisfaction. More women than men felt that the mediator listened to their concerns, and fathers were more likely to feel that mothers had an unfair advantage in mediation. Women were more likely than men to report that they felt too intimidated to say what they really felt in the 1991 study, but this difference was not replicated in the 1993 study (Center for Families, Children and Courts, 1993a). Subsequent analyses suggested that feelings of intimidation were related less to gender dynamics than to clients' education and financial resources. Ethnic and income differences in satisfaction also emerged, with mediation seen as more helpful in several dimensions by parents with less education and lower income and by ethnic minorities (Center for Families, Children and Courts, Report 3, 1994).

The issue of mediator recommendation to the court continues to be a controversial one among outside observers, but not apparently for the parties. Seventy-four percent of parents in "recommending" counties versus 78 percent of parents in "nonrecommending" (confidential) counties were satisfied with the process and outcomes, a nonsignificant difference. Reaching an agreement in mediation was the stronger determinant of client satisfaction, with client ratings overall approximately 12 percent higher when compared to those who remained at impasse and therefore had to use other more adversarial court processes to get their disputed issues resolved (Center for Families, Children and Courts, 1994b).

• *Changes in participants' relationships.* Follow-up studies with 1,532 parents two years later indicated a decline in measures of satisfaction, including whether mediation was a good way to come up with custody and visiting plans (93 versus 67 percent) and whether the agreement was perceived to be a fair one (87 versus 68 percent). Satisfaction remained higher among those who reached agreement, compared to clients who did not reach agreement in mediation and used other court processes, particularly for mothers. Fathers using other court processes were the least likely to view the results as fair (55 versus 63 percent of fathers reaching mediated agreements). On ratings of severity of family problems, such as violence and abuse, there were no differences between the two-parent groups, which might account for these different levels in satisfaction (Center for Families, Children and Courts, 1994b). A more recent study (Center for Families, Children and Courts, 2000) of client feedback indicates that satisfaction rates remain high across many measures of process, with participants with lower education and income, and being in pro per, more satisfied than better-educated, higher-income parents.

Follow-up studies of 1,532 parents two years after the 1991 data collection found that 51 percent of parents who did not reach mediated agreements reported that the way they arrived at custody agreements (mediator recommendation, judicial settlement, or custody evaluation) had a negative effect on their relationship with the other parent, compared to 42 percent of those mediating their agreements, a significant difference. And 55 percent of parents using mediation to reach agreements said the procedure helped them to work together as parents, compared to 34 percent of those using other legal processes.

• *Outcomes.* The range of agreements resulting from mediation is comparable to those in the general divorcing population, with the most common outcome being joint legal custody and mother physical custody (27 percent of families). Although critics of mediation have claimed that women are forced to agree to joint physical time-sharing arrangements, the California court data do not support that view, nor do the data already cited regarding women's satisfaction with the mediation process (see also Kelly and Duryee, 1992). Sixteen percent of parents chose a joint time-sharing arrangement (defined as eight to twenty overnights with the mother in a four-week period), which was most often linked to experience with de facto custody arrangements prior to mediation (Center for Families, Children and Courts, 1994a).

• *Compliance with agreements.* Mediation parents more often reported that the mediated agreement had sufficient detail to guide them, compared to those using other court methods (64 versus 53 percent), and 55 percent of parents did not report difficulties in compliance with their agreements. Among the 45 percent with problems reported in sticking with the visitation schedule, there were no differences between parents who mediated agreements and those using other court processes.

Mediation of Parenting Time and Responsibilities in a Colorado Court

In order to determine if mediation of parenting disputes produced measurable benefits to the Colorado courts, ninety-two mediation cases were compared to one hundred cases that had not participated in mediation (Thoennes, 2002a).

Structural Elements of the Colorado Project. Research was conducted in the Tenth Judicial District, where mediation of domestic relations disputes was the largest component of alternative dispute resolution (ADR) services offered. The mediation cases were systematically referred by the court in the early stages of the dissolution (generally within forty-five days of filing) during 1999–2000; the comparison cases in the study had filed for dissolution during 1996–1997 and had child-related disputes but either did not attend mediation (the majority) or did so only at a much later stage (typically five or more months after filing). Waivers to exempt parents from mediation could be obtained for domestic violence or where participation would be a hardship. The final research sample had ninety-two families in the mediation group and one hundred in the comparison group. Baseline comparisons of the two samples indicated no significant differences in income, length of marriage to filing, and number or age of children. Indicators of disputes about children were similar in both groups. The training and qualifications of the mediators are not reported, nor was type of mediation offered and role of the mediator described. The program charged fifty dollars per party per hour, unless parties were indigent (the fee was waived) or low income (the fee was halved). Parties had a right to counsel. Thirty-four percent of the mediation and 24 percent of the comparison cases had at least one parent without legal representation, more often father. Most cases were handled in one session of approximately two hours.

Outcomes of Mediations in Colorado Tenth Judicial District. The outcomes studied in the Colorado research focused less on participants' perceptions and more on effectiveness of dispute processing.

- *Settlement rates.* In 39 percent of cases, the parents reached full agreement on all issues, an additional 55 percent reached agreement on some issues, and 6 percent reached no agreements. Families reaching partial agreement returned to the court with stipulations regarding the settled disputes and had hearings to resolve the rest of the disputed issues.
- *Satisfaction and changes in relationships.* These were not assessed in this study.
- *Efficiencies in dispute processing.* On the first outcome criterion, the amount of time that cases were open, the mediation group had significantly fewer days between filing and final orders (the mean was 334) than did the comparison group (the mean was 395). On the second, stipulated agreements, the mediation group was significantly more likely to present stipulations on parental decision making, child residence, and child support than did the comparison group, which saved judicial and court time. On additional criteria, the mediation group was significantly less likely than the comparison group to have a continuance (15 versus 31 percent), filed fewer motions than the comparison group cases (means of 2.4 versus 3.6 motions filed), and more mediated cases filed no motions (21 versus 8 percent). Twelve percent of mediated cases filed five or more motions, whereas 25 percent of the comparison group filed five or more motions. Finally, the amount of hearing time scheduled was significantly less for the mediation group than the comparison group (2.0 hours versus 3.6 hours), and only 5 percent of mediation cases had hearings scheduled for a full day, compared with nearly 25 percent of the comparison group. Thus, mediation produced a more efficient and timely flow of cases, with fewer unexpected delays and motions.
- *Relitigation.* Rates of relitigation are often cited as a measure of mediation effectiveness.[2]

Charlottesville Custody Mediation Project

Parents filing a petition for a custody or visitation hearing in a central Virginia court between 1983 and 1986 were randomly assigned to mediation or litigation and invited to participate in a study. Few differences were found between those who agreed or refused to participate or between the two groups, who were predominantly young, working-class parents. Excluded from the mediation group were residents at a battered women's shelter or when a domestic violence or child abuse charge was pending. Some participants indicated during the mediation that they experienced violence earlier in the relationship (R. Emery, personal communication, Dec. 9, 2003). Thirty-six families proceeded through the usual court procedures and thirty-five families entered the mediation service. In a replication study, fifteen mediation and sixteen litigation families were combined with the original sample, resulting in a sample size for follow-up studies, after attrition, of seventy-one families. This is the only random assignment study of the relative effectiveness of custody mediation, and despite the small sample size, it merits attention (see Emery, 1994).

Structural Elements in the Charlottesville Study. Participants with custody or visitation disputes were recruited immediately prior to the initial court hearing. For the mediation families, mediation was an early voluntary intervention, whereas the litigation group proceeded through the usual court processes, typically using attorneys. Mediations were conducted by pairs of male and female comediators, all of whom had at least a master's degree in a mental health field and training in mediation. Mediation was free of charge and limited to six two-hour sessions. Participants completed mediation in an average of 2.4 meetings. All participants in the study had a right to counsel. Descriptions of mediation sessions indicate a mix of facilitative, education, and more directive styles of mediation.

Outcomes of Charlottesville Custody Mediation Project. The Charlottesville research investigated a broad array of outcomes.

- *Settlement rates.* In the mediation group, 77 percent of the thirty-five families reached either written or verbal agreement regarding their child issues. Only four of the eight families not reaching agreement proceeded to court. Among the litigation group, 72 percent appeared for hearings in domestic relations court for judicial determination.
- *Satisfaction of participants.* Mothers reported more satisfaction on a number of measures assessing both process and outcomes than men in both the mediation and litigation groups. Compared to fathers who litigated, fathers who mediated were substantially more satisfied on all nineteen measures, including aspects of the process, its effects on them, their relationship with their children, and their relationship with their former spouses. Fathers in the litigation group were significantly less likely to feel

their rights were protected compared to fathers in the mediation group or either group of women.

In comparison with mothers who litigated, mothers who mediated were less satisfied with the process, including the fairness of decisions, but they did not differ on feeling their rights had been protected. They were more satisfied than mothers who litigated on several other measures, including feeling understood, concern shown for self and for children, and whether problems were caused with their spouse (Emery, Matthews, and Wyer, 1991). At a one-year follow-up, mothers who mediated were less satisfied with the process and outcome of dispute resolution than they had been previously, but attrition of satisfied mothers in the follow-up sample may have contributed to this change (Emery, Matthews, and Kitzmann, 1994). Women in both groups remained more satisfied than fathers on a number of other measures of outcome, and "the majority of the study's findings point to the disadvantage of men in litigation, not to the disadvantage of women in mediation" (Emery, 1994, p. 187). Mediation parents more often reported that they each had won "somewhat" of what they wanted, compared to litigation parents, where mothers felt they had won "quite a bit" of what they wanted and fathers had won only "a little" (Emery, 1994), providing empirical support for the claim that mediation is more likely to produce modest win-win feelings in both parents rather than the widely divergent win-lose feelings characteristic of adversarial processes. Gender differences in satisfaction, or lack of them as in the California custody and comprehensive mediation studies (Center for Families, Children and Courts, 1993a; Kelly, 1989), must be set within the context of the legal and social climate of the research setting. California adopted gender-neutral statutes regarding custody much earlier than did Virginia, and permitted joint legal and physical custody options earlier than most other states. Sole maternal legal and physical custody was the most common outcome in Virginia at the time this study was conducted (Emery, 1994). In contrast, by 1990 in California, approximately 85 percent of parents had joint legal custody and reached access agreements (or had orders imposed) that reflected a broader array of access or shared physical custody arrangements.

• *Changes in conflict and parent-child relationships.* One of the most striking findings of this project was that fathers who mediated remained more involved with their children one year and twelve years later, compared to fathers in the litigation group (Emery, 1994; Emery and others, 2001). There were modest reductions in parent conflict in the mediation group that were sustained over the first postresolution year as well. Mediation did not differentially improve adult mental health compared to the litigation group.

- *Efficiencies in time.* Mediation settlements were reached in half of the time required by the litigation group, and significantly reduced the number of hearings needed in the court (Emery, Matthews, and Wyer, 1991).
- *Outcome patterns.* Whereas sole maternal physical custody was the predominant outcome for both groups, joint legal custody was more often an outcome in the mediation sample compared to the litigation group (Emery, Matthews, and Wyer, 1991). Actual parenting time was not substantively different in the two groups, including the number of days with the nonresidential parent. As in other studies (Ellis and Stuckless, 1996; Kelly, 1993), mediated agreements were more detailed as to days and times of transitions, other child-related details, and child support, whereas litigated agreements contained more vague language (for example, "reasonable visitation to the father").
- *Compliance.* Fathers who mediated complied more often with child support orders than did fathers who litigated (Emery, Matthews, and Kitzmann, 1994).

Access and Visitation Grant Mediation Programs

The U.S. Department of Health and Human Services (2002) funded studies in five states that provide access mediation to the IV-D population, with the objective of determining if mediation would facilitate and increase access rights for noncustodial parents and increase visitation. Findings were from 254 cases: 190 cases combined from four states (Nevada, Connecticut, Oklahoma, and Illinois), and 64 cases, analyzed separately because of programmatic differences, in Georgia.

Structural Elements of the Access and Visitation Mediation Programs. Randomly selected cases from nine community and court-based programs offering mediation for access problems in 2001 were examined. Participants were mothers and fathers in the IV-D program, a child support agency funded for collecting and enforcing child support orders. Mediation and court files and child support payment records were reviewed, and a telephone survey was conducted for 125 parents. Information was not provided on the timing of the intervention, or on the training, qualifications, or orientation of the mediators. Services were offered free of charge, and the average mediation session was 1.4 hours. In the majority of programs, referrals came from child support offices and the courts, and attendance was voluntary; three programs had mandatory participation.

Outcomes of DHHS Access and Visitation Program Research. Both settlement rates and satisfaction were studied in the DHHS research.

- *Settlement rates.* In 76 percent of cases, mediation facilitated noncustodial (NCP) parents' access rights through an agreement on visitation plans. In 69 percent of cases, NCPs had no prior access rights, and of these, 77 percent gained access in a mediated visitation agreement. Access rights increased from zero to nineteen hours, on average, for standard visitation and from zero to thirteen days for vacations and holidays. Of the 31 percent of NCPs with prior access rights, 74 percent successfully reached a visitation agreement in mediation with the custodial parent (CP), and in this group, there was slightly increased access (U.S. Department of Health and Human Services, 2002).

- *Satisfaction of participants.* Parents were asked to what extent they would recommend or advise against the mediation program. Eighty-one percent of CPs would strongly or somewhat recommend, with no difference between those who did and did not reach agreement. Among NCPs, 71 percent of NCPs would recommend, with 74 percent of those who reached agreement versus 59 percent who did not reach agreement indicating they would recommend mediation.

- *Outcome patterns.* In follow-up telephone surveys of one hundred cases, 42 percent of parents who reached an agreement reported an overall increase in noncustodial parents' visits following mediation. Gender differences were found, with 39 percent of CPs and 53 percent of NCPs reporting that visits increased. For 33 percent, visits stayed the same, most often those parents who reached no agreement, and 11 percent reported a decrease in visitations. In the six months after reaching a mediated agreement, the majority of both CPs and NCPs reported that more weekly visits occurred compared to the six months prior to mediation; in addition, visits were more regularly scheduled and were cancelled less often. One-third of CPs and two-thirds of NCPs who reported increased visits reported an improvement in their child's behavior after mediation.

Based on a subset of 111 cases from four states, 61 percent of NCPs increased the percentage of current child support they paid after mediation and 27 percent decreased the percentage. Prior to mediation, NCPs paid 52 percent of what was owed in child support; after mediation, NCPs paid 70 percent of what was owed, significantly above what the national child support system collects.

Comprehensive Divorce Mediation Projects

Far fewer studies have assessed comprehensive divorce mediation encompassing division of property, spousal and child support, and child custody and access issues. Comprehensive divorce mediation is most often offered in the private sector on a fee-for-service basis by lawyers and mental health professionals. The two studies considered here, the Divorce and Mediation Project in California (Kelly, 1989, 1990, 1991a, 1991b, 1993) and the Divorce Mediation Pilot Study in Ontario, Canada (Ellis, 1994; Ellis and Stuckless, 1996), represent a private and a public sector project.

California Divorce and Mediation Project

The Divorce and Mediation Project was a multidimensional study of the comparative legal, economic, psychological, and relationship effects of mediation and adversarial divorce on the participants during and after the divorce process. The longitudinal study collected data at five points in time, where time 1 was the beginning of divorce, time 3 final divorce, and time 5 two years after the final divorce. At time 1, the mediation sample consisted of 212 individuals (106 couples), and the adversarial divorce group consisted of 225 respondents (including 47 couples). The overall sample of 437 was mostly well educated, primarily white, and middle class. The mediation sample had more education and minor age children compared to the adversarial group, but median income did not differ, and there were no differences in amount of marital conflict or anger at spouse as reported at the beginning of divorce.

Structural Elements in the Divorce and Mediation Project. This study compared process and outcomes in the private sector for two groups: those who voluntarily chose to mediate their divorces from 1983 through 1985 at a nonprofit mediation center and agreed to participate in the study, and those who filed a divorce petition between 1984 and 1986, were randomly selected from court records, agreed to participate in the study, and had an attorney representing them in divorce proceedings. For the mediation couples, the timing of the intervention varied, as one-third of couples had not yet separated at entry into mediation and the remaining couples began mediation several months to more than a year after separation.

Comediations were conducted by a lawyer and two psychologists specifically trained in mediating property, support, and custody issues and with knowledge of family law. The mediation was a task-focused, facilitative, and problem-solving model, and responsibility for decision making remained with the parties on all issues. Final agreements were recorded in detailed memoranda of understanding, and any issues not resolved in mediation were left for subsequent attorney negotiations or court hearings. The average number of mediation sessions for those reaching agreement on all issues was ten (approximately fifteen hours), which varied with the legal and psychological complexity of issues, amount of conflict, and motivation of clients. Sliding-scale fees ranged from $40 to $120 per hour per couple, with an average fee per couple of $110 per hour, which was comparable to family law attorney fees at that time. Mediation respondents were encouraged to consult attorneys as needed and used counsel to prepare the legally binding marital settlement agreement and to file divorce papers. The mediation clients had high levels of self-determination with respect to selecting and ordering issues for discussion and negotiation, length of sessions, the pace of the mediation, the use of outside counsel and additional experts, and all temporary and final decisions.

Outcomes of California Divorce and Mediation Project. This comparative research provides insights on a variety of outcome measures.

- *Settlement rates.* Four groups were distinguished within the mediation sample. "Comprehensive completers" (50 percent) reached agreement on all issues pertaining to their divorces, resulting in a memorandum of understanding. They were not more cooperative than the other subgroups, but both spouses reported similar levels of knowledge about finances. A second group, "partial completers" (8 percent), were able to reach full written agreement within a particular area, usually custody and parenting or child support, but not reach full resolution on the other issues. This group was more likely to have attorneys active on their behalf prior to coming to mediation and had the largest discrepancy between the husbands' and wives' self-ratings of financial knowledge. Thus, the overall rate of reaching partial and full agreement was 58 percent. Among those who terminated mediation were two groups: the "productive terminators" (15 percent) resolved one or more critical issues, most often related to details of their separation including visitation or temporary support, but did not return to negotiate final divorce issues. This group scored highest on "interest in reconciliation," and a number later reached agreement on their own. The "true terminators" (26 percent) were unable to reach agreement on anything, and as a group they were more likely to report that they had an angry, demeaning spouse or an emotionally unstable, substance-abusing spouse. They also gave the lowest ratings of their spouses' honesty, fair-mindedness, and level of cooperation. These settlement rates are somewhat lower than rates reported in the court-based custody mediation studies in Virginia and Colorado but comparable to a large Canadian study of court-based comprehensive divorce mediation, which found full agreement in 49 percent of cases, partial agreement on 15 percent, and 64 percent when combined (Richardson, 1988). Comprehensive divorce mediation involves settling multiple complex issues, which requires an ability to comprehend all the issues and remain in mediation for the longer course.

• *Satisfaction with mediation.* Significant group differences were found on eighteen of forty items from a fifty-four-item Client Assessment of Mediation Services (CAMS) scale assessing participants' perceptions of and satisfaction with their respective divorce processes (see Kelly and Gigy, 1988; Kelly, 1989). Between 65 and 82 percent of all respondents viewed their mediators and attorneys as warm, sympathetic, and sensitive to feelings; helpful in standing up for their rights in disagreements with spouses; staying focused on the important issues; and having clear and sufficient information for decision making, with no group differences. The mediation group rated their mediators as more skillful and more helpful in proposing ways to resolve disagreements and getting to workable compromises, compared to the litigation group ratings of their attorneys. Mediation clients, particularly women, viewed mediation as more empowering than did the adversarial men and women in helping them assume greater responsibility in managing their financial affairs, and in better understanding their spouses' points of view. Men in both groups rated their attorneys or mediators as more often favoring their spouses' point of view than did the women, but there were no sex differences within just the mediation group. Seventy-six percent of mediation women and 62 percent of the men indicated that mediation helped them to become more reasonable with each other, compared to 26 and 39 percent of the adversarial men and women, respectively. More than half of the adversarial group reported that the divorce process had caused a deterioration in their communication compared to 11 percent of the mediation group. Finally, on a global measure of satisfaction, 69 percent of mediation respondents were somewhat to very satisfied, compared to 47 percent of adversarial men and women, with no sex differences.

• *Changes in conflict and coparental relationships.* Mediation respondents with minor children reported less conflict during the divorce process, at final divorce, and in the first year after final divorce on a number of measures compared to parents in the adversarial group. Since there were no group differences at time 1 on these measures, it appeared that mediation had the effect of diffusing and reducing interparental conflict, compared to the adversarial process, at least for a period of more than two years. By two years postdivorce, there were no longer any group differences in frequency of conflict, as the adversarial group gradually reduced their conflict. However, when conflict occurred, the mediation parents used a more direct and mutual style of resolving their conflict, compared to the adversarial parents, who most often avoided each other (Kelly, 1991a).

Compared to the adversarial process, mediation was more effective in increasing the general level of cooperation between beginning of divorce and final divorce, after controlling for initial baseline differences. These differences were still evident at the end of the first year of divorce but were no longer significant two years postdivorce. However, mediation parents continued at two years postdivorce to seek parenting help from each other more often than the adversarial parents, were more likely to accommodate any requested changes in parenting schedules, and could communicate by telephone with their children whenever they or the children wanted to compared to adversarial parents (Kelly, 1991a). These findings may be related to the fact that at final divorce, the mediation group indicated more beneficial effects on their ability to be reasonable with each other and that communication improved somewhat compared to the adversarial respondents. They also perceived their former spouses as less angry, even though objective measures of anger of former spouse did not significantly differ (Kelly, 1989).

Divorce mediation was not more beneficial than the adversarial process on a number of standardized and objective measures of psychological adjustment. Instead, the passage of time was associated with a reduction of symptoms, such as depression, anxiety, and paranoia, for both groups at final divorce, and at one and two years postdivorce (Kelly, 1990, 1991a). Furthermore, no changes in children's adjustment were associated with either dispute process. Similar findings were reported elsewhere (Emery, 1994; Walker, McCarthy, and Timms, 1994). The claims that mediation would improve psychological adjustment were quite unrealistic, particularly given the specific dispute resolution focus of mediation and the brevity of the intervention.

- *Efficiencies in time.* No differences were evident in the length of time it took mediation and adversarial group respondents to obtain their final divorce. There were, however, significant links between marital and psychological variables and the number of hours required to complete mediation and the costs associated with adversarial divorce.
- *Outcome patterns.* In mediation, parents agreed to joint legal custody more often than did the adversarial parent group, as was reported in other studies (Emery, 1994; Pearson, 1991; Richardson, 1988). Mediation also resulted in parenting plans that were more generous in parenting time with children for the noncustodial parent (Kelly, 1993). Mediation parents more often negotiated fathers' time with children in the range of 20 to 39 percent, compared to the adversarial parent outcomes, in which fathers more often had time with their children between 0 and 20 percent (every other weekend or less). These findings of more time allocated between fathers and children in the mediation sample are in contrast to Emery's custody mediation study (1994), where contact with children every other weekend was most common in both groups. Mediators in that project discouraged parents from negotiating more extended contacts or shared physical custody parenting when there was high conflict or other difficult issues, which may have contributed to the differences (Emery, 1994). In the California study, mediators did not directly caution parents who were discussing higher amounts of parenting time with fathers, but focused on creating conflict-free transitions of children and parental communication regarding their children. The agreements of mediation parents contained much greater specificity about decision making regarding children, parenting plan details, and parental responsibilities for health insurance and unreimbursed medical costs.

No differences were found in child support between mediation and adversarial groups, but the mediation fathers did pay for more "extras" for their children, including lessons and extracurricular activities, and were more likely to make some agreements regarding their children's college expenses and support beyond age eighteen than did the adversarial group. More recent research suggests that such extras may be associated with fathers' having more time with their children rather than an effect of mediation (Fabricius and Braver, 2003). No analysis of property division was conducted because of the complexity of analysis required and some expectation that the fifty-fifty community property division laws might not result in differences between the two processes (Pearson, 1991). The mediation clients rated their division of property as fairer than did the adversarial respondents (Kelly, 1990).

- *Cost savings.* The combined couple costs for the adversarial group were 134 percent higher than for the mediation group, despite comparable hourly fees for both groups. For the mediation group, total costs included all mediation hourly fees (the mean was $2,224), and external consulting attorney, accountant, and appraisal fees associated with the divorce for each spouse, for a mean total of $5,234 (the median was $3,428). The mean total costs for couples in the adversarial sample were $12,226 (for men, $6,850; for women, $5,376). The two groups did not differ on a divorce issues complexity scale or in the extent of marital conflict, initial level of anger at spouses, cooperation at beginning of divorce, amount of anticipated disagreement about issues to be resolved, or household income (Kelly, 1991). Thus, there is strong support for assuming that the differential cost of divorce was the result of the mediation process itself.

The inclusion of marital and psychological variables in this research provided a unique opportunity to explore divorce costs related to other dimensions. When spouses in mediation reported that they divorced primarily because of a high-conflict or demeaning relationship or because of a substance-abusing or emotionally unstable spouse, mediation took longer and therefore cost more (see Gigy and Kelly, 1992, for analyses of reasons for divorce). Similarly, poorer-quality marital communication, poorer cooperation, and perceptions of the spouse as dishonest, or taking advantage of the respondent, or lacking in fair-mindedness were all associated with longer and more costly mediations, although these partners did manage to complete the process. In contrast, mediation clients who rated their spouses as "good spouses" (a three-item scale measuring flexibility, fair-mindedness, and ability to compromise) had lower mediation costs. Interestingly, neither depression nor level of anger toward the spouse correlated with the time required to complete mediation (Kelly, 1990). Among the adversarial sample, attorney fees were higher for the men when they rated their spouses as dishonest and felt taken advantage of by them. For women, higher legal fees were associated with being angrier at their spouses, perceiving their spouses to be dishonest, lacking in fair-mindedness, and to have taken advantage of them during the marriage. In the adversarial group, neither level of cooperation nor reason for divorce was related to attorney fees.

- *Compliance.* The majority of respondents in both groups were complying with the terms of their final divorce orders, perhaps consistent with the relatively advantaged socioeconomic status of participants. But there was significantly more compliance immediately after divorce in the mediation group on an eleven-item compliance scale, compared to the adversarial sample, and more compliance on the separate items of paying spousal support, final division of personal property and household furnishings, and division of community property. These differences were still evident at one year postdivorce but disappeared at two years postdivorce, in part because the adversarial group become more compliant over time in child support payments. Women in both groups reported less compliance with child support orders than did men. Noncompliance in the mediation group was primarily late payments, whereas in the adversarial group, noncompliance was nonpayment or paying less than ordered. Many variables expected to contribute to noncompliance at two years postdivorce did not, including satisfaction with the divorce outcome, divorce process group, conflict in the marriage, and the amount of anger at spouse at final divorce and two years later.

Family Mediation Pilot Project-Ontario, Canada

This study focused on 361 men and women who were means tested and approved to receive a legal aid certificate for immediate assistance with separation and divorce, and who selected either a lawyer negotiation or mediation path for resolution of their disputed issues. Canadian lawyers are required by law to describe mediation as one option for resolving marital matters.

Structural Elements of the Family Mediation Pilot Project. Participants in this court-connected mediation study were voluntary and self-selected into either a mediation or adversarial sample on the basis of the information provided by lawyers and on referral from the court. Spouses indicating an interest in using mediation had the opportunity to attend a separate family law information meeting prior to beginning mediation, followed by an individual interview and screening for abuse and large power imbalances to confirm the choice and feasibility of mediation. Some settings used open mediation, involving recommendation to the court, and others were closed mediations, that is, confidential. Clients who selected lawyer negotiations were seen in the attorney's private practice. Services for both groups were offered free of charge.

The Hamilton Unified Family Court mediation settings offered comprehensive mediation for custody and access, support, and property division. More than two-thirds of clients in both samples indicated that access (visiting) was the major issue to be settled, 40 percent wanted the issues of custody and child support settled, and 10 percent wanted spousal support settled. The timing of both interventions was from five to twelve months after separation disputes were apparent, during which time some participants initiated motions and other legal action. Clients who chose lawyer negotiations were poorer, less well educated, had been separated for a longer period of time, and had been more recently abused by their partners, compared with those who chose mediation. Women were also more likely to choose lawyer negotiations than were men (Ellis, 1996). Mediators were trained and experienced in family law mediations.

Outcomes of Family Mediation Pilot Project. The Family Mediation Pilot Project studied standard outcomes like settlement rates and satisfaction, but also looked at spousal violence rates.

• *Settlement rates.* Along the four major issues of access, custody, child support, and property division, settlement rates in the mediation sample ranged from 40 to 80 percent, with an average rate of 60 percent, compared to approximately 80 percent in the lawyer negotiation group. Settlement rates were higher when mediation occurred prior to parties' being involved in any legal proceedings.

• *Satisfaction with process.* Among the 169 mediation clients, 66 percent indicated they participated in a process they judged to be the best way for them, in contrast to 48 percent of the 192 lawyer clients who thought that process was the best way. Far more lawyer than mediation clients indicated they had participated in a process they believed was the worst way for them to settle issues of separation and divorce (28 versus 1 percent). Clients who reached agreement in both processes were more satisfied than those who did not, and mediation clients were more satisfied than those participating in adversarial processes (Kelly, 1989). On each separate issue in contention, the percentage of satisfied mediation clients was higher than the settlement rate percentage. In contrast, in the lawyer negotiation group, satisfaction percentages were lower than settlement rates in each area, with the exception of custody, where women in the lawyer group were more satisfied than the men, and the men and women in the mediation group. These women were most likely to petition for and receive sole custody through negotiations, hearings, or trial compared to the mediation group. The least satisfied of all groups were men in the adversarial group, also reported elsewhere (Emery, 1994; Kelly, 1989). In the Canadian study, when lawyers participated in mediation sessions as comediators (and gave advice), mediation clients were less satisfied than were clients where no lawyers (or judges) were involved.

- *Spousal violence.* Three forms of abuse (emotional, verbal, and physical) were studied pre- and postprocessing for both groups. On a four-item composite abuse scale (also including intentional hurting), a greater number of mediation clients reported being physically, emotionally, and verbally abused prior to the mediation than did lawyer clients. However, the differences were no longer significant postintervention, suggesting that mediation made a greater contribution to reducing the violence than did lawyer processing. The use of affidavits (declarations) in the lawyer process that were personally attacking and hurtful rather than fact based accounted in part for the continuing violence in the lawyer group (Ellis and Stuckless, 1992). The most important factor responsible for decreases in abuse postintervention was physical separation, which decreased opportunities for both conflict-instigated and control-instigated abuse in both groups. All three forms of abuse decreased over time following the lawyer and mediation processes, with verbal and emotional abuse decreasing more for mediation clients in the first twelve months (Ellis and Stuckless, 1996). These researchers (1992) also found more postprocess violence in a one-session coerced mediation provided by Legal Aid when compared to court-connected voluntary mediation (publicly funded) averaging six sessions.

- *Outcome patterns.* Women in the mediation sample were more likely to get (and be satisfied with) the child support amount they wanted compared to the adversarial women. A greater proportion of adversarial group women got the sole custody they wanted compared to the mediation women (85 versus 67 percent). More joint legal custody agreements were reached in the mediation group than in the lawyer negotiation group, similar to Emery (1994) and Kelly (1990, 1993). In the mediation sample, abused and nonabused wives were equally likely to say that they were equal to or better able than their partners to stand up for themselves and state their positions (Ellis and Stuckless, 1996). Differences between husbands and wives in the mediation group in income and various measures of marital power were not significant predictors of custody, access, support, or property division outcomes.

- *Compliance.* Compliance problems were reported in greater numbers in the adversarial compared to the mediation group, and within the mediation group, those participating in one-session mediations reported more compliance problems than did those in multiple sessions. Wife abuse during the six months prior to separation was a significant predictor of compliance problems reported by female mediation clients. As in the California study, the presence of children was associated with more compliance problems.

Child Protection Mediation

In response to an increase in child maltreatment filings in the 1980s and the recognition that traditional adversarial processes had serious limitations in settling these cases, a number of courts initiated programs that offered mediation in the dependency courts. The earliest program was started in 1983 in Los Angeles Juvenile Court, and twenty-one programs were operating in California in 2002 (Center for Families, Children and Courts, 2003b). Three research programs in California, Colorado, and Ohio are described.

Child Protection Mediation in Five California Courts

Five pilot child protection mediation programs were given the opportunity to customize their services based on their own needs and caseloads. Four programs used mediation at the first major legal step: whether the child in out-of-home placement should be placed under the authority of the court. Mediation occurred at the next major step of case disposition in nearly all the counties, when a plan was developed to indicate which programs and services parents would need to attend to aid in reunification with the child. Most often, both the petition and the treatment plan were mediated in the same session. Several courts also used mediation at later stages in the cases, including at the permanency planning hearing, and dealt with noncompliance and problems with the placements (Thoennes, 1997).

Judges had discretion to refer cases to mediation, typically when jurisdiction and disposition were contested, and parent participation was mandatory with such referrals. Additional participants often included a representative of the child protection agency, the parents' attorneys, or other family caretakers. A confidential facilitative mediation model, free for parents, was provided by trained and experienced mediators in teams or solo, generally for more than ninety minutes. Data were collected for 606 mediated cases and 223 nonmediated cases.

Outcomes of California Child Protection Mediation Project Evaluation

Outcomes in child protection mediation are similar to those studied in other forms of family mediation.

- *Settlement rates.* Based on mediator ratings, between 60 and 80 percent of cases reached full agreements, and 90 percent reached some form of agreement. Cases were more likely to settle at the disposition or postdisposition stages rather than earlier. These families had serious problems: many had been in the child protection system before, half had a known drug problem, and one-third had been the subject of a criminal court filing (Thoennes, 1997).

- *Satisfaction.* More than 90 percent of parents felt that they had been understood in mediation, had a chance to talk about important issues, and felt mediation clarified what they needed to do in order for the agency to close their case. Most parents felt mediation was better than a court hearing. Initial resistance among all professionals to participating in mediation was short-lived.

- *Outcome patterns.* Mediated agreements were more detailed on specifics of visitation arrangements and more generous, and they included more specific services to be provided to the child when compared to non-mediated agreements. In addition, communication problems between parents and caseworkers were more often addressed, and parents were more likely to acknowledge that they needed to cooperate with the treatment plan and needed help in changing behaviors.

- *Cost savings.* Mediation of child protection cases in the long run appeared to help courts avoid repeated hearings on the same case. At six months postdisposition, based on data from four sites, 88 percent of the mediated cases did not require a contested review compared to 53 percent of the control cases. Many professional participants cautioned that while mediation may avoid repeat hearings and three- to four-day trials, appropriate mediation services take resources and commitment to making it work.

- *Compliance.* Combined site data indicated that there was complete compliance for 42 percent of the mediation cases compared to 25 percent of the comparison group at six-months postdisposition.

Child Protection Mediation in the Colorado Fourth Judicial District

Information from 243 child protection mediations completed between 1997 and 1999 and 49 cases from court records of comparable cases without mediation that had court action between 1997 and 1998 was collected to assess the effectiveness of mediated cases and participants' reactions (Thoennes, 2000).

Structural Elements in the Colorado Program. Mediated cases were evenly divided between predisposition and postdisposition cases and between families that been the subject of previous dependency filings and those that were in the court system for the first time. All cases in which a contested hearing or trial was requested were automatically ordered into mediation by judges. The most common types of maltreatment alleged were neglect (61 percent) and physical abuse (29 percent), and the majority of parents were rated as having major problems such as substance abuse or mental disabilities. The average mediation was 1.8 hours (the range was one to five sessions), with most cases resolved in a single session (Thoennes, 2000). Mediators were experienced professionals who viewed their role as a facilitator, not an evaluator or decision maker. The average number of participants in the mediation was 6.5, with a mean of 4.3 professionals in attendance.

Outcomes of Colorado Fourth Judicial District Child Protection Mediation. This research reports positive effects of child protection mediation.

• *Settlement rates.* Nearly 70 percent of the mediation cases reached consensus about all issues pending in the case, 20 percent reached partial agreement, and 11 percent reached no agreement in mediation. Settlement rates did not differ based on type of maltreatment, the stage at which the case was mediated, or the issues being discussed.

• *Satisfaction.* Initial reservations of professional participants about mediating these cases were significantly diminished, with professionals indicating they would not want to return to adversarial processes for handling these cases. Mediation provided a critical time in a child protection case when everyone was present and prepared to discuss the case.

• *Cost efficiencies.* Using conservative cost estimates of avoidance of trials, expert witnesses and repeated psychological evaluations, and trial preparation time for attorneys and caseworkers, analyses projected that the child protection mediations allowed the Fourth Judicial District to reduce its cost per case by 13 percent.

Hamilton County Permanent Custody Mediation Program

The Juvenile Court of Hamilton County (Cincinnati, Ohio) received U.S. Department of Health and Human Services funding to provide and evaluate mediation services to families that were the subject of permanent custody filings. Cases randomly assigned to the mediation and control groups resulted in forty-nine cases with a permanent custody mediation and thirty-seven comparable cases assigned to the control group. The focus of the study was whether mediation would shorten the time between filing and the termination hearing, whether biological parents in mediation would be more involved in the permanency planning process, and whether mediated termination agreements would include more provisions for information sharing or some contact between adoptive parents and biological parents.

Structural Elements in the Permanent Custody Mediation Program. This program compared mediated and contested cases in the last and most difficult stage of child protection cases, that of a filing for termination of parental rights. Parent participation was mandated, and mediations usually included the mother, mother's attorney, caseworker, attorney for the agency, and the child's advocate. Fathers attended in 38 percent of mediated cases.

Mediators used a facilitative model of confidential mediation and emphasized that parents had the right to choose not to make an agreement and the right to go to court. Parents were informed about binding and nonbinding agreements and the permanency of termination of parental rights. If an agreement was reached, parents would meet immediately with the magistrate and have the stipulated agreement entered into the court record if it was determined that they understood the terms of the agreement, had entered into it voluntarily, and alternatively could go to court. Mediators were required to have fifty-two hours of mediation training and a four-day training specific to child protection laws, roles and practices, types of cases, and violence, and comediated with experienced dependency mediators.

Outcomes of the Permanent Custody Mediation Program. As with other forms of family mediation, the results of this research confirm mediation efficacy.

- *Settlement rates.* Nearly 40 percent of mediated cases reached an agreement about permanent custody, which is remarkable given the emotionally difficult issue in dispute. While settlement did not appear to be influenced by the type of maltreatment, a prior history of child protection reports, or mental or physical health issues for the children, the length of time a child had been in out-of-home placement was related to settlement, with a settlement rate of 57 percent among those with children in placement for more than a year versus 31 percent for those in placement for less than a year. The settlement rate was also higher in families where just one child was the subject of the permanent custody filing (56 percent), as contrasted to a 30 percent settlement rate when two or more children were involved (Thoennes, 2002b). In approximately half of cases mediating agreement that discussed open adoption, some form of continued visiting or periodic exchanges of written information was agreed on, the former more often with children permanently placed with relatives.

- *Satisfaction of participants.* Most parents expressed satisfaction with aspects of the process, saying they felt heard and understood (74 percent), were given a chance to talk about what they really wanted (87 percent), and were treated with respect (83 percent). Overall, nearly 70 percent of parents felt mediation was better than going to court, with satisfaction higher among the settlement group. Despite disapproval of mediation at the beginning, rates of satisfaction among professionals ranged from 70 to 100 percent (Thoennes, 2002b).

- *Efficiencies in time and money.* About 70 percent of cases reaching agreement proceeded directly to the court to enter the agreement on the record. Using an analysis of estimated costs per case in mediation and the comparison sample, the resolution by mediation of a permanent custody case was estimated to cost 39 percent less than processing a case in the absence of mediation (Thoennes, 2002b).

Summary of Findings

Using a variety of methodologies, measures, and samples, the nine studies described suggest strong support for the use of mediation in family disputes. In public and private sectors, in voluntary and mandatory services, and when provided both early and late in the natural course of these disputes, family mediation has been consistently successful in resolving custody and access disputes, comprehensive divorce disputes, and child protection disputes. Mediation has given evidence of its power to settle complex, highly emotional disputes and reach agreements that are generally durable.

Settlement rates in custody, comprehensive divorce, and child protection mediations generally range between 50 and 90 percent, with the exception of the most difficult cases involving parental termination. Mediation appears to work with angry clients and sometimes for those with serious psychological and family problems. What is required are experienced and trained mediators. However, profound distrust and a lack of fairmindedness on the part of one or both partners more often interfere with reaching agreements (as is true in litigation processes as well).

Client satisfaction has been surprisingly high in all studies and settings on a large number of process and outcome measures. As would be expected, satisfaction is higher when clients reach agreement as opposed to no agreement, and those who use custody mediation are substantially more satisfied than parents using other court processes. Repeatedly, clients indicated that they felt heard, respected, given a chance to say what is important, not pressured to reach agreements, helped to work together as parents, and felt their agreements would be good for their children. Mediation clients in the private sector are significantly more satisfied on almost all measures of process and outcome than are those using adversarial divorce processes. Where gender differences in satisfaction were found, the legal context appears to be an important factor, as are the issues in dispute.

While mediation does not improve psychological adjustment in measurable ways, there are other important benefits for all family members. When contrasted to parents in adversarial processes, parents using a more extended mediation process experience a decrease in conflict during divorce, and in the first year or two following divorce, they are more cooperative and supportive of each other as parents and communicate more regarding their children, after controlling for any preintervention group differences. One astonishing result has been that twelve years following divorce, fathers in mediation remained more involved with their children compared to the litigation fathers.

Cautions as well emerge from the literature. Consistently, 15 to 20 percent of parents of both sexes are dissatisfied with aspects of mediation process and outcomes. Although this represents half the rate of dissatisfaction of adversarial clients, it is important to know if this reflects a more rushed or coercive mediation process, untrained or inept mediators, or parents who are angry and dissatisfied with any divorce process and outcome that does not produce what they expected or wanted. With the trend to limit court custody mediation to one session, more difficult cases with multiple serious issues most likely will not be given sufficient opportunity to settle, and settlement rates may decline.

Future Directions in Family Mediation Research

Family mediation research has been elucidating and promising, and has generated far more understanding than the scant and mostly superficial assessments of various adversarial divorce processes, arbitration, or collaborative law. To date, however, this research has not led to more complex second-generation research, in part due to a chronic lack of research funding for mediation, the complexity of what is required, and an apparent diminishing interest in research questions in the field.

Among the issues that need investigation are the relative merits of different mediation models used in family mediation, including facilitative, problem-solving, transformative, and more evaluative models of mediation (for descriptions of these models, see Folberg, Milne, and Salem, 2004). No empirical research exists that explores and compares the efficacy of these different models, the purity of their processes and practices, for whom and what type of disputes they are most effective, and their respective outcomes. This is surprising given the ongoing and somewhat contentious debate regarding these models. No research has yet investigated the relative effectiveness of mediation models that work with couples conjointly compared to models that use separate sessions exclusively. Are there different outcomes in client conflict, cooperation, and postdivorce communication for parents? Newer hybrid models, such as parenting coordination, which combine mediation, arbitration, and education for high-conflict parents, have also received little research attention (Kelly, 2002). The exception has been research conducted on specialized strategies and mediation models developed for high-conflict and violent parents who continue to chronically litigate child issues after the divorce (Johnston, 1994; Johnston and Campbell, 1988; Kelly, 2002; Smyth and Moloney, 2003; Pruett and Johnston, 2004). These more intensive therapeutic mediation models, typically longer in length, integrate individual and group mediation sessions with counseling and have been demonstrated to be effective with this difficult population.

A related issue is what type of mediation models and services are necessary and most effective for participants when there is a history of domestic violence, particularly since a sizable number of both women and men enter, and sometimes prefer, mediation to other adversarial alternatives (Ellis and Stuckless, 1996; Newmark, Harrell, and Salem, 1995). Since many states quickly passed legislation prohibiting custody mediation where domestic violence had occurred or was alleged, further study was discouraged. These statutes and policies were based on the belief that domestic violence was primarily that of males battering women. Recent research documents other less severe, nonescalating, and more commonly occurring categories of violence in relationships, including bidirectional or common couple violence, female violence, and separation-engendered violence, each with its distinctive features and histories. Among these partners are many who are not afraid of each other, cease their violence at separation, and are capable of mediating (see Johnson and Ferraro, 2000; Johnston and Campbell, 1993; Statistics Canada, 2001).

Research in mediation process issues remains quite limited, in part because such research is complex, expensive, and time-consuming (Kelly, 1996). The field would be advanced considerably if analyses were conducted of mediator behaviors and interventions, participant characteristics and behaviors, and the relationship of these to outcomes. As an example of the latter, couples with high mean dyad levels of anger did less problem solving, as did those with higher mean contentious behaviors, compared to those with disparate levels of anger. Each of these was among the best predictors of failure to reach agreement (Bickerdike and Littlefield, 2000). Such research has implications for mediation process and the active use of mediator techniques such as conflict management and structuring behaviors. Understanding the interaction of emotions and personality attributes that individuals bring to the mediation setting, and the styles and behaviors of mediators that diminish or enhance the likelihood of reaching agreements, would help the field define and refine practices, improve effectiveness, and promote excellence in the field.

Notes

1. Research was conducted under the auspices of the Administrative Offices of the Courts, Judicial Council of California. See www.courtinfo.ca.gov/programs/cfcc/resources/publications/articles.

2. Relitigation rates in child custody matters do not necessarily represent a failure or breakdown of the mediation agreement, or, for that matter, a failure of attorney-negotiated or judicially imposed orders. Relitigation may serve legitimate purposes and point to breakdowns in agreements among contentious parents. Some parents must relitigate when a parent relocates to modify future parenting arrangements, others return to renegotiate a more appropriate parenting plan as children's developmental needs change, and still others return when parents are not meeting their parenting responsibilities or are interfering with access. In Colorado, in the first two years following final divorce orders, 38 percent of the comparison group returned to court compared to 24 percent of the mediation group. On three specific issues relitigated (parenting time modifications, child support contempt, and other modifications), significant differences again favored the mediation group (Thoennes, 2002). In the Charlottesville project, relitigation rates were quite high in both groups during the first two years (nearly two-thirds returned to court). In contrast, in the California divorce and mediation project, at one and two years

postdivorce, relitigation rates were much lower in both groups (15 percent of all respondents and 20 percent among the parent subsample). In the Canadian study, adversarial clients reported higher rates of relitigation during the first two years postdivorce, but by five years after divorce, there were no differences, as 10 percent in both groups returned to court (Ellis, 1996).

References

Beck, C.J.A., and Sales, B. D. "A Critical Reappraisal of Divorce Mediation Research and Policy." *Psychology, Public Policy, and Law,* 2000, *6* (4), 989–1056.

Bickerdike, A. J., and Littlefield, L. "Divorce Adjustment and Mediation: Theoretically Grounded Process Research." *Mediation Quarterly,* 2000, *18* (2), 181–201.

Center for Families, Children and Courts. *Client Evaluations of Mediation Services: Perspectives of Mothers and Fathers.* San Francisco: Administrative Office of the Court, Judicial Council of California, 1993a.

Center for Families, Children and Courts. *Client Evaluations of Mediation Services: The Impact of Case Characteristics and Mediation Service Models.* San Francisco: Administrative Office of the Court, Judicial Council of California, 1993b.

Center for Families, Children and Courts. *Mediated Agreements on Child Custody and Visitation.* San Francisco: Administrative Office of the Court, Judicial Council of California, 1994a.

Center for Families, Children and Courts. *Client Feedback: Retrospective Results from the California Child Custody Project.* San Francisco: Administrative Office of the Court, Judicial Council of California, 1994b.

Center for Families, Children and Courts. *Preparing Court-Based Child-Custody Mediation Services for the Future.* San Francisco: Administrative Office of the Court, Judicial Council of California, 2000.

Center for Families, Children and Courts. *Custody Mediation and Ethnic Diversity in California.* San Francisco: Administrative Office of the Court, Judicial Council of California, 2001.

Center for Families, Children and Courts. *Domestic Violence in Court-Based Child Custody Mediation Cases in California.* San Francisco: Administrative Office of the Court, Judicial Council of California, 2002.

Center for Families, Children and Courts. *Difficult Cases in California Court-Based Child Custody Mediation.* San Francisco: Administrative Office of the Court, Judicial Council of California, 2003a.

Center for Families, Children and Courts. *Court-Based Juvenile Dependency Mediation in California.* San Francisco: Administrative Office of the Court, Judicial Council of California, 2003b.

Ellis, D. *Family Mediation Pilot Project.* Toronto: Attorney General of Ontario, 1994.

Ellis, D., and Stuckless, N. "Pre-Separation Abuse, Marital Conflict Mediation and Post-Separation Abuse." *Mediation Quarterly,* 1992, *9,* 205–226.

Ellis, D., and Stuckless, N. *Mediating and Negotiating Marital Conflicts.* Thousand Oaks, Calif.: Sage, 1996.

Emery, R. E. *Renegotiating Family Relationships: Divorce, Child Custody, and Mediation.* New York: Guilford Press, 1994.

Emery, R. E., Matthews, S. G., and Kitzmann, K. M. "Child Custody Mediation and Litigation: Parents' Satisfaction and Functioning One Year After Settlement." *Journal of Consulting and Clinical Psychology,* 1994, *62* (1), 124–129.

Emery, R. E., Matthews, S. G., and Wyer, M. M. "Child Custody Mediation and Litigation: Further Evidence on the Differing Views of Mothers and Fathers." *Journal of Consulting and Clinical Psychology,* 1991, *59* (3), 410–418.

Emery, R. E., and others. "Child Custody Mediation and Litigation: Custody, Contact, and Coparenting Twelve Years After Initial Dispute Resolution." *Journal of Consulting and Clinical Psychology,* 2001, *69,* 323–332.

Fabricius, W. V., and Braver, S. L. "Non-Child Support Expenditures on Children by Nonresidential Divorced Fathers: Results of a Study." *Family Court Review,* 2003, *41,* 321–336.

Folberg, J., Milne, A. L., and Salem, P. *Divorce and Family Mediation: Models, Techniques, and Applications.* New York: Guilford Press, 2004.

Gigy, L., and Kelly, J. B. "Reasons for Divorce: Perspectives of Divorcing Men and Women." *Journal of Divorce,* 1992, *18* (1/2), 169–187.

Johnson, M. P., and Ferraro, K. J. "Research on Domestic Violence in the 1990s: Making Distinctions." *Journal of Marriage and Family,* 2000, *62,* 948–963.

Johnston, J. R. *Developing Preventative Interventions for Children of Severe Family Conflict and Violence: A Comparison of Three Treatment Models.* San Francisco: Administrative Office of the Court, Judicial Council of California, 1994.

Johnston, J. R., and Campbell, L. G. *Impasses of Divorce: The Dynamics and Resolution of Family Conflict.* New York: Free Press, 1988.

Johnston, J. R., and Campbell, L. G. "A Clinical Typology of Interparental Violence in Disputed-Custody Divorces." *American Journal of Orthopsychiatry,* 1993, *63,* 190–199.

Kelly, J. "Mediated and Adversarial Divorce: Respondents' Perceptions of Their Processes and Outcomes." *Mediation Quarterly,* 1989, *24,* 71–88.

Kelly, J. *Mediated and Adversarial Divorce Resolution Processes: An Analysis of Post-Divorce Outcomes.* Washington, D.C.: Fund of Research in Dispute Resolution, 1990.

Kelly, J. B. "Parent Interaction After Divorce: Comparison of Mediated and Adversarial Divorce Processes." *Behavioral Sciences and the Law,* 1991a, *9* (4), 387–398.

Kelly, J. B. "Is Mediation Less Expensive? Comparison of Mediated and Adversarial Divorce Costs." *Mediation Quarterly,* 1991b, *8* (1), 15–26.

Kelly, J. B. "Developing and Implementing Post-Divorce Parenting Plans: Does the Forum Make a Difference?" In C. E. Depner and J. H. Bray (eds.), *Non-Residential Parenting: New Vistas in Family Living.* Thousand Oaks, Calif.: Sage, 1993.

Kelly, J. B. "A Decade of Divorce Mediation Research: Some Answers and Questions." *Family and Conciliation Court Review,* 1996, *34* (3), 373–385.

Kelly, J. B. "Psychological and Legal Interventions for Parents and Children in Custody and Access Disputes: Current Research and Practice." *Virginia Journal of Social Policy and the Law,* 2002, *10* (1), 129–163.

Kelly, J. B., and Duryee, M. "Women's and Men's Views of Mediation in Voluntary and Mandatory Mediation Settings." *Family and Conciliation Courts Review,* 1992, *30* (1), 34–49.

Kelly, J. B., and Gigy, L. "Client Assessment of Mediation Services (CAMS): A Scale Measuring Client Perceptions and Satisfaction." *Mediation Quarterly,* 1988, *19,* 43–52.

Newmark, L., Harrell, A., and Salem, P. "Domestic Violence and Empowerment in Custody and Visitation Cases." *Family and Conciliation Courts Review,* 1995, *33,* 30–62.

Pearson, J. "The Equity of Mediated Divorce Agreements." *Mediation Quarterly,* 1991, *7,* 347–363.

Pruett, M. K., and Johnston, J. R. "Therapeutic Mediation with High-Conflict Parents: Effective Models and Strategies." In J. Folberg, A. Milne, and P. Salem (eds.), *Mediating Family and Divorce Disputes.* New York: Guilford Press, 2004.

Richardson, C. *Court-Based Divorce Mediation in Four Canadian Cities: An Overview of Research Results.* Ottawa: Department of Justice, 1988.

Smyth, B., and Moloney, L. "Therapeutic Divorce Mediation: A Review." *Journal of Family Studies,* 2003, *9* (2), 161–186.

Statewide Office of Family Court Services. "California Family Court Services Mediation 1991. Report 1—Overview. Families, Cases, and Client Feedback." San Francisco: Administrative Office of the Courts, Judicial Council of California, 1992.

Statistics Canada. *Family Violence in Canada: A Statistical Profile, 2001.* Ottawa: Minister of Industry, 2001.

Thoennes, N. "An Evaluation of Child Protection Mediation in Five California Courts." *Family and Conciliation Courts Review,* 1997, *35* (2), 184–195.

Thoennes, N. "Dependency Mediation: Help for Families and the Courts." *Juvenile and Family Court Journal,* Spring 2000, pp. 14–22.

Thoennes, N. *Mediating Disputes Including Parenting Time and Responsibilities in Colorado's Tenth Judicial District: Assessing the Benefits to Courts.* Denver: Center for Policy Research, Aug. 2002a.

Thoennes, N. "Hamilton County Juvenile Court Permanent Custody Mediation." Denver: Center for Policy Research, Oct. 2002b.

U.S. Department of Health and Human Services. *Effectiveness of Access and Visitation Grant Programs.* Washington, D.C.: U.S. Government Printing Office, 2002.

Walker, J., McCarthy, P., and Timms, N. *Mediation: The Making and Remaking of Co-Operative Relationships.* Newcastle upon Tyne, UK: University of Newcastle upon Tyne, Relate Centre for Family Studies, 1994.

Joan B. Kelly, a psychologist, was director of the Northern California Mediation Center in Corte Madera, California, for twenty years. Her research, writing, and practice of over thirty-five years focused on children's adjustment to divorce, custody and access issues, and divorce mediation. She was a founding board member and former president of the Academy of Family Mediators. She is currently teaching seminars and writing.

Commentary: The Future of the History of Family Mediation Research

DONALD T. SAPOSNEK

The field of family mediation has indeed come of age. Joan Kelly's summary of the documented empirical research gives substance to what front-line practitioners have observed over the two and a half decades in the trenches: that it works, but not quite as comprehensively as we had hoped.

I was one of the early mediators who, in the late 1970s and early 1980s, believed that family mediation was truly revolutionary and the panacea to the then presumed negative effects of divorce. To us in the field at the time, it all seemed intuitively obvious, both theoretically and experientially, that these would be the rewards reaped by most of the families who went through mediation, save those couples who clearly could not benefit from the process and were destined to fail (see Folberg and Taylor, 1984; Haynes, 1981; Saposnek, 1983). Moreover, we all knew the toll that the contrasting adversarial system took on families. As Schepard (2004, pp. 175–176) summarized:

> The adversary system paradigm assumes that one parent is more important to the child's future than another, and that a court can identify that parent through courtroom combat. . . . The conflict-management paradigm, in contrast, assumes, 1) that parents, not judges or mental health experts, should determine how a child of divorce is parented, 2) that both parents are important to the child's future, and 3) that carefully structured interventions can encourage parents to place their children's interests above their anger and pain. . . . These assumptions . . . are more attractive morally than the assumptions of the adversary system/sole custody paradigm in that they appeal to the better instincts of people—and parents.

Through research efforts over the next several decades, we began to understand the complexities of our craft and the limited range of our reach. Indeed, the glowing research outcomes from the early years of mediation turned out to be in contrast to the more sobering outcomes of current research (Beck and Sales, 2001; Beck, Sales, and Emery, 2004). As Irving and Benjamin (1995) aptly explain, "Early research in mediation was, in part, intended to sell mediation to policymakers, for whom it was still novel and untested. That is no longer true" (p. 423).

Making matters more problematic is the fact that the population of our craft has been changing dramatically. Compared to disputed divorce cases in the 1980s, contemporary disputed divorce cases (the bulk of them seen by mediators within the family courts) involve families with more serious and multiple problems, who use a plethora of public agencies (child protective services, criminal court, welfare services, district attorney child support offices, and others) and disproportionately use the court's resources (Center for Families, Children and Courts, 2003). Mediation approaches and techniques that worked quite well in the past often are inappropriate today. Because of the multiproblem families that now frequent family courts, the one-size-fits-all mediation model is no longer tenable. Schepard's proposal (2004) of a multileveled, interdisciplinary array of services to divorcing families makes much sense at a pragmatic level. Moreover, theory that guides our research needs to heed this reality. Complexities of the present have overshadowed simplicities of the past in both practice and theory. It is no longer meaningful to argue whether a facilitative, evaluative, or transformative mediation model is best for divorcing couples. As Irving and Benjamin (1995) observed, "The critical policy question now is not whether mediation is useful, but rather how to use it to best advantage" (p. 423).

Let us now explore where future research needs to go within each of five pertinent areas: research design, antecedent conditions (premediation interventions), screening of cases (triage), mediation process, and mediation outcome.

Research Design: From Ideal to Realistic

As Kelly noted, most of the research conducted to date on family mediation has been flawed by methodological limitations. Such limitations prevent us from clearly assessing the strengths and weaknesses of mediation for families in dispute. Beck and Sales (2001) published what is likely the most detailed analysis to date of the limitations of our current mediation research and note a number of salient points. Comparing family mediation research design to its next closest cousin, psychotherapy research, they conclude that the former has lacked very basic rules for research evidence needed to acquire valid knowledge and establish cause-and-effect relationships. We have developed many assumptions about what in mediation works, what the essential elements are, and why they work. Such assumptions, however, are often conflicting and have not yet been placed under the scientific scrutiny necessary to draw valid and useful conclusions to guide social policy development.

Although it would be logistically challenging for mediation research, Beck and Sales suggest that an ideal research design would minimally have a control group to which to compare results of the mediation group, a random assignment of clients to groups (for equivalence of groups), a step-by-step manual detailing a clear definition of the particular mediation intervention, a check on the intervention actually delivered to the clients (for example, through videotaping) so as to be able to replicate the study, and agreed-on measures of outcome, making possible comparisons across studies. We at least need to closely approximate such ideal research designs if we are to gain valid understandings of what is best of our interventions.

Some might argue that we cannot afford the slow, methodical, and restrictive pace at which basic research takes place, as we have potentially volatile problems impinging daily on both the courts and the lives of the participants, with serious and intensely emotional, social, and legal consequences. Unlike psychotherapy research, which has no similarly pressing public agenda, the domain of divorce disputes (particularly with child custody contests) is extremely politically sensitive and driven by policy-based funding, which is known for its restrictive interests in agreement rate outcomes (Irving and Benjamin, 1995). Resolving a custody dispute feels to divorcing parents as pressing as accessing an experimental drug feels to a terminal cancer patient, even before the research demonstrating its efficacy is explored. Nonetheless, with the scaffolding of basic research methods in place, we could build a more valid and useful database for guiding social policy in conflict resolution.

Deutsch (2000) offers an expanded and fresh perspective on research methods (using the context of conflict resolution training). He suggests that we not take such a narrow view of research methodology, but rather consider that there are different kinds of research, each with merit. Among these research types are *basic* (fundamental questions), *developmental* (how a skill should be taught), *field* (identifying features of the political, cultural, or organizational structure that help or hinder skill development), and *consumer* (customer satisfaction). Moreover, there are different audiences for the research (such as funding agencies, practitioners, executives, and administrators and researchers), with the particular audience framing the research questions and strategies needed to address the questions posed. Such a perspective opens the gates for creatively adapting research methods to the specific questions asked, to the person or persons asking, and to the ultimate purpose of the inquiry.

Antecedent Conditions

Two essential aspects that are antecedent to family mediation need research exploration: prevention of family disputes through early education and preparation for mediation.

It seems reasonable that early efforts at preventing family conflict will benefit later efforts at family mediation. We need to develop new, or evaluate existing, public education protocols aimed at helping children form positive and satisfying peer friendship relationships as early as preschool and continuing into middle school. In high school, this would include developing and assessing the impact of educational curricula about adult relationships, marriage, and divorce on the development of adult relationships. We need rigorous longitudinal research to determine to what degree teaching young people effective communication skills, ways to select a compatible partner, and strategies for maintaining a good marriage would result in better relationships, prevent divorce, or minimize higher-conflict divorces. Or does such early education have little or no effect on later relationship development and management of family conflicts? Moreover, while we know of the relationship between higher-conflict divorces and failure in mediation, we do not know whether this outcome is due to personal characteristics of one or both of the participants that inevitably lead to conflict or to lack of earlier education in relationships, marriage, and divorce.

Once a couple chooses to part, how can we best prepare them to maximize successful negotiations in mediation? One of the most promising methods used in many court jurisdictions is the use of divorce education classes or workshops prior to beginning mediation. Kelly notes that such premediation interventions, referred to in her article as orientation and parent education, are offered in over half of the family court mediations conducted in California. In a national survey, Geasler and Blaisure (1998) report that 1,516 counties in the United States reported having court-connected divorce education programs. Such programs range from short-term, two-hour, universal programs, to multiple-session, skills-training interactive workshops (Braver, Salem, Pearson, and DeLuse, 1996; Goodman, Bonds, Sandler, and Braver, 2004). Evaluative research has shown that parents who attend such programs (even if mandated) rate the programs highly, learn useful parenting and communications skills, commit to lowering the exposure of their children to parental conflict (Arbuthnot and Gordon, 1996), reduce actual interparental conflict (Bacon and McKenzie, 2004), and relitigate at a significantly lower rate than those not taking the course, though only when mastery of behavioral skills of better coparenting was evident (Arbuthnot, Kramer, and Gordon, 1997), and their attendance is correlated with a lower use of court resources (Ellis and Anderson, 2003).

We have evidence that such programs can influence the thinking and behavior of participants toward a less conflictual attitude, especially when the program format fits specific client populations (Fuhrman, McGill, and O'Connell, 1999). This suggests that we might even better prepare disputants for more productive negotiations in mediation (clinical anecdotes from court-related mediators support this hunch). Such a model for individualized interventions of premediation personal coaching is already a component in the practice of collaborative divorce (Fagerstrom, 1997) and in certain models of collaborative law (Tesler, 2001).

We need validating research to determine whether, and to what degree, such classes, workshops, and personal coaching increase readiness for, or result in more favorable outcomes from, mediation. Moreover, we need comparative research to determine which formats work best for which types of separating or divorcing clients and which aspects of these programs produce enduring changes.

A related and intriguing area for research (with very minimal available data) is the relationship between client attitudes and expectations regarding mediation and outcomes of mediation. Herrman, Hollett, and Gale (2004), referring to these as "disputant beliefs and attitudes," suggest that these variables may have an important influence on the mediation process and outcome. Fountain (2001), defining client satisfaction as the gap between one's expectations of a service and the perceived performance of the service, led researchers of the California study (Center for Families, Children and Courts, 2004) to suggest that mediators might include in premediation orientation (for example, within divorce education classes, in separate premediation coaching sessions, or at the beginning of mediation sessions) realistic information about what mediation can and cannot offer, in attempts to influence client expectations in more positive directions. For example, clients could be told that an hour or two of mediation is unlikely to "transform intense marital conflict into affectionate cooperation, and intense distress into positive postdivorce family adjustment" (Irving and Benjamin, 1995, p. 423).

Prior to their decision to divorce and attend mediation, many couples attempt marital therapy. However, we know very little about what effect the timing, type, and duration of predivorce marital therapy actually have on the mediation process and outcome. Does such therapy immediately prior to the start of mediation differ from therapy attempted years earlier in its effect on the process and outcome of mediation? Research is needed on this widely used premediation intervention.

Screening and Triage of Cases

If we are to maintain some form of mandatory mediation in the courts (highly recommended by Schepard, 2004, and Behrman and Quinn, 1994), we need to develop screening methods that have proved empirically to predict success or failure in mediation. With the increase in multiproblem cases coming to family courts, we can no longer operate from a policy dictating that all cases should first try mediation, based on the outdated premise that all cases will benefit from it. In fact, it is very likely that for some cases, mediation will make things worse, perhaps increasing conflict, delaying resolution of conflict, and delaying the setting in place of needed coparenting structures for the safety and welfare of the children. Efficiently routing these cases into more relevant methods for conflict resolution could serve them and the court system well.

The differentiated case management model suggested by Schepard (2004) is a viable system in which a family court triages its cases and devotes more intensive resources to more troubled families. Some of the pertinent and unanswered research questions that emerge from this model are: Which cases should be screened out of mediation? What data are essential to gather for making this decision? What level of screener experience is needed to make a valid judgment? Although we generally consider high-conflict couples less amenable to mediation, how do we protect the rights of one individual who tries to cooperate with the partner and might well be able to mediate, when his or her partner unilaterally provokes conflict and does not fit the criteria for being able to mediate (Friedman, 2004)?

In planning research on screening methods, we must also consider that the definition of *mediation* stands as a proverbial pink elephant in the room. As Kelly notes, in the California family courts (which has often presaged the development of protocols for other courts across the country), there is a mandate for all parents in custody or visitation disputes to first attend a session of mediation. When this mandate was implemented in 1981, the cases were simpler and the interventions were few. As the cases increased in difficulty and complexity, methods for triage and expanded modes of intervention emerged out of necessity. However, they evolved without the support of empirical data and differently in each of California's fifty-eight counties. Within the court system, the definition of and the actual current practices of what is called mediation have parted ways, resulting in serious theoretical and practice inconsistencies. The mandate to mediate is being interpreted and implemented in practice as if the statute read: *Parties in dispute must attend a session with a court counselor who may mediate, arbitrate, recommend, refer, or terminate the case.* With such a range of options for action, research on "mediation" in the courts is actually studying a grab-bag of interventions that likely represents neither consistent nor comparable samples for researchers. We need to clarify and perhaps redefine what is actually meant by a *mandate* for mediation to one that is based on empirical, predictive data to screen for success in mediation. Minimally, we need to operationally define the term *mediation.*

An ideal research design would substantiate essential variables of predictability for success in various intervention processes (in both public and private settings) and contribute to the development of a computerized grid of known variables, matched by an array of available (and affordable) services through which to route the cases. The pertinent research questions would, for example, include the following: From an individual psychology point of view, which client characteristics and which mediator characteristics (see Bowling and Hoffman, 2003; Lang and Taylor, 2000) are predictive of success and failure in mediation? And from a family systems point of view, which dynamics of couples, with what degree of conflict, with how many issues to resolve, and at what time period in their separation or divorcing process are predictive of success and failure in mediation?

Combining these antecedent variables would likely increase the predictability of screening for success in mediation. The grid would allow one to sort cases into empirically researched specific interventions by case needs. These would include short-term, medium-term, and long-term interventions, within a variety of intervention models that includes confidential self-determined mediation, temporary or short-term recommendations, parenting coordinating, mini and comprehensive evaluations, supervised visitation, collaborative divorce models, individual and couples psychotherapy, and family group therapy—services that combine to make a veritable family conflict resolution clinic that expands well beyond a traditional family mediation service.

Process Research

We do not know much of what actually happens in mediation or what degree of consistency there is within a given mediator's model and across mediators and their methods. Irving and Benjamin's suggestion (1995) that we need a process approach to family mediation is very much on target. After caseloads are culled to select those appropriate for mediation, what are the process elements that contribute to effective mediation? A number of mediation models have been posed, but with little research on their efficacy, although we do know that the process is more complex than what a particular model asserts.

One promising approach to process research was undertaken by Becker-Haven (1990). Rather than attempt to validate a given theoretical model of mediation (facilitative, problem-solving, transformative, or evaluative model), she conceptualized specific mediation interventions as modes: "A mode serves as a conceptual framework within which a set of complex behaviors can be coordinated. Each mode regards the central challenge in mediation—that is, overcoming impasses—from a characteristic perspective. Each of the four modes can be distinguished by its view of the function of mediation and the corresponding role of the mediator; *Rational/Analytic Mode* (mediator as decision manager); *Therapeutic Mode* (mediator as healer); *Educational Mode* (mediator as teacher); *Normative Mode* (mediator as monitor)." This heuristic model, developed through field observations using objective raters, gets more directly to the root of mediation process. It allowed Becker-Haven to visually map out the process of each mediation session, using continuous colored bar graphs showing the amount of time a mediator spent in each mode. It also allowed her to conclude, "Individual mediators were shown to have distinctive styles that could be expressed as combinations of these four modes, and most of the mediators used each of the four modes at some time during the mediation." In addition, most mediators used a predominant mode.

The conceptual flexibility of this empirical work demonstrated that there is as much art and style to the process work of mediators as there is science (see Lang and Taylor, 2000; Saposnek, 1993, 2003). Indeed, as Korchin and Sands (1983) concluded, effective, experienced therapists of whatever specific theoretical models may practice more similarly than they preach, and it appears that this may also likely be the case for mediators. Although it may seem compelling to spend time and money testing differences in efficacies among theoretical models as practiced by random (average) mediators, it would likely be more fruitful to study intensively the processes of expert mediators. Then, in order to learn what actual structures and processes go into a grid of predictive variables for successful mediation, we should explore how to optimally match client capacities, style, and needs with the fluid, eclectic use of multiple modes and multiple models of mediation (facilitative, problem solving, evaluative, transformative).

Irving and Benjamin (1995) suggest that our current priorities for service are, ironically, the reverse of what is needed. Complex cases need more flexible, more intensive, more therapeutic, and longer-term services than do less complex cases (Pruett and Johnston, 2004). Yet most complex cases typically are serviced by the courts, which often restrict cases to about an hour or so of service. Moreover, they tend to use a limited, single model of mediation and, when impasse is reached, intervene quickly with evaluations and recommendations rather than giving the parties a chance to sort out their emotional issues. These authors suggest that research be directed toward finding a way to fund the servicing of these complex cases in the private sector, offering a greater chance for more suitable interventions. Although the costs would initially be increased, the likelihood of more permanent conflict resolution or management would result in public savings in the long run.

The basic question of process research is, "What are the elements that make mediation successful or unsuccessful? This indeed is a question of great complexity, with many subtle facets. One example of the more subtle aspects of conducting process research is the timing of the research. Because couples going through the separation and divorce process frequently manifest extreme emotional dynamics, it is very likely that researchers comparing the mediation process of couples fresh from a separation with those four to six months after a separation will not have comparable samples. There is a layer of ongoing emotional turmoil that fluctuates across the first several years following a separation (Kaslow and Schwartz, 1987) that challenges process research. Much of the process research to date has not taken into account this critical variable of research timing.

In addition to the process variables, many structural and practice setting variables of mediation likely influence its outcome. Because intervention rituals and practice conventions, which are based largely on practice setting and economic limitations, have preceded efficacy research, we do not yet know the answers to the following structural questions:

- After a decision to separate or divorce is reached, when is the optimal time to begin mediation? What effect does time since separation have on mediation process and outcome?

- What is the optimal duration and number of sessions? Experience suggests that more than three hours may be necessary for more complex cases and that fewer than two hours with most cases may be less than optimal.

- What intersession time intervals are optimal? Experience suggests this as an important variable (see Saposnek, 1983, 1998).

- What patterns of follow-up sessions help to maintain longer-term gains from mediation? Some research suggests that six to eight weeks after completion of mediation is optimal (Irving and Benjamin, 1995; Saposnek, Hamburg, Delano, and Michaelson, 1984).

- What differences in outcome are there if clients are seen in individual caucuses versus always together?

- Should children participate in mediation, and if so, in what fashion (Drapkin and Bienenfeld, 1985; Kelly, 2002; Sanchez and Kibler-Sanchez, 2004; Saposnek, 1991, 2004)?

- Would there be better success if child support were mediated along with the parenting plan? Irving and Benjamin (1995) note that multiple-issue cases afford mediators more flexibility than single-issue cases.

- What essential modifications need to be made to the mediation model and process to accommodate cultural and language differences? In California, for example, the issue is challenging, since no one race or culture is in the majority (Center for Families, Children and Courts, 2001) and 224 languages are spoken (Ricci, 2004). There is some evidence that cultural or ethnic similarity between mediator and clients facilitates the mediation process.

- What are the optimal models for training of content, process, and essential skills of family mediators? Course work? Comediation? Trial by fire? Internships?

Outcome Research

Although outcome research has largely been the focus for justifying mediation programs, it is not without its problems. Using the criteria of settlement rates, satisfaction of participants, and cost and time efficiencies does not necessarily answer important questions about mediation. For one, the debate continues as to whether merely getting an agreement in mediation is a sure sign of success. Some researchers assert that if the mediation process focuses on relational issues with therapeutic objectives (Irving and Benjamin, 1995) or with emotionally transformative goals (Bush and Folger, 1994), agreement is not the only important criterion for an outcome of success.

There is evidence that satisfaction with the process can be more important than satisfaction with the outcome of a court-related procedure. The California Client Feedback Study (Center for Families, Children and Courts, 2004, p. 3) concluded, "It is very important for people to feel that they have been treated with respect and given the opportunity to voice their concerns. If they feel that fair processes were used to come to a decision, they are more likely to accept and to comply with the outcome, regardless of whether the outcome favors them or the other party. This is especially important in the context of child custody disputes. In a large number of cases it is unlikely that both parents will be satisfied with the agreement or other outcome because they have to reach some kind of compromise." (Also see Lind and Tyler, 1988, and Tyler, 2000, for discussions of procedural justice and the experience of fairness and satisfaction.) Kelly notes that this finding also holds true with child protection mediation cases.

Moreover, some unknown percentage of couples settle outside mediation (for example, in the parking lot) and decide to treat their children differently as a result of mediation intervention and education, even if they could not reach agreement in mediation. Yet in such cases, the mediator may conclude that the case was unsuccessful. Moreover, if a couple comes back months later to modify their agreement (about a third of California courts' "successfully" mediated cases return for such modifications), does that indicate success or failure on the first round of mediation? Clearly we do not have a consensual definition of success in mediation.

Research findings show that client satisfaction is higher in mediation than in litigation, but there is no statistical difference when comparing satisfaction within the models of confidential mediation and recommending mediation. This is puzzling, since client self-determination, generally considered an essential element of mediation, is not clearly present in the recommending model, with the latter actually representing a wide range of process and procedural options (see Ricci, 2004; Shienvold, 2004). Kelly concludes that reaching agreement is more important than the actual intervention model for getting there. Since this finding begs the question of mediator neutrality, more research needs to be conducted to tease out the essential differences between these seemingly radically different models of mediation.

Economic and temporal efficiencies seem like obviously positive outcome criteria but can be shortsighted as goals. In consideration of limited court budgets, we need to study ways to reapportion budgets—getting away from funding one-size-fits-all thinking and moving more toward funding programs that distribute services more precisely, using need-based models. In this way, there could be an overall monetary savings while providing more effective and efficient services. Again, we need to develop and fund research that predicts the specific cases in which mediation will be most effective, within a broader model of interdisciplinary, dispute resolution services (Firestone and Weinstein, 2004; Schepard, 2004).

Since a large portion of the divorce mediation enterprise is about creating better outcomes for children, we need more research with this focus. Current research shows no relationships between children's adjustment to the divorce and the use of mediation or, for that matter, of litigation. Partly this attests to the powerful influences of the many changes children endure after parental separation. While we know that effective mediation tends to reduce interparental fighting—and this is one of the strongest predictors for more favorable outcome for the children—it is not the only predictor. Preseparation adjustment of the children is also a strong predictor of postdivorce adjustment, regardless of the type of intervention. We need more research to better understand what other specific variables prior to and within the mediation process result in better outcomes for children. Moreover, future mediation outcome research needs to enlarge the frame of variables studied to date and conduct direct assessments of children before and following mediation interventions. Relying on parent report is not enough, since parents tend to report from less-than-objective vantage points (see Saposnek, Hamburg, Delano, and Michaelson, 1984; Wenar, 1961).

The findings showing that mediation has been unable to improve the relationship between parting spouses, and unable to improve compliance with the agreements, are no surprise. They simply attest to the limitations of our brief models of mediation and to the strength of the emotional interactional patterns built up over the years of the relationship, as well as to the power of intervening life events. Also, the dynamics of mediation are inherently in opposition to the goals of the couple and thus create a dilemma: mediators are trying to get the divorcing couples to work together and cooperate, while the couples are trying to get apart emotionally—actively manifesting the very absence of cooperation that broke them apart in the first place. We need more research on what mediation models and processes (perhaps those with more active educational and therapeutic components) might facilitate the development of better quality and compliance of the coparenting relationship after divorce.

Last, given the increase in divorcing families with children with special needs, we need to explore ways to increase mediators' knowledge about and sensitivity to the unique features required in negotiating and drafting parenting plans for children with serious life-threatening medical problems, chronic developmental disabilities, and severe emotional and behavioral problems (Saposnek, Perryman, Berkow, and Ellsworth, forthcoming). There has been virtually no empirical research on this neglected but important area of intervention. There are potentially profound and long-term consequences (in some cases, life or death) on the children when mediators do not develop special coparenting provisions. We need to know the incidence of mediation cases involving these children and what happens to the children when their special needs are not specifically addressed.

Conclusions

The complexity of the research questions that remain to be answered about the effectiveness of family mediation is probably best represented in the following hypothetical grid. To better understand the nature of family mediation, we need to know which clients, with what personal and interpersonal dynamics, with what length and quality of preseparation relationship, with how many children, at what ages, at how long since separation, with what preseparation experience and quality of individual or marital counseling, with what number and complexity of issues in dispute, with what extended family or new partner's involvement, in what mediation setting (court or private), with what experience level and training of the mediator, using what model and processes of mediation, for how many sessions, with what frequency of sessions, with what kinds of follow-up interventions and referrals.

Family mediation has proved to be a sound, dynamic, effective, and well-liked process. Future empirical research that further documents what we have learned to date will help to validate, direct, and facilitate the future growth of our field.

References

Arbuthnot, J., and Gordon, D. A. "Does Mandatory Divorce Education Work? A Six-Month Outcome Evaluation." *Family and Conciliation Courts Review,* 1996, *34* (1), 60–81.

Arbuthnot, J., Kramer, K. M., and Gordon, D. A. "Patterns of Relitigation Following Divorce Education." *Family and Conciliation Courts Review,* 1997, *35* (3), 269–279.

Bacon, B. L., and McKenzie, B. "Parent Education After Separation/Divorce: Impact of the Level of Parental Conflict on Outcomes." *Family Court Review,* 2004, *42* (1), 85–98.

Beck, C.J.A., and Sales, B. D. *Family Mediation: Facts, Myths, and Future Prospects.* Washington, D.C.: American Psychological Association, 2001.

Beck, C.J.A., Sales, B. D., and Emery, R. E. "Research on the Impact of Family Mediation." In J. Folberg, A. L. Milne, and P. Salem (eds.), *Divorce and Family Mediation: Models, Techniques, and Applications.* New York: Guilford Press, 2004.

Becker-Haven, J. F. *Modes of Mediating Child Custody Disputes.* Palo Alto, Calif.: Stanford Center on Conflict and Negotiation, 1990.

Behrman, R. E., and Quinn, L. S. "Children and Divorce: Overview and Analysis." *Future of Children (Children and Divorce),* 1994, *4* (1), 4–14.

Bowling, D., and Hoffman, D. (eds.). *Bringing Peace into the Room: How the Personal Qualities of the Mediator Impact the Process of Conflict Resolution.* San Francisco: Jossey-Bass, 2003.

Braver, S. L., Salem, P., Pearson, J., and DeLuse, S. R. "The Content of Divorce Education Programs: Results of a Survey." *Family and Conciliation Courts Review,* 1996, *34* (1), 41–59.

Bush, R.A.B., and Folger, J. P. *The Promise of Mediation: Responding to Conflict Through Empowerment and Recognition.* San Francisco: Jossey-Bass, 1994.

Center for Families, Children and Courts. *1999 Client Baseline Study.* San Francisco: Administrative Office of the Courts, Judicial Council of California, 2001.

Center for Families, Children and Courts. *Difficult Cases in California Court-Based Child Custody Mediation.* San Francisco: Administrative Office of the Courts, Judicial Council of California, Mar. 2003.

Center for Families, Children and Courts. *Client Feedback in California Court-Based Child Custody Mediation.* San Francisco: Administrative Office of the Courts, Judicial Council of California, Apr. 2004.

Deutsch, M. "A Framework for Thinking About Research on Conflict Resolution Training." In M. Deutsch and P. T. Coleman (eds.), *The Handbook of Conflict Resolution: Theory and Practice.* San Francisco: Jossey-Bass, 2000.

Drapkin, R., and Bienenfeld, F. "The Power in Including Children in Custody Mediation." *Journal of Divorce,* 1985, *8* (3/4), 63–95.

Ellis, D., and Anderson, D. Y. "The Impact of Participation in a Parent Education Program for Divorcing Parents on the Use of Court Resources: An Evaluation Study." *Conflict Resolution Quarterly,* 2003, *21* (2), 169–187.

Fagerstrom, F. *Divorce: A Problem to Be Solved, Not a Battle to Be Fought.* Orinda, Calif.: Brookwood Publishers, 1997.

Firestone, G., and Weinstein, J. "In the Best Interests of Children: A Proposal to Transform the Adversarial System." *Family Court Review,* 2004, *42* (2), 203–215.

Folberg, J., and Taylor, A. *Mediation: A Comprehensive Guide to Resolving Conflicts Without Litigation.* San Francisco: Jossey-Bass, 1984.

Fountain, J. E. "Paradoxes of Public Sector Customer Service." *Governance: An International Journal of Policy and Administration,* 2001, *14* (1), 55–73.

Friedman, M. "The So-Called High-Conflict Couple: A Closer Look." *American Journal of Family Therapy,* 2004, *32,* 101–117.

Fuhrman, G.S.W., McGill, J., and O'Connell, M. E. "Parent Education's Second Generation: Integrating Violence Sensitivity." *Family and Conciliation Courts Review,* 1999, *37* (1), 24–35.

Geasler, M. J., and Blaisure, K. R. "1997–1998 Nationwide Survey of Court-Connected Divorce Education Programs." *Family and Conciliation Courts Review,* 1998, *37,* 36–63.

Goodman, M., Bonds, D., Sandler, I., and Braver, S. "Parent Psychoeducational Programs and Reducing the Negative Effects of Interparental Conflict Following Divorce." *Family Court Review,* 2004, *42* (2), 263–279.

Haynes, J. M. *Divorce Mediation: A Practical Guide for Therapists and Counselors.* New York: Springer, 1981.

Herrman, M. D., Hollett, N., and Gale, J. *Mediation from Beginning to End: A Testable Theory-Driven Framework.* Athens, Ga.: Skills Project, University of Georgia, 2004.

Irving, H. H., and Benjamin, M. *Family Mediation: Contemporary Issues.* Thousand Oaks, Calif.: Sage, 1995.

Kaslow, F. W., and Schwartz, L. L. *The Dynamics of Divorce: A Life Cycle Perspective.* New York: Brunner/Mazel, 1987.

Kelly, J. B. "Psychological and Legal Interventions for Parents and Children in Custody and Access Disputes: Current Research and Practice." *Virginia Journal of Social Policy and the Law,* 2002, *10* (1), 129–163.

Korchin, S. J., and Sands, S. H. "Principles Common to All Psychotherapies." In C. E. Walker (ed.), *The Handbook of Clinical Psychology.* Homewood, Ill.: Dow Jones-Irwin, 1983.

Lang, M., and Taylor, A. *The Making of a Mediator: Developing Artistry in Practice.* San Francisco: Jossey-Bass, 2000.

Lind, E., and Tyler, T. *The Social Psychology of Procedural Justice.* New York: Plenum, 1988.

Pruett, M. K., and Johnston, J. R. "Therapeutic Mediation with High-Conflict Parents: Effective Models and Strategies." In J. Folberg, A. L. Milne, and P. Salem (eds.), *Divorce and Family Mediation: Models, Techniques, and Applications.* New York: Guilford Press, 2004.

Ricci, I. "Court-Based Mandatory Mediation: Special Considerations." In J. Folberg, A. L. Milne, and P. Salem (eds.), *Divorce and Family Mediation: Models, Techniques, and Applications.* New York: Guilford Press, 2004.

Sanchez, E. A., and Kibler-Sanchez, S. "Empowering Children in Mediation: An Intervention Model." *Family Court Review,* 2004, *42* (3), 554–575.

Saposnek, D. T. *Mediating Child Custody Disputes: A Systematic Guide for Family Therapists, Court Counselors, Attorneys, and Judges.* San Francisco: Jossey-Bass, 1983.

Saposnek, D. T. "The Value of Children in Mediation: A Cross-Cultural Perspective." *Mediation Quarterly,* 1991, *8* (4), 325–342.

Saposnek, D. T. "The Art of Family Mediation." In D. T. Saposnek (ed.), *Beyond Technique: The Soul of Family Mediation.* San Francisco: Jossey-Bass, 1993.

Saposnek, D. T. *Mediating Child Custody Disputes: A Strategic Approach.* San Francisco: Jossey-Bass, 1998.

Saposnek, D. T. "Style and the Family Mediator." In D. Hoffman and D. Bowling (eds.), Bringing *Peace into the Room: The Personal Qualities of the Mediator.* San Francisco: Jossey-Bass, 2003.

Saposnek, D. T. "Working with Children in Mediation." In J. Folberg, A. L. Milne, and P. Salem (eds.), *Divorce and Family Mediation: Models, Techniques, and Applications.* New York: Guilford Press, 2004.

Saposnek, D. T., Hamburg, J., Delano, C. D., and Michaelson, H. "How Has Mandatory Mediation Fared? Research Findings of the First Year's Follow-Up." *Conciliation Courts Review,* 1984, *22* (2), 7–19.

Saposnek, D. T., Perryman, H., Berkow, J., and Ellsworth, S. "Special Needs Children in Family Court," forthcoming.

Schepard, A. I. *Children, Courts, and Custody: Interdisciplinary Models for Divorcing Families.* Cambridge: Cambridge University Press, 2004.

Shienvold, A. "Hybrid Processes." In J. Folberg, A. L. Milne, and P. Salem (eds.), *Divorce and Family Mediation: Models, Techniques, and Applications.* New York: Guilford Press, 2004.

Tesler, P. H. *Collaborative Law: Achieving Effective Resolution in Divorce Without Litigation.* Chicago: American Bar Association, 2001.

Tyler, T. "Social Justice: Outcome and Procedure." *International Journal of Psychology,* 2000, *35* (2), 117–125.

Wenar, C. "The Reliability of Mothers' Histories." *Child Development,* 1961, *32,* 491–500.

Donald T. Saposnek is a clinical-child psychologist, family therapist, family mediator, trainer, and consultant. He is director of Family Mediation Service of Aptos, California, and a psychology faculty member of the University of California, Santa Cruz. He is the editor of the Association for Conflict Resolution's *Family Mediation News* and the editor of the Family Section of www.mediate.com. He is also on the editorial boards of the *Family Court Review* and *Conflict Resolution Quarterly.*

The Effectiveness of Court-Connected Dispute Resolution in Civil Cases

ROSELLE L. WISSLER

This article reviews the empirical research on mediation and neutral evaluation, two court-connected dispute resolution processes in which the third party does not have decision-making power. Mediation has been used in small claims cases, general jurisdiction trial cases, and appellate cases; neutral evaluation has been used primarily in general jurisdiction cases. Because the program structure and the nature of the mediation process differ across the three court levels, the research findings are presented separately for each type of court as well as for each dispute resolution process.

I review the data sources and methodology used in the studies examined here, describe the dispute resolution process and the structure of the programs in order to provide a context for interpreting the research, present the empirical findings regarding program outcomes, and report findings regarding the impact of program structure on outcomes.[1]

Mediation in Small Claims Cases

The findings of ten small claims mediation studies are discussed in this section (Goerdt, 1993; Hermann, LaFree, Rack, and West, 1993; McEwen and Maiman, 1981; Maiman, 1997; Olexa and Rozelle, 1991; Raitt, Folberg, Rosenberg, and Barrett, 1993; Roehl, Hersch, and Llaneras, 1992; Russell, 1998; Vidmar, 1984; Wissler, 1995). Five of the studies relied primarily on telephone or in-person interviews with participants, which averaged thirty minutes in length and were conducted from immediately after the session up to four months later (Hermann, LaFree, Rack, and West, 1993; McEwen and Maiman, 1981; Roehl, Hersch, and Llaneras, 1992; Vidmar, 1984; Wissler, 1995), and three studies relied

NOTE: *Thanks to Bob Dauber, Craig McEwen, and Donna Stienstra for their comments and Beth DiFelice, Connie Strittmatter, and Kerry Skinner for their assistance.*

instead on participant exit questionnaires (Goerdt, 1993; Maiman, 1997; Russell, 1998). Two studies included a follow-up questionnaire or interview to obtain information on compliance (Hermann, LaFree, Rack, and West, 1993; Russell, 1998), and one also interviewed litigants prior to mediation (Vidmar, 1985). Several studies supplemented participant data with observations of mediation sessions (Hermann, LaFree, Rack, and West, 1993; McEwen and Maiman, 1981; Roehl, Hersch, and Llaneras, 1992; Vidmar, 1985) or information from mediator questionnaires or reports (Hermann, LaFree, Rack, and West, 1993; McEwen and Maiman, 1981) or from court records (McEwen and Maiman, 1981; Vidmar, 1985). Two studies relied solely on information from court records or court personnel (Olexa and Rozelle, 1991; Raitt, Folberg, Rosenberg, and Barrett, 1993).[2]

Seven of the studies included a comparison group of tried cases for one or more outcome measures (Goerdt, 1993; Hermann, LaFree, Rack, and West, 1993; McEwen and Maiman, 1981; Olexa and Rozelle, 1991; Roehl, Hersch, and Llaneras, 1992; Vidmar, 1986; Wissler, 1995). Only one study essentially randomly assigned cases to either mediation or trial (Roehl, Hersch, and Llaneras, 1992). Accordingly, the comparative findings should be interpreted with caution. Several studies, however, reported that mediation versus adjudication differences in outcomes generally remained when the case and litigant characteristics on which these two groups differed were taken into consideration (McEwen and Maiman, 1987; Vidmar, 1986; Wissler, 1995).

Program Structure

The small claims court divisions in the programs studied handled civil actions involving debt or damages below eight hundred dollars to five thousand dollars. In most cases, neither litigant had counsel (Hermann, LaFree, Rack, and West, 1993; McEwen and Maiman, 1981; Roehl, Hersch, and Llaneras, 1992), although in most courts they had the right to retain counsel (but see Goerdt, 1993). Some mediation programs were administered by court staff (Goerdt, 1993; Maiman, 1997), while others were administered by an outside organization (Goerdt, 1993; Hermann, LaFree, Rack, and West, 1993; Maiman, 1997; Wissler, 1995). In all programs, mediation took place in the courthouse at no cost to the litigants.

Mediation was held on the date of trial in most programs (Goerdt, 1993; McEwen and Maiman, 1981; Maiman, 1997; Olexa and Rozelle, 1991; Raitt, Folberg, Rosenberg, and Barrett, 1993; Roehl, Hersch, and

Llaneras, 1992; Russell, 1998; Wissler, 1995), and cases that did not settle in mediation generally had a trial the same day. In a few programs, however, mediation took place before the scheduled trial date (Hermann, LaFree, Rack, and West, 1993; Raitt, Folberg, Rosenberg, and Barrett, 1993; Vidmar, 1984). Mediation typically involved a single session that averaged between thirty and sixty minutes (Goerdt, 1993; McEwen and Maiman, 1981; Olexa and Rozelle, 1991; Roehl, Hersch, and Llaneras, 1992; Vidmar, 1985; Wissler, 1995; but see Raitt, Folberg, Rosenberg, and Barrett, 1993; Russell, 1998). The mediator generally did not receive information about the case prior to the session.

In some programs, litigants in cases in which both parties appeared for trial were required to attend mediation or were so "strongly encouraged" that few refused (Goerdt, 1993; McEwen and Maiman, 1981; Olexa and Rozelle, 1991; Roehl, Hersch, and Llaneras, 1992; Russell, 1998; Vidmar, 1985; Wissler, 1995; but see Hermann, LaFree, Rack, and West, 1993). In other programs, however, mediation was voluntary, and both litigants had to agree to use mediation (Goerdt, 1993; McEwen and Maiman, 1981; Maiman, 1997; Olexa and Rozelle, 1991; Raitt, Folberg, Rosenberg, and Barrett, 1993; Wissler, 1995).

The mediators generally were volunteers (Goerdt, 1993; Hermann, LaFree, Rack, and West, 1993; Maiman, 1997; Olexa and Rozelle, 1991; Roehl, Hersch, and Llaneras, 1992; Russell, 1998; Wissler, 1995; but see Goerdt, 1993; Raitt, Folberg, Rosenberg, and Barrett, 1993). They were either laypeople or a combination of lawyers, law students, and laypeople (Goerdt, 1993; Roehl, Hersch, and Llaneras, 1992; Wissler, 1995). Most programs provided mediation training (Goerdt, 1993; Hermann, LaFree, Rack, and West, 1993; Maiman, 1997; Russell, 1998; Vidmar, 1985; Wissler, 1995; but see Roehl, Hersch, and Llaneras, 1992) that ranged from sixteen to over forty hours (Goerdt, 1993; Hermann, LaFree, Rack, and West, 1993; Olexa and Rozelle, 1991; Russell, 1998).

In a number of programs, the mediator training stressed a facilitative mediation model (Olexa and Rozelle, 1991; Roehl, Hersch, and Llaneras, 1992), a principled negotiation model (Wissler, 1995), or a model that explicitly avoided assessing the legal merits of the case (Hermann, LaFree, Rack, and West, 1993). But in one program, the nonlawyer mediators took special law classes (Vidmar, 1985). Observers described the mediations in the latter program as being fairly legalistic and directive and focused largely on factual and legal issues (Vidmar, 1985). Observers in another program noted that the style of different mediators varied from restrained to very active, and the sessions typically focused more on issues relating to the claim and responsibility than on broader issues (McEwen and Maiman, 1981).

Outcomes

A variety of outcomes has been examined in this research.

Settlement Rate. Virtually all studies examined the rate of settlement in mediation. Most studies reported a settlement rate between 47 and 78 percent (Goerdt, 1993; Hermann, LaFree, Rack, and West, 1993; McEwen and Maiman, 1981; Maiman, 1997; Olexa and Rozelle, 1991; Raitt, Folberg, Rosenberg, and Barrett, 1993; Roehl, Hersch, and Llaneras, 1992; Russell, 1998; Vidmar, 1985), but a few reported a lower (25 percent; Raitt, Folberg, Rosenberg, and Barrett, 1993) or higher settlement rate (84 to 95 percent; Goerdt, 1993; Maiman, 1997; Raitt, Folberg, Rosenberg, and Barrett, 1993).[3]

Participants' Assessments. The seven studies that examined litigants' assessments of the process, the neutral, and the outcome reported highly favorable views. A majority of litigants felt that the mediation process, session, or procedures were fair (Goerdt, 1993; Maiman, 1997; Roehl, Hersch, and Llaneras, 1992; Wissler, 1995) and that mediation gave them full opportunity to present their case (McEwen and Maiman, 1981; Maiman, 1997; Wissler, 1995) and take part in its resolution (Maiman, 1997; Wissler, 1995). Most litigants thought the mediator was neutral and had a good understanding of their dispute (Hermann, LaFree, Rack, and West, 1993; McEwen and Maiman, 1981; Maiman, 1997; Roehl, Hersch, and Llaneras, 1992; Wissler, 1995). A majority of litigants felt that the mediated agreement was fair (Goerdt, 1993; Hermann, LaFree, Rack, and West, 1993; McEwen and Maiman, 1981; Roehl, Hersch, and Llaneras, 1992; Wissler, 1995). In two studies, almost twice as many litigants whose case went to trial after not settling in mediation said they would prefer to use mediation rather than trial in a future case (Roehl, Hersch, and Llaneras, 1992; Wissler, 1995), but one study found no differences in their process preferences (Hermann, LaFree, Rack, and West, 1993).

The studies that included a comparison group of adjudicated cases generally found that litigants in mediated cases had more favorable assessments of the process and the third party than did litigants in tried cases (Hermann, LaFree, Rack, and West, 1993; McEwen and Maiman, 1981; Roehl, Hersch, and Llaneras, 1992; Wissler, 1995), but one study found no differences (Goerdt, 1993). In four studies, litigants felt the mediated agreement was more fair than the adjudicated decision (Goerdt, 1993; Hermann, LaFree, Rack, and West, 1993; McEwen and Maiman, 1981; Roehl, Hersch, and Llaneras, 1992), but two studies found no differences (Vidmar, 1985; Wissler, 1995).

Impact on the Litigants' Relationship. The findings of the three studies that examined this outcome present a mixed picture. In one study, litigants in mediation were about as likely to think that the process had not improved their relationship as to think it had (Maiman, 1997). In a second study, litigants had less negative views of the other party, and those involved in an ongoing relationship felt the dispute had a less negative impact on their relationship if they settled in mediation than if they did not settle in mediation or only went to trial (Wissler, 1995). In a third study, litigants reported being less angry and upset at the end of mediation than did litigants at the end of trial (McEwen and Maiman, 1981).

Macrojustice. Several studies explored case outcomes and found fairly consistent differences between mediated and adjudicated cases in the nature of the outcome and the dollar amount received. Mediated agreements were more likely than judicial decisions to include nonmonetary provisions (Hermann, LaFree, Rack, and West, 1993; Wissler, 1995), the immediate payment of at least some of the money (McEwen and Maiman, 1981; Roehl, Hersch, and Llaneras, 1992; Wissler, 1995), and installment payments (McEwen and Maiman, 1981; Hermann, LaFree, Rack, and West, 1993; Wissler, 1995). In cases with monetary outcomes, plaintiffs were more likely to receive at least some money in mediated cases than in tried cases (McEwen and Maiman, 1981; Roehl, Hersch, and Llaneras, 1992; Vidmar, 1985). Two studies found that mediated agreements represented a smaller percentage of the plaintiff's claim than adjudicated decisions (McEwen and Maiman, 1981; Roehl, Hersch, and Llaneras, 1992), but two other studies found no differences (Hermann, LaFree, Rack, and West, 1993; Vidmar and Short, 1984).

Durability of Settlement. Eight studies assessed compliance with the mediated agreement, typically between one and six months after mediation, and found the rate of full compliance to be between 62 and 90 percent (Hermann, LaFree, Rack, and West, 1993; McEwen and Maiman, 1981; Olexa and Rozelle, 1991; Raitt, Folberg, Rosenberg, and Barrett, 1993; Roehl, Hersch, and Llaneras, 1992; Russell, 1998; Vidmar, 1984; Wissler, 1995). Of the subset of studies that involved a comparison group of tried cases, most found a higher rate of full or partial compliance with mediated agreements than with trial decisions (Hermann, LaFree, Rack, and West, 1993; McEwen and Maiman, 1981; Olexa and Rozelle, 1991; Roehl, Hersch, and Llaneras, 1992; Vidmar, 1984), but one found no differences (Wissler, 1995). There were no differences, however, between litigants whose case settled in mediation and litigants whose case was resolved at trial in their perceptions of whether the dispute was really settled (Roehl, Hersch, and Llaneras, 1992; Wissler, 1995) or in their reports of subsequent problems with the other party (Roehl, Hersch, and Llaneras, 1992).

Impact of Program Structure on Outcomes

The few studies to examine outcomes in relation to structural elements of programs found virtually no effects of structure.

Mode of Referral. Both studies that examined the impact of the mode of referral found no differences in the rate of settlement between cases that entered mediation voluntarily and cases ordered to mediation (McEwen and Maiman, 1981; Wissler, 1995). The mode of referral also did not result in differences in the size or nature of the mediated outcome (Wissler, 1995), compliance with the agreement (McEwen and Maiman, 1981; Wissler, 1995), improvement in the litigants' relationship (Wissler, 1995), or litigants' assessments of the process, mediator, or outcome (Wissler, 1995).

The Mediators. The single study to examine the effect of different types of mediators found that whether the mediator was a volunteer attorney, a court law clerk, or a volunteer layperson did not affect the settlement rate (Roehl, Hersch, and Llaneras, 1992). The only differences that independent observers reported between the lawyer and lay mediators was that lawyers were more likely to have a better understanding of the dispute and to refuse to hear some evidence.

Case Characteristics. The likelihood of settlement did not vary with general case-type categories in two studies (Roehl, Hersch, and Llaneras, 1992; Wissler, 1995), but another study found differences, with settlement most likely in cases involving unpaid bills and private sales and least likely in traffic accident cases (McEwen and Maiman, 1981). The findings of the latter study, however, might in part reflect that cases in which the defendant admitted owing some or all of the plaintiff's claim were more likely to settle than if the defendant denied all liability (Hermann, LaFree, Rack, and West, 1993; Roehl, Hersch, and Llaneras, 1992; Vidmar, 1984; but see Wissler, 1995). Four studies found no relationship between settlement and the contentiousness, nature, or length of the relationship between the litigants (McEwen and Maiman, 1981; Roehl, Hersch, and Llaneras, 1992; Vidmar, 1984; Wissler, 1995).[4]

Mediation in General Jurisdiction Civil Cases

The findings of twenty-seven general civil mediation studies are discussed in this section (Amis and others, 1998; Averill, 1995; Bergman, 1998; Bickerman, 1998; Clarke and Gordon, 1997; Daniel, 1995; Dichter, 1998; Estee, 1987; Fix and Harter, 1992; Hann and Baar, 2001; Herman, 2001; Kakalik and others, 1996, chaps. 5–8; Kobbervig, 1991; McEwen, 1992a; Macfarlane, 1995, 2003; Maiman, 1997; *Report on Mediation*, 2002; Schildt, Alfini, and Johnson, 1994; Schultz, 1990; Stienstra, Johnson, and Lombard, 1997, chaps. 5, 6; Wissler, 2002; Woodward, 1990). A majority of the studies relied on questionnaire data from litigants, attorneys, and usually also from mediators (Clarke and Gordon, 1997; Daniel, 1995; Hann and Baar, 2001; Herman, 2001; Kakalik and others, 1996, chaps. 5–8; Kobbervig, 1991; Macfarlane, 1995; Maiman, 1997; *Report on Mediation*, 2002; Schildt, Alfini, and Johnson, 1994; Schultz, 1990; Wissler, 2002). Several studies surveyed attorneys but not litigants (Averill, 1995; Estee, 1987; Stienstra, Johnson, and Lombard, 1997, chaps. 5, 6; Woodward, 1990). Instead of or in addition to questionnaires, several studies used litigant and attorney interviews (Fix and Harter, 1992; Macfarlane, 1995; Schildt, Alfini, and Johnson, 1994) or focus groups (Hann and Baar, 2001; Macfarlane, 2003). Several studies relied exclusively on court or mediation program records (Amis and others, 1998; Bergman, 1998; Bickerman, 1998; Dichter, 1998); most other studies used these records to supplement information from participants. Three studies included observations of mediation sessions (Clarke and Gordon, 1997; Stienstra, Johnson, and Lombard, 1997, chaps. 5, 6).[5]

Fifteen of the studies included a comparison group of nonmediation cases for one or more outcome measures (Clarke and Gordon, 1997; Estee, 1987; Fix and Harter, 1992; Hann and Baar, 2001; Kakalik and others, 1996, chapters. 5–8; Kobbervig, 1991; McEwen, 1992a; Macfarlane, 1995; Schildt, Alfini, and Johnson, 1994; Stienstra, Johnson, and Lombard, 1997, chaps. 5, 6; Wissler, 2002). Only four of these studies randomly assigned mediation-eligible cases to either a mediation or a non-mediation group (Kakalik and others, 1996, chaps. 5, 6; McEwen, 1992a;

Stienstra, Johnson, and Lombard, 1997, chap. 5; the last two studies had a third group of cases that entered mediation voluntarily, which were analyzed separately). One study compared mediation cases to a sample of nonmediation cases that were closed prior to the implementation of the mediation program (Hann and Baar, 2001). Several additional studies that had randomly assigned cases to be eligible for referral to mediation nonetheless involved an element of party or judicial selection in which some of those cases ultimately went to mediation (Clarke and Gordon, 1997; Kobbervig, 1991; Macfarlane, 1995). Comparisons from Kakalik and others (1996, chap. 8) were not included in this review because the authors reported the mediation cases were more complex and tougher to settle than the nonmediation cases. Because mediation and nonmediation cases in other studies that did not use random assignment also might differ from each other in important ways, the comparative findings should be interpreted with caution. An additional caution is that some studies did not report statistical significance tests for some or all of the comparisons; accordingly, some apparent differences might not be statistically significant or true differences.

Program Structure

General jurisdiction civil courts typically handled all civil actions other than small claims, domestic relations, and probate cases. Different programs excluded different types of cases from mediation, such as prisoner petitions, social security, and declaratory relief (Estee, 1987; Kakalik and others, 1996, chaps. 5–8; Stienstra, Johnson, and Lombard, 1997, chaps. 5, 6), motor vehicle claims (Macfarlane, 1995; Maiman, 1997), or medical malpractice cases (McEwen, 1992a). Most of the programs were administered by the court, but a few were administered by an outside organization (Kobbervig, 1991; Maiman, 1997). Although most programs offered mediation at no cost, litigants paid some or all of the mediator and administrative fees in some programs (Clarke and Gordon, 1997; Hann and Baar, 2001; Kakalik and others, 1996, chaps. 7, 8; Kobbervig, 1991; McEwen, 1992a; Maiman, 1997; Schultz, 1990).

The mediation session was held, on average, within six months after filing in some programs (Hann and Barr, 2001; Kakalik and others, 1996, chaps. 6, 7; Macfarlane, 1995; Stienstra, Johnson, and Lombard, 1997, chap. 5), between seven and twelve months after filing in other programs (Clarke and Gordon, 1997; Kakalik and others, 1996, chap. 8; McEwen, 1992a; Wissler, 2002), and a year or more after filing in yet other programs (Estee, 1987; Kakalik and others, 1996, chap. 5; Schildt, Alfini, and Johnson, 1994; Woodward, 1990). In some programs, a majority of cases had completed most or all discovery before the mediation session (Daniel, 1995; Dichter, 1998; Fix and Harter, 1992; Kobbervig, 1991; Stienstra, Johnson, and Lombard, 1997, chap. 6; Woodward, 1990), but in other programs, mediation occurred earlier in the discovery process, sometimes even before it had started (Hann and Baar, 2001; Macfarlane, 1995, 2003; Stienstra, Johnson, and Lombard, 1997, chap. 5; Wissler, 2002). A few programs noted they required all dispositive or significant motions to be heard before mediation took place (McEwen, 1992a; Stienstra, Johnson, and Lombard, 1997, chap. 6; Woodward, 1990). The mediator typically received information about the case prior to the session (Daniel, 1995; Estee, 1987; Kakalik and others, 1996, chaps. 5–7; McEwen, 1992a; Schildt, Alfini, and Johnson, 1994; Schultz, 1990; Stienstra, Johnson, and Lombard, 1997, chaps. 5, 6; Wissler, 2002; but see Kakalik and others, 1996, chap. 8).

Most programs involved mandatory referral of eligible cases to mediation on an automatic basis, on a judge's order, or at the request of one party. In only a few programs was mediation totally voluntary, requiring both parties to request or agree to use it (Estee, 1987; Maiman, 1997; Schildt, Alfini, and Johnson, 1994; *Report on Mediation,* 2002). Other programs assessed both parties' willingness to mediate prior to referral or permitted parties to opt out after referral (Bickerman, 1998; Daniel, 1995; Estee, 1987; Kakalik and others, 1996, chaps. 7, 8; Kobbervig, 1991; Macfarlane, 1995, 2003). The attorneys and litigants or persons with settlement authority were required to attend mediation in most programs (Bergman, 1998; Clarke and Gordon, 1997; Dichter, 1998; Estee, 1987; Kakalik and others, 1996, chaps. 5, 7, 8; McEwen, 1992a; Macfarlane, 1995; Schildt, Alfini, and Johnson, 1994; Stienstra, Johnson, and Lombard, 1997, chaps. 5, 6; Wissler, 2002; but see Kakalik and others, 1996, chap. 6; Woodward, 1990).

Most cases had a single mediation session in most programs (Clarke and Gordon, 1997; Hann and Baar, 2001; Kakalik and others, 1996, chaps. 6–8; McEwen, 1992b; Macfarlane, 2003; Stienstra, Johnson, and Lombard, 1997, chap. 6; Wissler, 2002), but half or more of the cases had more than one session in several programs (Daniel, 1995; Kakalik and others, 1996, chap. 5; Stienstra, Johnson, and Lombard, 1997, chap. 5). The length of the average mediation session was two to three hours in most programs (Clarke and Gordon, 1997; Hann and Baar, 2001; McEwen,

1992b; Macfarlane, 1995, 2003; Schildt, Alfini, and Johnson, 1994; Stienstra, Johnson, and Lombard, 1997, chaps. 5, 6; Wissler, 2002), but was less than two hours in one program (Kakalik and others, 1997, chap. 6) and from four to eight hours in other programs (Estee, 1987; Kakalik and others, 1996, chaps. 5, 7, 8; Kobbervig, 1991).

The mediators served partially or fully pro bono in some programs (Bergman, 1998; Bickerman, 1998; Daniel, 1995; Dichter, 1998; Estee, 1987; Kakalik and others, 1996, chaps. 5, 6; Schildt, Alfini, and Johnson, 1994; Stienstra, Johnson, and Lombard, 1997, chap. 6; Wissler, 2002; Woodward, 1990), were paid by the parties in other programs (Clarke and Gordon, 1997; Hann and Baar, 2001; Kakalik and others, 1996, chaps. 7, 8; Kobbervig, 1991; McEwen, 1992a; Maiman, 1997; Schultz, 1990), and were employed by the court in a few programs (Stienstra, Johnson, and Lombard, 1997, chap. 5; Wissler, 2002). The mediators in most programs were attorneys who had substantial litigation experience or had been a magistrate or a judge; only a few programs used both attorney and lay mediators (Averill, 1995; Kakalik and others, 1996, chap. 7; Macfarlane, 2003; Maiman, 1997). The mediators either had prior mediation training or experience or were trained by the program (Averill, 1995; Bergman, 1998; Bickerman, 1998; Clarke and Gordon, 1997; Daniel, 1995; Dichter, 1998; Kakalik and others, 1996, chaps. 5, 7, 8; McEwen, 1992b; Maiman, 1997; *Report on Mediation,* 2002; Schildt, Alfini, and Johnson, 1994; Schultz, 1990; Stienstra, Johnson, and Lombard, 1997, chap. 6; Wissler, 2002; Woodward, 1990).

Two programs adopted primarily a facilitative, nonevaluative approach (Macfarlane, 2003; Schildt, Alfini, and Johnson, 1994). In several programs, some of which were labeled "facilitative" (Kakalik and others, 1996, chaps. 6–8), mediators engaged in one or more of the following actions in from roughly one-fourth to three-fourths of the cases: evaluated the strengths and weaknesses of each side's case, suggested settlement options, predicted the outcome, or assessed or recommended the settlement value of the case (Herman, 2001; Kakalik and others, 1996, chaps. 5, 6, 8; McEwen, 1992b; Wissler, 2002; but see Kakalik and others, 1996, chap. 7). Several studies noted the mediators' approach varied among the mediators (Estee, 1987; McEwen, 1992b; Wissler, 2002) and over the course of a session (Dichter, 1998).

Outcomes

This research emphasizes settlement rates, participant satisfaction, and time and cost savings.

Settlement Rate. Virtually all studies examined the rate of settlement in mediation. The settlement rate in most studies was between 27 and 63 percent (Averill, 1995; Bergman, 1998; Bickerman, 1998; Clarke and Gordon, 1997; Daniel, 1995; Dichter, 1998; Estee, 1987; Fix and Harter, 1992; Hann and Baar, 2001; Herman, 2001; Kakalik and others, 1996, chaps. 5, 7, 8; Kobbervig, 1991; McEwen, 1992a; Macfarlane, 1995; Maiman, 1997; *Report on Mediation,* 2002; Schildt, Alfini, and Johnson, 1994; Schultz, 1990; Stienstra, Johnson, and Lombard, 1997, chaps. 5, 6; Wissler, 2002; Woodward, 1990), but a few studies reported a lower (13 to 22 percent; Kakalik and others, 1996, chap. 6; Macfarlane, 2003) or higher settlement rate (71 to 80 percent; Amis and others, 1998; Maiman, 1997). Of the eight studies that included a comparison group of non-mediation cases, half found that cases referred to mediation tended to have a somewhat higher rate of settlement, or a somewhat lower rate of trial or judgment on a dispositive motion, than did cases not referred to mediation (Kakalik and others, 1996, chaps. 5, 7; McEwen, 1992a; Stienstra, Johnson, and Lombard, 1997, chap. 5), but half found no differences (Clarke and Gordon, 1997; Kakalik and others, 1996, chap. 6; Kobbervig, 1991; Wissler, 2002).

Participants' Assessments. The sixteen studies that examined litigants' assessments of the process, the neutral, and the outcome found highly favorable views. Most litigants said the mediation process was fair (Clarke and Gordon, 1997; Herman, 2001; Kakalik and others, 1996, chaps. 5–8; Kobbervig, 1991; Maiman, 1997; *Report on Mediation,* 2002; Schildt, Alfini, and Johnson, 1994; Schultz, 1990; Wissler, 2002) and gave them sufficient opportunity to present their case (Clarke and Gordon, 1997; Daniel, 1995; Fix and Harter, 1992; Kobbervig, 1991; Macfarlane, 1995; Maiman, 1997; *Report on Mediation,* 2002; Wissler, 2002). A majority of litigants felt they had control over the process or had input in determining the outcome (Maiman, 1997; Schildt, Alfini, and Johnson, 1994; Wissler, 2002; but see Clarke and Gordon, 1997). Most litigants thought the mediator was neutral (Clarke and Gordon, 1997; Daniel, 1995; Macfarlane, 1995; Maiman, 1997; *Report on Mediation,* 2002; Schildt, Alfini, and Johnson, 1994; Wissler, 2002), did not pressure them to settle (Macfarlane, 1995; Schildt, Alfini, and Johnson, 1994; Wissler, 2002), understood their views and the issues in dispute (Hann and Baar, 2001; Maiman, 1997; *Report on Mediation,* 2002; Wissler, 2002), and treated them with respect (*Report on Mediation,* 2002; Wissler, 2002). A majority of litigants felt the mediated settlement was fair (Kobbervig, 1991; Macfarlane, 1995; Schildt, Alfini, and Johnson, 1994; Wissler, 2002) or were satisfied with it

(Daniel, 1995; Fix and Harter, 1992; Maiman, 1997; Schildt, Alfini, and Johnson, 1994).

The twenty studies that examined attorneys' assessments consistently reported high ratings of the mediation process and the mediator. Most attorneys said the mediation process was fair (Averill, 1995; Herman, 2001; Kakalik and others, chaps. 5–8; Kobbervig, 1991; Macfarlane 1995; Maiman, 1997; *Report on Mediation,* 2002; Schildt, Alfini, and Johnson, 1994; Schultz, 1990; Stienstra, Johnson, and Lombard, 1997, chap. 6; Wissler, 2002; Woodward, 1990) and gave sufficient opportunity to present the issues (Daniel, 1995; Fix and Harter, 2002; Kobbervig, 1991; Macfarlane, 1995; Maiman, 1997; *Report on Mediation,* 2002; Woodward, 1990). Most said they would recommend mediation to others or would use mediation again (Averill, 1995; Daniel, 1995; Estee, 1987; Hann and Baar, 2001; Herman, 2001; Macfarlane, 1995; Maiman, 1997; Schildt, Alfini, and Johnson, 1994; Stienstra, Johnson, and Lombard, 1997, chap. 5; Wissler, 2002). A majority of attorneys said the mediator was neutral (Daniel, 1995; Macfarlane, 1995; Maiman, 1997; *Report on Mediation,* 2002; Schildt, Alfini, and Johnson, 1994; Stienstra, Johnson, and Lombard, 1997, chap. 5; Wissler, 2002; Woodward, 1990), understood the issues (Hann and Baar, 2001; Maiman, 1997; *Report on Mediation,* 2002), was well prepared (Daniel, 1995; Stienstra, Johnson, and Lombard, 1997, chap. 5), and was effective in engaging the parties in a meaningful discussion (Daniel, 1995; Stienstra, Johnson, and Lombard, 1997, chap. 5; Wissler, 2002). Most attorneys felt that the mediated settlement was fair (Kobbervig, 1991; Macfarlane, 1995; Schildt, Alfini, and Johnson, 1994; Wissler, 2002) or were satisfied with it (Averill, 1995; Fix and Harter, 1992; Maiman, 1997; Schildt, Alfini, and Johnson, 1994; but see Daniel, 1995).

The subset of studies that compared participants' assessments in mediation and nonmediation cases produced mixed findings. Across all disposition types, two studies found no consistent overall differences in litigants' assessments between mediation and nonmediation cases (Clarke and Gordon, 1997; Macfarlane, 1995), but one study found that litigants in mediation cases had somewhat more favorable assessments (Kobbervig, 1991). Two studies found no consistent overall differences in litigants' assessments between cases that settled as a result of mediation versus negotiation (Clarke and Gordon, 1997; Fix and Harter, 1992). One study found no consistent overall differences in attorneys' assessments between mediation and nonmediation cases (Kobbervig, 1991).[6]

Impact on the Litigants' Relationship. The four studies that examined this outcome found that a minority of litigants (from 5 to 43 percent) thought that mediation improved their relationship with the other party (Hann and Baar, 2001; Herman, 2001; Macfarlane, 1995; Maiman, 1997). In two of the studies, a majority of the litigants felt that mediation had no effect on their relationship, and few felt mediation made their relationship worse (Herman, 2001; Macfarlane, 1995). A majority of attorneys thought that mediation either had no effect on or did not improve the litigants' relationship (Herman, 2001; Kakalik and others, 1996, chaps. 5–8; Stienstra, Johnson, and Lombard, 1997, chaps. 5, 6; Wissler, 2002).

Efficiencies in Dispute Processing. Five studies reported that mediation cases terminated faster than nonmediation cases (Clarke and Gordon, 1997; Hann and Baar, 2001; Kakalik and others, 1996, chap. 5; McEwen, 1992a; Stienstra, Johnson, and Lombard, 1997, chap. 5). However, four studies found no differences in disposition time (Kakalik and others, 1996, chaps. 6, 7; Kobbervig, 1991; Wissler, 2002), and one reported longer disposition times for mediation cases (Estee, 1987). The findings were mixed with regard to whether a majority of attorneys did (Daniel, 1995; Kakalik and others, 1996) or did not (Kakalik and others, 1996, chaps. 5, 6; Stienstra, Johnson and Lombard, 1997, chap. 6) think mediation reduced the time to disposition.

Macrojustice. The single study (Clarke and Gordon, 1997) to compare mediated and litigated outcomes found that plaintiffs were more likely to receive some money in cases that settled in mediation than in cases that went to trial, but the amount of money received in mediated settlements was smaller. No differences were found between settlements reached in mediation versus in bilateral negotiation.

Transaction Cost Savings. Three studies found no differences between mediation cases and nonmediation cases, when examining all disposition types combined, in the number of attorney work hours or in legal fees and litigation costs (Kakalik and others, 1996, chaps. 5–7). Another study found that attorneys' fees in cases that settled in mediation did not differ from those in cases that settled through negotiation, but that fees in both groups of settled cases were lower than in tried cases (Clarke and Gordon, 1997). The studies that obtained attorneys' views on costs were split between whether half or more of the attorneys (Hann and Baar, 2001; Kakalik and others, 1996, chaps. 7, 8; Macfarlane, 1995; Maiman, 1997;

Schultz, 1990; Stienstra, Johnson, and Lombard, 1997, chaps. 5, 6) or fewer than half of the attorneys (Clarke and Gordon, 1997; Daniel, 1995; Fix and Harter, 1992; Kakalik and others, 1996, chaps. 5, 6; Maiman, 1997; Wissler, 2002) thought that mediation reduced litigation costs.

Four studies found no differences between mediation and nonmediation cases in the number of interrogatories, depositions, or discovery motions filed (Kakalik and others, 1996, chaps. 5, 6, 8; Stienstra, Johnson, and Lombard, 1997, chap. 5), but two studies reported less discovery and fewer discovery requests and discovery motions filed in mediation cases (Kakalik and others, 1996, chap. 7; McEwen, 1992a). Five studies found no differences between mediation cases and nonmediation cases in the number of motions filed or decided (Clarke and Gordon, 1997; Kakalik and others, 1996, chaps. 6–8; Wissler, 2002), but two studies reported fewer motions in mediation cases (Kakalik and others, 1996, chap. 5; McEwen, 1992a). A majority of attorneys in several studies estimated there was little or no change in the amount of discovery needed or conducted (Clarke and Gordon, 1997; Herman, 2001; Kakalik and others, 1996, chaps. 5–8; Stienstra, Johnson, and Lombard, 1997, chap. 6) or in the number of motions filed (Stienstra, Johnson, and Lombard, 1997, chap. 6; Herman, 2001).

Durability of Settlement. The three studies that examined compliance found that the rate of compliance with mediated agreements was generally 90 percent or greater (Clarke and Gordon, 1997; Fix and Harter, 1992; Macfarlane, 2003). In one study, the rate of compliance with mediated agreements did not differ from the rate of compliance with negotiated settlements, although compliance with both types of settlements was greater than compliance with a trial verdict (Clarke and Gordon, 1997). In another study, mediation and nonmediation cases did not differ in the rate of full compliance or in reports of subsequent disputes (Fix and Harter, 1992).

Impact of Program Structure on Outcomes

Structural elements in these programs had a mixed effect on outcomes.

Timing. Two studies found that cases were more likely to settle if mediation was held sooner after the case had been filed (Schildt, Alfini, and Johnson, 1994; Wissler, 2002), while two other studies found no relationship between mediation timing and the likelihood of settlement (Schultz, 1990; Stienstra, Johnson, and Lombard, 1997, chap. 6). In cases with earlier sessions, fewer motions were filed and decided (Wissler, 2002), and the time to disposition was shorter (Stienstra, Johnson, and Lombard, 1997, chap. 5; Wissler, 2002). Three studies reported no relationship between the status of discovery and the likelihood of settlement (Schildt, Alfini, and Johnson, 1994; Stienstra, Johnson, and Lombard, 1997, chap. 6; Wissler, 2002), but in another study, there appeared to be a link (McEwen, 1992b). Settlement was less likely if dispositive or other motions were pending (Wissler, 2002).

Mode of Referral. Two studies found no differences in settlement rates by mode of referral to mediation (Estee, 1987; Wissler, 2002), and two other studies found that cases that entered mediation voluntarily settled at a higher rate than cases ordered to mediation (McEwen, 1992b; Stienstra, Johnson, and Lombard, 1997, chap. 5). Litigants' assessments of the fairness of the mediation process were not related to whether their side had requested mediation (Wissler, 2002), but attorneys who requested mediation had more favorable assessments of mediation (Stienstra, Johnson, and Lombard, 1997, chap. 5; Wissler, 2002).

The Mediators' Approaches. All three studies that examined this issue found that settlement was more likely if the mediators were more active and disclosed their views about the strengths and weaknesses of the case, case settlement value, or likely court outcome than if they did not (McEwen, 1992b; Wissler, 2002; Woodward, 1990). In the single study that examined the impact of mediator actions on participants' assessments (Wissler, 2002), litigants were more likely to feel the mediation process was fair and did not feel more pressured to settle when the mediators evaluated the case merits than when they did not. However, litigants were more likely to feel pressured to settle by the mediator and were less likely to feel the mediation process was fair if the mediators recommended a particular settlement than if they did not.

The Mediators. Both studies that examined the impact of mediator experience on settlement found that mediators who had mediated more cases had a higher rate of settlement than those with less experience (Hann and Baar, 2001; Wissler, 2002). Mediation experience, however, was not related to litigants' or attorneys' assessments of the fairness of the mediation process (Daniel, 1995; Wissler, 2002). The amount of mediation training was not related to settlement (Wissler, 2002) or to litigants' or attorneys' assessments of the fairness of mediation (Daniel, 1995; Wissler, 2002). And the mediator's familiarity with the substantive issues in the case was not related to the likelihood of settlement or to litigants' and attorneys' assessments of the fairness of the mediation process (Wissler, 2002).

Case Characteristics. Several studies found no differences in settlement rates among general case type categories (Kakalik and others, 1996; McEwen,1992a; Macfarlane, 1995; Schultz, 1990; Wissler, 2002). Two studies found differences in settlement rates by case type: personal injury cases appeared to have a higher rate of settlement than contract cases in one study (Schildt, Alfini, and Johnson, 1994) but a lower rate in the other study (Macfarlane, 2003). Other studies suggested that differences in the rate of settlement might be found by looking at subtypes of cases within these broad case categories (Hann and Baar, 2001; Schultz, 1990). Participants' assessments of the process (Schildt, Alfini, and Johnson, 1994) or the outcome (Schultz, 1990) did not vary by case type. Nor was the monetary value of the case related to the likelihood of settlement (Macfarlane, 1995).

Several other case characteristics were related to the increased likelihood of settlement in mediation: less disparity in the parties' positions at the start of mediation (Wissler, 2002), liability being contested to a lesser degree (Wissler, 2002), and fewer named parties (Hann and Baar, 2001). Greater party preparation for mediation was related to an increased likelihood of settlement, to litigants' feeling less pressured by the mediator to settle, and to litigants' and attorneys' viewing the mediation process as fairer (Wissler, 2002). The complexity of the issues was not related to settlement in two studies (Schildt, Alfini, and Johnson, 1994; Woodward, 1990), but another study found a higher settlement rate in less complex cases (Wissler, 2002). The contentiousness of the litigants' relationship was not related to the likelihood of settlement (Macfarlane, 1995; Wissler, 2002). Greater cooperativeness of opposing counsel during mediation, however, was related to an increased likelihood of settlement and to litigants' and attorneys' viewing the mediation process as fairer (Wissler, 2002).

Mediation in Appellate Cases

The findings of fifteen appellate mediation studies are discussed in this section (Aemmer, 1997; Birnbaum and Ellman, 1976; Cohen and Mashburn, 1999; Eaglin, 1990; FitzGibbon, 1993; Ganzfried, 1997; Hanson, 1991; Hanson and Becker, 2002; McNally, 2000; Note, 1979; Partridge and Lind, 1983; Riselli, 2001; Steelman and Goldman, 1986; Task Force, 2001; Torregrossa, 2002).[7] Only one study surveyed litigants (Task Force, 2001);[8]

seven studies used attorney questionnaires (Eaglin, 1990; Hanson, 1991; Hanson and Becker, 2002; Note, 1979; Partridge and Lind, 1983; Steelman and Goldman, 1986; Task Force, 2001). A few studies supplemented these data sources with mediator logs (Eaglin, 1990; Task Force, 2001) or observations of mediation sessions (Eaglin, 1990; Hanson and Becker, 2002). All studies obtained data from court or program records.

Six of the studies included a comparison group of nonmediation cases for one or more outcome measures. Five of these studies had essentially randomly assigned mediation-eligible cases to either a mediation or a nonmediation group (Aemmer, 1997; Eaglin, 1990; Hanson, 1991; Partridge and Lind, 1983; Steelman and Goldman, 1986). The remaining study compared mediation cases to a sample of nonmediation cases that were closed prior to the implementation of the mediation program (Note, 1979). The comparative findings should nonetheless be interpreted with caution because some studies did not report tests of statistical significance for some or all of the comparisons.

Program Structure

Appellate mediation programs typically excluded prisoner petitions and cases in which parties were not represented by counsel (Aemmer, 1997; Cohen and Mashburn, 1999; Eaglin, 1990; Hanson, 1991; Hanson and Becker, 2002; McNally, 2000; Partridge and Lind, 1983; Riselli, 2001; Steelman and Goldman, 1986; Torregrossa, 2002). State court programs, which involved domestic relations cases as well as general civil cases, typically also excluded appeals involving custody, paternity, or termination of parental rights (Cohen and Mashburn, 1999; FitzGibbon, 1993; McNally, 2000; Steelman and Goldman, 1986) or juveniles (Hanson, 1991; Steelman and Goldman, 1986). All programs were administered by the court, and virtually all offered mediation at no cost to the parties (but see McNally, 2000; Task Force, 2001). Several programs noted that they attempted to settle not only the appeal but also related matters at both the trial and appellate levels (Aemmer, 1997; McNally, 2000; Riselli, 2001; Task Force, 2001).

The initial mediation session was held in most programs within one to two months after the notice of appeal had been filed (Birnbaum and Ellman, 1976; Cohen and Mashburn, 1999; Eaglin, 1990; Hanson, 1991; Hanson and Becker, 2002; Partridge and Lind, 1983; Steelman and Goldman, 1986; Task Force, 2001), but was held four to five months after filing in a few programs (FitzGibbon, 1993; Steelman and Goldman, 1986). Mediation typically took place before briefing and oral argument (but see Steelman and Goldman, 1986). The mediator generally received information about the case prior to the session (Aemmer, 1997; Birnbaum and Ellman, 1976; Cohen and Mashburn, 1999; Eaglin, 1990; Ganzfried, 1997; Hanson and Becker, 2002; Note, 1979; Task Force, 2001; Torregrossa, 2002).

Mediation was totally voluntary, requiring the agreement of both parties, in only one program (Steelman and Goldman, 1986). All other programs involved mandatory referral of eligible cases to mediation on an automatic basis, on a judge's order, or at the request of one party. A few programs sought attorney input prior to referral or permitted parties to opt out after referral (FitzGibbon, 1993; Task Force, 2001; Torregrossa, 2002). Counsel's participation in mediation generally was required (Aemmer, 1997; Birnbaum and Ellman, 1976; Cohen and Mashburn, 1999; Eaglin, 1990; FitzGibbon, 1993; Ganzfried, 1997; Hanson, 1991; Note, 1979; Partridge and Lind, 1983; Steelman and Goldman, 1986; Torregrossa, 2002). Most programs also required the participation of litigants or persons with settlement authority (Birnbaum and Ellman, 1976; Cohen and Mashburn, 1999; Hanson, 1991; Riselli, 2001; Steelman and Goldman, 1986; Task Force, 2001; Torregrossa, 2002) or their availability for consultation (Note, 1979). Other programs welcomed or encouraged, but did not require, litigant participation (Aemmer, 1997; McNally, 2000; Steelman and Goldman, 1986).

Some programs, especially those in courts that covered a large geographical area, held mediation sessions primarily by telephone to minimize litigants' costs (Aemmer, 1997; Eaglin, 1990; Hanson and Becker, 2002; Riselli, 2001), while others tended to hold in-person sessions (Cohen and Mashburn, 1999; FitzGibbon, 1993; Hanson, 1991; McNally, 2000; Note, 1979; Steelman and Goldman, 1986; Task Force, 2001; Torregrossa, 2002). The length of the typical initial mediation session was sixty to ninety minutes in some programs (Eaglin, 1990; Partridge and Lind, 1983), but in other programs it was as short as thirty minutes (FitzGibbon, 1993) or as long as four to six hours (McNally, 2000; Task Force, 2001). The mediator generally engaged in extensive follow-up with the attorneys to monitor the progress of negotiations and to hold additional caucuses or joint sessions as the negotiations continued (Aemmer, 1997; Eaglin, 1990; FitzGibbon, 1993; McNally, 2000; Torregrossa, 2002). Accordingly, appellate mediation in a single case could span weeks or months (FitzGibbon, 1993).

The mediators were employed by the court in most programs; in two programs, however, the mediators served partially or fully pro bono (Ganzfried, 1997; Task Force, 2001). The mediators consisted of attorneys with substantial prior litigation experience (Aemmer, 1997; Ganzfried, 1997; Hanson and Becker, 2002; Partridge and Lind, 1983; Riselli, 2001), sitting or retired judges (Birnbaum and Ellman, 1976; Cohen and Mashburn, 1999; FitzGibbon, 1993; Hanson, 1991; Steelman and Goldman, 1986), or a combination of attorneys and judges (Note, 1979; Torregrossa, 2002). Sitting judges who served as mediators were automatically disqualified from hearing the case (but see Steelman and Goldman, 1986). Only one program used experienced nonattorney mediators, comprising a majority of that program's mediators (Task Force, 2001). Some programs noted that the mediators had prior mediation experience or received mediation training (Ganzfried, 1997; Hanson, 1991; Hanson and Becker, 2002; Riselli, 2001; Task Force, 2001).

Although variation in mediator approach within a program was noted, in most programs the mediators tended to engage participants in a discussion of the strengths and weaknesses of the case, the litigants' interests, various settlement options, and the risks and benefits of settlement and non-settlement (Aemmer, 1997; Birnbaum and Ellman, 1976; Eaglin, 1990; FitzGibbon, 1993; Ganzfried, 1997; Hanson, 1991; Hanson and Becker, 2002; McNally, 2000; Task Force, 2001; Torregrossa, 2002). A few studies noted that the mediators sometimes (FitzGibbon, 1993; Partridge and Lind, 1983) or frequently (Note, 1979) predicted the outcome of the appeal.

Outcomes

This research focused mainly on settlement rates, attorney's assessments, and efficiencies of dispute processing.

Settlement Rate. All studies examined the rate at which cases were settled, withdrawn, or voluntarily dismissed prior to the submission of briefs, oral argument, or a judicial decision on the merits.[9] In most programs, between 29 and 47 percent of the cases were resolved before argument (Aemmer, 1997; Birnbaum and Ellman, 1976; Eaglin, 1990; FitzGibbon, 1993; Ganzfried, 1997; Hanson and Becker, 2002; McNally, 2000; Note, 1979; Partridge and Lind, 1983; Steelman and Goldman, 1986; Task Force, 2001; Torregrossa, 2002), but several programs had a higher rate of preargument disposition, ranging from 56 to 76 percent (Cohen and Mashburn, 1999; Hanson, 1991; Riselli, 2001; Steelman and Goldman,

1986). Most of the subset of studies that included a comparison group of nonmediation cases found that cases assigned to mediation were 10 to 20 percent more likely than cases not assigned to mediation to be resolved before briefing or argument (Aemmer, 1997; Eaglin, 1990; Hanson, 1991; Note, 1979; Partridge and Lind, 1983; Steelman and Goldman, 1986), but one study reported no differences in two programs (Steelman and Goldman, 1986).

Participants' Assessments. The only study to obtain litigants' assessments found they gave high ratings to the mediator's impartiality and knowledge, as well as to the fairness, confidentiality, and opportunity for participation the mediation process provided (Task Force, 2001). The six studies that obtained attorneys' assessments consistently found high ratings of the mediator and the mediation process. Most attorneys felt that the mediator was neutral (Hanson and Becker, 2002; Task Force, 2001), did not apply undue settlement pressure (Note, 1979; Partridge and Lind, 1983), and was knowledgeable about mediation and the subject matter (Task Force, 2001). Most attorneys supported the continuation of the mediation program (Hanson, 1991; Note, 1979), preferred participation in the program to the usual appeals process (Eaglin, 1990; Partridge and Lind, 1983), and would use mediation again or recommend it to others (Hanson and Becker, 2002; Task Force, 2001). Most attorneys reported that the mediation agreement was clear, workable, and fair to both sides (Hanson and Becker, 2002).

Efficiencies in Dispute Processing. In five of the studies that examined this outcome, the time from filing the appeal to case disposition (for all modes of disposition combined) was one to three months shorter for cases assigned to mediation than for cases not assigned to mediation (Eaglin, 1990; Hanson, 1991; Note, 1979; Partridge and Lind, 1983; Steelman and Goldman, 1986).[10] One study, however, found no reduction in the time to disposition in two programs (Steelman and Goldman, 1986).

Transaction Cost Savings. The single study to compare cases assigned to mediation with cases not assigned to mediation did not find differences in attorneys' reports of time spent on the appeal or transcript and reproduction costs in any of the three programs examined (Steelman and Goldman, 1986). With regard to the potential for cost savings for the courts, several studies calculated that the mediation program resolved a number of cases equal to the caseload of one to two judges and their staff (Eaglin, 1990; Hanson and Becker, 2002; Partridge and Lind, 1983).

Impact of Program Structure on Outcomes

The structural elements examined in these programs had limited effects on outcomes.

In-Person Versus Telephonic Mediations. Although no data were provided to support their conclusions, one program noted that experimental telephone conferences "were found to be effective" (Eaglin, 1990, p. 14), another reported that their "experience" suggested that in-person mediations were more productive than those conducted by telephone (Torregrossa, 2002, p. 1070), and a third program reported "no appreciable difference" in settlement rates between in-person and telephonic mediations (Riselli, 2001, p. 60).

Case Characteristics. Four studies found no substantial differences in the likelihood of settlement in mediation based on the subject matter of the case (Eaglin, 1990; FitzGibbon, 1993; Hanson and Becker, 2002; Note, 1979), but one study (Task Force, 2001) found differences that family law and probate cases were more likely to settle than contract and personal injury cases, which in turn were more likely to settle than employment and insurance cases. One study found that participation in alternative dispute resolution (ADR) in an earlier stage of the case reduced the likelihood the appeal would settle in mediation (Task Force, 2001). Another study found that the presence of a decision maker in mediation affected settlement, such that settlement was least likely when neither side had a decision maker present and most likely when both sides did (McNally, 2000). Settlement rates were not related to several other case characteristics, including the number of parties (Note, 1979), whether the plaintiff sought monetary or other relief (Note, 1979; Partridge and Lind, 1983), or whether the appeal was from an agency or a court decision and, if the latter, whether from trial or summary judgment (Note, 1979).

Neutral Evaluation in General Jurisdiction Civil Cases

The findings of four neutral evaluation studies are discussed in this section (Fitzhugh, 1998; Kakalik and others, 1996, chaps. 9, 10; Rosenberg and Folberg, 1994).[11] All studies obtained information from court or program records; three also reported data from questionnaires completed by litigants, attorneys, and evaluators (Kakalik and others, 1996, chaps. 9, 10; Rosenberg and Folberg, 1994). One study supplemented questionnaire data with interviews, focus groups, and observation of sessions (Rosenberg and Folberg, 1994).

All four studies included a comparison group of cases not assigned to neutral evaluation. Only one study randomly assigned eligible cases to neutral evaluation (Rosenberg and Folberg, 1994). One study used a comparison group of cases that were managed by a magistrate judge but did not go to neutral evaluation (Kakalik and others, 1996, chap. 10). Two studies used a comparison group of cases that were closed prior to the implementation of the neutral evaluation program (Fitzhugh, 1998; Kakalik and others, 1996, chap. 9). Comparisons from the latter study were not included in this review, however, because the court instituted earlier and more intensive case management at the same time as the neutral evaluation program; accordingly, any differences between the outcomes of the two groups of cases could not be attributed to the program alone. Because the other studies did not report tests of statistical significance for some or all of the comparisons, the comparative findings should be interpreted with caution.

Program Structure

Neutral evaluation generally involved the discussion of settlement possibilities, accompanied by the evaluator's assessment of the strengths and weaknesses of each side's case and a prediction of the likely trial outcome (Fitzhugh, 1998; Rosenberg and Folberg, 1994). If a settlement was not reached, the evaluator typically explored case management issues, such as information sharing, discovery, and motions (Fitzhugh, 1998; Kakalik and others, 1996, chap. 9; Rosenberg and Folberg, 1994). Different programs excluded different types of cases, most commonly those involving prisoner petitions, social security, bankruptcy, or injunctive relief (Fitzhugh, 1998; Kakalik et al., 1996, chap. 9; Rosenberg and Folberg, 1994). All programs were administered by the court, and most offered neutral evaluation at no cost to the litigants (but see Fitzhugh, 1998).

In two programs, the neutral evaluation session was held in a majority of cases four to five months after the case was filed (Kakalik and others, 1996, chap. 9; Rosenberg and Folberg, 1994), but in another program the session was held on average a year after filing (Kakalik and others, 1996, chap. 10). Most cases had a single session in most programs, but about half of the cases had two or more sessions in one program (Kakalik and others, 1996, chap. 9). In all programs, a majority of the sessions lasted two to six hours. The evaluators received information about the case prior to the session in all programs.

All programs primarily involved mandatory referral of cases to neutral evaluation; parties in one program could opt out, but few did (Rosenberg and Folberg, 1994). The attorneys and litigants or persons with settlement authority typically were required to attend the session in all programs.

In two programs, the evaluators were attorneys with substantial litigation experience who served pro bono (Kakalik and others, 1996, chap. 10; Rosenberg and Folberg, 1994). In another program, the evaluators were magistrate judges who were supervising discovery (Kakalik and others, 1996, chap. 9). In the fourth program, the evaluators were paid by the parties (Fitzhugh, 1998). One court provided a two-day training for evaluators who did not have prior ADR training or experience (Fitzhugh, 1998), and another provided a several-hour training program and written materials for new evaluators (Rosenberg and Folberg, 1994).

Across programs and across evaluators within a program, the evaluator's approach ranged from mediation to "hard-nosed" settlement tactics (Fitzhugh, 1998; Rosenberg and Folberg, 1994, p. 1495). In two programs, the evaluators gave an evaluation to each side in two-thirds to three-fourths of the cases (Kakalik and others, 1996, chaps. 9, 10). In another program, evaluators reported they assessed the strengths and weaknesses of the parties' positions in 80 percent of the cases, but they went further and predicted the trial outcome in 45 percent of cases, estimated the costs of trial in 35 percent, and recommended a specific settlement value in 29 percent of cases (Rosenberg and Folberg, 1994). This study also reported that a majority of evaluators gave their evaluation in the course of settlement discussions, while 20 percent gave their evaluation only after negotiations bogged down, and 5 percent offered their evaluation at the start of the session (Rosenberg and Folberg, 1994).

Outcomes

Once again, standard outcomes have been examined.

Settlement Rate. All four studies examined the rate of settlement as a result of neutral evaluation, which ranged from 23 percent to 51 percent. The single study to compare the trial rate for cases assigned to neutral evaluation with that of cases not assigned to neutral evaluation found that neutral evaluation cases were slightly less likely to have a trial (Kakalik and others, 1996, chap. 10).

Participants' Assessments. The three studies that reported participants' assessments consistently found them to be highly positive. Most litigants and attorneys thought the neutral evaluation process was fair (Kakalik and others, 1996, chaps. 9, 10; Rosenberg and Folberg, 1994) and worth the resources they devoted to it (Rosenberg and Folberg, 1994). In one study, a majority of litigants and attorneys thought the evaluator listened carefully to them and understood their perspectives, was an expert in the subject matter in their case, accurately analyzed the legal and factual issues, and was interested in exploring creative solutions, and a majority of attorneys thought the evaluator was neutral and well prepared (Rosenberg and Folberg, 1994). In two studies, most litigants and attorneys thought the neutral evaluation program was good and should be continued (Kakalik and others, 1996, chaps. 9, 10).

Impact on the Litigants' Relationship. In the two studies that examined this outcome (Kakalik and others, 1996, chaps. 9, 10), 41 percent and 46 percent of attorneys, respectively, said that neutral evaluation helped to improve the relationship between the parties; an equal or larger percentage of attorneys said neutral evaluation had no effect on the parties' relationship. Few attorneys, however, thought neutral evaluation had a detrimental effect on the parties' relationship.

Efficiencies in Dispute Processing. Both of the studies that examined the length of time from filing to disposition found no differences between cases assigned to neutral evaluation and cases not assigned to neutral evaluation (Fitzhugh, 1998; Kakalik and others, 1996, chap. 10). Slightly more attorneys thought that neutral evaluation had no effect on disposition time than thought it reduced disposition time (Kakalik and others, 1996, chaps. 9, 10; Rosenberg and Folberg, 1994); few thought it increased disposition time (Kakalik and others, 1996, chaps. 9, 10).

Transaction Cost Savings. The single study to examine objective measures of costs found no differences between cases assigned to neutral evaluation and cases that were not assigned to neutral evaluation in attorneys' reports of hours worked and fees and costs (Kakalik and others, 1996, chap. 10). The same study reported that fewer motions were filed in cases assigned to neutral evaluation than in cases not assigned to neutral evaluation (Kakalik and others, 1996, chap. 10). In three studies, about half of the attorneys thought neutral evaluation reduced litigation costs, whereas roughly one-fourth thought it increased costs (Kakalik and others, 1996, chap. 10; Rosenberg and Folberg, 1994).

Impact of Program Structure on Outcomes

Few studies examined whether structural elements were related to outcomes.

Timing. The one study that examined the effect of the timing of the neutral evaluation session found it was not related to litigants' or attorneys' satisfaction with the session (Rosenberg and Folberg, 1994).

The Evaluators' Approach. The single study that examined the effects of the evaluators (Rosenberg and Folberg, 1994) found that attorneys were more satisfied with the neutral evaluation process when the evaluator spent more time preparing for a session. Attorneys also were more satisfied with the neutral evaluation process when the evaluators spent less time in private caucuses, gave an evaluation of the case, made suggestions to facilitate and organize discovery, and gave their views on litigation procedure. Attorneys generally were more satisfied with the process when their expectations about how the session would be conducted were closer to the actual approach used. The timing of the evaluation also made a difference: litigants and attorneys were less satisfied with neutral evaluation if the evaluators gave their case assessments before beginning settlement discussions, rather than during the discussions or after negotiations bogged down.

Case Characteristics. The single study to examine the impact of case characteristics (Rosenberg and Folberg, 1994) found that litigants' and attorneys' satisfaction with neutral evaluation was not related to the type of case, the amount of the claim, or the number of parties. Litigant and attorney preparation for the session was not related to their satisfaction with neutral evaluation, but the degree of attorney cooperation during the session was.

Comparison of Outcomes in Mediation and Neutral Evaluation in General Jurisdiction Civil Cases

Only one study has compared the outcomes of mediation and neutral evaluation in a single court (Stienstra, Johnson, and Lombard, 1997, chap. 4).[12] This study relied on questionnaire data from attorneys and neutrals, as well as court record data. Mediation and neutral evaluation were two of several ADR processes administered by the court from which the parties could choose or to which they could be referred by a judge or assigned by a clerk. The attorneys and litigants were required to attend the session in both processes. The neutrals received training through the court and served pro bono for the first four hours of the session; the parties split the neutral's fees if additional time was needed.

There were no differences between mediation and neutral evaluation, or any of the other processes, in the following outcomes: whether the case settled; attorneys' perceptions of the fairness of the procedures and whether the benefits of ADR outweighed the costs; and attorneys' estimates of the effect of ADR on the time to disposition, litigation costs, the cost to prepare for and participate in the session, the amount of discovery conducted, or the number of motions filed. Because cases were not randomly assigned to dispute resolution processes, however, it is unclear whether there were no underlying differences in the effectiveness of the processes or whether parties or judges correctly matched cases to the processes for which they were best suited.

Data from this study and several other multioption or screening conference programs do not reveal a consistent preference for one process over the other. More cases selected, or were referred to, neutral evaluation than mediation in one study (Stienstra, Johnson, and Lombard, 1997, chap. 4), but the pattern was reversed in another study (Stuart and Savage, 1997). And two studies of a single program in different years reported opposite findings: in the first, more cases selected case evaluation (Lowe and Keilitz, 1992), while in the second, more cases selected mediation (Maiman, 1997). In addition, one study found that most tort cases selected case evaluation, whereas most contract cases selected mediation (Lowe and Keilitz, 1992).

Conclusion

In small claims, general civil, and appellate court settings, the empirical research indicates that mediation and neutral evaluation settle cases and that participants view the process and outcome as fair. On these dimensions, as well as with regard to compliance, improving the parties' relationship, and reducing the time and cost of resolution, however, the findings are mixed with regard to whether mediation and neutral evaluation outperform or simply do as well as traditional litigation. In addition, the pattern of findings differs across the three court levels.

In small claims cases, a majority of studies find that compared to trial, mediation receives more favorable assessments from litigants, reduces the rate of noncompliance, and at least in cases that settle, has more positive effects on the parties' relationship. In general civil jurisdiction cases, a majority of studies find no differences between mediation cases and non-mediation cases in participants' assessments, transaction costs, the amount of discovery, and the number of motions filed. The findings are mixed with regard to whether mediation does or does not increase the rate of settlement or reduce the trial rate, reduce the time to disposition, and enhance compliance compared to the traditional litigation process. The few studies of neutral evaluation in general civil cases suggest it does not reduce the time to disposition or transaction costs, but might reduce the number of motions and trials. In appellate cases, a majority of studies find that mediation reduces the rate of cases that go to oral argument and reduces the time to disposition compared to cases that are not assigned to mediation. Mediation does not, however, appear to reduce transaction costs in appellate cases.

The impact that program structural elements have on outcomes also varies across studies. The mode of referral to mediation does not affect the likelihood of settlement or participants' assessments in some studies, but in others the voluntary use of mediation has positive effects. Earlier sessions reduce the time to disposition and the number of motions filed, and in some studies also increase the likelihood of settlement; but in other studies, timing has no impact on settlement. With regard to mediator qualifications, a majority of studies find that more mediation experience is associated with more settlements, but mediation training and subject matter expertise do not affect settlement rates. A majority of studies find that when the neutral plays a more active role, the settlement rate increases. The impact of the neutral's approach on participants' assessments seems to vary depending on what the mediators do, when they do it, and what approach was expected. A majority of studies find that neither the general case type category nor the litigants' relationship is related to settlement, but some studies suggest that other case characteristics might play a role.

To date, some mediation outcomes have been examined in many studies, but other outcomes have been assessed in only a few studies. The neutral evaluation process has received scant empirical attention. Our ability to draw clear conclusions about the relative effectiveness and efficiency of court-connected mediation, neutral evaluation, and traditional litigation is limited by the small number of studies with reliable comparative data based on the random assignment of cases to dispute resolution processes and the use of statistical significance tests. The variation in findings across studies and across court levels also might reflect the use of different measures in different studies or differences in program design or the court context in which different programs operate. Only a handful of studies have systematically varied and assessed elements of program structure, and the litigation context's impact on the efficiency and effectiveness of court-connected mediation and neutral evaluation has seldom been considered. Future studies need to address these gaps in the research.

Notes

1. If multiple studies were conducted on a single program, only the most recent study is included here. If multiple reports were written for a single study, only one report was cited for any given proposition, even if several of the reports contained the same finding, so that readers can more easily discern the number of studies supporting a particular finding. If a single report included data from multiple programs and reported differences among the programs in their structure or outcomes, that report is cited for each proposition it supported and thus would appear multiple times for a single issue.

For brevity, throughout the article "most programs" means "most programs for which empirical data are available." The features of these programs are the ones most relevant for interpreting the research findings discussed. Describing "the" structure of some programs was difficult because different mediators or evaluators in a single program, and different judges in a single court, often adopted different practices with regard to the ADR process. Studies that presented findings for different types of dispute resolution processes combined (such as "multidoor courthouse" programs) were not included because the effects attributable to the different processes could not be ascertained. Studies of programs that involved a single category of case or party, such as programs involving only medical malpractice cases or cases in which a state agency was a party, were not included to maximize the comparability across the studies reviewed.

The few studies that have systematically examined the impact of different program structures on outcomes were included in this review. No conclusions about the relationship between program characteristics and program outcomes based on comparisons across programs were included because such comparisons are likely to be misleading, given that mediation programs often differ on multiple characteristics, any of which could mask or enhance the effects of a particular factor (Beck and Sales, 2000; Hensler, 1999).

2. Several studies incorporated data from more than one program or from more than one court (Goerdt, 1993; McEwen and Maiman, 1981; Maiman, 1997; Raitt, Folberg, Rosenberg, and Barrett, 1993; Wissler, 1995). To increase the comparability of the studies reviewed, the findings from Roehl, Hersch, and Llaneras (1992) discussed in this article are based only on the small claims cases, not the special civil or justice center cases, included in that study.

3. The wide range of reported settlement rates in this and subsequent sections could in part be due to different studies measuring settlement in different ways. Some studies categorized as settled only cases in which a full settlement was

reached by the end of the mediation session, others included settlements that occurred after mediation but before trial, and other studies did not clearly define their use of the terms *settled* or *resolved.*

4. It was beyond the scope of this article to review the research findings regarding the effect of litigant characteristics on mediation outcomes. Readers are referred to a number of small claims mediation studies (Hermann, LaFree, Rack, and West, 1993; McEwen and Maiman, 1981; Maiman, 1997; Roehl, Hersch, and Llaneras, 1992; Vidmar, 1984; Wissler, 1995) and several general civil mediation studies (Clarke and Gordon, 1997; Maiman, 1997; Wissler, 2002) that have examined the impact of litigant characteristics, including gender, race, education, income, and goals; familiarity with mediation and litigation; status as an individual litigant or business representative; and role as plaintiff or defendant.

5. Several studies incorporated data from more than one program or from more than one court (Amis and others, 1998; Clarke and Gordon, 1997; Hann and Baar, 2001; Kakalik and others, 1996; McEwen, 1992a, 1992b; Stienstra, Johnson, and Lombard, 1997; Wissler, 2002). For the two studies that reported the findings pertaining to each program in a separate chapter (Kakalik and others, 1996; Stienstra, Johnson, and Lombard, 1997), the findings are referenced by chapter.

6. Litigants' and attorneys' views of the court's overall management of the case (for example, Kakalik and others, 1996; Stienstra, Johnson, and Lombard, 1997) were not discussed in this review because of the impossibility of attributing those assessments specifically to the mediation process.

7. For brevity, all appellate programs reviewed in this section are referred to as "mediation programs" and all third parties as "mediators," even though some programs used different labels (such as Civil Appeals Management Plan, settlement conference, or preargument conference; staff or conference attorney, settlement conference judge). The process used in most programs, based on the limited description typically provided, appeared to be consistent with the term *mediation,* but in a few programs (Birnbaum and Ellman, 1976; Cohen and Mashburn, 1999; Note, 1979; Partridge and Lind, 1983; Steelman and Goldman, 1986), it was not entirely clear whether the process should be considered evaluative mediation, neutral evaluation, or some other process. Programs whose primary goal was something other than settlement, such as improving brief quality, were not included in this review.

8. The findings from McNally (2000) discussed in this article are based only on data from the permanent program. One study (Steelman and Goldman, 1986) reported separate findings for programs in three different states.

9. Most studies did not report separately the percentage of cases that settled, but only reported the combined percentage of cases with these different dispositions. Some studies did not clearly define their use of the terms *settled* or *disposed.* In addition, some studies assessed the rate of disposition before briefing, others before oral argument, and others before a decision was rendered. These measurement differences could in part explain the variation in "settlement" rates observed in different studies.

10. In examining time to disposition, as well as the transaction costs reported in the following section, none of the studies included the length of time or costs incurred after case disposition in the appellate court but before the final resolution of the case, such as would occur with further trial or appellate proceedings. One study noted that roughly one-quarter of trial court judgments were reversed, and most of those cases were remanded to the trial court (Task Force, 2001). Another study reported that most of the cases that settled in mediation also resolved related matters at both the trial and appellate levels (Riselli, 2001). If there were differences between mediation and nonmediation cases in the breadth or finality of case resolution at this stage, then the findings would underestimate the impact of mediation on litigation time and costs (Aemmer, 1997; Partridge and Lind, 1983).

11. Kakalik and others (1996) reported the findings pertaining to two different programs in separate chapters; the findings are referenced by chapter. To increase the comparability of the studies reviewed, studies of two neutral evaluation programs were not included because the consequences for accepting or rejecting the evaluation in those programs were different than in most neutral evaluation programs and more akin to court-connected non-binding arbitration.

12. This study was not included in the mediation or neutral evaluation sections because it reported only whether there were differences among the dispute resolution processes in the outcomes, not what those outcomes were (for example, the percentage of settled cases) for each process. Other studies of mediation (Herman, 2001) and neutral evaluation (Rosenberg and Folberg, 1994) in the same court, however, were discussed in those sections of the article.

References

Aemmer, D. "Appellate Mediation in the Tenth Circuit." *Colorado Lawyer,* 1997, *26* (10), 25–28.

Amis, M., and others. "The Texas ADR Experience." In E. J. Bergman and J. G. Bickerman (eds.), *Court-Annexed Mediation: Critical Perspectives on Selected State and Federal Programs.* Bethesda, Md.: Pike and Fisher, 1998.

Averill, T. "Assessing the Orleans Parish Civil District Court Pilot Mediation." *Louisiana Bar Journal,* 1995, *43* (2), 150–154.

Beck, C.J.A., and Sales, B. D. "A Critical Reappraisal of Divorce Mediation Research and Policy." *Psychology and Public Policy,* 2000, *6,* 989–1046.

Bergman, E. J. "Mediation Program of the United States District Court, District of New Jersey." In E. J. Bergman and J. G. Bickerman (eds.), *Court-Annexed Mediation: Critical Perspectives on Selected State and Federal Programs.* Bethesda, Md.: Pike and Fisher, 1998.

Bickerman, J. G. "The Mediation Program of the United States District Court for the District of Columbia." In E. J. Bergman and J. G. Bickerman (eds.), *Court-Annexed Mediation: Critical Perspectives on Selected State and Federal Programs.* Bethesda, Md.: Pike and Fisher, 1998.

Birnbaum, A., and Ellman, S. "Pre-Argument Settlement Process in an Intermediate Appellate Court: The Second Department Experience." *Brooklyn Law
Review,* 1976, *43,* 31–46.

Clarke, S. H., and Gordon, E. E. "Public Sponsorship of Private Settling: Court-
Ordered Civil Case Mediation." *Justice System Journal,* 1997, *19,* 311–339.

Cohen, L. J., and Mashburn, W. "The Ten Principles of Successful Appellate
Mediation in Nevada." *Nevada Lawyer,* 1999, *7* (12), 19–22.

Daniel, J. *Assessment of the Mediation Program of the U.S. District Court for the District of Columbia.* Washington, D.C.: Administrative Conference of the
United States, 1995.

Dichter, F. R. "A Study of the Northern District of Oklahoma Settlement Program." In E. J. Bergman and J. G. Bickerman (eds.), *Court-Annexed Mediation: Critical Perspectives on Selected State and Federal Programs.* Bethesda, Md.:
Pike and Fisher, 1998.

Eaglin, J. B. *The Pre-Argument Conference Program in the Sixth Circuit Court of
Appeals: An Evaluation.* Washington, D.C.: Federal Judicial Center, 1990.

Estee, S. L. *Civil Mediation in the Western District of Washington: A Brief Evaluation.* San Francisco: Judicial Council for the U.S. Courts for the Ninth
Circuit, 1987.

FitzGibbon, S. F. "Appellate Settlement Conference Programs: A Case Study."
Journal of Dispute Resolution, 1993, *1993,* 53–107.

Fitzhugh, J. "Report Card on ENE: Early Neutral Evaluation in the Vermont
Federal District Court." *Vermont Bar Journal and Law Digest,* 1998, *24* (3),
44–46.

Fix, M., and Harter, P. J. *Hard Cases, Vulnerable People: An Analysis of Mediation
Programs at the Multi-Door Courthouse of Superior Court of the District of
Columbia.* Washington, D.C.: Urban Institute, 1992.

Ganzfried, J. J. "Bringing Business Judgment to Business Litigation: Mediation
and Settlement in Federal Courts of Appeals." *George Washington Law Review,*
1997, *65,* 531–541.

Goerdt, J. A. "How Mediation Is Working in Small Claims Courts: Three Urban
Court Experiments Evaluated." *Judges' Journal,* 1993, *32* (4), 13–16, 45–50.

Hann, R. G., and Baar, C. *Evaluation of the Ontario Mandatory Mediation Program
(Rule 24.1): Final Report—The First 23 Months.* Toronto: Ontario Ministry of
the Attorney General, Queens Printer, 2001. [www.attorneygeneral.jus.gov.
on.ca/html/MANMED].

Hanson, R. *An Evaluation of the Florida Fourth District Court of Appeal's Settlement Conference Program.* Williamsburg, Va.: National Center for State
Courts, 1991.

Hanson, R. A., and Becker, R. "Appellate Mediation in New Mexico: An Evaluation." *Journal of Appellate Practice and Process,* 2002, *4,* 167–188.

Hensler, D. "A Research Agenda: What We Need to Know About Court-
Connected ADR." *Dispute Resolution Magazine,* 1999, *6* (1), 15–17.

Herman, H. "Preliminary Report of Responses to Mediation Questionnaires." Paper presented at the American Bar Association Dispute Resolution Section, Washington, D.C., Apr. 26–28, 2001.

Hermann, M., LaFree, G., Rack, C., and West, M. B. *The MetroCourt Project Final Report.* Albuquerque: Institute of Public Law, University of New Mexico, 1993.

Kakalik, J. S., and others. *An Evaluation of Mediation and Early Neutral Evaluation Under the Civil Justice Reform Act.* Santa Monica, Calif.: RAND, 1996.

Kobbervig, W. *Mediation of Civil Cases in Hennepin County: An Evaluation.* St. Paul, Minn.: Office of the State Court Administrator, 1991.

Lowe, R. A., and Keilitz, S. L. *Middlesex Multi-Door Courthouse Evaluation Project, Final Report.* Andover, Mass.: National Center for State Courts, 1992.

Macfarlane, J. *Court-Based Mediation for Civil Cases: An Evaluation of the Ontario Court (General Division) ADR Centre.* Windsor, Ontario: University of Windsor, 1995.

Macfarlane, J. *Learning from Experience: An Evaluation of the Saskatchewan Queen's Bench Mandatory Mediation Program.* Windsor, Ontario: University of Windsor, 2003.

Maiman, R. J. *An Evaluation of Selected Mediation Programs in the Massachusetts Trial Court.* Boston: Massachusetts Supreme Judicial Court, 1997.

McEwen, C. A. "An Evaluation of the ADR Pilot Project." *Maine Bar Journal,* 1992a, *7* (5), 310–311.

McEwen, C. A. *An Evaluation of the ADR Pilot Project: Final Report.* Brunswick, Me.: Bowdoin College, 1992b.

McEwen, C. A., and Maiman, R. J. "Small Claims Mediation in Maine: An Empirical Assessment." *Maine Law Review,* 1981, *33,* 237–268.

McEwen, C. A., and Maiman, R. J. "The Relative Significance of Disputing Forum and Dispute Characteristics for Outcome and Compliance." *Law and Society Review,* 1987, *21,* 155–164.

McNally, J. N. "Lessons Learned in the Court of Appeals Settlement Program." *Michigan Bar Journal,* 2000, *79* (5), 488–493.

Note. "The Minnesota Supreme Court Prehearing Conference: An Empirical Evaluation." *Minnesota Law Review,* 1979, *63,* 1221–1257.

Olexa, J. S., and Rozelle, D. *Small Claims Mediation Project in the District Court of the State of Oregon for Multnomah County.* Portland: Fourth Judicial District of the State of Oregon for Multnomah County, 1991.

Partridge, A., and Lind, A. *A Reevaluation of the Civil Appeals Management Plan.* Washington, D.C.: Federal Judicial Center, 1983.

Raitt, S. E., Folberg, J., Rosenberg, J., and Barrett, R. "The Use of Mediation in Small Claims Courts." *Ohio State Journal on Dispute Resolution,* 1993, *9,* 55–94.

Report on Mediation. Lincoln, Neb.: U.S. District Court for the District of Nebraska, 2002. [http://www.ned.uscourts.gov/mediation/medweb/report-02.pdf.]

Riselli, D. "Appellate Mediation at the First District Court of Appeal: How and Why It Works." *Florida Bar Journal,* 2001, *75* (1), 58–61.

Roehl, J. A., Hersch, R., and Llaneras, E. *Civil Case Mediation and Comprehensive Justice Centers: Process, Quality of Justice, and Value to State Courts, Final Report.* Washington, D.C.: Institute for Social Analysis, 1992.

Rosenberg, J. D., and Folberg, H. J. "Alternative Dispute Resolution: An Empirical Analysis." *Stanford Law Review,* 1994, *46,* 1487–1537.

Russell, S. L. "Latah County Small Claims Mediation Program Is a Success." *Advocate (Idaho),* 1998, *41* (11), 17–19.

Schildt, K., Alfini, J. J., and Johnson, P. *Major Civil Case Mediation Pilot Program: 17th Judicial Circuit of Illinois.* DeKalb: Northern Illinois University, 1994. [http://www.caadrs.org/studies].

Schultz, K. D. *Florida's Alternative Dispute Resolution Demonstration Project: An Empirical Assessment.* Tallahassee, Fla.: Florida Dispute Resolution Center, 1990.

Steelman, D. D., and Goldman, J. "Preargument Settlement Conferences in State Appellate Courts." *State Court Journal,* 1986, *10* (4), 4–13.

Stienstra, D., Johnson, M., and Lombard, P. *Report to the Judicial Conference Committee on Court Administration and Case Management: A Study of the Five Demonstration Programs Established Under the Civil Justice Reform Act of 1990.* Washington, D.C.: Federal Judicial Center, 1997.

Stuart, K. K., and Savage, C. A. "The Multi-door Courthouse: How It's Working." *Colorado Lawyer,* 1997, *26* (10), 13–17.

Task Force on Appellate Mediation. *Mandatory Mediation in the First Appellate District of the Court of Appeal: Report and Recommendations.* San Francisco: California Court of Appeal, 2001. [http://www.courtinfo.ca.gov/reference/4_reports.htm#ADR].

Torregrossa, J. A. "Appellate Mediation in the Third Circuit—Program Operations: Nuts, Bolts and Practice Tips." *Villanova Law Review,* 2002, *47,* 1059–1087.

Vidmar, N. "The Small Claims Court: A Reconceptualization of Disputes and an Empirical Investigation." *Law and Society Review,* 1984, *18,* 515–550.

Vidmar, N. "An Assessment of Mediation in a Small Claims Court." *Journal of Social Issues,* 1985, *41,* 127–144.

Vidmar, N. "Assessing the Effects of Case Characteristics and Settlement Forum on Dispute Outcomes and Compliance." *Law and Society Review,* 1986, *20,* 439–447.

Vidmar, N., and Short, J. "Social Psychological Dynamics in the Settlement of Small Claims Court Cases." In D. J. Muller, D. E. Blackman, and A. J. Chapman (eds.), *Psychology and Law: Topics from an International Conference.* New York: Wiley, 1984.

Wissler, R. L. "Mediation and Adjudication in the Small Claims Court: The Effects of Process and Case Characteristics." *Law and Society Review,* 1995, *29,* 323–358.

Wissler, R. L. "Court-Connected Mediation in General Civil Cases: What We Know from Empirical Research." *Ohio State Journal of Dispute Resolution,* 2002, *17,* 641–703.

Woodward, J. G. "Settlement Week: Measuring the Promise." *Northern Illinois University Law Review,* 1990, *11,* 1–54.

Roselle L. Wissler is director of research of the Lodestar Dispute Resolution Program, Arizona State University College of Law. Dr. Wissler has served as a research consultant to several courts to examine the effectiveness of ADR programs and address program design questions. The author can be reached by e-mail at rwissler@asu.edu.

Commentary: Focusing on Program Design Issues in Future Research on Court-Connected Mediation

JOHN LANDE

Court-connected mediation often works very well. That is a fair conclusion based on evidence summarized in Roselle Wissler's meticulous review of court-connected mediation. Analyzing studies of small claims, general civil, and appellate mediation programs, her review suggests that mediation is usually evaluated very favorably and is rated as highly as or better than the alternatives on virtually all outcome indicators.[1] In other words, almost all of these studies find that the results are either better in mediation or that there are no significant differences.

This suggests that mediation has the potential to be quite effective in producing various desired results and that whether a mediation program actually generates such results depends on how well it is designed and fits with the local practice culture. Mediation is a highly variable process that program designers and users can readily adapt. As McEwen (1988) suggests, instead of "asking whether mediation works or not, we need to examine how and why parties and lawyers 'work' mediation in varying ways" (p. 3).[2] McEwen's suggestion can be extended to analyze how mediators and program designers "work" mediation processes. Thus, this article analyzes prior research to determine why some mediation programs did not outperform traditional litigation while others did.[3] It illustrates how researchers and program designers might analyze past research findings, design programs to produce desired results, and then empirically test the effectiveness of such design efforts.[4]

This article also suggests that researchers increase the use of outcome measures in addition to traditional measures of efficiency, satisfaction, and perceived fairness. These include substantive justice, empowerment and recognition, and interest-based problem solving. Given intense concerns about mediator evaluation and party self-determination, researchers should also examine these issues further.

Research on Mediation Efficacy

Most research on court-connected mediation analyzes a few key outcomes including settlement rates, time savings, cost savings, and participants' assessments of the process.

Settlement Rates

Future research should try to identify the most important factors affecting participants' decisions whether to reach agreement in (or soon after) mediation. Settlement rates are a common benchmark of success used by mediators, programs, and program sponsors.[5] Moreover, settlement may affect many other important outcomes, such as efficiency of and satisfaction with the process. Wissler finds that small claims programs had settlement rates between 25 and 95 percent, general civil mediation programs had settlement rates between 13 and 80 percent, and appellate mediation programs had settlement rates between 29 and 76 percent. Although settlement rates in most programs were well within these ranges, nevertheless there was tremendous variation on this dimension. There was also great variation about whether mediated cases had higher settlement rates greater than nonmediated cases did. Although most of the appellate studies found a greater resolution rate for mediated cases, most of the studies of trial court civil cases showed no difference in settlement rates.

Wissler notes a range of findings in the relationship between settlement and other variables. Studies have found that settlement was related to the extent to which liability was contested, the amount of disparity in the parties' positions, the extent of party preparation, whether parties with decision-making authority attended, whether dispositive motions were pending, whether mediators took an active role and analyzed the strengths and weaknesses of the case, and the amount of mediators' mediation experience. There were mixed findings about whether settlement was related to whether the mediation was conducted early in the dispute, case type, the complexity of issues, whether the referral was voluntary or mandatory, and the extent to which discovery had been completed. Some studies found that settlement rates were not related to the number of named parties; the nature, contentiousness, or length of parties' relationship; the amount at issue in the case; whether the parties sought nonmonetary relief; the mediator's familiarity with the substantive issues in the case; the mediator's professional role (whether the mediator is an attorney, law clerk, or nonattorney); and the amount of mediator's mediation training.

It would be helpful to replicate these findings (some of which are based on a single study) and determine the most important causes for variation in settlement rates. Because of the large number of possible causes and the likely interrelationship among many of them, researchers should use multivariate analyses to separate possible causal factors. Moreover, some of the variables are likely to be proxies for more fundamental causes. For example, some of the variables may be related to the reasonableness of party expectations, relative assessments of their substantive and procedural alternatives to agreement in mediation, risk preferences, extent to which offers satisfied participants' interests, whether important information was missing or seriously disputed, the mediators' and participants' motivation or skill, and perhaps other factors. Obviously settlement rates are affected by mediation program decisions about which cases are mediated. Presumably, programs have higher settlement rates if they select cases for mediation that are more likely to settle.[6] Thus, analysis of screening procedures and criteria may also help explain variations in settlement rates.

Time Savings

Future research should try to reconcile previous findings regarding the effect on case disposition time of the timing of referral to and holding of mediation and should also investigate whether other factors have significant impact. Wissler reports that program evaluations found mixed results about whether mediation programs reduced the length of litigated cases. Although most of the appellate court mediation programs and about half of the civil mediation programs reported faster dispositions in the mediation group, about half of the civil mediation programs and two appellate programs found no differences. This pattern may be related to the fact that the mediation group includes cases regardless of whether they settled in mediation. Although many studies finding no difference overall did not report separately based on whether the cases settled, some studies did find, not surprisingly, that cases settling in mediation had faster disposition times than those that did not do so (Wissler, 2002). This suggests that settlement at mediation (or soon afterwards) may be a key factor in expediting resolution, and thus research on factors promoting resolution (discussed above) may be critical in reducing disposition time.

The mediation referral procedure itself may contribute to increased disposition time and should be a key independent variable in future studies. In a study of the program in federal court in the Western District of Missouri, cases were randomly assigned to three groups: those ordered to mediate early in the case, those precluded from mediating, and those with the option of mediating. The study found that the cases ordered to mediate had the shortest disposition times. In the mediation-optional group, however, the nonmediated cases terminated an average of about one month faster than the mediated cases. The researchers suggested that this difference may be due to the time required to decide whether to mediate and set up the mediation, which was not needed in the automatic referrals to mediation (Stienstra, Johnson, and Lombard, 1997, chap. 5). Timing of referral to and holding of mediation are significant factors in the only study in which Wissler finds a study showing a group of mediation cases performing significantly worse than nonmediated cases. In the program in that study, disposition time for mediated cases was longer than nonmediated cases. This was apparently due to the fact that the referral to mediation occurred relatively late in the case (an average of 10.3 months after filing), and it took an average of four additional months before mediators were selected (Estee, 1987).

Reports about differences in timing of mediation referrals relate to a controversy about the best time to refer cases to mediation regarding whether parties have conducted discovery and courts have ruled on significant motions (see Guthrie and Levin, 1998). Although Wissler cites some research on the effect of mediation on the amount of discovery, there is apparently little or no research experimenting with various scheduling policies where the independent variable is the timing of mediation in relation to discovery and motions. The latter design would be helpful to determine whether courts can devise scheduling practices to save time and money by facilitating settlements at the earliest appropriate time.

Cost Savings

Wissler's summary showing that most studies do not find a significant reduction of litigation costs, motions, or discovery in mediated cases suggests the need to focus on causal factors in the few studies that do find significant cost savings. In one study finding reduced discovery (and presumed litigation costs), the mediation referral order suspended formal discovery during the pendency of the order (McEwen, 1992). In practice, legal communities are likely to differ about whether they would suspend discovery or adopt similar practices. In another study, Clarke and Gordon (1997) found lower litigation costs for cases that settle, with or without mediation, than those that go to trial. Litigation costs for cases settled in mediation were much closer to costs of nonmediation cases that settled. Like measures of time to disposition, litigation costs seem strongly related to whether cases settle. Thus, researchers should study factors leading to settlement and whether these factors lead in turn to time and cost savings. In the meantime, the research findings suggest that mediation proponents should avoid claiming that mediation results in cost savings to litigants.

Participants' Assessments of the Process

Wissler's review shows consistent findings that mediation participants generally had very positive assessments of the process. The studies found that most participants believed they had an opportunity to present their case, and the mediators understood the issues and the participants' views, treated them with respect, and were neutral, well prepared, and effective. They generally believed the mediation process was fair and said that they would use mediation again. Future research should focus on identifying factors causing such positive assessments, especially factors that program designers can adjust.

Many studies of small claims mediation and some general civil mediation found that parties have more favorable assessments of mediation than litigation. There were some exceptions, especially in studies of general civil mediation. In some studies, the lack of significant difference was due to generally favorable assessments of both mediation and adjudication (Goerdt, 1993; Kobbervig, 1991) and does not reflect any design deficiency in mediation. Other studies found no difference in assessment based on whether the case was mediated, which researchers attributed to failure of some cases to settle in mediation (Fix and Harter, 1992) or dissatisfaction with the outcome (Clarke and Gordon, 1997). If the latter two findings are replicated and the causal order can be established, it might suggest appropriate program design changes. It would be helpful to know, for example, how much the fact of settlement contributes to perceptions of process fairness and how much those perceptions contribute to parties deciding to settle.

Suggestions for Research on Court-Connected Mediation

The existing body of research addresses the following issues to a limited extent. These issues deserve more study, especially in the context of court programs.

Mediator Evaluation, Party Autonomy, and Settlement Pressure

Mediators have vigorously debated the ethics and impact of using evaluative techniques in mediation. Wissler's study of civil mediation programs

(2002) helps explain the impact of separate elements of evaluation. She found that when mediators evaluated the case, parties felt the mediation process was fairer and did not feel more pressured to settle, whereas when mediators made recommendations, parties felt that the process was less fair and did feel pressured to settle. This study is intriguing because it finds beneficial (albeit modest) effects of mediator evaluation, contrary to the expectations of facilitation proponents, who believe that mediator evaluations necessarily create harmful settlement pressure and reduce parties' autonomy in making decisions. Additional research would be helpful to replicate Wissler's study, examine additional elements of evaluation (such as predicting court outcomes or urging parties to settle), consider the context of mediators' evaluative moves (such as whether the participants requested or desired the evaluative move, whether they were done in caucus, or whether participants felt that they had presented their case sufficiently before mediators did the evaluative moves), and analyze the effect of whether parties had lawyers at mediation and the perceived efficacy of lawyers' advocacy (see Lande, 1997; Riskin, 1996, 2003; Welsh, 2001a, 2001b).

Effect of Mediation on Substantive Justice

Courts are supposed to dispense justice in addition to resolving disputes, so it would be important to know more about the objective consequences of mediation processes and how to assess the substantive fairness of the results (see Bush, 1989; Galanter, 1974; Garth, 2002; Hyman and Love, 2002; Menkel-Meadow, 1999). Researchers should be creative in conceptualizing substantive justice to include a wider range of measures of justice. This is an extremely difficult endeavor, which may explain why researchers have generally studied outcome indicators relying on participants' perceptions rather than objective results. The MetroCourt report (Hermann, LaFree, Rack, and West, 1993; LaFree and Rack, 1996) is an important study of differences by gender and ethnicity in objective and subjective outcomes. The study reports surprising findings, including that despite the fact that minority claimants received lower monetary awards in mediation, they expressed more satisfaction than whites did. The study found no significant differences in awards, however, based on ethnicity of the parties when the comediators were both minorities. Just as intriguing, the study found that white women defendants achieved better objective results in mediation as compared with the other three ethnic and gender groups, but were less likely to see the mediation process as fair.

The findings of this study call out for further studies to replicate and extend this inquiry. Considering historical disadvantages that women and minorities have encountered, research exploring racial, ethnic, and gender issues focuses on an important measure of justice. Gender and ethnicity are imperfect proxies for analyzing substantive justice, however, because women and minorities may not be disadvantaged and the law may require rejections of their requests for relief in particular cases.

Research should also examine how the have-nots fare (especially in disputes with the haves), how plaintiffs fare against defendants, and how individuals fare against organizations. Again, these are important but imperfect ways of operationalizing substantive fairness. Judging by norms of law and fairness, sometimes the have-nots deserve to lose. Moreover, although defining justice in terms of winning and losing is sometimes appropriate, a major lesson of the alternative dispute resolution (ADR) movement is that a win-lose paradigm itself can lead to poor results. Using legal rules may often be an appropriate standard of justice, yet the law is unpredictable and may itself be the source of some unfairness. Hyman and Love (2002) describe various conceptualizations of substantive justice, including reparative justice, retribution, distributive justice, and improvement of relationships. Researchers should use such alternative theories of justice in conceptualizing outcome measures.

Problem Solving

Interest-based negotiation, often called problem solving, is a major contribution of the ADR movement and is sometimes the main dynamic in mediation. Yet there has been remarkably little empirical research about use of interest-based negotiation in court-connected mediation, and researchers should investigate this more. Heumann and Hyman (1997) found that although 61 percent of the lawyers in their survey wanted greater use of problem solving in their negotiations, about 71 percent of the negotiations used positional methods (see also Schneider, 2002). Is there a similar phenomenon in mediation, where mediators, lawyers, and parties believe that problem solving should be used more often than they actually use it? How often is problem solving used in mediation? What are the barriers to increased use? How often do participants benefit from problem solving, and how often do they feel exploited after openly disclosing their interests?

Empowerment and Recognition

Bush and Folger (1994) challenged the mediation community to use mediation to increase empowerment and recognition (or "transformation") rather than settlement or problem solving. Some may doubt whether transformation should be the primary goal of court mediation programs or whether it is achievable in a court context (see, for example, Hensler, 2002). Even if transformation is not the sole or primary goal, it is certainly an important potential goal or outcome and is worth measuring. Although some might have been skeptical whether transformation would be a feasible goal in an institution like the U.S. Postal Service, there is substantial evidence that mediation increases empowerment and recognition in that context (Bingham, 2003).

Mediation Program Design

Mediation program planners may want to conduct research in their local areas to understand local legal and mediation cultures (Lande, 2000). For example, litigants and lawyers may differ in their attitudes about the best time to schedule cases for mediation, whether to use premediation memoranda and, if so, what should be included, how much litigants should talk in mediation sessions (as compared with how much their lawyers talk), how much time should be spent in caucus, whether mediators should express opinions about various aspects of the case, and numerous other procedural features of mediation. Local cultures also may vary on what Riskin (2003) calls meta-procedural issues–decisions about making procedural decisions–such as whether mediators, litigants, or lawyers should make procedural decisions. Moreover, local legal communities are likely to differ on the extent to which the goals in mediation should be settlement, problem solving, substantive justice, empowerment and recognition, or perhaps a combination of goals. Presumably such factors affect people's behavior in mediation and the results of the process. Courts using a formal planning or dispute system design process for their mediation programs may be especially interested in conducting research about their local areas (Lande, 2002). Some of this research should involve experiments that vary program features to see if such adjustments affect outcomes of interest. Moreover, researchers should study courts' program design processes to find out how to make them as successful as possible.[7]

Conclusion

No further research should be needed to persuade policymakers about the potential efficacy of court-connected mediation programs. Although mediation is not necessarily superior to available procedural alternatives, the experience and evidence amassed to date about mediation is generally quite positive. If policymakers have not yet been persuaded of the benefits of court-connected mediation, further studies are unlikely to convince them to adopt or maintain these programs.

Future research should focus on program design choices rather than trying to establish the general efficacy of mediation programs. Many prior studies have focused on a single program where the program design and local culture are invariant. In the future, some researchers should compare programs that have varying design features and that operate in different cultural environments to test the effects of these variations. Future research on individual programs should focus on program features and local practice culture that bear on local policy options.

Whenever appropriate, research should use multivariate analyses to identify potential causal relationships between various independent variables (especially program and process features that can be adjusted) and outcome measures of interest. Research should expand the range of outcome measures to include substantive justice, problem solving, and empowerment and recognition.

Notes

1. Wissler provides an excellent description of limitations of the data in the studies. Because of these limitations, readers should interpret the studies with some caution.

2. Like much other literature on the subject, this article uses the term *mediation* for simplicity in referring to quite diverse and complex processes. It is particularly problematic to use *mediation* as the subject of a sentence as if the process is the active agent rather than the individuals and institutions involved. Although this article follows that convention for ease of understanding, readers should understand that the term is just a convenient placeholder for certain concerted activities (McEwen, 1998).

3. Scientific norms require researchers to assume that there is no difference between comparison groups unless the evidence shows that the probability that observed differences would have occurred by chance is less than a specified level, often 5 percent. Given these norms, researchers may conclude that there is no

difference when there is such a difference but the data do not provide a sufficient level of confidence that it exists. These "false-negative" results may occur for many reasons, including small sample sizes, problematic research design and implementation, and random events. Thus, the absence of observed differences at specified levels of confidence should not lead to the conclusion that there necessarily are no differences. If researchers suspect that findings are false negatives, the solution is to replicate the study and correct problems suspected to have caused the erroneous conclusion.

4. Wissler (2002) provided an excellent, detailed review of the empirical literature with suggestions for further research (see also Hensler, 1999). I do not attempt here to duplicate Wissler's review. Instead, I highlight a few issues that Wissler (2002 and in this volume) discusses and identify others that have not been studied much.

5. Many mediators and programs use settlement rates as a key measure of success because they value settlement as an end in itself, they can collect and interpret these data relatively easily, and they can use settlement rates to justify their work to program sponsors. Settlement is the primary goal of some, but certainly not all, mediators and programs (Bush and Folger, 1994). Sander (1995) appropriately cautions about having an "obsession" with settlement rates for many reasons, including that excessive attention to settlement rates does not recognize other values, such as opportunities to discuss issues in a safe environment regardless of the outcome.

6. This is not to imply that programs should focus only or primarily on the goal of settlement or necessarily screen out cases that may be less likely to settle. Although settlement can lead to benefits such as time and cost savings as well as greater satisfaction, there is an intrinsic value in trying to understand the other parties and negotiate even if the parties do not settle.

7. The Civil Justice Reform Act of 1990 required federal courts to use advisory groups to make recommendations about court program design. For examples of studies of the operation of this program design process, see Kakalik and others (1996), Robel (1993), and Somerlot and Mahoney (1998).

References

Bingham, L. B. "Mediation at Work: Transforming Workplace Conflict at the United States Postal Service." 2003. [http://www.businessofgovernment.org/pdfs/Bingham_Report.pdf].

Bush, R.A.B. "Defining Quality in Dispute Resolution: Taxonomies and Anti-Taxonomies of Quality Arguments." *Denver University Law Review,* 1989, *66,* 335–380.

Bush, R.A.B., and Folger, J. P. *The Promise of Mediation: Responding to Conflict Through Empowerment and Recognition.* San Francisco: Jossey-Bass, 1994.

Clarke, S. H., and Gordon, E. E. "Public Sponsorship of Private Settling: Court-Ordered Civil Case Mediation." *Justice System Journal,* 1997, *19,* 311–339.

Estee, S. L. *Civil Mediation in the Western District of Washington: A Brief Evaluation.* Judicial Council for the United States Courts for the Ninth Circuit, 1987.

Fix, M., and Harter, P. J. *Hard Cases, Vulnerable People: An Analysis of Mediation Programs at the Multi-Door Courthouse of Superior Court of the District of Columbia.* Washington, D.C.: Urban Institute, 1992.

Galanter, M. "Why the 'Haves' Come Out Ahead: Speculations on the Limits of Legal Change." *Law and Society Review,* 1974, *9,* 95–127.

Garth, B. G. "Tilting the Justice System: From ADR as Idealistic Movement to a Segmented Market in Dispute Resolution." *Georgia State University Law Review,* 2002, *18,* 927–953.

Goerdt, J. A. "How Mediation Is Working in Small Claims Courts: Three Urban Court Experiments Evaluated." *Judges' Journal,* 1993, *32,* 13–16, 45–50.

Guthrie, C., and Levin, J. "A 'Party Satisfaction' Perspective on a Comprehensive Mediation Statute." *Ohio State Journal on Dispute Resolution,* 1998, *13,* 885–907.

Hensler, D. "A Research Agenda: What We Need to Know About Court-Connected ADR." *Dispute Resolution Magazine,* Fall 1999, pp. 15–17.

Hensler, D. R. "Suppose It's Not True: Challenging Mediation Ideology." *Journal of Dispute Resolution,* 2002, *6,* 81–99.

Hermann, M., LaFree, G., Christine Rack, C., and West, M. B. *The MetroCourt Project Final Report.* Albuquerque: Center for the Study and Resolution of Disputes, University of New Mexico, 1993.

Heumann, M., and Hyman, J. M. "Negotiation Methods and Litigation Settlement Methods in New Jersey: 'You Can't Always Get What You Want.'" *Ohio State Journal on Dispute Resolution,* 1997, *12,* 253–310.

Hyman, J. M., and Love, L. P. "If Portia Were a Mediator: An Inquiry into Justice in Mediation." *Clinical Law Review,* 2002, *9,* 157–193.

Kakalik, J. K., and others. *Implementation of the Civil Justice Reform Act in Pilot and Comparison Districts.* Santa Monica, Calif.: RAND Institute for Civil Justice, 1996.

Kobbervig, W. *Mediation of Civil Cases in Hennepin County: An Evaluation.* St. Paul, Minn.: Office of the State Court Administrator, Minnesota Judicial Center, 1991.

LaFree, G., and Rack, C. "The Effects of Participants' Ethnicity and Gender on Monetary Outcomes in Mediated and Adjudicated Civil Cases." *Law and Society Review,* 1996, *30,* 767–797.

Lande, J. "How Will Lawyering and Mediation Practices Transform Each Other?" *Florida State University Law Review,* 1997, *24,* 839–901.

Lande, J. "Getting the Faith: Why Business Lawyers and Executives Believe in Mediation." *Harvard Negotiation Law Review,* 2000, *5,* 137–231.

Lande, J. "Using Dispute System Design Methods to Promote Good-Faith Participation in Court-Connected Mediation Programs." *UCLA Law Review,* 2002, *50,* 69–141.

McEwen, C. A. "An Evaluation of the ADR Pilot Project." *Maine Bar Journal,* 1992, *7* (5), 310–311.

McEwen, C. A. "Managing Corporate Disputing: Overcoming Barriers to the Effective Use of Mediation for Reducing the Cost and Time of Litigation," *Ohio State Journal on Dispute Resolution,* 1998, *14,* 1–27.

Menkel-Meadow, C. "Do the 'Haves' Come Out Ahead in Alternative Judicial Systems? Repeat Players in ADR." *Ohio State Journal on Dispute Resolution,* 1999, *15,* 19–61.

Riskin, L. R. "Understanding Mediators' Orientations, Strategies, and Techniques: A Grid for the Perplexed." *Harvard Negotiation Law Review,* 1996, *1,* 7–51.

Riskin, L. R. "Decisionmaking in Mediation: The New Old Grid and the New New Grid System." *Notre Dame Law Review,* 2003, *79,* 1–53.

Robel, L. K. "Grass Roots Procedure: Local Advisory Groups and the Civil Justice Reform Act of 1990." *Brooklyn Law Review,* 1993, *59,* 879–908.

Sander, F.E.A. "The Obsession with Settlement Rates." *Negotiation Journal,* 1995, *11,* 329–332.

Schneider, A. K. "Shattering Negotiation Myths: Empirical Evidence on the Effectiveness of Negotiation Style." *Harvard Negotiation Law Review,* 2002, *7,* 143–233.

Somerlot, D. K., and Mahoney, B. "What Are the Lessons of Civil Justice Reform? Rethinking Brookings, the CJRA, Rand, and State Initiatives." *Judges' Journal,* 1998, *37,* 4–6, 61–63.

Stienstra, D., Johnson, M., and Lombard, P. *Report to the Judicial Conference Committee on Court Administration and Case Management: A Study of the Five Demonstration Programs Established Under the Civil Justice Reform Act of 1990.* Washington, D.C.: Federal Judicial Center, 1997.

Welsh, N. A. "Making Deals in Court-Connected Mediation: What's Justice Got to Do with It?" *Washington University Law Quarterly,* 2001a, *79,* 787–861.

Welsh, N. A. "The Thinning Vision of Self-Determination in Court-Connected Mediation: The Inevitable Price of Institutionalization?" *Harvard Negotiation Law Review,* 2001b, *6,* 1–96.

Wissler, R. L. "Court-Connected Mediation in General Civil Cases: What We Know from Empirical Research." *Ohio State Journal of Dispute Resolution,* 2002, *17,* 641–703.

John Lande is director of the LL.M. Program in Dispute Resolution and associate professor at the University of Missouri-Columbia School of Law. His publications discuss how lawyering and mediation practices will transform each other, business lawyers' and executives' opinions about litigation and ADR, designing court-connected mediation programs, and collaborative law.

The Evolution and Evaluation of Community Mediation: Limited Research Suggests Unlimited Progress

TIMOTHY HEDEEN

Building meaningful community capacity and changing conflict patterns are the most powerful tools provided by community mediation programs. Many of the elements of true democracy are present in the work we do. I believe that if, in any given situation, there is a community and a conflict, placing everyone together in one room and working through the mediation process will result in the most equitable and elegant solution possible.

—*Scott Bradley, former executive director, Mediation Network of North Carolina*

Community mediation in the United States is the product of thirty years of inspiration, innovation, and improvisation. A broad array of players—working often in concert, but sometimes at cross purposes—have constructed a remarkable field that handles an estimated 100,000 conflicts each year (National Association for Community Mediation, 2003), primarily through the services of highly trained volunteer mediators.

While domestic community mediation builds on traditions from around the world and across many generations (Auerbach, 1983), the contemporary field is a uniquely American experience. The goals for community mediation are many, and they are lofty. With its emphases on individual self-determination, community self-reliance, and equal access to justice for all, community mediation is truly dispute resolution "of the people, by the people, and for the people."

This article seeks to present the structure, accomplishments, and unfinished work of community mediation centers in the United States. Following an overview of the evolution of the field and consistent with the other articles in this volume, the article is organized around the structural elements of community mediation and concludes with a discussion of the future opportunities for research, policy, and practice.

A Brief History of Community Mediation in the United States

Community mediation represents the confluence of two streams of innovation, each flowing forth from a deep well-spring of inspiration. Social trends of the 1960s and 1970s set the stage for community mediation's inception: the highly mobile and urbanizing population moved further from traditional informal dispute resolvers (extended family, clergy, long-time neighbors) and closer to anonymous strangers and insular lives; the attendant delay and high costs of the courts led to popular frustration with the functioning of the justice system; and many judges, scholars, and other observers began to question the appropriateness and effectiveness of the court case process for certain types of disputes (McGillis, 1997).

One stream was formed of a primarily governmental justice reform program in the mid-1970s, the Neighborhood Justice Centers (NJC) project, as a response to the perceived inadequacy of the courts to handle both the nature and number of cases that deluged its dockets. Chief Justice Warren E. Burger repeatedly asserted the need for "a better way" to address minor civil and criminal matters, including his address before the National Conference on the Causes of Popular Dissatisfaction with the Administration of Justice in 1976 (Burger, 1976). This conference convened a range of interested parties who reflected on the event quite differently: law professor Frank Sander described the conference as "damage control" to relieve the overburdened courts (2003), while anthropologist Laura Nader argued that the event was less about justice and more about "efficiency and harmony, or how to rid the country of confrontation and the courts of 'garbage cases'" (1992, p. 12). Proponents and practitioners of community mediation held forth against such a critique, refuting claims of "second-class justice" by emphasizing the high rates of agreement and disputant satisfaction with this "first-class process" (Christian, 1986).

The central recommendation of the conference was to establish neighborhood justice centers to "make available a variety of methods of processing disputes, including arbitration, mediation, referral to small claims courts as well as referral to courts of general jurisdiction" (McGillis and Mullen, 1977, p. 29). Six NJC programs were established on an experimental basis over the next three years. These programs worked toward the following goals (McGillis, 1986):

- Screening cases to determine whether charges should be brought against the respondent
- Diverting cases from the court caseload
- Providing more efficient and accessible services to citizens
- Reducing case processing costs to the justice system
- Improving the image of the justice system
- Providing a more appropriate process for certain cases

The same report outlined the goals of the complementary stream, which sprung forth from a tradition of community empowerment and mobilization:

- Decentralization of control of decision making
- Development of indigenous community leadership
- Reducing community tensions

Community mediation programs designed around the latter set of goals were quite distinct from the NJCs in emphasis and direction:

> Community mediation was embraced as an empowerment tool for individuals and communities to take back control over their lives from a governmental institution (the courts) that was seen not only as inefficient, but oppressive and unfair. This vision included equipping citizens to resolve their own disputes and the building of a truly alternative system that would keep many disputants from seeing the inside of a courthouse (Hedeen and Coy, 2000, p. 352).

Programs such as the Community "No-Fault" Boards in San Francisco and the Community Dispute Settlement Center in Delaware County, a suburb of Philadelphia, were designed to provide "first-resort conflict-settlement service[s] for local residents outside the perimeters of the formal legal system" (Shonholtz, 1993, p. 205). Many supporters and scholars hoped that these programs would be not only providers of mediation services, but resources for the development of community capacity and leadership (Merry, 1982). The words of Elise Boulding (1986) reflect the inspiration for many: "Cultures are not created in the halls of parliaments and presidential palaces; they are created locally and only later drawn on nationally. Therefore the cultures of mediation and peacemaking must begin locally" (p. iv).

These movements shared the broad goals of increasing access to justice and developing appropriate processes to produce fitting resolutions, even as they held considerably different—and sometimes contradictory—hopes and motivations. While some programs may be considered primarily justice based and others community based, a majority of the centers in the field have joined together to form a national organization that seeks to support the work of all types of community mediation.

The National Association for Community Mediation (NAFCM) boasts some 321 member centers in the United States (A. Hardin, telephone conversation with the author, Oct. 22, 2003). While estimates of the number of extant centers range from 300 to 550, an exact count remains elusive; not only is there difficulty in tallying very small operations or programs that are housed under broad umbrella organizations, but there are fundamental questions of definition.

A 1991 National Institute for Dispute Resolution (NIDR) manual observed that "the major factor distinguishing . . . [community mediation] is that volunteers play a major role in delivering services" (Fn'Piere, 1991, p. 2). A more robust definition may be gleaned from NAFCM, which enumerates nine characteristics of community mediation programs. Four are considered core characteristics, and to qualify for membership as a community mediation center, programs must:

1. Be a private non-profit or public agency or program thereof, with mediators, staff, and governing/advisory board representative of the diversity of the community served.

2. Use trained community volunteers as providers of mediation services; the practice of mediation is open to all persons (volunteers are not required to have academic or professional credentials).

3. Provide direct access to the public through self referral and strive to reduce barriers to service, including physical, linguistic, cultural, programmatic, and economic [barriers]; and

4. Provide services to clients regardless of ability to pay [NAFCM Board of Directors meeting minutes, Apr. 2003].

The Structure of Community Mediation

Observers have long sought to classify community mediation programs into one taxonomy or another, beginning with Wahrhaftig's three categories in the late 1970s. He identified three types of programs: those sponsored by the justice system, those sponsored or hosted by a nonprofit, and those that were "community based" (1979). Through a 1982 nationwide survey of programs, McGillis reclassified programs into three groups: "justice-system-based, community-based, and composite" (1986, p. 20). Almost two decades later, he revised this typology, observing that "programs do not lend themselves to ready categorization, but two basic types of project structures and goals exist: government-sponsored programs and community-based programs" (1997, p. 8).

Paralleling McGillis's lines of distinction, Shonholtz (2000) described two models: the neighborhood justice center and the community mediation center. The former "serves as a diversionary channel for cases considered by justice and similar governmental institutions as more appropriate for informal, nonbinding, local dispute settlement mechanisms," while the latter is "organized around a different perception of need and a different understanding of the opportunities provided through community-based conciliation mechanisms" (2000, pp. 331–332); those opportunities include building community capacity to prevent, deescalate, and resolve conflicts among its members through the efforts of only its members.

Most recently, research on the broader field of dispute resolution has contributed two taxonomies useful in understanding community mediation. In a study of seven mediation programs in Florida, including community mediation as well as other mediation resources, researchers identified three types of relationships between mediation providers and the court system: autonomous, synergistic, and assimilative (Folger, Della Noce, and Antes, 2001). And in a study of restorative justice agencies in British Columbia, sociolegal scholars coined distinct groups organized around communitarian or governmentalist interests (Ratner and Woolford, 2003). Where the Florida study underscores the predominance of court-related functions and interests in mediation, the British Columbia study emphasizes the dynamic tension between formal and informal justice, leaving dispute resolution in an oscillating space.

The various typologies presented reflect the rich history and diversity of the community mediation field and hint at the limitations of broad generalization concerning centers or their services. Beer (1986) highlighted the importance of and variation in program models nearly twenty years ago, and her observations hold true today:

> The appearance and soundness of a house are determined by the frame and foundation which hold it together. Any program model is shared around goals and philosophy, whether or not those are consciously laid out. The form is further set by external factors such as money, location, connections with the community, and staff skills. While everyone agrees that a sound foundation of practice and purpose are basic to building a sturdy program, the young community mediation movement is still experimenting with organizational blueprints [p. 145].

With the recognition that the field continues to experiment with blueprints, I now present the structural elements and aspirations of the field of community mediation.

The Sector

The vast majority of community mediation programs are nonprofit agencies, either stand-alone centers or programs under the umbrella of a larger nonprofit social service organization, while a substantial number of programs are public agencies, typically housed within justice systems or local government operations. The NAFCM membership rolls are likely the best source of program data nationwide, and as of 2003, eight of nine member centers (89 percent) were private nonprofit organizations (or agencies of them). Public agencies, administered through city, county, or state offices, constitute the remaining 1 percent (E. H. Acerra, e-mail to the author, Oct. 24, 2003).

While the NJC programs were funded initially in large part, if not in full, through the federal Law Enforcement Assistance Administration, community mediation programs today receive very limited financial support from federal sources. Returning to the earlier question of definition, the NIDR Community Justice Task Force offered a fitting summary of the unique sector of community mediation: "Sponsorship, funding sources, and methods of case referral [differ], but the use of trained volunteers [is] the common denominator" (Fn'Piere, 1991, p. 2).

The Overall Dispute System Design

Community mediation programs may take many forms, but in most interactions with individual disputants, referral agencies, or training clients, they are essentially outside contractors. Programs contract with a wide range of public and private organizations, including courts, law enforcement agencies, schools, and private corporations. For most individuals, the programs represent social service providers. Even for programs that function as part of governmental offices, and therefore do not appear to be outside contractors, the services delivered—usually mediation or conflict resolution training—are most often provided on a case-by-case, short-term basis.

Mediation practitioners across almost every context jealously protect their neutrality and independence (as perceived by clients), as these qualities provide mediators their credibility. To maintain the trust of a broad audience with sometimes contradictory interests, community mediation programs appreciate the value of holding an independent contractor role. Where sponsorship or affiliation may compromise a program's perceived neutrality, centers have taken steps to diversify their boards, staff, and volunteer rosters to demonstrate their commitment to impartiality.

Around the country, many community mediation centers handle disputes under federal legislation; these cases are usually channeled through related state offices. In Michigan, Nebraska, New York, North Carolina, and Oklahoma, the federal requirement of the Individuals with Disabilities Education Act of 1997 to provide mediation is fulfilled through local community mediation centers (P. Moses, telephone conversation with the author, Apr. 1, 2004). Many states also contract with community mediation programs to serve cases related to the American with Disabilities Act of 1990, the Agricultural Credit Act of 1987, and the Vocational Rehabilitation Act of 1973 (Wilkinson, 2001; Community Dispute Resolution Centers Program, 2003). Furthermore, some state mediation associations serve as intermediaries for the intake and referral of agricultural, lemon law, or manufactured homes disputes to community mediation centers (New York State Dispute Resolution Association, 2003). In these arrangements, community mediation programs are networked providers of contracted services.

A similar arrangement was employed for another national initiative, the training of AmeriCorps members between 1995 and 1999. Through an agreement with the federal Corporation for National Service, NAFCM oversaw the development of an outstanding training curriculum in communication and conflict resolution skills, and contracted with community mediation centers nationwide to deliver the training locally. Whether through national or state networks, such training arrangements realize a tremendous opportunity for the localized implementation and delivery of programs across a broad geographical area.

Predictably, mediation services represent the bulk of most centers' activities. The types of disputes handled include minor criminal matters, civil small claims, custody and visitation issues, landlord-tenant matters, neighborhood concerns such as noise and property boundaries, school-related issues of behavior, victim-offender restorative justice efforts, interpersonal differences, and large-group concerns around public policy, environmental, and community issues. What is not readily apparent from the diversity of this caseload is that the majority of cases are not initiated by parties but rather referred through the courts.

The reliance on courts to resolve concerns was a product of many social trends. It was a project of the Department of Justice to pilot the concept of mediation for low-level civil and criminal matters. It began in 1978 and many of the centers created through the project live on. The final report on the NJC Field Test explained:

> The courts have not actively sought to become the central institution for dispute resolution; rather the task has fallen to them by default as the significance and influence of other institutions has waned over the years. . . . Many of the disputes which are presently brought to the courts would have been settled in the past by the family, the church, or the informal community leadership. While the current role of these societal institutions in resolving interpersonal disputes is in doubt, many citizens take their cases to the courts [Cook, Roehl, and Sheppard, 1980, p. 2].

Through referral partnerships with community mediation centers, courts direct many cases on to mediation as a more appropriate or efficient process; this flow of cases often represents the lion's share of a center's caseload. For illustration, consider that of all cases handled by centers in recent years in Michigan and North Carolina, court referrals accounted for nearly 60 percent and over 75 percent, respectively (Community Dispute Resolution Program, 2002; Mediation Network of North Carolina, 2000). Furthermore, a national survey of NAFCM member centers found that 46 percent of the programs received at least half of their cases through the courts (including 28 percent of the membership that received at least three-quarters of their cases as court referrals; Hedeen and Acerra, 2003). This proximity has led practitioners to observe, "We haven't created an alternative to the courts. We've become an alternative to the courtroom" (quoted in Beer, 1986, p. 206). Such close ties have led some to question whether this arrangement risks the neutrality and integrity of mediation (Hedeen and Coy, 2000), while others view this level of coordination and institutionalization as the field's greatest promise (Hedeen, 2003).

Level of Self-Determination Available to Disputants

Community mediation centers place a high priority on self-determination at every stage of conflict. Disputants retain decision-making authority with regard to attendance at mediation, the extent of their participation within mediation, and the outcome of the mediation. Where community mediation programs are operated with extensive community participation and governance, disputants have a further voice in the design of delivery of the program's services. It should be noted that anecdotal evidence demonstrates that high levels of community participation and governance are relatively rare.

Efforts to Implement and Publicize the Program and Referral Processes

The authors of a chapter on marketing community mediation open with a straightforward summation of one of the field's greatest challenges: "Mediation, ancient as a skill, is a relatively new concept as it is offered to the general public. . . . It can be ineffectual unless those in need of it are aware of its availability and understand what it is" (Hicks, Rosenthal, and Standish, 1991, p. 73). Efforts to raise public awareness have ranged from traditional media to statewide declarations of Mediation Day or Week, from door-to-door outreach to the distribution of telephone stickers and refrigerator magnets. The NAFCM Regional Training Institute module on Public Education provides examples of articles published in local newspapers and offers important counsel such as, "Don't turn down 6 A.M. interviews! Lots of people listen to them, even on Sunday mornings" (Weinstein, 2003, p. 24). Through surveys of both disputants and referrals sources, Mika's research (1997a) has found that the most powerful influence toward referring cases is a word-of-mouth recommendation.

Based on the very large proportion of cases referred through another agency or program, coordination with referral sources is critical for community mediation. Despite this fact, a study of Michigan's statewide network of programs concluded that "few written agreements or contracts exist between local programs and their referral sources that articulate expectations, processes, and problem-solving strategies. The norm is that referral sources receive little or no feedback" (Mika, 1997a, p. 18). Prevalent efforts to educate referrers about mediation services include presentations at staff meetings or police roll calls, as well as in-service staff development training that concludes with a short plug for the mediation program. And to facilitate referrals further, many centers have developed flyers to insert with court filing materials and tear-off referral cards with one part for the disputant, one for the mediation center, and one for the police officer to track activity.

Structural Support and Institutionalization

The external structural support provided to community mediation varies greatly across the country. In some states, there exist nonprofit associations of centers, while in others there are state offices specifically designed to support community mediation, and in still other states there are both. Consider New York, which hosts both the New York State Dispute Resolution Association and the Community Dispute Resolution Centers Program of state court office of alternative dispute resolution (ADR). By legislation, the latter provides over $6 million annually to fund community mediation program work in community and family cases in all of the state's sixty-two counties; these funds represent approximately half of a typical center's budget (Community Dispute Resolution Centers Program, 2003). States fund community mediation in a variety of ways, including a filing fee surcharge as in California and Michigan or a legislative appropriation, such as in North Carolina, or both, as in Nebraska. On the broader national scale, the Washington, D.C.–based National Association for Community Mediation provides technical assistance and a voice for the field in the nation's capital. The American Bar Association Section of Dispute Resolution maintains the Community-Based and Peer Mediation Committee, and the Association for Conflict Resolution hosts the Community Section; both organizations offer community mediation–relevant sessions at their annual conferences and collaborate with NAFCM and local centers to advance the field. For many years, the National Conference on Peacemaking and Conflict Resolution has attracted a large number of community mediation practitioners, along with academics and researchers. There is also a natural connection between the Victim-Offender Mediation Association and community mediation centers that provide restorative justice services.

A crucial form of support is funding, and the funding of community mediation has led to a spirited discussion within the field and its literature.

Centers that participate in NAFCM's Regional Training Institutes are counseled to seek funding from a diversity of sources; the seven types of funds identified within the Fund Development module are individual donations, fees for services, special projects or events, community funds such as the United Way, corporate giving, foundations, and government grants (Brown, 2001). This echoes the counsel offered in a 1991 NIDR manual subtitled *Insights and Guidance from Two Decades of Practice,* which emphasized the importance of establishing viable fundraising plans and building diverse funding bases for community centers (Fn'Piere, 1991). Programs that attain a patchwork quilt of funding are often exemplars of public-private partnerships.

Many programs "have attained success by embedding themselves within a specific financial structure, such as by a single large contract with a court system or local government . . . such 'sole source' arrangements create vulnerability to the vagaries of other institutions' fortunes" (Honeyman, 1995, n.p.). Just as Honeyman identifies the financial dangers of overreliance, Hedeen and Coy (2000) highlight the possible compromises to a program's mission and direction: "When mediation programs are funded in large part by any one source, the potential for control or even undue influence that a funding agency has over aspects of the mediation program is likely to increase" (p. 356). It is worthy to note that these questions of funding are not recent developments, as nearly twenty-five years ago Wahrhaftig advised critical examination of "the political consequences of program sponsorship" (1979, n.p.) and not long after, with the benefit of careful research and observation, Davis (1986) pronounced that programmatic structure does not follow function so much as "form follows funding" (p. 35).

Sociolegal and organizational scholars have demonstrated that not only does form follow funding, but that mediation programs may adjust their practices and processes to mimic those of their primary funding and referral sources. Morrill and McKee (1993) studied the "institutional isomorphism" of a center in the Southwest, observing many points of assimilation into the culture of the court system. Their findings were consistent with those of more recent studies of organizational change within community mediation (Folger, Della Noce, and Antes, 2001; Hedeen and Coy, 2003), which have identified a tendency away from "the emphases on access, diversity, volunteerism, and change [which] represent community ownership of disputes and dispute resolution" (Hedeen 2003, p. 276), and a shift toward greater routinization and efficiency.

Due Process Protections

The community mediation process, like other forms of mediation, is some-times described as facilitated negotiation, and as in direct negotiation, there are limited procedural safeguards for participants. At the same time, the voluntary nature of community mediation services affords disputants con-siderable opportunity to opt out of mediation and to initiate or continue proceedings that provide greater due process protections. It should be noted that cases involving relationships marked by severe power imbalances, including those with past violence or abuse, deserve and receive special screening and case management (Gerencser, 1995). Similarly, mediation centers bear a responsibility to ensure that participants can make full use of the mediation process; individuals without such capacity are often accom-panied by and assisted in mediation by support persons: translators, coun-selors, attorneys, or relatives, for example (Coy and Hedeen, 1998). To the extent possible, disputants are encouraged to participate directly in media-tion; thus, surrogate or proxy representation is discouraged. Given these conditions, even the staunchest proponents of community mediation recognize that this forum does not fit every fuss (Sander, 1976).

Accessibility is a hallmark of due process, and a defining characteristic of community mediation and programs is that they work tirelessly to ensure the broadest access possible to serve mediation-appropriate cases. Among the features designed to maximize the accessibility of justice are five listed in *Community Dispute Resolution Programs and Public Policy*: "(1) not charging for services, (2) not requiring lawyers, (3) holding hearings at times con-venient to all parties to the dispute, including nights and weekends, (4) pro-viding readily understandable procedures and rules, and (5) providing multilingual staffs to serve non-English speaking disputants" (McGillis, 1986, p. 87). In addition, the location of mediation matters. The Maryland Mediation and Conflict Resolution Office (MACRO, 2002) has adopted a nine-point model for community mediation in that state, including two concerning the location of services: "(3) Hold mediations in neighbor-hoods where disputes occur" and "(4) Schedule mediations at a time and place convenient to the participants." One center, the Baltimore City Mediation Program, has coordinated with other services to offer mediation at over one hundred sites.

The Nature of the Intervention

Almost by definition, community mediation centers provide mediation services. Few centers, if any, provide only mediation services. The range of services varies by center, but a national survey turns up centers providing conflict resolution and communication skills training, meeting facilitation, public policy mediation, organizational consulting including dispute system design and strategic planning, conciliation (that is, attaining a resolution through communication with both parties but without convening all parties at any time, also known as telephone mediation), arbitration, restorative justice processes such as conferencing and circles, and in Cleveland, a homeless prevention program, the Cleveland Mediation Center, which disburses rent assistance (McGillis, 1997; Wilkinson, 2001; National Association for Community Mediation, 2003).

Mediation is not a monolithic process, so some qualification of various approaches employed at community mediation centers is required. On Riskin's facilitative-to-evaluative, narrow-to-broad continua (1994), most community mediators have been trained in a facilitative, broad model of mediation. To elaborate, mediators facilitate dialogue and decision making by the parties without offering the mediator's own assessment or evaluation of the matters under negotiation; furthermore, mediators encourage parties to discuss a broad range of issues related to their conflict instead of narrowly focusing on the legal facts or facets of the dispute.

Many community mediation programs have embraced the transformative model of mediation, based on the transformative framework outlined in Bush and Folger's book, *The Promise of Mediation* (1994). This model emphasizes two important shifts that may occur in mediation: empowerment and recognition. The empowerment shift is the restoration of a disputant's confidence in self, and in turn, his or her capacity to resolve the conflict constructively; the recognition shift represents a disputant's openness and respect for the other disputant. A number of centers participate in Community Centers in Transition, a project to support programs as they shift their mediation services toward the transformative approach.

Alongside approaches to mediation intervention are questions of the interveners, specifically, How many mediators? A large proportion, perhaps a majority (figures are unavailable, but anecdotal evidence suggests this), of community mediation centers employ comediation or panel mediation models. A perceived advantage of these models is that "multiple mediators can be selected to represent the range of gender or ethnic diversity of disputants" (McGillis, 1997, p. 12). Furthermore, some models of community dispute resolution intentionally draw on a group, not just a pair, of citizens to serve as intermediaries. Prior to the recent emergence of community conferencing and circle processes as services of the formal justice system, especially in restorative justice efforts, there was the pioneering boards model of the San Francisco Community Boards program, which typically involved between three and five panelists (not mediators; Shonholtz, 1993).

Arbitration is widely employed in the labor arena, with arbitrators provided through federal, state, or private agencies, but is conducted in only a handful of community mediation centers. Of those centers offering arbitration services, most do so in small civil claims or in specialized environments, In New York, for example, many centers handle lemon law arbitration through a contract between the New York State Dispute Resolution Association and the state attorney general's office (Community Dispute Resolution Centers Program, 2003). The hybrid practice of mediation-then-arbitration (med-arb) has been provided by a limited number of centers in the past, but its use has waned considerably (McGillis, 1997).

The facilitation of public policy and intergroup conflict appears to be an area of growth for community mediation centers. Center staff and volunteers bring years of experience and credibility to the task of facilitating public meetings, as well as specific knowledge of the local culture around conflict. Community mediation resources such as the program in Orange County, North Carolina, have created full-time staff positions for public disputes (McGillis, 1998); the center has conducted cases regarding housing shortages and the siting of landfills. And centers as far apart as New Mexico and New York City have facilitated meetings to address gang-related issues in schools and communities (McGillis, 1997). Through collaborations among centers, state offices, universities, and nonprofit organizations, an ever-increasing number of centers are developing the capacity to conduct community problem-solving initiatives. A presentation at the 2003 conference of the Association for Conflict Resolution showcased recent efforts in Maryland, North Carolina, and Virginia (Dukes, Parker, and Dunne, 2003).

A commonly overlooked service of many community mediation programs is education. Centers routinely provide educational materials and conduct outreach efforts to raise public awareness of mediation and other dispute resolution options, and many centers provide skills training in communication and conflict resolution skills in a variety of contexts. These contexts include formal educational structures such as K–12 schools and colleges, with centers heavily involved in initiatives ranging from peer mediation programs to peaceable schools efforts (see Jones, this volume), as well as informal, popular education efforts. Popular education in conflict resolution may take the form of workshops or seminars offered to community members at low or no cost, as well as self-instructional materials like brochures, handbooks, refrigerator magnets, and even widely accessible Web pages (see Community Mediation Services, 2003).

Participation: Voluntary, Opt Out, or Mandatory

The voluntary nature of mediation is held to be fundamental, as demonstrated by the prominent placement of self-determination as the first standard in the field's most widely recognized code of ethics, the *Model Standards of Conduct for Mediators* (1995): "Self-Determination: A mediator shall recognize that mediation is based on the principle of self-determination by the parties" (p. 1). The many facets of self-determination include freedom from pressure to accept specific (or any) agreements, freedom to leave the process at any point, freedom to share information selectively, and freedom to choose whether to mediate at all. A common argument for keeping participation in mediation voluntary comes from the early days of the mediation movement: agreements reached in mediation are more durable and fitting than court decisions because the parties design them at their pleasure and discretion (Aaronson and others, 1977; Wahrhaftig, 1978). This is consistent with theories and studies of procedural justice, which demonstrate higher satisfaction with, and durability of, outcomes reached through fair processes (Thibaut and Walker, 1975; Lind and Tyler, 1988). "Volition is the key to successful outcomes—volition validates those [mediated] outcomes; compulsion does not" (Nicolau, 1995, p. 1), and therefore, "Voluntariness is vital" (Nicolau, 1986, p. 1).

Only a few years into the enterprise of community dispute resolution, McGillis (1986) recognized a continuum of coercion levels in operation: "Very low coercion—Moderate coercion—Quite high coercion—Very high coercion—Outright referral to the program" (p. 43). Referrals often take the form of a judge's recommendation or are delivered in writing, on the letterhead of the court of the prosecutor (McGillis and Mullen, 1977; Hedeen and Coy, 2000). A number of early studies found that increased coercion leads to higher rates of attendance: the initial three neighborhood justice centers employed low to moderate coercion and attained mediation sessions in 35 percent of cases, while five Florida court-sponsored programs employed "quite high" coercion and attained sessions in 56 percent of their cases, and a Minnesota project sponsored by the prosecutor employed "very high" coercion and attained sessions in 90 percent of its cases (McGillis, 1986). Different case streams within the NJCs led to different rates of participation, In Kansas City, for example, "a mediation hearing was held in 86 percent of the cases referred by the criminal justice system where an arrest charge was involved. In those cases referred by criminal justice agents without charges pending . . . only 38 percent participated in a hearing" (Harrington, 1985, p. 121). Consistent with these earlier findings, a recent study of Baltimore's community mediation program has found that a greater proportion of court-referred cases proceed to mediation than that of self-referred cases (Charkoudian, 2001). And a large-scale study of the caseload of New York's network of programs found that the greater the perceived coercive power of the referring agency, the greater the likelihood of participation in mediation; however, the same study found that the greater the perceived coercive power of the referring agency, the lower the likelihood of agreement (Hedeen, 2001). Even without the benefit of the research findings presented here, Merry (1982) observed over twenty years ago, "Rates of appearance for hearings seem to vary with the coercive powers of the referral source" (p. 179).

Participation in community mediation is ultimately a choice made by disputants. The limited research on the topic, including interviews with case managers and intake staff, indicates that disputants are often motivated to attend mediation when they believe there will be negative repercussions for failure to participate. Consider the words of a case manager in New York, reflecting on years of caseloads: "I don't know that there are any consequences [for not participating], I think there are perceptions of consequences. . . . It's eventually going to end up back in front of the judge, so if you can say you made an effort, you won't be hurt. . . . I think a lot of people who perceive that type of pressure participate as a pre-emptive action" (Hedeen, 2001, p. 31). The interviews further suggest that community mediation staff emphasize the voluntary nature of mediation to clients at many points of case development in an effort to maintain the disputants' self-determination throughout the case.

Timing of the Intervention

The timing of community mediation services varies considerably, and is difficult to track. While NAFCM member centers are committed to "providing a forum for dispute resolution at the earliest stage of conflict," the court-referral figures already presented clearly demonstrate another commitment: to provide an "alternative to the judicial system at any stage of a conflict" (National Association for Community Mediation, 2003). The high proportion of court referrals reflects that many cases have escalated to the point of court action, even prior to reaching community mediation centers. An innovative statewide research project in Maryland is under way to collect data on the history of community mediation cases, including each conflict's length and any prior attempts toward resolution, but the results of this study are not yet available.

The Nature, Training, and Other Qualifications of the Neutrals

Davis's definition of community mediation focuses on the mediators: "Three distinguishing features of community mediation programs are (1) their use of volunteers (2) who come from all types of backgrounds and (3) who begin providing service after a relatively brief period of training" (1991, p. 206). Indeed, community mediators come from all walks of life, representing every conceivable demographic in the United States. Despite this significant diversity and the characterization of the training as relatively brief, they share a remarkable identity: community mediators are among the most trained dispute resolvers nationwide. Even a casual review of the training requirements set forth by state legislatures, courts, and centers demonstrates that community mediators' basic training, apprenticeship, and continuing education and mentorship total more hours of training than is provided to almost any other group of mediators or arbitrators (the states reviewed were Maryland, Minnesota, Nebraska, New York, and North Carolina).

The introductory mediation training length is typically between thirty and fifty hours for community mediators, and it is common for centers or other regulating bodies to require at least six hours of continuing education and the conduct of three or more cases each year. For illustration, consider the recently revised guidelines of the New York Community Dispute Resolution Centers Program. In addition to an initial training of thirty hours, new mediators are "required to mediate two structured role-plays, observe at least one mediation, mediate or co-mediate at least five cases, and mediate or co-mediate at least one case followed by either a debriefing session with staff or completing a self-evaluation form" (Community Dispute Resolution Centers Program, 2002, p. 6) and must complete six hours of continuing training each year. It should be noted that there are over two thousand active volunteer mediators in New York, with an average (mean) length of service of eight years (Community Dispute Resolution Centers Program, 2003).

Prior to even the introductory training, many centers conduct recruitment and screening efforts. Although there exist no uniform guidelines for screening, "some important considerations to use the selection process are whether the individual is willing to make a commitment to the program and whether his or her attitude is congruent with program goals and philosophy" (Fn'Piere, 1991, p. 41). Consistent with NAFCM's characteristics and Davis's descriptions, these considerations do not include academic or professional credentials. Paradoxically, while these diverse volunteer mediators are among the most trained dispute resolvers in the country, many would be willing to donate more hours than they already do. In interviews with community mediators, most indicate that they are underused, as many centers rely on a small cadre of volunteers who have both strong skills and (probably more importantly) regular, broad availability due to flexible schedules (Rogers, 1991).

The Financial or Professional Incentive Structure

Community mediators are seldom compensated for their work, although many centers provide support for transportation (for example, reimbursement for subway fare or parking costs in large cities or for mileage in rural areas). Why, then, do individuals serve as mediators? While anecdotal evidence suggests that many volunteers view community mediation as an opportunity to hone their skills or as a stepping-stone toward professional practice (note that many mediation trainings offer no opportunity for apprenticeship, leaving participants to seek out venues such as community mediation programs), the limited research on the issue emphasizes more selfless goals.

Survey research has demonstrated that most volunteers are motivated by altruism. Mediators in the surveyed population ranked "helping others" and "building the community" along with "learning new skills" as their greatest motivations (Rogers, 1991). These interests fall neatly within Harrington and Merry's delineation (1988) of three distinct goals of community mediation: the delivery of dispute resolution services, social transformation, and personal growth and development. Building on research findings regarding intrinsically motivated behavior, Olczak, Grosch, and Duffy (1991) suggest that "mediators who enjoy mediating cases might feel less motivated if they were paid for rendering the same service" (p. 331). As a community service or as a pro bono service by some professionals, mediation provides valuable benefits to the community as well as valuable life skills to the volunteers.

Many community mediation centers provide stipends to their mediators, especially in specialized or lengthy cases. In some cities, the professionalization of mediation has created pressure on community programs to pay mediators for service (L. Baron, telephone conversation with the author, Dec. 9, 2003). And in rural areas, where mediators often log extensive travel time, some compensation is necessary to allow volunteers to take time off work to provide mediation services.

Accomplishments: Measures of Community Mediation

The following quotation captures both the potential of community mediation and the still incomplete documentation of the field's accomplishments: "Everyone involved with community mediation in Maryland believes that it provides an affordable service that goes a lot further than easing court dockets and reducing police calls. Community mediation programs preserve relationships and yield long-lasting results. The research on community mediation programs is only beginning to document its dynamism and potential for community-wide success" (quoted in Wilkinson, 2001, p. 46).

Like the elephant and the six blind men, the impact of community mediation may be considered from many reference points. While the men, respectively, ascertained that the elephant was similar to a wall, a spear, a snake, a tree, a fan, and a rope, it is most relevant to recall the poem's concluding lines: "Though each was partly in the right/They all were in the wrong." Analogously, studies of community mediation often focus on only one or two measures of effectiveness, assessing these without addressing other dimensions or indicators of effectiveness.

We review empirical findings related to a variety of measures: the resolution rate; participants' satisfaction with the process, the mediators, and any resolution reached; perceptions of fairness; the durability of resolutions; and the cost and time efficiencies realized through the process. Readers will note the relative dearth of evaluation research, as well as the limited scope of measures employed.

Resolution Rate

Across the many contexts in which the process is employed, the most prevalent measure of mediation success is the proportion of mediations that conclude in resolutions, known as the settlement rate or agreement rate. The frequent use of this measure stems in large part from its apparent ease of measurement: Did the parties to a mediation arrive at an agreement, or did they not? "For many analysts, the ambiguities of the terms *effectiveness* and *success* have led them to categorize simply reaching a settlement with the participation of a mediator to be a successful mediation. If the overt struggle continues, the mediation is regarded as failed" (Kriesberg, 1998, p. 242). Although this measure has been widely adopted, a consensus among researchers and practitioners is emerging that it fails to capture much of mediation's value; this misrepresentation is perhaps nowhere greater than in community dispute resolution. Mediation may lead to improved or restored relationships, greater understanding of others' perspectives, resolution of some (but not all) issues, and movement toward later resolution; none of these might show up on the "resolved" side the ledger. Furthermore, as methodologists have observed, "The simple achievement of an agreement . . . , while significant, can represent anything from a highly comprehensive and sensitive settlement reflecting an effort to solve the entire range of problems embedded in the dispute to an agreement by the parties regarding a marginal issue that may have some limited importance but leaves the vast bulk of the conflict unresolved" (McGillis, 1997, p. 50).

. . . These critiques notwithstanding, community mediation programs have diligently recorded their settlement rates. In a ten-year sample of some 426,000 cases handled through the statewide network of centers in New York, 80 percent of mediated cases concluded in agreement (Hedeen, 1999). The Michigan network reported agreements in 71 percent of cases that reached mediation in 2002 (Community Dispute Resolution Program, 2002), and the Nebraska statewide network of centers reported full or partial agreements in 81 percent of mediated cases (Nebraska Office of Dispute Resolution, 2003). These rates are consistent with earlier studies of community mediation, as the NJC Field Test produced an agreement rate of 82 percent for the three programs in Atlanta, Kansas City, and Los Angeles (Cook, Roehl, and Sheppard, 1980), while a study of five citizen dispute resolution projects in Florida found an agreement rate of 81 percent (Bridenback, 1979).

Satisfaction with the Mediation Process

In their work to assess litigants' experience with and attitudes toward the trial process, social psychologists Thibaut and Walker developed a measure that has become a mainstay in the evaluation of mediation and other forms of dispute resolution: "satisfaction with the process" (1975, p. 73). Satisfaction with the mediation process is viewed as critical, as it represents the participants' sense of procedural justice and correlates well with their compliance with the outcome (see Wissler, 2002). Studies of community mediation demonstrate high levels of satisfaction with the mediation process.

Research on the NJC programs found that 84 percent of initiating parties or complainants were satisfied with the mediation, alongside

89 percent of responding parties (Cook, Roehl, and Sheppard, 1980), while more recent statewide studies have led to similar findings. In Michigan, 84 percent of disputants indicated they would use the process again, and 88 percent would recommend the process to others (Mika, 1997a); in North Carolina, 96 percent of initiating parties reported satisfaction with the mediation process, along with 90 percent of responding parties (Clarke, Valente, and Mace, 1992). The 2002–2003 annual report on Nebraska's statewide network presents findings from client surveys that 89 percent were satisfied with their mediation (Nebraska Office of Dispute Resolution, 2003), and the New York programs found that 95 percent of those who reached agreement and even 63 percent of those who did not reach agreement reported that "mediation was a good way to attempt to resolve this dispute" (Community Dispute Resolution Centers Program, 1999, p. 7). The NJC study went a step further, comparing the satisfaction levels of mediation participants to those of disputants in similar cases that proceeded to court. While the questions were not identical and thus direct comparisons cannot be made, a greater proportion of respondents in the mediation sample reported satisfaction. Consider the more than 80 percent figures for mediation above with the following proportions of those involved in court-resolved matters: in Atlanta, only 42 percent of participants believed their case was handled well in court, and in Kansas City only 33 percent reported the same.

Satisfaction with the Mediators

Mediators provide the critical facilitating role within the mediation session, engaging in a broad array of steps and behaviors to support the disputants in addressing the issues before them. Survey research has documented similarly high rates of satisfaction with mediators' performance as well. In the North Carolina study, 98 percent of initiating parties and 100 percent of responding parties were satisfied with the efforts of their mediators (Clarke, Valente, and Mace, 1992), while the NJC evaluation found that 88 percent of all disputants reported satisfaction with the mediators, as compared to 64 percent of disputants in court-handled cases who reported satisfaction with the judge (Cook, Roehl, and Sheppard, 1980).

Regardless of approach or style, mediators usually employ listening skills extensively in mediation. One of the measures of procedural justice is voice, that is, the extent to which a disputant was able to relate her or his concerns and to feel heard. Researchers of community mediation services in criminal cases in Brooklyn found that 94 percent of complainants and

90 percent of defendants reported that they felt their story was heard by the mediator; in comparison, in similar cases handled by the criminal court, the study found that only 65 percent of complainants and 44 percent of defendants felt heard by the judge (Davis, Tichane, and Grayson, 1980).

Satisfaction with the Mediation Resolution

Surveys of mediation participants consistently demonstrate high levels of satisfaction with mediated outcomes. In the NJC evaluation, with its comparison to court-processed cases, 86 percent of mediation participants reported satisfaction with their agreement, while only 33 percent of individuals in court-handled cases were satisfied with their outcome (Cook, Roehl, and Sheppard, 1980). The Brooklyn study found that 73 percent of complainants and 79 percent of defendants in mediated cases were satisfied with their outcome, while only 54 percent of complainants and 67 percent of defendants in court cases were satisfied with the outcome (Davis, Tichane, and Grayson, 1980).

Fairness

The perceived fairness of mediation processes, practitioners, and outcomes speaks directly to a center's credibility and legitimacy in a community. In a comparative study of the mediation and court handling of criminal cases in Brooklyn, researchers found that a higher proportion of the mediation group found case outcomes fair (77 percent of complainants and 79 percent of respondents) compared to that of the court group (56 percent and 59 percent, respectively) (Davis, Tichane, and Grayson, 1980). The same samples reported mediators to be fair (88 percent of complainants and 89 percent of defendants) slightly more often than judges (76 percent and 86 percent, respectively). Of participants surveyed in a family mediation program, 95 percent of parents and 84 percent of children reported that they considered their agreements to be fair (Merry and Rocheleau, 1985). Focusing on perceptions of mediator fairness, a survey of mediation participants found that 99 percent of those who reached agreement and 91 percent of those who did not reach agreement reported that their mediators were fair (Community Dispute Resolution Centers Program, 1999).

Durability of Resolutions

The stability of mediated resolutions over time is a measure valuable for many reasons. First, it represents disputants' abilities to fashion a fitting solution to their differences and to comply with the terms of any agreement made.

Furthermore, it indicates that the participants will not require the intervention of the courts, police, mediation center, or other resources. The NJC evaluation study conducted interviews of disputants six months after their mediations to learn how well the agreements stood up. More than two-thirds of all disputants reported that the other participant had upheld all terms of the resolution (Cook, Roehl, and Sheppard, 1980). A similar follow-up study found that 59 percent of initiating parties and 62 percent of respondents reported long-term compliance (Pruitt and others, 1993), and the same research found that over three-quarters of all disputants reported that no subsequent problems had arisen since the mediation. In the NJC sample, only 28 percent of initiating parties and 2 percent of respondents reported new disputes with the other party (Cook, Roehl, and Sheppard, 1980). Through follow-up surveys, the Michigan programs reported a 93 "agreement compliance rate" in a recent year (Community Dispute Resolution Centers Program, 2002).

Cost Efficiency

The cost efficiency, or cost-effectiveness, of community mediation is a complex measure. A 1985 study of the Durham Dispute Settlement Center compared the average costs to local and state governments for the center's processing of a case to those costs for court processing of the same case (Sheppard, 1985). The study arrived at an average cost of $72 per mediated case and $186 per court-handled case. A 2002 report prepared by the City of Portland Office for Neighborhood Improvement compiled self-reported data from fifty-seven community mediation programs, of which thirty-three were located in cities similar to Portland in size and outside Oregon, while the remaining twenty-four were within various-sized communities within Oregon. The cost-per-case figures over the aggregate sample of 47,357 cases ranged from $50 to $1,500, with a mean of $274 (Office of Neighborhood Involvement, 2002). Coincidentally, while the Portland study did not include figures from any centers in New York, the state office there maintains some of the most comprehensive data in the country.

The 2002–2003 annual report from the New York Community Dispute Resolution Centers Program (CDRCP) presents cost figures on two bases: the first employs the total number of cases as the unit of measure, while the second includes only cases mediated or otherwise resolved through the center. For the 51,899 cases handled that year, the cost per case was $131 and the cost per mediation, conciliation, or arbitration was $239 (Community Dispute Resolution Centers Program, 2003). The same report notes that over two thousand volunteers were active in resolving those cases, donating some 88,500 hours; while the assignment of a per-hour wage or other valuation to these services is beyond the scope of this article, it is clear that community mediation leverages considerable services on behalf of citizens and communities.

An additional measure of cost efficiency may be derived from the cost of services saved, that is, those services that were not required or delivered due to the successful resolution of concerns through mediation. Just as the research on the Durham center identified the potential court costs saved, another study has found that police referrals can lead to a decrease in return calls for service (Charkoudian, 2001), leading to direct cost savings for municipalities.

Time Efficiency

Community mediation centers achieve high efficiency in case processing time. The turnaround time between intake and disposition is a common measure of social services, reflecting an agency's responsiveness to clients. The New York CDRCP tracks the operations of the statewide network of programs, a network that handles some fifty thousand cases each year, and reported in a recent year an average case processing time of eighteen days for mediated cases that concluded in a single session (Community Dispute Resolution Centers Program, 2003). Similarly, the Michigan Community Dispute Resolution Program reported a period of twenty-four days (Community Dispute Resolution Centers Program, 2002).

These recent figures are slightly higher than those found in the NJC Field Test and an early study of programs in Florida. The Florida evaluation found the average processing time was eleven days (Bridenback, 1979) while the NJC research reported an average processing time of ten days for mediated matters and fourteen days for unresolved cases; these compared quite favorably to court processing of similar cases, which took ninety-eight days to reach trial in Atlanta and sixty-three days in Kansas City (Cook, Roehl, and Sheppard, 1980). This documented, demonstrated efficiency is among the strongest selling points for community mediation in both policy discussions and case intake conversations.

Conclusion: Challenges, Opportunities, and the Great Unknown

Reflecting on the short history of community mediation up to the late 1980s, Fee (1988) observed, "Nothing in dispute resolution has been more daring—and audacious—than the creation of scores of community justice centers" (p. 2). That pioneers of the young field would presume a role alongside the formal justice system to resolve differences through the delivery of a "grass-roots, imperfectly understood service" was bold indeed, and yet the accomplishments detailed here demonstrate much of the field's success over the past three decades. Research has shown that community mediation centers handle a broad array of case types in an appropriate, respectful, and cost- and time-efficient manner. However, the prevalent measures of community mediation fail to capture many of the field's broader goals, leaving some large questions unanswered. Merry identified this gap as early as 1982, when she observed an important trend in community mediation: "Centers are restructured in order to generate large caseloads and reduce costs while evaluations stress the number of cases handled and the potential reduction of demands on the criminal and civil justice systems. . . . Other goals for neighborhood justice centers have been virtually ignored, both in the planning process and in the bulk of evaluation studies" (p. 181).

Alongside Merry's concern about the lack of research on the community-oriented goals of community mediation, Lowry (1993) has lamented the general paucity of available research on community mediation: "There is a small and aging evaluative literature on community-justice programs. Some of it is published, but there are few recent published studies. Most evaluations remain in the 'gray literature': unpublished, minimally circulated papers and reports assessing the success or effectiveness of particular programs in particular settings" (p. 89). One need only consider this article's heavy reliance on research findings from the 1970s and 1980s and a handful of states' annual reports to appreciate the need for contemporary research on this vibrant field. This lack of up-to-date knowledge of the field affects many stakeholders, including funders and referrers who seek demonstration of the field's impact. But perhaps the most affected group are the staff and volunteer practitioners: Without data and analysis, on what basis does the practice of community mediation improve?

Research on community mediation is required at many levels, and many scholars have offered valuable lists of research topics requiring attention (see Duffy, Grosch, and Olczak, 1991; McGillis, 1986). These topics may be organized by the level of analysis: individual, organizational, or societal. The first of these has received the bulk of research attention to date, but all require further study.

At the individual level of analysis, researchers may focus on disputants, mediators, cases, and the role of support persons. Further study of disputants' motivations to participate in mediation (or not), of the past attempts toward resolution of a given matter, and of their perceptions of procedural justice in mediation, would provide important information for policymakers, mediation center staff and volunteers, and academics alike. Similarly, research into which mediator behaviors promote self-determination and procedural justice, facilitate appropriate agreements, and provide a safe environment for all involved would enhance the delivery of services. There are case- and process-related questions at this level too, including examination of the appropriate participation of support persons, of which cases require specialized case management or services, and of the factors contributing to the durability or stability of agreements.

Research concerning the volunteer mediator base is needed, too, as the use of volunteers is arguably the most unique quality of the community mediation enterprise. Rogers (1991) employed survey methods to glean insights from a sample of mediators about motivations and experiences, and her work opens the door to broader questions of impact at the individual and community levels. In what ways do volunteers use their skills within and outside mediation? Do they employ mediation skills in other community-building contexts?

Organizational-level research into case screening criteria and methods, referral systems and funding relationships, program accessibility, and outreach efforts will benefit the field greatly, providing the basis for informed planning and decision making, as well as enhanced services. The issue of funding is fundamental to any social service, even one that relies heavily on volunteer labor, and the need for stable and diverse funding streams is repeated through the literature on community mediation (Fn'Piere, 1991; Mika, 1997a; McGillis, 1997; Hedeen and Coy, 2000). Innovative funding arrangements may be linked to performance standards; one measure of interest to referrers and centers alike is the utilization rate of mediation in mediation-appropriate disputes. When researchers in North Carolina examined this question within the court context, they found that fewer than a quarter of mediation-eligible cases were referred to mediation (Clarke, Valente, and Mace, 1992). Greater benefits might accrue to the courts and other agencies through the development and evaluation of initiatives aimed at increasing use and decreasing case attrition between intake and mediation.

In addition, attention must be paid to organizational collaboration. For example, through work with Department of Justice-sponsored

Community-Oriented Policing Services and Weed and Seed initiatives, community mediation centers have gained service opportunities through ties to governmental agencies. The benefits and costs of such affiliations deserve careful consideration, as early critics of community mediation voiced concerns that the field may represent an extension of social control (see Abel, 1982; Hofrichter, 1987) or little more than an appendage of government (Wahrhaftig, 1979; Hedeen and Coy, 2000; Hedeen, 2003). Efforts to ensure accessibility of services deserve further attention too, as access is among the hallmarks of community mediation. Anecdotal evidence aside, there has been little documentation of program designs to enhance access and their effects. The Maryland funding model requires centers to deliver mediation in the disputants' neighborhood and at times convenient to all (Maryland Mediation and Conflict Resolution Office, 2002); the hope is that the measurable effects of such policy will be seen in coming years.

The most difficult level of research is, predictably, that which has received the least attention: the effects of community mediation on society. Does community mediation democratize justice? Does it lead to greater self-sufficiency? Research is sorely needed to measure the spillover effects of mediation and mediation programs. Does the "peace virus" hypothesis— the proposition that constructive, nonviolent behavior by some will lead to the same behavior by those with whom they interact—hold any weight with regard to community mediators? Studies in community (Henderson, 1986) and school (Crary, 1992) contexts have demonstrated partial support for the hypothesis, highlighting the need for research into social capital production through community mediation. Furthermore, what are the effects of individuals' assuming the role of "small 'm' mediator" (Beer, 1997, p. 136), providing mediation services flexibly and informally to friends, colleagues, or other disputants to whom the mediator is known?

These questions speak to community capacity building, an endeavor based largely in education. Many centers conduct training in communication and conflict resolution skills for formal education systems, ranging from preschool through law school. While the benefits of conflict resolution education in schools are well documented elsewhere in this volume (see the article by Jones), community mediation centers have a unique opportunity to enhance popular justice through processes of popular education (Freire, 1970). Development of centers' educational programming and research on its effectiveness should assist the field in plotting future directions.

The value of community mediation has been demonstrated in hundreds of communities across the United States, through the efforts of thousands of volunteers and staff members, for the benefit of hundreds of thousands of individuals. The task remains to document and analyze this value. Anecdotal evidence supports the claims of greater individual self-determination, increased community self-reliance, and enhanced access to justice, but more rigorous and comprehensive research is needed. Innovative and appropriate research methodologies—perhaps refinements of Mika's combination of site visits, extensive interviewing, organizational audits, multiple surveys of stakeholders, and analysis of case data in his evaluation of Michigan's programs (1997b)—can facilitate the progressive development of mediation services "of, by, and for the people."

References

Abel, R. L. (ed.). *The Politics of Informal Justice.* Orlando, Fla.: Academic Press, 1982.

Aaronson, D., and others. *The New Justice: Alternatives to Conventional Criminal Adjudication.* Washington, D.C.: Institute for Advanced Studies in Justice, American University, 1977.

Auerbach, J. S. *Justice Without Law? Resolving Disputes Without Lawyers.* New York: Oxford University Press, 1983.

Beer, J., with Stief, E. *The Mediator's Handbook.* (3rd ed.) Gabriola Island, B.C.: New Society Publishers, 1997.

Beer, J. E. *Peacemaking in Your Neighborhood: Reflections on an Experiment in Community Mediation.* Philadelphia: New Society Publishers, 1986.

Boulding, E. "Foreword." In J. Beer, *Peacemaking in Your Neighborhood: Reflections on an Experiment in Community Mediation.* Philadelphia: New Society Publishers, 1986.

Bridenback, M. *The Citizen Dispute Settlement Process in Florida: A Study of Five Programs.* Tallahassee: Florida Supreme Court, Office of the State Courts Administrator, 1979.

Brown, G. *Fund Development Module: Regional Training Institute Participant Manual.* Washington, D.C.: National Association for Community Mediation, 2001.

Burger, W. E. "Agenda for 2000 A.D.: A Need for Systematic Anticipation." Paper delivered at the National Conference on the Causes of Popular Dissatisfaction with the Administration of Justice, 1976.

Bush, R. B., and Folger, J. *The Promise of Mediation.* San Francisco: Jossey-Bass, 1994.

Charkoudian, L. "Economic Analysis of Interpersonal Conflict and Community Mediation." Unpublished doctoral dissertation, Johns Hopkins University, 2001.

Christian, T. "Community Dispute Resolution: First-Class Process or Second-Class Justice?" *New York University Review of Law and Social Change,* 1986, *14,* 771–783.

Clarke, S. H., Valente, Jr., E., and Mace, R. R. *Mediation of Interpersonal Disputes: An Evaluation of North Carolina's Programs.* Chapel Hill: Institute of Government, University of North Carolina, 1992.

Community Dispute Resolution Centers Program. *Annual Report, 1998–1999.* Albany: New York Unified Court System Office of Alternative Dispute Resolution, 1999.

Community Dispute Resolution Centers Program. *Annual Report, 2001–2002.* Albany: New York Unified Court System Office of Alternative Dispute Resolution, 2002.

Community Dispute Resolution Program. *Annual Report, 2002.* Lansing: Michigan Office of Dispute Resolution, 2002.

Community Dispute Resolution Centers Program. *Annual Report, 2002–2003.* Albany: New York Unified Court System Office of Alternative Dispute Resolution, 2003.

Community Mediation Services. "Tips to Prevent Conflicts with Neighbors," 2003. [http://www.ci.vancouver.wa.us/chservices/mediation/Tips_M.htm].

Cook, R. F., Roehl, J. A., and Sheppard, D. I. *Neighborhood Justice Centers Field Test: Final Evaluation Report.* Washington, D.C.: Department of Justice, 1980.

Coy, P. G., and Hedeen, T. "Disabilities and Mediation—Readiness in Court-Referred Cases: Developing Screening Criteria and Service Networks." *Mediation Quarterly,* 1998, *16* (2), 113–127.

Crary, D. "Community Benefits from Mediation: A Test of the 'Peace Virus' Hypothesis." *Mediation Quarterly,* 1992, *9,* 241–252.

Davis, A. *Community Mediation in Massachusetts: A Decade of Development, 1975–1986.* Salem, Mass.: Administrative Office of the District Court, 1986.

Davis, A. "How to Ensure High-Quality Mediation Services: The Issue of Credentialing." In K. G. Duffy, J. Grosch, and P. Olczak (eds.), *Community Mediation: A Handbook for Practitioners and Researchers.* New York: Guilford Press, 1991.

Davis, R., Tichane, M., and Grayson, D. *Mediation and Arbitration as Alternatives to Criminal Prosecution in Felony Arrest Cases: An Evaluation of the Brooklyn Dispute Resolution Center (First Year).* New York: Vera Institute of Justice, 1980.

Duffy, K. G., Grosch, J. W., and Olczak, P. V. (eds.). *Community Mediation: A Handbook for Practitioners and Researchers.* New York: Guilford Press, 1991.

Dukes, E. F., Parker, L., and Dunne, T. "Community Solutions: Preparing and Promoting Community Mediation to Resolve Community-wide Public Disputes." Paper presented at the Annual Conference of the Association for Conflict Resolution, Orlando, Fla., Oct. 15–18, 2003.

Fee, T. "Introduction." In *National Institute for Dispute Resolution (NIDR) Forum: The Status of Community Justice.* Dec. 1988.

Fn'Piere, P. (ed.). *Community Dispute Resolution Manual: Insights and Guidance from Two Decades of Practice.* Washington, D.C.: National Institute for Dispute Resolution, 1991.

Folger, J. P., Della Noce, D. J., and Antes, J. A. *A Benchmarking Study of Family, Civil, and Citizen Dispute Mediation Programs in Florida.* Tallahassee: Florida Dispute Resolution Center, 2001.

Freire, P. *Pedagogy of the Oppressed.* (M. B. Ramos, Trans.). New York: Continuum, 1970.

Gerencser, A. "Family Mediation: Screening for Domestic Abuse." *Florida State Law Review,* 1995, *23,* 43–69.

Harrington, C. *Shadow Justice: The Ideology and Institutionalization of Alternatives to Court.* Westport, Conn.: Greenwood Press, 1985.

Harrington, C., and Merry, S. "Ideological Production: The Making of Community Mediation." *Law and Society Review,* 1988, *22,* 709–737.

Hedeen, T. "From Intake to Mediation: Where Do All the Cases Go?" *Community Mediator, Newsletter of the National Association for Community Mediation.* Summer 1999.

Hedeen, T. "The Influence of Referral Source Coerciveness on Mediation Participation and Outcomes." Unpublished doctoral dissertation, Syracuse University, 2001.

Hedeen, T. "Institutionalizing Community Mediation: Can Dispute Resolution 'of, by, and for the People' Long Endure?" *Penn State Law Review,* 2003, *108,* 265–276.

Hedeen, T., and Acerra, E. Unpublished survey of National Association for Community Mediation membership documents, 2003.

Hedeen, T., and Coy, P. G. "Community Mediation and the Court System: The Ties That Bind." *Mediation Quarterly,* 2000, *17* (4), 351–367.

Hedeen, T., and Coy, P. G. "The Community Mediation Movement and Political Cooptation: A Theoretical Analysis." Paper presented at the Law and Society Association Annual Meeting, Pittsburgh, Pa., June 6–8, 2003.

Henderson, M. "Coordinating an Innovative Mediation Program." *Mediation Quarterly,* 1986, 12.

Hicks, L., Rosenthal, L. J., and Standish, L. "Marketing Mediation Programs." In K. G. Duffy, J. W. Grosch, and P. V. Olczak (eds.), *Community Mediation: A Handbook for Practitioners and Researchers.* New York: Guilford Press, 1991.

Hofrichter, R. *Neighborhood Justice in a Capitalist Society.* Westport, Conn.: Greenwood Press, 1987.

Honeyman, C. *Financing Dispute Resolution.* San Francisco: William and Flora Hewlett Foundation, 1995. [http://www.convenor.com/madison/fdr.htm].

Kriesberg, L. *Constructive Conflict: From Escalation to Resolution.* Lanham, Md.: Rowman and Littlefield, 1998.

Lind, E. A., and Tyler, T. *The Social Psychology of Procedural Justice.* New York: Plenum Press, 1988.

Lowry, K. "Evaluation of Community-Justice Programs." In S. E. Merry and N. Milner (eds.), *The Possibility of Popular Justice.* Ann Arbor: University of Michigan, 1993.

Maryland Mediation and Conflict Resolution Office. *The 9-Point Community Mediation Model.* Towson, Md.: Maryland Mediation and Conflict Resolution Office, 2002.

McGillis, D. *Community Dispute Resolution Programs and Public Policy.* Washington, D.C.: National Institute of Justice, 1986.

McGillis, D. *Community Mediation Programs: Developments and Challenges.* Washington, D.C.: National Institute of Justice, 1997.

McGillis, D. *Resolving Community Conflict: The Dispute Settlement Center of Durham, North Carolina.* Washington, D.C.: National Institute of Justice, 1998.

McGillis, D., and Mullen, J. *Neighborhood Justice Centers: An Analysis of Potential Models.* Washington, D.C.: Department of Justice, 1977.

Mediation Network of North Carolina. *Annual Report, 1999–2000.* Chapel Hill: Mediation Network of North Carolina, 2000.

Merry, S. E. "Defining 'Success' in the Neighborhood Justice Movement." In R. Tomasic and M. Feeley (eds.), *Neighborhood Justice: An Assessment of an Emerging Idea.* White Plains, N.Y.: Longman, 1982.

Merry, S. E., and Rocheleau, A. M. *Mediation in Families: A Study of the Children's Hearings Project.* Cambridge, Mass.: Children's Hearing Project of Cambridge, 1985.

Mika, H. *An Evaluation of Michigan's Community Dispute Resolution Program: Detailed Findings, Recommendations, and Appendices.* Lansing: Michigan Supreme Court State Court Administrative Office, 1997a.

Mika, H. *An Evaluation of Michigan's Community Dispute Resolution Program: A Methodology for Multi-Site Community Dispute Resolution Program Evaluation.* Lansing: Michigan Supreme Court State Court Administrative Office, 1997b.

Model Standards of Conduct for Mediators. Published jointly by the American Bar Association, the Society of Professionals in Dispute Resolution, and the Academy of Family Mediators, 1995.

Morrill, C., and McKee, C. "Institutional Isomorphism and Informal Social Control: Evidence from a Community Mediation Center." *Social Problems,* 1993, *40,* 445–463.

Nader, L. "Trading Justice for Harmony," *NIDR Forum,* 1992, Winter, 12–16.

National Association for Community Mediation. *Membership Directory.* Washington, D.C.: National Association for Community Mediation, 2003. [www.nafcm.org].

National Conference on Causes of Popular Dissatisfaction with the Administration of Justice, 1976 April 7–9, St. Paul, Minn.

Nebraska Office of Dispute Resolution. *Annual Report, July 2002–June 2003.* Lincoln: Administrative Office of the Courts/Probation, 2003.

New York State Dispute Resolution Association. Albany, 2003. [http://www.nysdra.org].

Nicolau, G. "Community Mediation: Progress and Problems." In *Massachusetts Association of Mediation Programs.* Boston, 1986.

Nicolau, G. "Where Goeth ADR—Ruminations of an Older Warrior." In *Massachusetts Association of Mediation Programs and Practitioners.* Boston, 1995.

Office of Neighborhood Involvement. *Community Mediation Services in Portland, Oregon, Report and Recommendations to City Council, City of Portland.* Portland, Ore.: Office of Neighborhood Involvement, 2002.

Olczak, P. V., Grosch, J. W., and Duffy, K. G. "Toward a Synthesis: The Art with the Science of Community Mediation." In K. G. Duffy, J. W. Grosch, and P. V. Olczak (eds.), *Community Mediation: A Handbook for Practitioners and Researchers.* New York: Guilford Press, 1991.

Pruitt, D. G., and others. "Long-Term Success in Mediation." *Law and Human Behavior,* 1993, *17,* 313–330.

Ratner, R. S., and Woolford, A. "Nomadic Justice? Restorative Justice on the Margins of Law." *Social Justice,* 2003, *30* (1), 117–194.

Riskin, L. "Mediator Orientations, Strategies and Techniques." *Alternatives,* 1994, *12,* 111–114.

Rogers, S. J. "Ten Ways to Work More Effectively with Volunteer Mediators." *Negotiation Journal,* 1991, *7,* 201–210.

Sander, F.E.A. "Varieties of Dispute Processing." *Federal Rules Decisions* 1976, *77,* 111–123.

Sander, F.E.A. "ADR—Promise and Prospects." Keynote address at the Tenth Annual ADR Institute and the 2003 Neutrals' Conference, Lake Lanier Islands, Ga., Nov. 20, 2003.

Sheppard, B. "Report to the Durham Dispute Settlement Center on the Comparative Costs of Going to Court Versus Mediation." Durham, N.C.: Duke University, 1985.

Shonholtz, R. "Justice from Another Perspective: The Ideology and Developmental History of the Community Boards Program." In S. Merry and N. Milner (eds.), *The Possibility of Popular Justice.* Ann Arbor: University of Michigan, 1993.

Shonholtz, R. "Community Mediation Centers: Renewing the Civic Mission for the Twenty-First Century," *Mediation Quarterly,* 2000, *17* (4), 331–350.

Thibaut, J., and Walker, R. *Procedural Justice.* New York: Wiley, 1975.

Wahrhaftig, P. "Citizens Dispute Resolution: A Blue Chip Investment in Community Growth." *Pretrial Services Annual Journal,* 1978.

Wahrhaftig, P. "A Time to Question Direction." *Perspective,* 1979.

Weinstein, M. *Public Education and Marketing Module, Regional Training Institute Training Manual.* Washington, D.C.: National Association for Community Mediation, 2003.

Wilkinson, J. *Community Mediation Trends and Needs: A Study of Virginia and Ten States, Final Report and Recommendations.* Charlottesville: Institute for Environmental Negotiation, University of Virginia for the Virginia Association for Community Conflict Resolution, 2001. [http://www.gmu.edu/departments/nvms/PDFs/Study.pdf].

Wissler, R. "Court-Connected Mediation in General Civil Cases: What We Know from Empirical Research." *Ohio State Journal on Dispute Resolution,* 2002, *17,* 641–703.

Timothy Hedeen is assistant professor of Conflict Management at Kennesaw State University. He serves as chair of the Community-Based and Peer Mediation committee of the American Bar Association's Section of Dispute Resolution, as chair of the Learning Networks' committee of the Association for Conflict Resolution's research section, as editor of the community section of Mediate.com, and is a former cochair of the National Association for Community Mediation.

Commentary: The Case for the Field of Community Mediation

LINDA BARON

Timothy Hedeen's overview of the history of mediation, the underlying characteristics of the model, and the major research findings is comprehensive and insightful and clearly identifies areas where research is needed. In this commentary, I discuss five components of a strategy to strengthen community mediation: data collection, research, and distribution; training and leadership development; funding and development of national, state, and community-based organizations; policy research, analysis, and development; and public relations, public education, and marketing. I will also describe how funding for those elements will make a difference and outline some policy concerns of the field.

Strategy for Action

There are several components to be addressed in articulating the strategy for action.

Data Collection, Research, and Distribution

Hedeen has identified the need for additional research regarding the effectiveness of community mediation at the individual, organizational, and societal levels of analysis. The ability to do this research would be enhanced if there were a mechanism for collecting case data on a consistent basis, similar to the mechanisms that exist for collection of court data and crime statistics. Many community mediation centers purchased case management data through a subsidy made available through the National Association for Community Mediation (NAFCM) from a Hewlett grant. The project designers hoped that the software would not only help centers manage cases more efficiently, but would also make it possible for large quantities of case data to be pooled and analyzed. By using compatible software and collecting common data, information about referral sources, relationships of parties, nature of disputes, and disposition of cases could be collected at multiple centers. The project has not fulfilled all the expectations of its designers, largely because many centers do not have staff resources to use the program and enter data consistently, but NAFCM has used the pooled data to generate some descriptive statistics and crosstabulations about the caseloads in the participating centers and with additional resources could provide assistance to the centers so that more case data could be collected and analyzed.

Centers are frequently required to support their requests for funding with proof of the effectiveness of their programs. They are seeking "sound bites" that will help convince funders and referral sources that mediation works. In the same way that we have come to believe that "seat belts save lives" and "milk builds strong bones," community mediation centers would like to be able to say that "mediation works." In an effort to make the results of research more accessible to centers for these purposes, NAFCM, with grant money from Hewlett, reviewed the research literature in the conflict resolution field and prepared abstracts in language accessible to program administrators and funders. The abstracts will be disseminated to centers and can be used to inform funders, local governments, courts, and social service agencies about the benefits of mediation. Additional resources will be needed to create an ongoing program to identify, abstract, and disseminate research relevant to community mediation. In addition, individual centers, statewide networks, and national associations need to develop ongoing partnerships with researchers so that the work that the centers are doing can be evaluated and the benefits disseminated.

Training and Leadership Development

The case for community mediation can also be enhanced by strengthening training and leadership development in the field to ensure the quality of the services provided by centers. Staff of existing centers can benefit from training programs that cover a variety of topics, including center administration, program development, fund development, case management, program evaluation, public education, and government relations. Training on general nonprofit management topics as well as issues specific to community mediation also needs to be available for individuals creating new centers. (While the community mediation field needs to identify areas currently underserved by community mediation centers and explore strategies to stimulate development of new centers, if funding for existing centers is insecure, it may not be advisable to encourage development of new centers but instead to focus on finding ways to support existing centers.)

Conferences have traditionally been used as training opportunities, but there is no conference specifically designed to address the needs of community mediation centers other than the regional training institutes that NAFCM convenes twice each year. Community mediation centers have traditionally participated in the National Conference on Peacemaking and Conflict Resolution, and this organization is currently exploring the idea of convening a conference with several other organizations in the field, including PeaceWeb, the Victim-Offender Mediation Association, the National Coalition on Dialogue and Deliberation, and the Practitioner's Research and Scholars Institute.

Many community mediation centers provide training not just for the volunteers who mediate for the center, but also for the wider community. Some training programs focus on teaching third-party skills such as mediation, community conferencing, and facilitation. Other programs teach more general skills such as conflict management and systems design. These training programs help to infuse conflict management and conflict resolution skills in the wider community, but also generate much-needed program revenue for the centers. In some centers, however, the emphasis on training has detracted from the primary mission of providing dispute resolution services. In addition, when training programs are primarily intended to raise revenue and offered only to those able to pay for training, the center's mission of serving the all segments of the community may be compromised. Research into the effectiveness of a variety of types of training programs will help the community mediation field decide how to focus limited training resources.

Funding and Development of National, State, and Community-Based Organizations

Funding is needed to support development of local centers and the state and national entities that link and support them. Local centers need funding for innovative, sustainable, and replicable projects. Funding is also needed for peer-to-peer technical assistance to support the exchange of technical expertise among centers and for evaluation of these projects. State coordinating entities play an important role in supporting centers by fostering exchange of information and serving as a voice for community mediation in policymaking at the state level. They can also serve as central points for distribution of information and technical assistance among centers and for collection of data from centers. Ideally, these coordinating entities would not be tied to state administrative offices or to the entity that distributes funding, but should be free-standing associations of community mediation centers. Funding is also needed to create new networks in states without such networks. In addition, financial support is needed for national membership-based organizations such as the National Association for Community Mediation and the Victim Offender Mediation Association so that those organizations can continue to provide technical assistance, facilitate networking and information exchange, and represent the interests of community mediation in professional organizations in the field and in national legislative and regulatory processes.

For community mediation in particular, community foundations may be a natural source of support. Community mediation centers not only need to inform community foundations about their work, but can also make the case for how they can support community foundations in the foundation's work in convening community members around significant communitywide issues. In that way, the partnership is not solely one of funder to fundee, but a mutually beneficial partnership in which community mediation centers can provide services that help enhance the work of community foundations. The community mediation field also needs to develop partnerships with other foundations, particularly those supporting civic engagement and deliberative democracy initiatives.

Community mediation needs to enlist the support of other allies, including many current leaders in the dispute resolution field—practitioners, academics, administrators, and program administrators—who were introduced to mediation through community mediation centers and received their first training and experience there. Many of these individuals may now be able to contribute to the community mediation field in a variety of ways, including financial contributions and contributions of their time and expertise in areas such as research or strategic planning, or may be able to use their current connections and affiliations to help community mediation centers develop strategic relationships with other national and community-based institutions. The corporate donor community, including alternative dispute resolution providers in the private sector, also needs to be approached for support.

More than a dozen states currently have a role in providing funding and support for community mediation centers. Funding is generally provided from filing fees and court surcharges and through legislative appropriations. NAFCM has researched these mechanisms and will be publishing a report describing them in detail and offering a number of recommendations. Among the report's recommendations is the suggestion that states fund mediation centers through multiple funding mechanisms and encourage both basic and innovative processes. States are encouraged to reward a number of factors, including quality performance measures, outreach, diversity of referral sources and populations served, and service to underserved populations and areas. They are also urged to create legislation that will foster stability of centers and establish state offices to work with centers to coordinate advocacy and technical assistance.

Policy Research, Analysis, and Development

The issue of quality assurance, credentialing, and certification for mediators has received considerable attention for many years. As conflict resolution organizations grapple to set standards for the field, it is critical that community mediation be represented at the table and participate in the development of national and local policies. Areas where collaboration would be beneficial include national-level deliberations about model standards, mediator certification and trainer credentialing, and state-level policies regarding funding for mediation and other legislation and regulations that will have an impact on the work of community mediation centers.

NAFCM supports a broad approach to quality assurance that advocates self-determination by centers, recognizes the uniqueness of community mediation, and facilitates the continued high quality of service provided by community mediation centers. Centers can participate in NAFCM's quality assurance initiative by implementing a quality improvement program using NAFCM's *Quality Assurance Self-Assessment Manual* (Broderick and Carroll, 2002). The manual provides a checklist of factors covering all aspects of management and operations for centers to consider. The approach is intended to be aspirational, not prescriptive. Twelve centers are currently participating in a pilot project to test this approach. Each of the centers in the pilot writes its own quality improvement plan and is partnered with another center. During the six months of the pilot, each pair meets monthly by conference call with an NAFCM board member and staff to share ideas and discuss progress on their individual plans.

Public Relations, Public Education, and Marketing

If community mediation is going to thrive, communications strategies need to be devised to raise awareness about these services. In designing these strategies, it will be important to understand how community mediation is perceived by the general public, consumers, referring agencies, funders, and policymakers. The audiences for the messages need to be identified and messages need to be tailored for each audience. Then the message needs to be delivered. Materials for electronic and print media need to be developed. New strategic alliances must be formed with local, state, and national non-profits and government that are concerned with the needs of youth, families, and communities. Internal allies for community mediation need to be identified in federal agencies for the purpose of securing grants and contracts. Such agencies might include the Departments of Justice, Health and Human Services, Housing and Urban Development, and Agriculture. Partnerships also need to be developed with national organizations with local affiliates that could or do refer cases to community mediation centers. Examples include professional organizations such as the American Planning Association and the International City Managers' Association; public interest groups such as the League of Cities and the National Civic League; groups that represent law enforcement, schools, and human relations commissions; organizations that promote bias awareness, diversity, and inclusion; and groups promoting dialogue and civic engagement. Discussions with these national entities can help community mediation centers develop strategies for using national organizations to promote their work. The top-down approach needs to be balanced by a bottom-up approach in which local centers position themselves as the resolution experts when community conflicts arise. Centers need to continuously seek to understand their own communities and identify ways that they can serve their neighbors.

How Funding Could Make a Difference

The community mediation model, with its reliance on trained volunteers, might seem an inexpensive proposition. But functioning centers need staff to provide training, manage cases, supervise volunteers, negotiate contracts, raise funds, and do all the other things that nonprofit agencies do. Centers also need offices, furniture, utilities, computers, telephones, supplies, and all the other items that for-profit businesses and nonprofit providers require. In addition, the commitment to providing services to clients regardless of their ability to pay means that centers cannot expect to receive significant revenue from clients. In some ways, this business model seems to doom centers to a short, but idealistic, life span. Centers have managed to survive, but for most centers, seeking funding consumes a significant portion of the energies of center staff and volunteers, and funding is always somewhat precarious.

One of the consequences of shaky funding is that centers have challenges employing and keeping qualified staff. Too frequently experienced employees leave for other opportunities when centers are not able to compensate them appropriately or when funding reductions require staff cuts. If centers received sufficient resources, they would not only be able to hire and retain staff, but could also relieve staff of the ongoing burden of fundraising. In a survey of centers conducted in 2003, twenty-one of the twenty-two centers that responded stated that funding, financial stability, and sustainability were a challenge for the field over the next three to five years. When asked what the most critical challenge was for centers, eighteen identified financial stability and funding; and when asked what NAFCM programs were most beneficial, the most common response, coming from fourteen centers, was that the most beneficial programs were the minigrants that member centers are eligible to apply for.

In most centers, the majority of the caseloads consists of interpersonal disputes: minor commercial and criminal cases—referred by courts. These cases typically require moderate amounts of case management, and relatively little time is spent with clients prior to mediation. With more funding, centers would also be able to provide mediation, facilitation, and other problem-solving services in larger and more complex cases. More complex cases often require time-consuming case management, including more time identifying and interviewing parties and preparing them to participate in the mediation process. Community mediation centers that are well known and trusted in their communities can be effective interveners in these kinds of cases, but they are often reluctant to do so because they lack the resources to manage the cases properly.

Community mediation centers would have no problem listing additional ways that they could serve their communities if they had more funding. There are unlimited training needs in schools, workplaces, and other areas of community life, and additional funding would enable centers to conduct training without having training compete with providing dispute resolution services. Additional funding would also enable centers to conduct more outreach to all parts of their communities, take risks and experiment with new and innovative programs and practice models, research community needs, and conduct evaluations to measure the effectiveness of their work.

National and state organizations provide technical assistance and networking, and they serve as a voice for the community mediation field in policy deliberations. They are an important part of the infrastructure of the community mediation field, yet they face funding challenges that are similar to the challenges of the centers. Many are membership-based associations and rely on members as the base of their financial support. But, community mediation centers themselves have limited resources and are therefore limited in their ability to pay dues or participate and pay for revenue-generating activities provided by state and national networks, such as conferences and training. Like centers, they have difficulty hiring and retaining qualified staff and are burdened by the ongoing need to raise funds not only for special projects but for operating expenses as well. This challenge can subject them to what in the nonprofit sector is referred to as "mission drift," that is, the tendency to cast such a broad net in seeking funds that they stray from their initial and primary purpose: serving their members. State and national associations also need to avoid competing with their own members, but that restricts their revenue-generating activities. NAFCM, for example, has a policy of not applying for grants if its members are applying for the same grant and not offering services that its members provide. For this reason, NAFCM does not provide mediation training, since most of the centers provide such training. NAFCM does, however, offer training in the management and administration of mediation centers, since that training is not offered by members. Some state associations serve as brokers for cases from public agencies by contracting with state agencies and then referring those cases to centers.

With additional resources, state and national networks could engage in more of the kinds of activities that serve their members and are best done on a national or statewide basis. Public education, research, and policy analysis are all activities that can best be done by state and national networks working with and on behalf of their members. Community mediation remains little known and underused in large part because the public, including potential users and referral agencies, is unaware of its existence. In many ways, community mediators share this dilemma with other private mediation practitioners. Mediation centers cannot rely on word-of-mouth recommendations. Because of the confidentiality of the process, some parties believe they cannot even tell others that they participated in mediation. And because parties in mediation discuss difficult issues that they would often prefer not to disclose to others and because parties tend to be one-time consumers, even satisfied customers tend not to refer others to mediation. With additional resources, state and national networks could conduct coordinated efforts to raise awareness about the services of their members.

A great deal of work needs to be done to demonstrate empirically the effectiveness of community mediation. Research will require funding, and any large-scale research efforts will probably benefit from some coordination involving associations of centers. While centers and associations are generally enthusiastic about participating in research, they also need to be compensated for the time they devote to those activities.

Policy development for community mediation can also best be initiated by national and state associations working closely with local affiliates. Promoting and tracking of legislation and regulations can also be most efficiently and effectively conducted by networks rather than by individual centers, but associations will need funding to support these activities.

Policy Implications for the Current and Future State of Community Mediation

As the mediation field has moved in the direction of becoming a profession, community mediation centers have also moved toward a service model. Many question whether the creativity, autonomy, and adaptability that were the hallmark of community mediation will remain as centers struggle to survive as community institutions.

Reliance on trained volunteers has become a challenge as the nature of volunteerism has changed and as the broader field of mediation has evolved. While in some centers the capacity of the volunteer pool exceeds the caseload, many centers are not able to attract the volunteers they need most: volunteers who are available during the daytime and volunteers who speak languages other than English. Centers in rural areas find it difficult to find volunteers willing to travel long distances to mediate. And some centers in urban areas with markets for private mediators complain that they are training their own competition. And while centers aspire to reflect the diversity of the communities they serve, the mediators in most centers are rarely of the same class or culture of the majority of clients.

Community mediators do not advocate for one side or another in a conflict (rather, they are impartial third-party interveners), but most funders are interested in funding organizations that advocates for a particular cause or issue. Community mediation centers can argue that they are advocates for a process and that they prevent prolonged litigation, escalation of conflicts, and even violence by helping parties resolve conflicts peacefully, but it is difficult to prove the impact of such processes. NAFCM has been advised by a development consultant to consider focusing on an issue-oriented approach rather than a process-oriented approach to describe the impact that community mediation has on communities.

Some centers are now shifting their focus from interpersonal disputes to communitywide disputes. One center has even changed its name to the Center for Dialogue. Centers are training mediators to serve as facilitators of processes designed to address communitywide conflicts and are participating in civic engagement and deliberative democracy processes. Does this indicate a shift away from reliance on referral agencies back to a community service model, or does it suggest that community mediation centers are moving away from serving their communities and becoming consultants? Or is it simply another example of how wonderfully adaptive and creative community mediation can be?

The field of community mediation has accomplished a great deal and still faces significant challenges. A comprehensive strategy incorporating all the elements of the strategy described above, and the funding to implement the strategy, will enable the field of community mediation to grow and to fulfill the high ambition stated in NAFCM's preamble: "Community Mediation is designed to preserve individual interests while strengthening relationships and building connections between people and groups, and to create processes that make communities work for all of us."

Reference

Broderick, M., and Carroll, B. (eds.). *Community Mediation Center Self-Assessment Manual.* Washington, D.C.: National Association for Community Mediation, 2002.

Linda Baron is the executive director of the National Association for Community Mediation, a membership organization representing the interests of community mediation programs and practitioners across the United States. She has been a mediator and mentor with court and community-based programs since 1986.

Employment Dispute Resolution: The Case for Mediation

LISA B. BINGHAM

Employment dispute resolution (EDR) addresses conflict arising out of a continuing or terminated employment relationship. Typical cases include complaints of discrimination under state and federal equal employment opportunity (EEO) law; wrongful discharge under state law; whistle-blower retaliation; workers' compensation; wage and hour violations; occupational safety disputes; breach of contract; alleged violations of administrative policies on performance evaluation, supervision, or assignment of duties; communication problems in the chain of command; and similar matters. These claims are often outside the scope of a collective bargaining agreement. In the employer context, programs may exist in a nonunion workplace, or they may coexist with a union grievance procedure (Lipsky, Seeber, and Fincher, 2003). However, there are also programs offered by administrative agencies and courts for resolving employment disputes. Whether employer based or third party, programs may offer a variety of interventions, including an ombuds, early neutral assessment, fact finding, peer panels, mediation, or arbitration, or some combination of these.

Research on and evaluation of EDR has been influenced by the extensive literature on voice and grievance systems (Bies, 1987; Folger, 1977; Greenberg, 1996; Lewicki, Weiss, and Lewin, 1992; Lewin, 1987, 1999; Sheppard, Lewicki, and Minton, 1992; Sitkin and Bies, 1993), labor grievance mediation and arbitration in collective bargaining (Dunlop and Zack, 1997; Zack, 1997; Feuille, 1995; Ury, Brett, and Goldberg, 1989), negotiation and dispute resolution (Carnevale and Pruitt, 1992; Wall and Lynn, 1993), procedural justice (Lind and Tyler, 1988; Lind and others, 1990; Lind, Kulik, Ambrose, and de Vera Park, 1993; Tyler, 1988), and dispute system design (Costantino and Merchant, 1996; Slaikeu and Hasson, 1998; Ury, Brett, and Goldberg, 1989). This review is limited to field and applied research on third-party neutral processes in conflict arising from the employment relationship outside the context of collective bargaining. (For a previous review integrating literature from collectively bargained procedures, see Bingham and Chachere, 1999.)

The structural aspects of an EDR program affect its organizational function, effectiveness, and efficiency. This review is organized around these structural elements: sector or setting; overall dispute system design, including level of self-determination and institutionalization; nature of intervention; due process protections; voluntariness; timing; and quality and characteristics of neutrals. The evaluation and field research literature suggests that mediation produces better organizational outcomes than either no intervention or an adjudicatory one like arbitration.

The Sector or Setting for EDR

Context can shape dispute resolution procedures and their results (Kolb, 1989). Thus, EDR is affected by its setting in the private, nonprofit, or public sectors. In the private sector, arbitration is the dominant process; in the public sector, mediation predominates. The U.S. General Accounting Office (USGAO, 1997) also compared alternative dispute resolution (ADR) techniques used by five private sector companies and five federal agencies. It found that private companies more frequently used arbitration, and federal agencies more frequently used mediation. The settlement rate for mediation was comparable in the private and federal sectors, ranging from 60 to 80 percent.

EDR's legal setting differs from private to public sector. In the private sector, the U.S. Supreme Court has enforced mandatory arbitration agreements for claims of discrimination in employment on the theory that the Federal Arbitration Act preempts state efforts to regulate them (Dunlop and Zack, 1997; Stone, 1999; Zack, 1997). However, in the public sector, state law varies on the authority of government to use binding arbitration. At the federal level, the Administrative Dispute Resolution Act of 1996 authorizes a wide range of processes, including mediation and arbitration, but prohibits mandatory, adhesive arbitration (Evans, 1998).

Private Sector

A large-scale study of the Fortune 1000 general and litigation counsel revealed that by 1997, 87 percent of these companies had experience using mediation and 80 percent using arbitration at least once in the three years preceding the survey (Lipsky, Seeber, and Fincher, 2003). Over 10 percent reported they had experience using a broad range of other processes, including mediation-arbitration, in-house grievance systems, minitrials, fact finding, peer review, and ombudspersons. However, only about 19 percent reported frequent use of mediation, and 43 percent reported occasional use. There was a similar pattern for arbitration. The majority of cases involved a determination of rights, not interests. In other words, they were disputes about existing laws or contracts or policies, not efforts to negotiate new contracts. Under 40 percent had general policies favoring use of ADR. For employment disputes, almost 79 percent reported using mediation and 62 percent reported using arbitration. Mediation was by far the preferred process across all industry types. Across industry type, those reporting use of mediation for employment disputes varied from 64 to 91 percent, but again, this represents, on balance, occasional use.

Colvin (2003) found that both institutional pressures and human resource strategies are factors driving adoption of EDR. Private sector employers adopt mandatory arbitration to avoid individual employment rights litigation and because of expanded court deferral to arbitration. Union avoidance continues to be a factor predicting processes like peer review. In addition, there is a link between the use of high-performance work systems and EDR.

Federal Sector

In the federal sector, Congress enacted the Administrative Dispute Resolution Act (ADRA) in 1990 to spur agencies to consider using alternative dispute resolution (Dunlop and Zack, 1997). Five years later, a survey showed that the vast majority of cabinet- and noncabinet-level federal agencies were experimenting with the use of mediation in personnel and employment disputes (Bingham and Wise, 1996). Only a small minority of agencies made even limited use of arbitration, largely because of concerns over loss of control and delegation of governmental authority to a private decision maker.

Of federal agencies, in 1994 31 percent had some form of EDR (U.S. General Accounting Office, 1995); by 1996, this increased to 49 percent (U.S. General Accounting Office, 1997). At present, Equal Employment Opportunity Commission (EEOC) regulations mandate that all agencies make EDR available for complaints of discrimination (Senger, 2003; see www.adr.gov, the gateway Web site for all information on ADR in the federal government). In 2001, there were 2.5 million federal employees, about 15,000 of whom used EDR in an EEO case, with settlement rates ranging from over 50 to 64 percent. Federal agencies report improved case processing time with EDR. Federal agencies average three and a half years to process an EEO complaint; through EDR, the air force averages nine months. The U.S. Postal Service (USPS) is the single largest federal employer, with over 800,000 employees; its mediations average four hours in duration and result in a case closure rate of 60 to 80 percent. Canadian public service employees also have access to employment mediation for grievances; an evaluation of that program found a 50 percent settlement rate, with outcomes including practical solutions that would not have been available through adjudicative grievance proceedings, such that both parties reported interest in using mediation in the future (Zweibel, Macfarlane, and Manwaring, 2001).

There have been efforts to estimate cost savings when the federal government uses ADR for employment cases. Agencies have compared mediation costs to fully litigating a case, a method some would criticize as based on a false assumption: that the case would not have settled on its own. The Justice Department spends on average $1,007 to mediate and $17,000 to litigate the typical case. The air force estimates that it saves $14,000 and 276 labor hours when it uses EDR (Senger, 2003).

Federal agencies have also tracked disputant satisfaction with EDR. The EEOC reports that over 90 percent of the participants in its private sector EDR program said they would use the process again (Senger, 2003). The USPS reports consistent satisfaction rates of over 90 percent with the mediation process and the mediators over a period of five years during which it used mediation in ten thousand to fourteen thousand cases a year (Bingham, 2003).

State and Local Government

At the state and local government levels, there are approximately six comprehensive state offices of dispute resolution, thirty-eight offices focusing on courts, and thirty-four in universities and nonprofits (see www.policyconsensus.org). Some states have legislation similar to the federal ADRA (Texas is one of them), but many have more general authorizations as part of state administrative procedure acts. Generally, state government is lagging behind the federal government in its implementation of EDR. However, there is research or evaluation on experiments in the areas of workers' compensation for on-the-job injuries in California (Lipsky, Seeber, and Fincher, 2003), New York (Seeber, Schmidle, and Smith,

2001), and North Carolina (Clarke, 1997); on wrongful discharge and workplace grievances in Ohio (Hebert, 1999) and South Carolina (Youngblood, Trevino, and Favia, 1992); and on discrimination complaints in Kansas (Varma and Stallworth, 2002) and Massachusetts (Kochan, Lautsch, and Bendersky, 2002).

Clarke (1997) examined a North Carolina mediation program for workers' compensation cases. He used random assignment to allocate cases to either mediation or control groups. A state mediator reviewed the file, referred it to mediation if appropriate, and forwarded a list of mediators to the parties. Parties were required to attend; mediation took from two to six hours. Mediation settled 26.1 percent of the cases. In addition, some mediation group cases settled outside mediation, bringing the total settlements to 60.8 percent. In the control group, settlements were 47.6 percent. Mediation diverted some parties from bilateral settlement, but it also diverted some parties from a hearing. The program reduced median time to disposition by 60 days, from 372 days in the control to 312 days in the mediation group. Although legal counsel was present in many cases, not all parties had legal counsel in all cases. Legal counsel and mediators surveyed generally responded favorably about the program. The New York workers' compensation EDR system also produced significant favorable results (Lipsky, Seeber, and Fincher, 2003; Seeber, Schmidle, and Smith, 2001). Researchers found substantial efficiency improvements: of two thousand cases, all were resolved short of arbitration and few went to mediation. There was a significant reduction in time to disposition: 137 fewer days.

Youngblood, Trevino, and Favia (1992) examined the operation of a South Carolina conciliation office for employees not covered by a union, civil service protection, or other legislation. A statute gave the labor commissioner broad powers to deal with industrial disputes between employers and employees: to investigate, ascertain cause, and induce voluntary settlements. Researchers examined archival records and interviewed participants to determine why at-will employees viewed their dismissal as unjust and how they viewed third-party dispute resolution. They found that participants generally felt both the process and outcome of conciliation were unfair or unjust. Only 6 percent of the employees were reemployed after conciliation; 81 percent felt the outcome was unfair (distributive justice). Employees also complained the conciliation process was unfair. There usually was no face-to-face meeting or hearing; 75 percent of interviewees were dissatisfied with this process (procedural justice). Both distributive and procedural justice contributed to low employee satisfaction.

In Massachusetts, the Massachusetts Commission Against Discrimination (MCAD) provided mediation and arbitration for discrimination claims; it was designed in collaboration with the American Arbitration Association (AAA), which administered the program (Kochan, Lautsch, and Bendersky, 2002). Based on surveys and interviews with participants in 150 EDR and traditional cases, researchers found about a 33 percent mediation participation rate; disputants reported the chief reason they did not use EDR was that the other party would not agree. EDR cases had a 67 percent settlement rate; non-EDR cases settled at the rate of 21 percent (Lipsky, Seeber, and Fincher, 2003). Participants estimated that they had substantial cost savings, and 77 percent reported they would use the process again.

There are substantial differences across private, federal, and state sectors in the reasons for adopting EDR programs and designs; however, there is very little comparative research. Clearly, multivariate studies on factors that lead organizations to adopt different EDR designs need to control for sector and different legal and policy contexts. The absence of this research makes it more difficult to assess the degree to which the field can make general claims from program-specific research and evaluation.

Overall Design of an EDR Program for an Organization's Own Employees

Dispute system design determines many aspects of an EDR program (Ury, Brett, and Goldberg 1989; Costantino and Merchant, 1996). These designs include integrated conflict management systems, ombuds programs, and silo or stovepipe programs. Organizations may design these programs for conflict arising in-house among employees or with customers, consumers, contractors, and others. This section focuses only on in-house systems for employment conflict.

EDR at the System Level

Employers may adopt integrated conflict management systems, ombuds programs, or silo or stovepipe programs for EDR.

Integrated Conflict Management Systems. An integrated conflict management system (ICMS) is a coordinated network of options available to people for resolving conflict in an organization (Lipsky, Seeber, and Fincher, 2003). An ICMS is easily accessible to address disputes at the earliest time, most appropriate level, and in the most appropriate manner; they include rights-based, interest-based, and stakeholder-based options. Finally, they focus on the causes of conflict and provide a systematic approach to preventing, managing, and resolving conflict in organizations (Gosline and others, 2001; Rowe, 1997). Examples include the Massachusetts Institute of Technology, the National Institutes of Health (NIH), and the federal Agency for Healthcare Research Quality (AHRQ).

AHRQ at the Department of Health and Human Services (HHS) supports health care research through grants and contracts to improve the quality and reduce the costs of health care. With about three hundred full-time employees, AHRQ generates few EEO complaints. However, in 1996 and 1997, AHRQ scored the lowest among all HHS agencies on the Human Resources Quality of Worklife survey, suggesting that employees were dissatisfied with communication, trust, teamwork, and organizational structure at the agency. AHRQ used the ICMS as a model for its Ombuds program to address a broad range of workplace issues, including work environment, ethics, benefits, leadership, discipline, and research (Bingham and Nabatchi, 2003). Subsequently, AHRQ received the highest score on the 2000 Quality of Worklife Survey; previously, it ranked last within HHS. AHRQ's survey scores have increased a statistically significant amount each year since its program.

Ombuds Programs. A workplace ombuds is a neutral operating inside an organization to assist employees in resolving disputes informally through confidential means. Using qualitative interviews of key federal agency stakeholders, Meltzer (1998) found that an ombuds is likely to be most effective when the EEO office has too many non-EEO complaints; the employee assistance plan is receiving workplace complaints outside its mandate; personnel-related offices are not working together; employee morale is low; there is poor employee-management communication; significant workplace issues emerge and surprise management; there are poor labor-management relations; and there are frequent employee claims of retaliation. Meltzer also found that the agencies did not evaluate their ombuds program effectiveness but enjoyed management support.

Employers may distort the ombuds title in unilaterally adopted nonunion arbitration programs. One employer had its ombuds represent employees as their advocate in arbitration, and select the arbitrator on behalf of both parties; this resulted in repeated selection of the same arbitrator, who always ruled for management (Bingham, 1996). This structure gives at least the appearance of a conflict of interest.

Innovative research on the ombuds program at NIH suggests that such programs may help identify systemic problems. Using reflective practice to debrief practitioners, researchers found five categories of dispute factors: difficult individuals, problematic interpersonal dynamics, NIH's scientific and organizational culture, systemic problems in specific research environments, and leadership dysfunction (Kressel and others, 2004). Because an ombuds office is small and the ombuds is often a single person, these programs are particularly difficult to evaluate empirically.

The confidential nature of the work, combined with the ease of tracing a case to the parties, makes ombudspersons sometimes reluctant to cooperate with research or evaluation. Ombuds offices vary in design to fit the organization (Kolb, 1987), which makes it hard to compare one to the next.

Silo or Stovepipe Programs.   Programs are so-called silos or stovepipes when they are freestanding offices, not integrated into some other department or system for disputes. Most pilot programs start this way and become institutionalized. The U.S. Department of Agriculture (USDA) has programs across fifteen agencies, including workplace, EEO, and combined offices. Most operate as stovepipes, and as a result there are some concerns about competition and turf wars between the ADR programs and traditional complaint offices like EEO (Bingham, Pitts, and Salter, 2003). The U.S. Department of Labor (USDOL) created a stovepipe for mediating regulatory cases; it had trouble achieving permanency (Lipsky, Seeber, and Fincher, 2003; Schuyler, 1993). In contrast, management gave the USPS silo two years, followed by institutionalization within EEO; this program has achieved permanency. Clearly, how the design for an initial start-up of an EDR program affects institutionalization is a critical, underresearched issue.

Control over Dispute System Design

Control over dispute system design can affect the nature of the system and its outcomes (Bingham, 2002a, 2002b). Systems for handling employment disputes may be designed unilaterally by the employer, may be negotiated at arm's length by both parties, or may be the product of a third party with regulatory responsibility, like the EEOC.

One-Party Designs.   Employers in the public sector that have designed systems generally adopt mediation or ombuds programs. However, in the private sector, employers have adopted arbitration programs. One controversy in EDR surrounds the ability of an employer to structure employment arbitration systems unilaterally and impose them on employees as a condition of new or continued employment. The outcomes of such systems were examined in a series of studies on the employer as a repeat user of arbitration (Bingham, 1997, 1998, 2002b; Bingham and Sarraf, 2004). Looking at a sample of actual arbitration awards decided under AAA rules, Bingham (1997a, 1998) found that employers who make repeated use of arbitration have superior outcomes compared to employers that use arbitration only once in the sample and that they are more likely to be arbitrating pursuant to unilaterally imposed personnel manuals. In addition, the relative bargaining power of the employee, operationalized as white-, blue-, or pink-collar employment category, was also relevant to success in arbitration. White-collar employees did better (Bingham, 1997a). Employees arbitrating pursuant to unilaterally imposed personnel manuals did worse (Bingham, 1998). However, studies comparing outcomes before and after the Due Process Protocol for Mediation and Arbitration of Statutory Disputes Arising Out of the Employment Relationship (www.adr.org; Dunlop and Zack, 1997) found that the disparity between repeat player and nonrepeat player win rates declined in cases involving adhesive personnel manual clauses after the Due Process Protocol required procedural protections for employees (Bingham, 2002b; Bingham and Sarraf, 2004).

Hill (2004) created alternate formulations of the repeat player variable by examining capacity for repeat use instead of actual repeat use and replicated the result. Her explanation is that there is an "appellate effect," the result of large institutions with sophisticated human resource management operations resolving meritorious cases in house and that this cannot be isolated from the repeat player effect. This is directly related to the employer learning theory suggested by others. However, an appellate effect presumably would exist equally before and after the Due Process Protocol. The fact that this study finds evidence of different outcomes before and after the Due Process Protocol in personnel handbook cases suggests that there is more at work here than sophisticated human resource management.

One study found that employers with mandatory or binding arbitration plans are viewed less favorably than employers with voluntary or non-binding arbitration policies (Richey, Bernardin, Tyler, and McKinney, 2001). The researchers did a laboratory experiment manipulating voluntariness and binding or nonbinding arbitration independently. A follow-up study of employees in a Fortune 500 company found that employees had a strong preference for voluntary over mandatory programs and for mediation over binding arbitration or med-arb (Richey, Garbi, and Bernardin, 2002).

Two-Party Designs. Under the general supervision of a state agency, parties to a collective bargaining agreement negotiated a system for New York workers' compensation claims; it produced significant favorable results (Lipsky, Seeber, and Fincher, 2003; Seeber, Schmidle, and Smith, 2001). These disputes arise from on-the-job injuries; they concern medical treatment, return to work, and amount and duration of benefits. There were delays in administrative adjudication, scheduling, and incentive structures for legal counsel. The EDR system focused on one union contract covering twenty-five thousand workers and included an ombudsperson, nurse advocate, mediation, and arbitration. Using before and after comparisons, researchers found substantial efficiency improvements: of two thousand cases, all were resolved short of arbitration, and few went to mediation. There was a significant reduction in time to disposition: 137 fewer days. There was decreased reliance on outside counsel; employees got their questions answered without an advocate. The new system produced comparable substantive outcomes; there was no significant reduction in employee benefits. This is a litmus test evaluators have used in the past to judge the fairness of alternatives to the public justice system.

Third-Party Designs. In the employment arena, third-party designs are generally the product of the executive branch of government. Due to concern about the constitutionality of delegating to an arbitrator the power to decide these cases, mediation is the process of choice. Third-party designs include experiments by the MCAD (Kochan, Lautsch, and Bendersky, 2002) and the EEOC (McDermott, Obar, Jose, and Bowers, 2000); workers' compensation systems in California, New York (Seeber, et al. 2001), and North Carolina (Clarke, 1997); a wrongful dismissal claim system (Youngblood, Trevino, and Favia, 1992); and mediation in Canada for discrimination complaints (Zweibel and Macfarlane, 2001). In general, third-party designs have not been subject to the same commentator criticism as one-party designs. Most agencies involve stakeholders in the design process and solicit comment through the use of focus groups and other techniques. In assessments of procedural justice, the majority of participants generally report that mediation in this context is fair. However, there has been no explicit comparison of these with one- and two-party designs to examine patterns of difference in the structural features of the resulting system.

Institutionalization, Structural Support, and Efforts to Implement

One measure of a program's effectiveness is participation rate: Of those offered mediation or ADR, what proportion accepts? For EEO, participation rates varied widely across the various USDA agencies, with an overall department average of 23.3 percent, as contrasted with 75 percent at the USPS (Bingham, 2003); the USPS has one consistent national system integrated into the EEO function, and it conducted nationwide training and awareness efforts, including video presentations on its in-house television network. USDA key stakeholders reported that the three top incentives for using EDR were early resolution (46 percent), improving workplace climate (31.7 percent), and cost savings (28.6 percent) (Bingham, Pitts, and Salter, 2003). The top three obstacles or weaknesses were lack of awareness or appropriate marketing (42.9 percent), mistrust or skepticism about EDR (22.2 percent), and lack of resources (14.3 percent). Stakeholders recommended better marketing or improving awareness (19 percent), training managers and employees in conflict management (15.9 percent), and improving office communication or working to minimize turf wars (14.3 percent).

The USDOL had a sequence of pilot programs that it designed on a silo model for employment regulatory disputes; the USDOL is a party in an enforcement capacity. An early pilot provided mediation for wage-and-hour cases (Schuyler, 1993). Using incomplete data, the USDOL found a wage-and-hour case that used EDR had lower average administrative cost and required less time than a non-EDR case. This study did not use random assignment. The pilot, though a success, failed to attract more institutional resources at USDOL. More recently, the USDOL tried another pilot in collaboration with Cornell (Lipsky, Seeber, and Fincher, 2003). The design called for the solicitor's office to refer cases under any of the 180 statutes the department has responsibility to enforce. Cornell designed the pilot, developed the roster, and administered the program. After one year of operation, the program had handled only seventeen cases, although there was a 75 percent case closure rate (cases settled or withdrawn). Similarly, participation rates were lower in the MCAD program, averaging at about one-third (Kochan, Lautsch, and Bendersky, 2002). Researchers reported problems training MCAD employees and turnover within leadership as hindering implementation of the program; they found AAA administrative services to be essential. This points to one of the problems with silo programs: their very independence can create a barrier to institutional acceptance.

Nature of the Intervention: Mediation or Arbitration

Whether to have an ombuds, early neutral assessment, fact finding, peer panels, mediation, or arbitration, or some combination, is the critical choice in employment dispute system design. Lipsky and Seeber (1998) found that private companies used mediation because it allowed the parties to resolve the dispute themselves, gave them greater control, was a more satisfactory process, and preserved good relationships; they used arbitration because it is required by contract and better than litigation. Brett, Barsness, and Goldberg (1996) compared mediation and arbitration outcomes based on a sample of 449 cases administered by four different major ADR providers and found that mediation was less expensive and more satisfactory to the parties than arbitration.

Mediation. Employers have adopted mediation programs for nonunion workplace disputes (Bedman, 1995; Bingham, 1997b, 2003; Bingham, Chesmore, Moon, and Napoli, 2000; Bingham and Novac, 2001). State and federal agencies have adopted mediation programs for employment disputes over which they have regulatory or enforcement authority (Clarke, 1997; Kochan, Lautsch, and Bendersky, 2002; Lipsky, Seeber, and Fincher, 2003; Schuyler, 1993; Youngblood, Trevino, and Favia, 1992).

• *Models of mediation:* A largely unexplored area is the impact of different models of mediation on participant and organizational outcomes (Bingham, 2002a; Riskin, 2003). Mediation can be evaluative if the mediator gives an expert opinion on the merits of the dispute (Waldman, 1998). In a problem-solving or facilitative model, the mediator helps the parties identify and dovetail their interests (Fisher, Ury, and Patton, 1991; Waldman, 1998). Still less directive is transformative mediation (Bush and Folger, 1994; Folger and Bush, 1996), which focuses on empowering the parties to control all aspects of the mediation. Transformative mediators do not pressure parties to accept a settlement, but rather to clarify their own interests, goals, and choices. The mediator also fosters moments of recognition, in which each party reaches a better understanding or acknowledges the other's perspective. The USPS, the Transportation Security Administration, and Raytheon Corporation have adopted the transformative model; virtually all court- and agency-annexed programs use either facilitative or evaluative mediation.

The mediation model may influence participant and organizational outcomes, but there is limited systematic employment research comparing them. One study asked human resource practitioners to rate the effective-ness of different models of mediation at different stages of an EEO charge, and found they believed all models more effective precharge than in court; in general, mean effectiveness rankings fell below the midpoint on a five-point scale (Varma and Stallworth, 2001). Interestingly, they ranked trans-formative mediation more effective than facilitative or evaluative models. Unfortunately, the study had a small sample of only seventy-four; the response rate was 37 percent.

• *Employer programs:* The USPS mediation program REDRESS has generated the most comprehensive data (Lipsky, Seeber, and Fincher, 2003). The program uses transformative mediation (Bush and Folger, 1994). One study suggests that USPS dispute resolution specialists and mediators are generally focusing on opportunities for disputant empower-ment and mutual recognition of interests, concerns, and perspectives; in the USPS design, mediators may not evaluate the case or pressure the par-ties to settle (Nabatchi and Bingham, 2001). Bingham (1997b, 2003) found that USPS supervisors and employees were equally satisfied with the outside neutral mediator and the process of EEO dispute mediation, and that there was the same pattern with respect to satisfaction with outcome as in other procedural justice research; complainants were less satisfied with outcomes than respondents.

The USPS database contains over 180,000 exit surveys collected since the inception of the first pilot program in 1994. Contrary to critics' sug-gestions that mediation is a fad or disputants' satisfaction is the product of honeymoon or Hawthorne effects, the national USPS program has pro-duced consistently high participant satisfaction (over 90 percent with process and mediator, over 60 percent with outcome) for over five years (Bingham, 2003). Both complainants and respondents report satisfaction with how they can present their views in mediation (93 percent), can par-ticipate in the process of resolving the dispute (94 percent), and are treated in mediation (91 and 94 percent, respectively). On measures of respectful-ness, impartiality, fairness, and performance, between 96 and 97 percent of all complainants, respondents, and their respective representatives were either satisfied or highly satisfied with the mediators. Complainants and their representatives are satisfied with the mediators' impartiality (95 per-cent), although the USPS created the roster, assigns individual mediators to each case, and pays the full costs of the process. This suggests that the dispute system design has successfully addressed any latent concerns regarding mediator bias. Most employees and supervisors are satisfied or highly satisfied with the outcome (on average, 64 percent and 69 percent, respectively). Case closure rates have exceeded 60 percent during this period.

The REDRESS program is having a significant positive impact on the USPS conflict management system. Mediation has reduced USPS formal EEO complaint caseloads (Bingham and Novac, 2001). A multivariate linear regression on formal EEO complaint filings by geographical district, number of employees, number of informal complaints, and seasonal workload complaint fluctuations found that implementation of mediation was statistically significantly related to a subsequent drop in formal complaints; these declined by almost 30 percent from their peak at fourteen thousand complaints annually in 1998. This is proof that mediation is resolving workplace conflict at an earlier stage than the traditional EEO complaint process.

Moreover, the number of complainants is decreasing. Complaints now come from 40 percent fewer people; complainants are more likely to be repeat filers (Bingham, 2003). By providing an effective voice mechanism, mediation may be averting the creation of new chronic discontents. Whether repeated use of mediation will gradually address the challenge of repeat filers, who file as many as sixty EEO complaints a year, remains to be seen.

There has been little research on how mediation affects disputants' relationships. Both employees and supervisors at the USPS reported improved supervisor listening skills through participation in the mediation pilot (Anderson and Bingham, 1997). Listening helps participants move toward recognition. In exit surveys, 61 percent of complainants and 69 percent of supervisors agreed or strongly agreed that they acknowledged as legitimate the other person's perspective, views, or interests (Bingham, 2003). While most report they acknowledged the other, the other does not always hear it; fewer than half (complainants 49 percent and supervisors 45 percent) report that the other acknowledged them. However, these percentages suggest substantial exchange of perspectives.

The most telling indicator of recognition is the apology. Apology is not always possible in litigation, because it may be an admission against interest and evidence of liability. USPS complainants and supervisors report apologies to the complainant in about 29 to 30 percent of all exit surveys (Bingham, 2003). There is less agreement about complainants apologizing to supervisors; complainants report they apologize 23 percent of the time, while supervisors hear an apology in 16 percent of their exit surveys.

Clearly, the potential of a nonadversarial process to improve workplace relationships and climate remains a fertile area for research. For example, there are no systematic longitudinal panel studies on how participation in mediation may affect disputant conflict management skills or workplace climate. We also lack multivariate studies on the relationships between mediation and indicators of productivity, such as sick, personal, annual, unscheduled, or injury leaves; workplace injury claims for stress; unscheduled overtime; employee assistance plan referrals; and other grievance or claiming systems at the workplace. There is work in industrial relations and human resource management but not in examining EDR systems.

• *Agency programs:* The EEOC has institutionalized mediation and conducted extensive evaluations of its impact (Lipsky, Seeber, and Fincher, 2003; McDermott, Obar, Jose, and Bowers, 2000; Tajalli and Wright, 2002, 2003). The EEOC had mediation programs in each of its fifty field offices by 1998. In 2000, the program was voluntary and limited to cases with established cause and a possibility of settlement before trial (Lipsky, Seeber, and Fincher, 2003). Surveys from a large representative sample revealed that 90 percent were willing to mediate again. They felt the process was fair, they had adequate information, and they had a full opportunity to present their case. Satisfaction with mediators was also high, regardless of source (Federal Mediation and Conciliation Service, EEOC, or other external mediators). However, satisfaction with outcomes was related to perceptions that the settlement was more favorable to one party. Disputants viewing themselves as the relative losers were less satisfied. The San Antonio office replicated high satisfaction findings (means over 4 on a five-point scale) and found an overall settlement rate of 62.9 percent (Tajalli and Wright, 2002). A second study found a settlement rate of 55.8 percent but a low participation rate (19.6 percent of identified cases) (Tajalli and Wright, 2003).

Arbitration. Arbitration is a quasi-judicial process in which the disputants hire a third-party decision maker, the arbitrator, to adjudicate their dispute. Generally, arbitration takes the form of an informal adversarial hearing, allowing for broad admissibility of evidence and argument and resulting in a written award (Dunlop and Zack, 1997).

The legal context for employment arbitration differs significantly from that of mediation or ombudsperson programs. Mediation and ombudsperson programs are generally voluntary as to participation and outcome. Settlement usually takes the form of an enforceable contract. Most arbitration results in a final, binding award. There is a strong federal policy of enforcing nonunion employment arbitration clauses, giving rise to the term *mandatory arbitration* (Bales, 1994). An employer can force an employee to accept arbitration of all disputes as a condition of new or continued employment, including binding arbitration for statutory claims (for a review of the law, see LeRoy and Feuille, 2003, which also contains a comprehensive empirical review of how courts have attempted to regulate predispute arbitration clauses).

Theorists have suggested that mandatory arbitration of employment discrimination claims may have adverse effects on perceptions of both procedural and distributive justice (Cohen and Domagalski, 1998). Bingham (1995) examined whether the employer or employee was the claimant and whether the arbitrator was paid or worked pro bono in 1,992 commercial arbitration cases involving employment, and found that recoveries were lower in cases where the arbitrator was paid a fee, but there was no evidence of overall proemployer bias (Bingham, 1995). However, there was evidence of due process problems in employment arbitration in 1993 (Bingham, 1996).

Howard (1995) examined mean damage awards in discrimination cases, comparing litigated and arbitrated outcomes. Arguing in favor of employment arbitration, Howard observed that plaintiffs' lawyers will take only one in twenty cases, and then only when the employee is capable of advancing a retainer and has high provable damages; thus, a quick, economical, and final process could level the playing field. Comparing samples of cases litigated in federal court (21,518 cases) with arbitration awards issued under American Arbitration Association rules (510 cases) and arbitration awards issues in the securities industry where discrimination was alleged (61 awards), he found that employees recovered something in 71 percent of pre- and posttrial cases, but in only 28 percent of tried cases. They did better in jury trials (38 percent) than nonjury trials (19 percent). In AAA arbitration, employees recovered something in 68 percent of cases, but in only 48 percent of the securities arbitration cases. The problem with these comparisons is that the cases may be apples and oranges, that is, samples of fundamentally different kinds of cases as a result of selection bias inherent in the different systems. Howard also surveyed employment lawyers, finding that while 79 to 84 percent of cases settled prior to litigation, only 31 to 44 percent of arbitrated cases settled. Defense counsel estimated attorneys' fees at $96,000 for litigated employment discrimination cases but only $20,000 in arbitration.

Bickner, Ver Ploeg, and Feigenbaum (1997) surveyed employers to identify arbitration components of their dispute resolution plans. They found that about 25 percent of employers limit arbitration to dismissal cases and that most employers adopted their plans with little or no employee input out of a concern over perceived runaway jury awards.

The field needs a well-designed empirical examination of how arbitration compares to the traditional litigation process, preferably using random assignment or matched pairs of cases. This is information policymakers need in order to decide how to address competing claims about efficiency or bias in mandatory employment arbitration.

Due Process Protections

Researchers using the organizational justice literature have long established that perceptions of fairness are an important factor in assessing the effectiveness of EDR voice systems (for reviews, see Boroff, 1991; Blancero, 1995; and Phillips, 1996). Other research shows that positive organizational outcomes are associated with more methods to voice dissatisfaction in nonunion organizations (Spencer, 1986; Huselid, 1995). Due process protections may contribute to perceptions of fairness. EDR programs may limit the right to counsel, discovery, location of process, availability of class actions, availability of written opinion or decision, and other procedural safeguards usually available in courts. Particularly in binding arbitration, the availability of procedural safeguards may make a difference; this gave rise to the Due Process Protocol.

There is limited research on the extent of due process protections in employer-designed plans. Feuille and Chachere (1995) found that plans had limits on due process. Only 55 of 110 employers allowed employees to be accompanied by a representative, and 11 of 107 employers allowed the final decisions on grievances by independent decision making by outside arbitrators. Chachere (1999 reported similar results in a study of 393 hospital ADR procedures. Few employers (18 percent) used a standard of proof for evidence, although up to 52 percent allowed employees to call witnesses. Only 224 of 393 hospitals allowed employee representation, and 54 (13 percent) allowed for independent decision making by outside arbitrators.

There is research on the role of representatives in mediation. Bingham, Kim, and Raines (2002) examined the USPS mediation program, which allows employees to bring any representative they choose, including lawyers, union representatives, professional association representatives, and friends or family. Some employees chose not to bring a representative. The study examined 7,651 mediator data tracking reports and exit surveys (7,989 complainants and 6,794 respondents), with a response rate of 70.3 percent on surveys.

Researchers found that representation had a positive impact on settlement. The settlement rate for mediations where neither party was represented was 55 percent, whereas the settlement rate for mediations where both parties were represented was 61 percent, a statistically significant difference of 6 percent. Representation was also associated with longer mediation sessions. The mean duration for mediations where neither party was represented was 152 minutes, but that number rose to 184 minutes for mediations where both parties were represented. Researchers also compared resolution rates (full and partial) among different types of complainant representation: fellow employee, attorney, union representative, or "other." The highest rate (65 percent) occurred when complainants had a union or professional association representative. When they used fellow employees, there was a 60 percent resolution rate; complainants with attorneys had a 50 percent rate. However, cases with attorneys may be more difficult to settle because of attorney fees, making nonmonetary resolutions difficult. Attorneys may also hope to recover monetary damages in adjudication. Researchers have no way of assessing the relative merits of complaints across representation categories.

Representation also affected participant satisfaction with mediation fairness. Of complainants represented by union or professional associations, 91 percent reported being very or somewhat satisfied with mediation fairness, while 88 percent of those represented by fellow employees agreed, and only 76 percent of those with attorneys were satisfied. However, cases with attorney representatives had the lowest rate of resolution, and resolution correlates with perceptions of fairness. Complainants with no representation reported a 91 percent total satisfaction rate, with 67 percent reporting that they were "very satisfied." Participant satisfaction was generally high with all representatives. Allowing participants to bring whatever representative they prefer had no adverse impact on the program.

Varma and Stallworth (2002) surveyed human rights disputants who used mediation through a Kansas state program that employed an outside service provider. Again, there is a small sample size of forty-seven and a low response rate (17 percent), but the survey was comprehensive. Overall satisfaction rates averaged from 3.24 to 4.18 on a five-point scale (5 = very satisfied). Researchers found that attorney-represented clients had slightly higher satisfaction with the mediation process but slightly lower satisfaction with the mediation outcome than unrepresented or self-represented disputants. However, consistent with the USPS study, unrepresented or self-represented disputants reported higher satisfaction with their opportunity to present their side of the dispute and level of participation. Perceptions of fairness were the same for both groups. Attorney-represented disputants reported lower satisfaction with mediators' skills. The majority of both were happy to have a mediation provider appoint the mediator rather than select the mediator themselves. The more experience they had with mediation, the higher were their levels of satisfaction.

Voluntary, Opt-Out, or Mandatory Interventions

Brett, Barsness, and Goldberg (1996) found that mediation settled about 78 percent of cases including employment contract disputes, whether mandatory or voluntary. The USPS program is voluntary for complainants, but mandatory for the respondents as representatives of the organization; it has a 75 percent participation rate (Bingham, 2003). The MCAD program was entirely voluntary; its participation rate was about 33 percent because both disputants did not always agree to use the process (Kochan, Lautsch, and Bendersky, 2002). Court-annexed ADR research suggests that opt-out programs will generate participation almost as high as mandatory ones. Human resource practitioners reported support for legislation mandating participation in mediation by both parties, even where only one party expressed a desire to mediate (Varma and Stallworth, 2001).

Timing of the Intervention

The timing of an intervention may affect program-level outcomes. The intervention may occur anytime in a case; most often, it coincides with the four classic points of settlement: before a written complaint, immediately after a written complaint, after discovery is completed, or on the eve of trial. An intervention may affect all subsequent steps; mediation may occur in the shadow of arbitration (Dunlop and Zack, 1997). Federal EEO settlement rates vary with when ADR occurs: 56.1 percent at the informal complaint, 64.3 percent at the formal complaint, and over 50 percent in federal court (Senger, 2003). In federal government civil litigation, including employment cases, a multivariate analysis determined that earlier ADR correlated with shorter time to disposition (Bingham, Nabatchi, Jackman, and Senger, 2004). Using matched pairs, it showed no statistically significant differences between ADR and litigation for the outcome of a case, defined as the ratio of relief recovered to amount in the demand.

Varma and Stallworth (2001) found that human resource practitioners believed EEO mediation was most effective used early in cases other than dismissal. Similarly, a survey of human rights disputants revealed a strong correlation between early mediation and higher satisfaction with process, mediator skills, and outcome (Varma and Stallworth, 2002).

The Nature, Training, Qualifications, or Demographics of the Neutrals

Third parties come from a variety of backgrounds and institutions. In employment programs, they may be lawyers, businesspeople, counselors, clergy, psychologists, social workers, peers, or volunteers. Little research systematically compares third parties along any of these dimensions or on demographic lines. Commentators have suggested that while there may be core common skills for high-quality mediators (including substantive knowledge, experience, facilitation skills, breadth of approach, communication and problem-solving skills), the skills necessary may vary depending on case context (Mareschal, 1998).

Demographics

There is debate over whether administrators should match a third party to disputants based on race, ethnicity, gender, or other demographic variables. Varma and Stallworth (2002) found minority disputants more strongly agreed that the mediator's race makes a difference. There is limited research on the demographics of disputants; one evaluation found that females decline mediation at the EEOC more than males do (Tajalli and Wright, 2003), but otherwise found no relationship between gender and employer sector (public or private). One study found no relationship between human rights disputants' income and satisfaction with mediation, but found that females were more satisfied overall than males and that whites were more satisfied than nonwhites (Varma and Stallworth, 2002).

Inside versus Outside Neutrals

During 1995 to 1997, some USPS regions implemented an inside-neutral mediation model. Inside neutrals are fellow employees trained as mediators. Outside neutrals are outside hired contractors. Generally, USPS inside neutrals were employees who administered the EEO complaint process. In 1998, all regions began using the national outside neutral model, with independent contractors trained in transformative mediation under the supervision of Robert A. Baruch Bush and Joseph Folger. This allowed a direct comparison of participant judgments of the two models (Bingham, Chesmore, Moon, and Napoli, 2000). Participants reported higher satisfaction with the outside mediators than the insiders; they reported full or partial resolution in 75 percent of the surveys in the outside model but in only 56 percent in the inside model, despite case selection bias in the inside model designed to produce settlements by identifying cases perceived as easier to resolve. Those who participated in the inside model were statistically significantly less satisfied with the fairness of the process, mediator impartiality and fairness, and mediator skill and performance.

However, in the EEOC San Antonio District, researchers found that EEOC inside neutrals outperformed outsiders in a third-party design (Tajalli and Wright, 2002). In this case, the insiders were independent of both employer and employee. The inside neutrals had a higher resolution rate (69.6 percent) than the outsiders (55.7 percent). Moreover, they found participants were statistically significantly more satisfied with inside neutrals on every indicator of process and mediator performance. Inside EEOC mediators might be perceived as having more power to influence the disposition of the complaint if it failed to settle; these dynamics might explain both higher satisfaction and resolution rates for insiders. However, these results must be treated with some caution because EEOC staff had access to the surveys; they were not entirely confidential. This too could skew responses in favor of the insiders.

Shared Neutrals

Hebert (1999) evaluated shared neutrals in an Ohio pilot program. Three state agencies contributed employees who were trained as mediators and comediated. Researchers surveyed mediators, participants, and agency coordinators, with response rates ranging from 48 to 63 percent, but the overall sample size was low (twenty-nine for three groups). Almost 90 percent of mediated cases reached full settlement; the remaining cases settled in part. Shared neutrals had positive views of the comediation model, feeling that it made mediation go more quickly, smoothly, and successfully. Disputant surveys reported mediators were both facilitative and evaluative.

Arbitration Panels

Bingham and Mesch (2000) used a hypothetical employee dismissal case to examine differences across four groups of actual arbitrators: AAA labor arbitrators, National Academy of Arbitrators (NAA) members, AAA Commercial panel for employment, and graduate students. They found that employment arbitrators reinstate employees less frequently than labor arbitrators, NAA members, or students. However, when they controlled for arbitrator characteristics such as education and experience, this difference was no longer significant. The result suggested systematic differences in the arbitrator panels.

The Future and Opportunities for EDR Research

Few studies in this review use multivariate techniques to answer certain questions critical to policymakers. There are two major sets of questions that call out for ongoing research: those regarding the most effective dispute system design (DSD) and those addressing the impact of EDR on justice. Underresearched questions about DSD include what dispute system design is most effective for enhancing interest-based dispute resolution, improving workplace climate, increasing productivity, and reducing rights-based complaint filing and claiming. What about the impact of EDR on personal efficacy and the relationship between disputants? Moreover, does the best dispute system design depend on context? What factors predict adoption of a particular dispute system design in the public, private, or nonprofit sector?

The second set of questions that should concern policymakers explores the impact of private dispute resolution systems on public law and social justice. Few of the cited studies answer EDR critics' concerns that private processes are ways to convert discourse about civil rights of importance to our public community into negotiation about personal interests. How would we know whether EDR is undermining enforcement of public law? The answer to these questions would depend on large-scale macrojustice studies, that is, quantitative research comparing the outcomes of similarly situated cases in EDR and the public justice system or allowing for random assignment between the two. We have no adequate studies like this to date.

There are real barriers to conducting this research, but they are not insurmountable. EDR processes are generally confidential; this distinguishes them from the public justice system. Research requires some degree of disclosure. There are a few public federal sources of data, for example, those maintained by the EEOC on federal agency ADR use for cases of employment discrimination. However, there are virtually no data on private employers. Employers are concerned that system-level data might get used against them in litigation. For example, what if system-level data reveal that female claimants get higher dollar amount settlements than minority claimants? While statistically significant, the difference might be legally meaningless, but the mere prospect has caused some employers to refuse to collect the data, since they cannot be forced to disclose what they do not have. Moreover, ADR service providers are reluctant to release data for research that may adversely affect their ability to market their services.

This is a structural impediment to the next generation of EDR research: How can the field collect data in a way that will minimize an organization's exposure to risk? This very structural impediment provides an opportunity for foundations and government organizations that would support the research to make a significant difference. It is at least in theory possible to pool EDR data. It is possible for key stakeholders to negotiate an agreement that analyses of this pooled data would not identify an individual ADR provider or employer.

There is already precedent for national players in EDR to negotiate agreements that shape the field. The Due Process Protocol is one such agreement involving major third-party providers and professional organizations of mediators and arbitrators. Similarly, there is a national Alliance for Education in Dispute Resolution administered through Cornell University's School of Industrial and Labor Relations. The solution to this structural impediment requires a national alliance to create a repository of data on EDR. While archives of selected arbitration awards and other documents exist (notably at Cornell), the few electronic databases in which there are comprehensive case data are proprietary, that is, they represent trade secrets of the organizations that created them. A negotiated agreement would have to address what entity should house the repository, protections of confidentiality for organizations providing the data, and conditions for access to the data set. Until we have better sources of data, we will have trouble answering some of the most important EDR research questions.

Conclusion

A fair reading of this substantial and growing body of research suggests that the case has been made for mediation as compared to arbitration in the field of employment disputes. It is perceived as fairer and consistently produces high satisfaction and settlement rates among disputants, and there is growing evidence that a well-designed program may produce efficiencies in terms of dispute processing time and early resolution of employment-related conflict. There is no evidence to date that arbitration produces these efficiencies. Moreover, there is at least preliminary evidence that mediation produces upstream effects in terms of disputants' conflict management skills. There is no similar evidence for arbitration. At the workplace, mediation works.

We cannot yet answer all the questions policymakers should ask us about the function of EDR systems. We do not have adequate quantitative, multivariate research on what factors best predict the adoption, design, and function of dispute resolution systems and what designs produce the best outcomes. We cannot answer questions on the impact of these private systems on public justice. This research will require better data. To get better data, the field needs to explore the possibilities of collaboration.

References

Anderson, J. F., and Bingham, L. B. "Upstream Effects from Mediation of Workplace Disputes: Some Preliminary Evidence from the USPS." *Labor Law Journal,* 1997, *48,* 601–615.

Bales, R. *A New Direction for American Labor Law: Individual Autonomy and the Compulsory Arbitration of Individual Employment Rights.* 30 Hous. L. Rev. 1863 (1994).

Bedman, W. L. "From Litigation to ADR: Brown and Root's Experience." *Dispute Resolution Journal,* 1995, *50* (4), 8–14.

Bickner, M. L., Ver Ploeg, C., and Feigenbaum, C. "Developments in Employment Arbitration: Analysis of a New Survey of Employment Arbitration Programs." *Dispute Resolution Journal,* 1997, *52* (1), 8–15, 78–84.

Bies, R. J. "The Predicament of Injustice: The Management of Moral Outrage." In L. L. Cummings and B. M. Staw (eds.), *Research in Organizational Behavior, 9.* Greenwich, Conn.: JAI Press, 1987.

Bingham, L. B. "Is There a Bias in Arbitration of Nonunion Employment Disputes? An Analysis of Actual Cases and Outcomes." *International Journal of Conflict Management,* 1995, *6* (4), 369–386.

Bingham, L. B. "Emerging Due Process Concerns in Employment Arbitration." *Labor Law Journal,* 1996, *47* (2), 108–126.

Bingham, L. B. "Employment Arbitration: The Repeat Player Effect." *Employee Rights and Employment Policy Journal,* 1997a, *1* (1), 189–220.

Bingham, L. B. "Mediating Employment Disputes: Perceptions of Redress at the United States Postal Service." *Review of Public Personnel Administration,* 1997b, *17* (2), 20–30.

Bingham, L. B. "On Repeat Players, Adhesive Contracts, and the Use of Statistics in Judicial Review of Arbitration Awards." *McGeorge Law Review,* 1998, *29* (2), 223–260.

Bingham, L. B. "Why Suppose? Let's Find Out: A Public Policy Research Program on Dispute Resolution." *Journal of Dispute Resolution,* 2002a, *2002* (1), 101–126.

Bingham, L. B. "Self-Determination in Dispute System Design and Employment Arbitration." *University of Miami Law Review,* 2002b, *56* (4), 873–908.

Bingham, L. B. *Mediation at Work: Transforming Workplace Conflict at the United States Postal Service.* Washington, D.C.: IBM Center for the Business of Government, 2003.

Bingham, L. B., and Chachere, D. R. "Dispute Resolution in Employment: The Need for Research." In A. E. Eaton and J. H. Keefe (eds.), *1999 Industrial Relations Research Association Research Volume: Employment Dispute Resolution and Worker Rights in the Changing Workplace.* Champaign, Ill.: Industrial Relations Research Association, 1999.

Bingham, L. B., Chesmore, G., Moon, Y., and Napoli, L. M. "Mediating Employment Disputes at the United States Postal Service: A Comparison of In-House and Outside Neutral Mediators." *Review of Public Personnel Administration,* 2000, *20* (1), 5–19.

Bingham, L. B., Kim, K., and Raines, S. "Employment Mediation: Exploring the Role of Representation at the USPS." *Ohio State Journal of Dispute Resolution,* 2002, *17* (2), 341–378.

Bingham, L. B., and Mesch, D. "Decision-Making in Employment and Labor Arbitration." *Industrial Relations,* 2000, *39* (4), 671–694.

Bingham, L. B., and Nabatchi, T. "Dispute System Design in Organizations." In W. J. Pammer Jr. and J. Killian (eds.), *The Handbook of Conflict Management.* New York: Marcel Dekker, 2003.

Bingham, L. B., Nabatchi, T., Jackman, M. S., and Senger, J. M. *Before the Alternative Dispute Resolution Act of 1998: Comparing Litigation and ADR When the Federal Government Is a Civil Litigant.* Bloomington: Indiana Conflict Resolution Institute, 2004.

Bingham, L. B., and Novac, M. C. "Mediation's Impact on Formal Complaint Filing: Before and After the REDRESS Program at the United States Postal Service." *Review of Public Personnel Administration,* 2001, *21* (4), 308–331.

Bingham, L. B., Pitts, D., and Salter, C. R. *Incentives, Obstacles and Barriers to Alternative Dispute Resolution Use at the U.S. Department of Agriculture.* Bloomington: Indiana Conflict Resolution Institute, 2003.

Bingham, L. B., and Sarraf, S. "Employment Arbitration Before and After the Due Process Protocol for Mediation and Arbitration of Statutory Disputes Arising Out of Employment: Preliminary Evidence That Self-Regulation Makes a Difference." In S. Estreicher and D. Sherwyn (eds.), *Alternative Dispute Resolution in the Employment Arena: Proceedings of New York University Fifty-Third Annual Conference on Labor.* Norwell, Mass.: Kluwer, 2004.

Bingham, L. B., and Wise, C. R. "The Administrative Dispute Resolution Act of 1990: How Do We Evaluate Its Success?" *Journal of Public Administration, Research and Theory,* 1996, *6* (3), 383–414.

Blancero, D. "Non-Union Grievance Systems: Systems Characteristics and Fairness Perceptions." *Academy of Management Best Papers Proceedings,* 1995, *38* (1), 84–88.

Boroff, K. E. "Measuring the Perception of the Effectiveness of a Workplace Complaint System." In D. Sockell, D. Lewin, and D. Lipsky (eds.), *Advances in Industrial Relations, 5.* Greenwich, Conn.: JAI Press, 1991.

Brett, J. M., Barsness, Z. I., and Goldberg, S. B. "The Effectiveness of Mediation: An Independent Analysis of Cases Handled by Four Major Service Providers." *Negotiation Journal,* 1996, *12* (3), 259–269.

Briggs, S., and Gundry, L. "The Human Dimensions of Grievance Peer Review." *Journal of Collective Negotiations in the Public Sector,* 1994, *23* (2), 97–113.

Bush, R.A.B., and Folger, J. *The Promise of Mediation: Responding to Conflict Through Empowerment and Recognition.* San Francisco: Jossey-Bass, 1994.

Carnevale, P. J., and Pruitt, D. G. "Negotiation and Mediation." *Annual Review of Psychology,* 1992, *43,* 521–582.

Chachere, D. R. "Does Employee Voice Reduce Turnover? Some Evidence from Nonunion Grievance Procedures." Presented at the Industrial Relations Research Association Annual Meeting, New Orleans, January 5, 1999.

Child, J. "Predicting and Understanding Organizational Structure." *Administrative Science Quarterly,* 1973, *18,* 168–185.

Clarke, S. H. "Mandatory Mediation in On-the-Job Injury Cases." *Popular Government,* 1997, *63* (1), 19–26.

Cohen, C. F., and Domagalski, T. "The Effects of Mandatory Arbitration of Employment Discrimination Claims: Perceptions of Justice and Suggestions for Change." *Employee Responsibilities and Rights Journal,* 1998, *11* (1), 27–40.

Colvin, A.J.S. "Institutional Pressures, Human Resource Strategies, and the Rise of Nonunion Dispute Resolution Procedures." *Industrial and Labor Relations Review,* 2003, *56* (3), 375–391.

Costantino, C. A., and Merchant, C. S. *Designing Conflict Management Systems: A Guide to Creating Productive and Healthy Organizations.* San Francisco: Jossey-Bass, 1996.

Dunlop, J. T., and Zack, A. M. *The Mediation and Arbitration of Employment Disputes.* San Francisco: Jossey-Bass, 1997.

Evans, R. J. "Notes and Comments: The Administrative Dispute Resolution Act of 1996: Improving Federal Agency Use of Alternative Dispute Resolution Processes." *Administrative Law Review,* 1998, *50* (1), 217–233.

Feuille, P. "Dispute Resolution Frontiers in the Unionized Workplace." In S. E. Gleason (ed.), *Workplace Dispute Resolution: Directions for the Twenty-First Century.* East Lansing: Michigan State University Press, 1995.

Feuille, P., and Chachere, D. R. "Looking Fair or Being Fair: Remedial Voice Procedures in Nonunion Workplaces." *Journal of Management,* 1995, *21* (1), 27–42.

Fisher, R., Ury, W., and Patton, B. *Getting to Yes.* (2nd ed.) New York: Penguin Books, 1991.

Folger, J. P., and Bush, R.A.B, "Transformative Mediation and Third-Party Intervention: Ten Hallmarks of a Transformative Approach to Practice." *Mediation Quarterly,* 1996, *13* (4), 263–278.

Folger, R. "Distributive and Procedural Justice: Combined Impact of 'Voice' and Improvement on Experience Inequity." *Journal of Personality and Social Psychology,* 1977, *35,* 108–119.

Gosline, A., and others. *Designing Integrated Conflict Management Systems: Guidelines for Practitioners and Decision Makers in Organizations.* Ithaca, N.Y.: Cornell/PERC Institute on Conflict Resolution, 2001.

Greenberg, J. *The Quest for Justice on the Job: Essays and Experiments.* Thousand Oaks, Calif.: Sage, 1996.

Hebert, C. "Establishing and Evaluating a Workplace Mediation Pilot Project: An Ohio Case Study." *Ohio State Journal on Dispute Resolution,* 1999, *14* (2), 415–480.

Hill, E. "Employment Arbitration Under the Auspices of the American Arbitration Association: An Empirical Study." In S. Estreicher and D. Sherwyn (eds.), *Alternative Dispute Resolution in the Employment Arena: Proceedings of New York University Fifty-Third Annual Conference on Labor.* Norwell, Mass.: Kluwer, 2004.

Howard, W. M. "Arbitrating Claims of Employment Discrimination: What Really Does Happen? What Really Should Happen?" *Dispute Resolution Journal,* 1995, *50* (4), 40–50.

Huselid, M. A. "The Impact of Human Resource Management Practices on Turnover and Productivity." *Academy of Management Journal,* 1995, *38* (3), 635–672.

Kochan, T. A., Lautsch, B. A., and Bendersky, C. "An Evaluation of the Massachusetts Commission Against Discrimination Alternative Dispute Resolution Program." *Harvard Negotiation Law Review,* 2002, *5,* 233–278.

Kolb, D. M. "Corporate Ombudsman and Organization Conflict Resolution." *Journal of Conflict Resolution,* 1987, *31* (4), 673–691.

Kolb, D. M. "How Existing Procedures Shape Alternatives: The Case of Grievance Mediation." *Journal of Dispute Resolution,* 1989, *1989,* 59–87.

Kressel, K., and others. "Sources of Destructive Conflict in Scientific Research: Findings Using the Reflective Case Study Method." Paper presented at the Seventeenth Annual Conference of the International Association for Conflict Management, Pittsburgh, June 2004.

LeRoy, M. H., and Feuille, P. "Judicial Enforcement of Predispute Arbitration Agreements: Back to the Future." *Ohio State Journal on Dispute Resolution,* 2003, *18* (2), 249–341.

Lewicki, R. J., Weiss, S. E., and Lewin, D. "Models of Conflict, Negotiation and Third Party Intervention: A Review and Synthesis." *Journal of Organizational Behavior,* 1992, *13,* 209–252.

Lewin, D. "Dispute Resolution in the Nonunion Firm: A Theoretical and Empirical Analysis." *Journal of Conflict Resolution,* 1987, *31* (3), 465–502.

Lewin, D. "Theoretical and Empirical Research on the Grievance Procedure and Arbitration: A Critical Review." In A. E. Eaton and J. H. Keefe (eds.), *1999 Industrial Relations Research Association Research Volume: Employment Dispute Resolution and Worker Rights in the Changing Workplace.* Champaign, Ill.: Industrial Relations Research Association, 1999.

Lind, E. A., Kulik, C. T., Ambrose, M., and de Vera Park, M. V. "Individual and Corporate Dispute Resolution: Using Procedural Fairness as a Decision Heuristic." *Administrative Science Quarterly,* 1993, *38,* 224–251.

Lind, E. A., and Tyler, T. R. *The Social Psychology of Procedural Justice.* New York: Plenum Press, 1988.

Lind, E. A., and others. "In the Eye of the Beholder: Tort Litigants' Evaluations of Their Experiences in the Civil Justice System." *Law and Society Review,* 1990, *24* (4), 953–996.

Lipsky, D. B., and Seeber, R. L. "In Search of Control: The Corporate Embrace of ADR." *University of Pennsylvania Journal of Labor and Employment Law,* 1998, *1* (1), 133–157.

Lipsky, D. B., Seeber, R. L., and Fincher, R. D. *Emerging Systems for Managing Workplace Conflict: Lessons from American Corporations for Managers and Dispute Resolution Professionals.* San Francisco: Jossey-Bass, 2003.

Mareschal, P. M. "Providing High Quality Mediation: Insights from the Federal Mediation and Conciliation Service." *Review of Public Personnel Administration,* 1998, *18* (4), 55–67.

McDermott, E. P., Obar, R., Jose, A., and Bowers, M. *An Evaluation of the Equal Employment Opportunity Commission Mediation Program.* Washington, D.C.: Equal Employment Opportunity Commission, 2000.

Meltzer, D. L. "The Federal Workplace Ombuds." *Ohio State Journal on Dispute Resolution,* 1998, *13,* 549–609.

Nabatchi, T., and Bingham, L. B. "Transformative Mediation in the United States Postal Service REDRESS Program: Observations of ADR Specialists." *Hofstra Labor and Employment Law Journal,* 2001, *18* (2), 399–427.

Phillips, V. "Mediation: The Influence of Style and Gender on Disputants' Perception of Justice." *New Zealand Journal of Industrial Relations,* 1996, *21* (3), 297–311.

Richey, B., Bernardin, H. J., Tyler, C. L., and McKinney, N. "The Effect of Arbitration Program Characteristics on Applicants' Intentions Toward Potential Employers." *Journal of Applied Psychology,* 2001, *86* (5), 1006–1013.

Richey, B., Garbi, E., and Bernardin, H. J. "Is Alternative Justice Just: ADR Program Characteristics and Employee Fairness and Trust Perceptions." Unpublished manuscript, 2002.

Riskin, L. L. "Decisionmaking in Mediation: The New Old Grid and the New Grid System." *Notre Dame Law Review,* 2003, *79* (1), 1–53.

Rowe, M. P. "Dispute Resolution in the Non-Union Environment: An Evolution Toward Integrated Systems for Conflict Management?" In S. E. Gleason (ed.),

Workplace Dispute Resolution: Directions for the Twenty-First Century. East Lansing, Mich.: State University Press, 1997.

Schuyler, M. L. *A Cost Analysis of the Department of Labor's Philadelphia ADR Pilot Project.* Washington, D.C.: U.S. Department of Labor, 1993.

Seeber, R. L., Schmidle, T. B., and Smith, R. S. *An Evaluation of the New York State Workers' Compensation Pilot Program for Alternative Dispute Resolution.* Albany: New York State Workers' Compensation Board, 2001.

Senger, J. M. *Federal Dispute Resolution: Using ADR with the United States Government.* San Francisco: Jossey-Bass, 2003.

Sheppard, B. H., Lewicki, R. J., and Minton, J. W. *Organizational Justice: The Search for Fairness in the Workplace.* San Francisco: New Lexington Press, 1992.

Sitkin, S. B., and Bies, R. J. "Social Accounts in Conflict Situations: Using Explanations to Manage Conflict." *Human Relations,* 1993, *46* (3), 349–370.

Slaikeu, K. A., and Hasson, R. H. *Controlling the Costs of Conflict: How to Design a System for Your Organization.* San Francisco: Jossey-Bass, 1998.

Spencer, D. G. "Employee Voice and Employee Retention." *Academy of Management Journal,* 1986, *29* (3), 488–502.

Stone, K.V.W. "Employment Arbitration Under the Federal Arbitration Act." In A. E. Eaton and J. H. Keefe (eds.), *1999 Industrial Relations Research Association Research Volume: Employment Dispute Resolution and Worker Rights in the Changing Workplace.* Champaign, Ill.: Industrial Relations Research Association, 1999.

Tajalli, H., and Wright, W. A. *Evaluation of the Mediation Program of the San Antonio District Office of the U.S. Equal Employment Opportunity Commission.* San Antonio, Tex.: Equal Employment Opportunity Commission, 2002.

Tajalli, H., and Wright, W. A. *Analysis of Charges of Employment Discrimination Identified as Candidates for Mediation in the San Antonio District Office of the U.S. Equal Employment Opportunity Commission.* San Antonio, Tex.: Equal Employment Opportunity Commission, 2003.

Tyler, T. "What Is Procedural Justice? Criteria Used by Citizens to Assess the Fairness of Legal Procedures." *Law and Society Review,* 1988, *22* (1), 103–135.

U.S. General Accounting Office. *Employment Discrimination: Most Private-Sector Employers Use Alternative Dispute Resolution.* Washington, D.C.: U.S. General Accounting Office, 1995.

U.S. General Accounting Office. *Alternative Dispute Resolution: Employers' Experiences with ADR in the Workplace.* Washington, D.C.: U.S. General Accounting Office, 1997.

Ury, W., Brett, J., and Goldberg, S. *Getting Disputes Resolved: Designing Systems to Cut the Cost of Conflict.* San Francisco: Jossey-Bass, 1989.

Varma, A., and Stallworth, L. E. "The Use of Alternative Dispute Resolution Mechanisms in the Workplace: An Empirical Study." *Alternative Dispute Resolution in Employment,* 2001, *12* (3), 71–79.

Varma, A., and Stallworth, L. E. "Participants' Satisfaction with EEO Mediation and the Issue of Legal Representation: An Empirical Inquiry." *Employee Rights and Employment Policy Journal,* 2002, *6* (2), 387–418.

Waldman, E. A. "The Evaluative-Facilitative Debate in Mediation: Applying the Lens of Therapeutic Jurisprudence." *Marquette Law Review,* 1998, *82* (1), 155–170.

Wall, J. A., and Lynn, A. "Mediation: A Current Review." *Journal of Conflict Resolution,* 1993, *37* (1), 160–194.

Youngblood, S. A., Trevino, L. K., and Favia, M. "Reactions to Unjust Dismissal and Third-Party Dispute Resolution: A Justice Framework." *Employee Responsibilities and Rights Journal,* 1992, *5* (4), 283–307.

Zack, A. M. "Can Alternative Dispute Resolution Help Resolve Employment Disputes?" *International Labour Review,* 1997, *136* (1), 95–108.

Zweibel, E., and Macfarlane, J. "Systemic Change and Private Closure in Human Rights Mediation: An Evaluation of the Mediation Program at the Canadian Human Rights Tribunal." Unpublished manuscript, 2001.

Zweibel, E., Macfarlane, J., and Manwaring, J. "Negotiating Solutions to Workplace Conflict: An Evaluation of the Public Service Staff Relations Board Project." Unpublished manuscript, 2001.

Lisa B. Bingham is the Keller-Runden Professor of Public Service at the Indiana University School of Public and Environmental Affairs.

Commentary: Research on Employment Dispute Resolution: Toward a New Paradigm

DAVID B. LIPSKY

ARIEL C. AVGAR

The dramatic growth in the use of alternative dispute resolution (ADR) in employment relations over the past twenty-five years has sometimes been called a "quiet revolution." Before the revolution, the use of techniques such as mediation and arbitration was largely confined to the unionized segment of the American workforce. Some nonunion employers had grievance procedures or other forms of dispute resolution processes, but these employers rarely, if ever, relied on impartial third parties to resolve employment disputes (Lewin, 1987a, 1987b; Foulkes, 1980; McCabe, 1988). It is probably not an exaggeration to state that the landscape of employment dispute resolution has been transformed by the development of ADR over the past quarter-century.

Lisa Bingham's article is a comprehensive survey of the growing body of research on employment dispute resolution conducted in recent years. We commend her for performing this important service for scholars and practitioners in our field. Undoubtedly, her review of the literature will be a starting point for scholars contemplating new research projects. One of the strengths of her article is her use of a structural framework to organize her review of the research. By focusing on structural elements, Bingham aptly directs our attention to most of the critical—and frequently controversial—issues that have captured the attention not only of researchers but also of practitioners in the field. Her own research on the repeat-player effect in arbitration, the use of transformative mediation in the U.S. Postal Service, and other topics is testimony to the important role that research can play in an evolving field (Bingham, 1997a, 1997b, 1998; Bingham, Kim, and Raines, 2002).

Our argument in this article is greatly influenced by the work of Thomas Kuhn, who famously introduced the concept of a "paradigmatic shift" in his book *The Structure of Scientific Revolutions* (1962). Kuhn maintained that a paradigm was essential to scientific inquiry: "No natural history can be interpreted in the absence of at least some implicit body of intertwined theoretical and methodological belief that permits selection, evaluation, and criticism" (pp. 16–17). He argued that in any era, there is a dominant paradigm that provides the framework for research in a given field.

"Normal science," Kuhn argues, is devoted to explaining phenomena on the basis of the dominant paradigm (1962, p. 24). Over time, however, normal science uncovers "anomalies" that subvert the existing paradigm. The accumulation of these anomalies leads to a growing awareness that there are profound discrepancies between existing theories and observable facts that cannot be reconciled within an existing paradigm. These mounting "failures" result in a "crisis," but Kuhn notes that scientists seldom renounce the existing paradigm that led them into the crisis (Kuhn, 1962). Scientists resist abandoning an existing paradigm, even in the face of growing evidence that the paradigm is obsolete, until "an alternative candidate is available to take its place" (Kuhn, 1962, p. 77).

We maintain that the ADR revolution has been, in effect, a paradigmatic shift in the practice of employment dispute resolution. Prior to the shift, the existing paradigm of practice was rooted in an industrial relations framework, specifically the so-called New Deal industrial relations system, which Kochan, Katz, and McKersie (1986) claim was the dominant system of employment relations from the end of World War II to the 1970s. But beginning in the 1960s and 1970s, a combination of factors caused this system to come unstuck: globalization, technological change, deregulation, the decline of the labor movement, the increase in the statutory protection of individual rights, and the emergence of team-based production are some of these factors (Kochan, Katz, and McKersie, 1986; Lipsky, Seeber, and Fincher, 2003). Hindsight allows us to recognize that the ADR revolution was the product of a historic transformation of the American workplace.

Although we believe there has been a paradigmatic shift in practice, we do not believe there has been a paradigmatic shift in research on employment dispute resolution. Instead, the research so ably synthesized by Bingham appears to be an exercise in "normal science." Research, we maintain, has been conducted within paradigms that existed before the rise of ADR. The paradigm that has guided this research has depended on the discipline of the researcher. Lawyers, for example, use standard legal theory and doctrinal analysis, and specialists in labor relations use the industrial relations paradigm (influenced greatly by Dunlop, 1958). Although there have been many anomalies discovered in the research on ADR, there has yet to emerge a distinctive ADR paradigm for guiding such research. In sum, the preconditions Kuhn specified for the emergence of a new paradigm have been met by the existing research.

The research on employment dispute resolution has moved through three successive generations, and we believe a fourth generation is now emerging. The emergence of a new generation of research does not necessarily mean that the work associated with a preceding generation has been finished. On the contrary, in common with life in general, the work of one generation usually continues throughout successive generations.

We believe that this generational analysis of the evolution of ADR research is helpful in highlighting the avenues explored and those left uncharted. Each generation founded its research on a number of core assumptions about the nature of the phenomenon at hand. Thus, for example, the three generations differ with regard to their assumptions about the forces that influenced the rise of ADR. This variance has led the researchers of each generation to examine different aspects of ADR. One of the challenges facing the next generation of ADR researchers is the integration of these independent insights provided by their predecessors.

The First Generation: Dispute Resolution at the Societal Level

The first generation of research on ADR largely focused on legal questions and the implications of ADR for our legal system and social justice. This is not surprising since the birth of ADR is embedded in the search for extra-adjudicative procedures that would be superior in their procedural efficiency and their substantive outcomes to litigation.

The early legal literature, dating to the 1970s, did not focus specifically on ADR in the workplace but did deal with the desirability and legality of settling public claims in private forums. In short order, the practical relevance of these developments to workplace dispute resolution was recognized. Especially following the Supreme Court's decision in *Gilmer* v. *Interstate/Johnson Lane Corp.* (1991), which appeared to sanction the use of mandatory and binding arbitration in employment disputes, the questions addressed by legal scholars (such as the coverage of the Federal Arbitration Act) had obvious relevance for employment dispute resolution.

Since ADR developed as a reaction to procedural and substantive pathologies in the judicial system, the first generation examined the extent to which ADR was in fact a suitable and viable alternative. Legal scholars were divided on this question. On the one hand, many scholars argued that ADR had the potential to increase both procedural and substantive justice in the settlement of disputes. Auerbach (1983), for example, described the effectiveness of private dispute resolution methods in preserving and strengthening community norms and values. Bush (1989) maintained that mediation is unique in its capacity to empower the parties to control their dispute and therefore tailor a settlement to their specific needs and circumstances.

On the other hand, not all legal scholars were convinced of ADR's unequivocal superiority. For example, Abel (1982) objected to the concept of informal justice, arguing that merely settling disputes can be a means of denying the existence of more persistent conflict. ADR opponents maintained that denying conflict is counterproductive and prevents a healthy deliberation over norms in a heterogeneous society (see, for example, Nader, 1993). Critics contended that ADR dealt solely, if effectively, with procedural issues but ignored the question of substantive outcomes. Furthermore, they argued that ADR exacerbated preexisting imbalances of power. Fiss (1984) maintained that ADR procedures assume there is a balance of power between the disputing parties. Since this is clearly not the case in many disputes, Fiss argued that ADR contradicts the notion of equal access to justice regardless of a party's financial resources. Edwards (1986) warned that the substantial perils in the use of ADR had largely been overlooked. He maintained that although ADR may be suitable for "strictly private disputes," its application in disputes involving constitutional issues or public law risked the substitution of nonlegal values for the rule of law. Critics contended that ADR was a method to bypass legislative and constitutional requirements. ADR, as Fiss (1984) wrote, focuses on restoring the peace between the parties "while leaving justice undone."

Despite the debate, it is clear that the first generation agreed that societal forces of influence, exogenous to the specific settings in which ADR was used, gave rise to this paradigmatic shift of practice. Thus, the first generation of ADR researchers focused on important societal issues such as ADR's effect on procedural and substantive justice, the balance of power between disputants, and the appropriateness of using ADR to settle statutory disputes. But the ascendancy of ADR led the next generation of researchers to shift their focus from societal concerns to concerns at the organizational level.

The Second Generation: Dispute Resolution at the Macro-Organizational Level

In the mid-1980s, industrial relations and human resource scholars began to examine internal mechanisms of dispute resolution in nonunion settings (Foulkes, 1980; Lewin, 1987a, 1987b, 1990; Westin and Feliu, 1988; McCabe, 1988; Ewing, 1989). These researchers relied heavily on the existing industrial relations paradigm, which is associated with the work of scholars such as Dunlop, Kerr, McKersie, Kochan, and others (Dunlop, 1958; Kerr, Dunlop, Harbison, and Myers, 1960; Walton and McKersie, 1991; Kochan, Katz, and McKersie, 1986). Second-generation researchers assumed that what they had learned about dispute resolution under collective bargaining could be transferred to dispute resolution in nonunion settings. Research using the industrial relations paradigm has indeed produced some valuable results, but as Kuhn might have predicted, it has also produced anomalies inconsistent with that paradigm.

For example, in the 1980s, some of the industrial relations researchers cited above examined basic grievance and complaint-filing procedures, which by then had clearly become a more important phenomenon among nonunion employers. These procedures were a fairly unsophisticated version of present-day employment dispute resolution systems, but the studies by this generation of researchers provided an important foundation on which future ADR researchers could build.

Second-generation researchers attempted to gain an understanding of the types of procedures being used by nonunion employers, the types of employers using such procedures, and the situations in which they were used. The evidence suggested, for example, that much greater variety in nonunion dispute resolution procedures existed than was observed in union grievance procedures (McCabe, 1988). A distinguishing feature of this research was its attempt to analyze the effect of dispute resolution procedures on workplace outcomes, such as turnover rates and employee performance. This research demonstrated that although the use of dispute resolution procedures in nonunion settings was in many ways similar to the use of ADR in other settings, the use of ADR in employment relations required the consideration of characteristics uniquely associated with the workplace.

The second generation developed models that could explain non-union grievance procedures. For example, Lewin (1987a) studied nonunion appeals systems in three large companies. He developed a model for understanding grievance filing by nonunion employees that took into account employee characteristics such as age, race, and gender, the issues raised by the complainants, the level of settlement, and the identity of the prevailing party. Lewin also analyzed the effect of the outcomes of these grievance systems on factors such as turnover rates, promotion rates, and employee performance.

The exit-voice model, devised by Hirschman (1971), had proven useful in explaining the effect of unions on workplace outcomes, such as turnover and employee performance (Freeman and Medoff, 1984). But Lewin's analysis suggested that the exit-voice model did not seem to apply to nonunion dispute resolution procedures. For example, contrary to the predictions of the exit-voice model, Lewin found that turnover among employees filing appeals was higher than among their colleagues who did not. Furthermore, Lewin found that supervisors and managers involved in the appeals process also had higher turnover rates, lower promotion rates, and lower performance ratings than those who were not involved (Lewin, 1987a, 1987b). Within the standard industrial relations paradigm, these findings are clearly Kuhn-like anomalies.

In recent years, the macro-organizational perspective has reemerged in a number of studies that examine more complex complaint procedures yet follow in the tradition of the earlier research. Colvin (1999, 2003), for example, examined the factors that have motivated a growing number of nonunion organizations to adopt arbitration and peer review procedures in the workplace. Colvin analyzed the relationship between the adoption of high-performance work systems and environmental pressures (such as the threat of litigation and the threat of unionization), on the one hand, and the specific types of dispute resolution implemented by employers, on the other. Colvin found that the adoption of peer review procedures could be explained by both environmental pressures and the existence of a high-performance work system, but the adoption of arbitration was influenced primarily by the threat of litigation but not by the presence of a high-performance work system.

Following in the footsteps of second-generation researchers, Colvin (1999) also addressed some of the organizational dimensions associated with ADR, such as use rate, disciplinary outcomes, and quit rates. Colvin, similar to Lewin, found no support for the exit-voice hypothesis in the use of nonunion employment arbitration. He found, however, that the use of peer review was associated with lower quit rates. In a study that examined the relationship between employee voice and quit rates in the telecommunications industry, Batt, Colvin, and Keefe (2002) did not find any significant correlation between peer review procedures and quit rates.

Implicit in this generation's research is the assumption that although the use of ADR can be attributed to exogenous forces such as the threat of litigation and the potential for unionization (see Colvin, 2003), there are endogenous forces, namely organizational transformation, that are influencing an organization's decision to turn to new methods of resolving disputes (see, for example, Lipsky, Seeber, and Fincher, 2003; Stone, 2001; Cutcher-Gershenfeld and Kochan, 1997).

However, there is relatively little empirical research on the correlation between organizational changes that have taken place over the past three decades and ADR use. In this sense, we maintain that the potential vested in this generation's research direction has not yet been exhausted.

A variety of external and internal pressures have caused organizations to restructure their traditional bureaucratic models in search of alternatives that can increase their competitive viability (Appelbaum, Bailey, Berg, and Kalleberg, 2000; Appelbaum and Batt, 1994). As a consequence of this restructuring, the employment practices in many of these organizations have undergone drastic alterations. In the quest for increased competitiveness, organizations have been shedding their traditional, hierarchical, rigid rule-based practices. This shift is characterized by some as the emergence of a "high-performance" or a "postbureaucratic" organizational model (for a discussion on high-performance work systems, see Appelbaum, Bailey, Berg, and Kalleberg, 2000; in relation to ADR, see Lipsky, Seeber, and Fincher, 2003; for a discussion on the "postbureaucratic" organization, see Heckscher and Donnellon, 1994). As a growing number of organizations move away from the traditional bureaucratic model, it becomes all the more important to study the link between the transformation of organizations and the transformation in the way organizations manage conflict.

Thus, for example, one might explore the relationship between changes in organizational structure, work design, workforce heterogeneity, and the employment relationship and the implementation of internal systems for dispute resolution. In addition, it is important to examine the link between the emphasis on flexibility and reduction in formal rules in nontraditional organizational design and the implementation of formal dispute resolution systems.

The Third Generation: Dispute Resolution
at the Micro-Organizational Level

The third generation of ADR research, we maintain, is characterized by a focus on dispute resolution at the micro-organizational level. Bingham's structural analysis (in this issue) encompasses many of the micro-organizational studies. Third-generation researchers focus intently on the operation of processes and procedures and are concerned with their relative effectiveness. For example, some stress the effect of the characteristics of different procedures on the likelihood of disputants reaching settlement. Other researchers deal with the perceptions and behaviors of participants in these procedures. Bingham notes that the literature on ombuds and silo programs is highly descriptive and pays little attention to the effects of such programs on either workplace or macro-organizational outcomes.

Third-generation researchers have enriched our understanding of the significance of the procedural aspects of ADR. This focus can be attributed in part to the third generation's assumptions that various ADR procedures were developed as the result of efficiency considerations and pressures.

Bingham's structural analysis helps clarify the host of procedural considerations that are likely to affect the use of such procedures, settlement rates, and participant satisfaction. For example, as Bingham notes, the use and effectiveness of a given procedure are likely to depend on the timing of the intervention by a third party, the degree of voluntarism permitted by the procedure, and the precise nature of the intervention. This generation of research has also attempted to identify the contextual factors that affect the choice of the specific ADR intervention (Lewicki and Sheppard, 1985). Third-generation research has demonstrated that the type of process an organization uses has significant implications for employee perceptions of justice (Karambayya and Brett, 1989).

The second research generation glossed over the intricacies of specific ADR processes, but the third generation has studied them intensely. For example, the third generation delved into the implications of using different types of mediation (facilitative, evaluative, and transformative) and different types of arbitration (interest, rights, advisory, and others). Bingham's literature review demonstrates that the specific type of intervention affects the course of the dispute. Kolb's work (1983, 1994) also illustrates the effect of different mediator styles on the settlement process. In addition, their intense focus on process has led third-generation researchers to assess the influence of an array of third-party characteristics on dispute resolution.

Industrial relations scholars had virtually ignored the influence of character-istics such as the race and gender of the neutral on the dispute resolution process, but third-generation researchers began to analyze such effects. Sim-ilarly, these researchers have assessed the effectiveness of internal mediation versus external mediation and have also dealt with the relative effectiveness of supervisors versus peers in resolving disputes (Karambayya, Brett, and Lytle, 1992).

An additional item on this generation's research agenda is the exami-nation of the relationship between the perceptions and levels of satisfaction of the users of ADR procedures and the specific nature of those procedures. For example, some of the principal criteria Bingham used to evaluate the effectiveness of REDRESS, the U.S. Postal Service's dispute resolution program, are measures of the satisfaction of individual employees and supervisors with the program. Bingham's evaluation of the USPS program also depicts the influence that different ADR procedures have on the nature of individual-level relationships within the organization. For exam-ple, Bingham (1997b, 2003) analyzes the degree to which mediation can bring about the conditions for participants to acknowledge each other and apologize for their wrongdoings.

Third-generation researchers have also begun the intricate task of deter-mining whether arbitration awards are qualitatively or quantitatively differ-ent from court awards. Bingham notes that Howard (1995) compared damage awards in discrimination cases decided by litigation and by arbitra-tion and discovered that in many respects, employees did better in arbitration than they did in litigation. By contrast, in a recent study, Eisenberg and Hill (2003) compared arbitrated outcomes with court-tried outcomes for a large sample of employment discrimination cases and found no statistically significant differences in employee win rates and median award levels in this comparison. By analyzing the effect of procedures on outcomes, this research is similar in some respects to the research conducted by the second genera-tion. It is different in at least two respects: first, it does a much more careful job of parsing the effect of specific procedures on outcomes, and, second, it provides evidence that has implications for the societal consequences of ADR.

The third generation, in common with the first, is concerned with the extent to which employees are provided with due process protections. The principal difference between first- and third-generation researchers is that the former approach the topic from the perspective of the law, while the latter have developed models to test empirically the effect of variations in due process protections on dependent variables such as settlement rates, participant satisfaction, and perceptions of procedural fairness. Bingham's own research (1997a) on the so-called repeat player effect is a leading example of how a researcher can translate a conceptual concern for an imbalance of power in arbitration into concrete and testable hypotheses.

The Next Generation: Synthesizing Across Levels

We believe the next generation of researchers will have the task of synthesizing the disparate theories and empirical findings of the first three generations of researchers. They will need to do a better job of bridging the gap between practice and research and of building and testing empirical models based on sound theory. One of the principal questions frequently debated by first-generation researchers was the potential effects of ADR on the quality of justice in our society. We maintain that one of the principal tasks of the next generation of researchers will be to reexamine the societal implications of ADR, but to do so on the basis of rigorous empirical analysis rather than abstract debate. Has the transformation of employment dispute resolution in the United States strengthened or weakened employee rights and our system of social justice?

We know, for example, that there has been a dramatic shift in the resolution of many types of disputes from public forums to private ones. Some have claimed that this shift represents nothing less than the de facto privatization of our system of justice. One index of this transformation is the declining use of trials to resolve disputes. Samborn (2002), for example, reported a significant decrease in federal trials over the period 1970–2001: thirty years ago, 10 percent of the civil and criminal cases filed in federal courts were resolved after a jury or a bench trial; in 2001, although the number of federal cases had increased by nearly 150 percent, the proportion resolved by trial had declined to 2.2 percent. Samborn attributes "the vanishing of the trial" to the increasing reliance of the courts and the disputants on ADR.

The privatization of American justice is fertile territory for serious researchers, but to date there has been virtually an absence of rigorous, analytical research on the implications of this trend. This picture is not substantially different from the picture one might paint of the evolution of research on the societal effects of collective bargaining. The rise of collective bargaining in the United States, particularly after the 1930s, was accompanied by heated debates and controversies, but serious scholarly attempts to understand the societal effects of collective bargaining did not commence until the 1960s, when social scientists (aided by the development of computerization) began to analyze large bodies of empirical data (see, for example, Freeman and Medoff, 1984).

We also believe researchers should attempt to synthesize micro- and macro-organizational approaches to the study of employment dispute resolution systems. Specifically, efforts should be made to examine more carefully the effects of microvariations in dispute procedures on macrolevel outcomes, such as recruitment, retention, employee performance, productivity, employee satisfaction, and even profits and other bottom-line measures. Would the more precise specification of procedural variables help us confirm the predictions of the exit-voice model regarding workplace outcomes? Or would more careful specification uncover anomalies of the type discovered by Lewin and Colvin?

Similarly, we believe that researchers should begin to grapple with the divergent assumptions concerning the driving force behind ADR's diffusion in the workplace. Throughout our analysis of successive generations of research, we have emphasized the link between these different assumptions and each generation's primary focus. It is now time to develop a multidimensional framework for understanding the emergence of ADR, which will lead to a broader and more complex agenda for researching the phenomenon.

We also need to learn more about the effects of dispute resolution systems in one organization or sector on the behavior of employers and employees in other organizations or sectors; in the industrial relations literature, these are called spillover effects. Many employers engage in benchmarking the experience of other employers, and there are distinct patterns of ADR usage across industries (Lipsky and Seeber, 1998). Our understanding of cause and effect in this regard, however, is limited. At some point in the recent past, it appears that a so-called tipping point was reached in the use of ADR in employment relations (Lipsky, Seeber, and Fincher, 2003). Gladwell (2002) has analogized the diffusion of social innovations to an epidemic. We do not have a clear understanding of the factors that led to an ADR "epidemic" in the 1990s, and in the absence of an understanding we cannot predict whether ADR is likely to become institutionalized or will be just another passing management fad.

To address such questions, the next generation of researchers will need to do a better job of building multidimensional models and using multivariate statistical techniques to test hypotheses. A considerable amount of the research reviewed by Bingham consists of either qualitative analysis (such as case studies) or, if quantitative in nature, simple tabulations and correlations between variables of interest. To advance our knowledge of the effect of ADR procedures on outcomes of interest, multivariate models that control for the influence of organizational and environmental factors will need to be developed (see, for example, Lipsky, Seeber, and Fincher, 2003). The influence of ADR procedures on workplace outcomes is probably sensitive to the settings and contexts in which it is used, as Bingham indicates. But social scientists usually require a higher level of statistical proof of this proposition than has yet been provided by researchers.

Finally, an additional methodological challenge facing the next generation of ADR researchers is the need to develop a richer body of comparative studies that can serve to validate or refute the very foundation on which these procedures have been instituted—that they are a preferable alternative to traditional dispute resolution methods. We already noted that there is some third-generation research comparing ADR and litigation outcomes. Comparative ADR research, however, is still in its infancy and must be applied to first- and second-generation concerns as well. In addition, the ADR path must be compared to the traditional path as a coherent set of alternatives rather than merely as a specific procedure. To do this, researchers will need to develop a clear and structured set of criteria for evaluating and comparing ADR processes and outcomes. We believe that by doing so, ADR researchers will begin to bridge the generational gaps discussed throughout this commentary.

Toward a New Paradigm?

Our call for the next generation of researchers to engage in a synthesis of the work of earlier generations and to build more rigorous models requiring more sophisticated statistical techniques would be characterized by Kuhn (1962) as a recommendation consistent with the course of normal science. As we have noted, however, existing paradigms have not been able to explain many phenomena of interest in employment dispute resolution, and the number of anomalies continues to accumulate. We cannot discern the contours of a new paradigm, nor can we predict how soon it will arrive. We believe it is safe to predict, however, that when a new research paradigm emerges, it will permit "the prediction of phenomena that had been entirely unsuspected while the old paradigm prevailed" (Kuhn, 1962, p. 158).

References

Abel, R. L. "The Contradictions of Informal Justice." In R. L. Abel (ed.), *The Politics of Informal Justice.* Orlando, Fla.: Academic Press, 1982.

Appelbaum, E., Bailey, T., Berg, P., and Kalleberg, A. L. *Manufacturing Advantage: Why High Performance Work Systems Pay Off.* Ithaca, N.Y.: ILR Press, 2000.

Appelbaum, E., and Batt, R. *The New American Workplace: Transforming Work Systems in the United States.* Ithaca, N.Y.: ILR Press, 1994.

Auerbach, J. S. *Justice Without Law?* New York: Oxford University Press, 1983.

Batt, R., Colvin, A., and Keefe, J. "Employee Voice, Human Resource Practices, and Quit Rates: Evidence from the Telecommunications Industry." *Industrial and Labor Relations Review,* 2002, *55,* 573–594.

Bingham, L. B. "Employment Arbitration: The Repeat Player Effect." *Employee Rights and Employment Policy Journal,* 1997a, *1,* 189–220.

Bingham, L. B. "Mediating Employment Disputes: Perceptions of REDRESS at the United States Postal Service." *Review of Public Personnel Administration,* 1997b, *17,* 20–30.

Bingham, L. B. "On Repeat Players, Adhesive Contracts, and the Use of Statistics in Judicial Review of Arbitration Awards." *McGeorge Law Review,* 1998, *29,* 223–260.

Bingham, L. B. *Mediation at Work: Transforming Workplace Conflict at the United States Postal Service.* Washington, D.C.: IBM Center for the Business of Government, 2003.

Bingham, L. B., Kim, K., and Raines, S. S. "Exploring the Role of Representation in Employment Mediation at the U.S.P.S." *Ohio State Journal of Dispute Resolution,* 2002, *17,* 341–377.

Bush, R.B.A. "Efficiency and Protection, or Empowerment and Recognition? The Mediator's Role and Ethical Standards in Mediation." *Florida Law Review,* 1989, *41,* 253–286.

Colvin, A. J. "Citizens and Citadels: Dispute Resolution and the Governance of Employment Relations." Unpublished doctoral dissertation, Cornell University, 1999.

Colvin, A.J.S. "Institutional Pressures, Human Resource Strategies, and the Rise of Nonunion Dispute Resolution Procedures." *Industrial and Labor Relations Review,* 2003, *56,* 275–391.

Cutcher-Gershenfeld, J., and Kochan, T. A. "Dispute Resolution and Team-Based Work Systems." In S. E. Gleason (ed.), *Workplace Dispute Resolution: Directions for the Twenty-First Century.* East Lansing: Michigan State University Press, 1997.

Dunlop, J. T. *Industrial Relations Systems.* New York: Holt, 1958.

Edwards, H. T. "Alternative Dispute Resolution: Panacea or Anathema?" *Harvard Law Review,* 1986, *99,* 668–684.

Eisenberg, T., and Hill, E. *Employment Arbitration and Litigation: An Empirical Comparison.* New York: New York University School of Law, Mar. 2003.

[http://srn.com/abstract].

Ewing, D. W. *Justice on the Job: Resolving Grievances in the Nonunion Workplace.* Boston: Harvard Business School Press, 1989.

Fiss, O. "Against Settlement." *Yale Law Journal,* 1984, *93,* 1073–1090.

Foulkes, F. K. *Personnel Policies in Large Nonunion Companies.* Upper Saddle River, N.J.: Prentice Hall, 1980.

Freeman, R. B., and Medoff, J. L. *What Do Unions Do?* New York: Basic Books, 1984.

Gilmer v. *Interstate/Johnson Lane Corp.,* 500 U.S. 20 (1991).

Gladwell, M. *The Tipping Point.* New York: Little, Brown, 2002.

Heckscher, C., and Donnellon, A. *The Post-Bureaucratic Organization: New Perspectives on Organizational Change.* Thousand Oaks, Calif.: Sage, 1994.

Hirschman, A. O. *Exit, Voice, and Loyalty.* Cambridge, Mass.: Harvard University Press, 1970.

Howard, W. M. "Arbitrating Claims of Employment Discrimination: What Really Does Happen? What Really Should Happen?" *Dispute Resolution Journal,* 1995, *50,* 40–50.

Karambayya, R., and Brett, J. M. "Managers Handling Disputes: Third-Party Roles and Perceptions of Fairness." *Academy of Management Journal,* 1989, *32,* 687–704.

Karambayya, R., Brett, J. M., and Lytle, A. "Effects of Formal Authority and Experience on Third Party Roles, Outcomes, and Perceptions of Fairness." *Academy of Management Journal,* 1992, *35,* 426–438.

Kerr, C., Dunlop, J. T., Harbison, F., and Myers, C. *Industrialism and Industrial Man.* Cambridge, Mass: Harvard University Press, 1960.

Kochan, T. A., Katz, H. C., and McKersie, R. B. *The Transformation of American Industrial Relations.* New York: Basic Books, 1986.

Kolb, D. M. *The Mediators.* Cambridge, Mass.: MIT Press, 1983.

Kolb, D. M., and others. *When Talk Works: Profiles of Mediators.* San Francisco: Jossey-Bass, 1994.

Kuhn, T. S. *The Structure of Scientific Revolutions.* Chicago: University of Chicago Press, 1962.

Lewicki, R. J., and Sheppard, B. H. "Choosing How to Intervene: Factors Affecting the Use of Process and Outcome Control in Third Party Dispute Resolution." *Journal of Occupational Behavior,* 1985, *6* (1), 49–64.

Lewin, D. "Dispute Resolution in the Nonunion Firm: A Theoretical and Empirical Analysis." *Journal of Conflict Resolution,* 1987a, *13,* 465–502.

Lewin, D. "Conflict Resolution in the Nonunion High Technology Firm." In A. Kleingartner and C. S. Anderson (eds)., *Human Resource Management in High Technology Firms.* San Francisco: New Lexington Press, 1987b.

Lewin, D. "Grievance Procedures in Nonunion Workplaces: An Empirical Analysis of Usage, Dynamics, and Outcomes." *Chicago Kent Law Review,* 1990, *66,* 823–844.

Lipsky, D. B., and Seeber, R. L. *The Appropriate Resolution of Corporate Disputes: A Report on the Growing Use of ADR by U.S. Corporations.* Ithaca, N.Y.: Institute on Conflict Resolution, 1998.

Lipsky, D. B., Seeber, R. L., and Fincher, R. D. *Emerging Systems for Managing Workplace Conflict.* San Francisco: Jossey-Bass, 2003.

McCabe, D. M. *Corporate Nonunion Complaint Procedures and Systems: A Strategic Human Resources Management Analysis.* New York: Praeger, 1988.

Nader, L. "Controlling Processes in the Practice of Law: Hierarchy and Pacification in the Movement to Re-Form Dispute Ideology." *Ohio State Journal on Dispute Resolution,* 1993, *9* (1), 1–25.

Samborn, H. Jr. "The Vanishing Trial." *ABA Journal,* Oct. 2002, pp. 24–27.

Stone, K. V. "Dispute Resolution in the Boundaryless Workplace." *Ohio State Journal on Dispute Resolution,* 2001, *16,* 467–489.

Walton, R. E., and McKersie, R. B. *A Behavioral Theory of Labor Negotiations: An Analysis of a Social Interaction System.* (2nd ed.) Ithaca, N.Y.: ILR Press, 1991.

Westin, A. F., and Felieu, A. G. *Resolving Employment Disputes Without Litigation.* Washington, D.C.: Bureau of National Affairs, 1988.

David B. Lipsky is professor of Industrial and Labor Relations and director of the Institute on Conflict Resolution at Cornell University. In 2004 he became the president-elect of the Industrial Relations Research Association. He is the coauthor (with Ronald L. Seeber and Richard D. Fincher) of *Emerging Systems for Managing Workplace Conflict* (Jossey-Bass, 2003). Lipsky served as dean of the School of Industrial and Labor Relations at Cornell from 1988 until 1997.

Ariel C. Avgar is a doctoral student at the Cornell School of Industrial and Labor Relations. He received a B.A. in Sociology and an LL.B. in Law from the Hebrew University in Jerusalem. Prior to his admittance to the Israeli Bar he served as law clerk for the president of the Israeli National Labor Court. His research focuses on conflict and its resolution in the nonbureaucratic workplace.

What We Know About Environmental Conflict Resolution: An Analysis Based on Research

E. FRANKLIN DUKES

Environmental conflicts typically involve many different types of parties, issues, and resources. Such conflicts may occur upstream over policy, which means laws or regulations about how a particular issue or class of issues will be addressed, or downstream about place, which refers to what has occurred or will occur in a particular circumstance (O'Leary and Bingham, 2003).

Practically every community finds itself embroiled in periodic disputes over public land use and preservation, private land development, water quality or quantity, air quality, habitat for species, waste disposal, natural resource use and management, environmental hazards, and more. What is often at stake in such conflicts are fundamental issues: individual and community health, racial and ethnic justice, the survival or death of entire species, the integrity or destruction of whole ecosystems, and the economic or cultural viability of various human communities.

Environmental conflict is a subset of the larger category of public conflicts involving issues such as health and health care, race and ethnicity, economic development, and governance. Environmental conflict often includes some combination of these issues (d'Estrée, Dukes, and Navarette-Romero, 2002). It also may involve multiple jurisdictions and multiple levels of jurisdictions (international, federal, tribal, regional, state, and local), and the conflict may be less about the resources at stake than about issues of jurisdiction or precedent.

Early research and theory building in the environmental conflict resolution arena focused on mediation (Bacow and Wheeler, 1984; Bingham, 1986). The vocabulary that at one point favored *mediation* has expanded to include terms such as *consensus building* (Susskind, McKearnan, and Thomas-Larmer, 1999b), *collaboration* (Dukes and Firehock, 2001), *collaborative learning* (Daniels and Walker, 2001), *collaborative planning* (Innes and Booher, 1999), *collaborative natural resource management*

(Conley and Moote, 2001), *community-based collaboration* (see www. cbcrc.org), and *community-based conservation.* Many practitioners would include *enhanced public involvement* within their practice as well. Some work encompasses a combination of such processes.

For this article, *environmental conflict resolution* (ECR) serves as an umbrella term for this entire range of processes. The characteristics that identify an ECR process include direct, face-to-face discussions; deliberation intended to enhance participants' mutual education and understanding; inclusion of multiple sectors representing diverse and often conflicting perspectives; openness and flexibility of process; and consensus or some variation other than unilateral decision making as the basis for agreements. ECR may or may not include a third-party mediator or facilitator. The subject matter includes some environmental element, by which is meant the interconnected biophysical, economic, political, and social systems encompassing both natural and human systems (Glavovic, Dukes, and Lynott, 1997).

Key Structural Elements of Environmental Conflict Resolution

ECR provides an intriguing set of structural questions and challenges for sponsors, analysts, and researchers. The following categories reflect an effort to make sense of these structural issues, but these should not be thought of as representing any sort of consensus among analysts of ECR:

- The distinction between ECR processes and other ways of addressing environmental conflict
- The distinction between agreement-seeking processes and processes that seek to meet other goals
- The distinction between ECR processes that include independent third-party assistance and those that do not
- The distinction between public and private sponsorship of ECR and a related distinction between private and public interests and impacts
- The distinction between programmatic processes and those that develop organically
- The distinction between planning and policy (upstream) or place-based and site-specific (downstream) ECR
- The impact on any socioenvironmental system under consideration

Research and Environmental Conflict Resolution

Perhaps the most compelling question is how ECR compares to other ways of addressing environmental conflicts. Analysts of ECR, proponents and critics alike, commonly think of it as an alternative to other processes. These so-called traditional procedures include primarily legislation, administrative decision making (agency rules and regulations), and adjudication.

There are times when that distinction makes sense. But the risk is that we fail to appreciate that ECR processes are less often alternatives and more often one part of a complex and interdependent system of legal, legislative, or administrative processes (Dukes, 2004a).

Many environmental conflicts, and all complex and enduring ones, play themselves out in a number of forums involving a variety of processes. ECR influences and in turn is influenced by these other processes. Buckle and Thomas-Buckle (1986, p. 64) describe this interplay: "Indeed, for the parties, the relationships among mediation, direct negotiation among themselves, legislative politics, regulatory process, media-based efforts at persuasion, litigation, and many other events influencing the outcome of the conflict are typically complex, constantly variable and mutually interactive. . . . Even the parties to the six cases that reached a signed agreement through mediation expressed some ambiguities about just how the case could be said to have been processed."

Furthermore, the conflict behavior that some want to resolve is exactly the conflict behavior that others want to see. That is, the preferred alternative to ECR may actually be continuation or even escalation of the conflict. This is certainly true of some critics of ECR for whom the term *collaboration* or *mediation* too often equates with selling short the environment (Amy, 1987; McCloskey, 1996; Kenney, 2000).

Settlement Rates

Is there any way of gauging what proportion of cases handled by ECR processes reach agreement, and can that rate be compared in any meaningful way to non-ECR processes? Does that rate in fact mean anything?

The five studies that address this question present a conundrum. Because of the complexity and variability of environmental issues, a valid comparison of settlement rates between ECR and non-ECR cases appears nearly impossible. The three studies that directly make such a comparison are found in relatively large-volume programs that deal with issues of a similar type. Two other studies approach the question of settlement rates indirectly by asking participants their views about how likely a settlement would have been had they not used an ECR process. Such speculation is one valid way to ascertain participant satisfaction, but cannot offer sufficient rigor for any substantial claims about settlement.

The pilot mediation program in the U.S. District Court for the District of Oregon described in Kloppenberg (2002) is telling. Seventy-five environmental cases "not easily resolved by a judicial decision or by a traditional evaluative settlement conference" (p. 566) were screened for potential mediation during the pilot. Thirteen proceeded to mediation; seven were essentially distributive in nature, mostly involving cleanup costs. Of these seven, only two were resolved during mediation. One case was still under negotiation but likely to settle without a return to mediation. Two of the seven returned to litigation; one of those had used a settlement judge rather than an external mediator. One returned to litigation to address a single issue and then returned to mediation to work out an arbitration process. One went to mediation but paired the mediator with an expert adviser; the parties returned to further discovery even as mediation remained an option at the time the pilot ended. Of the six complex integrative cases that proceeded to mediation, three settled and one withdrew before agreeing on a mediator. One case was still pending, and one did not settle despite resolution of the major issues because "a dispute over attorney fees remained" (p. 573). Finally, twenty-three of the seventy-five reviewed cases that did not proceed to mediation settled before trial. One of the remaining cases was settled in a mediation conducted outside the pilot program, and one case that involved a former mediation participant reported using a similar process to reach settlement. Two cases settled using a settlement judge. That left thirty-six cases continuing in litigation as the study ended. (See Exhibit 1.)

This study illustrates the difficulty of isolating ECR from other processes. And this is the case in an environment circumscribed by the judicial system, whereas much, if not most, ECR work occurs outside the courts (no research delineates how much ECR work occurs and where).

Sipe (1998) evaluated ECR within the Florida Department of Environmental Protection, studying 21 mediations out of 150 enforcement actions filed between 1988 and 1990. The primary research questions were whether mediation of these enforcement actions that were at the point of impasse resulted in higher settlement rates and increased compliance than nonmediated techniques of unassisted negotiation, administrative hearings, or court trials. Twenty-one mediated cases were compared with 125 nonmediated cases and tracked over a five-year period.

Exhibit 1. Disposition of Seventy-Five Challenging Cases in the U.S. District Court, Oregon

---

Thirteen proceed to mediation.

 Six complex integrative cases

  Three were settled.

  One withdrew from mediation prior to selecting a mediator.

  One was pending when the study ended.

  One settled issues but not attorney fees.

 Seven distributive cases (mostly cleanup costs)

  Two were resolved.

  One was likely to settle without returning to mediation.

  Two returned to litigation. (One of the two used a settlement judge rather than an external mediator.)

  One returned to litigation to address a single issue and then returned to work out an arbitration process.

  One interrupted by discovery that may resume later.

Sixty-two proceeded to the judicial system,

 Twenty-three settled before trial.

 One settled in a nonpilot mediation.

 One settled using a mediation-like process.

 Two settled using a settlement judge.

 Thirty-five continued in litigation as the pilot ended.

For this universe of cases, the settlement rate was indeed high—4.6 percent—compared with a somewhat lower rate of 70.6 percent of the nonmediated cases of a similar set. Sipe speculates that preparing for mediation breaks the inertia of stalemate by focusing the parties' attention on settlement.

Sipe and Stiftel (1995) surveyed a similar set of mediated enforcement cases in Florida between 1990 and 1992. Of those nineteen cases, fourteen (74 percent) settled and five (26 percent) did not achieve a settlement with mediation. The survey response rate was 67 percent for unresolved cases and 76 percent for resolved.

The strength of these three carefully designed studies about Oregon's U.S. District Court and Florida's enforcement mediation—the comparison within a similar set of issues between mediated and nonmediated cases—also means that their results may be atypical. Many environmental disputes tend to be complex, with multiple parties and issues and dynamics that change over a long period of time. However fiercely fought they may be, enforcement disputes are generally less complex, with fewer parties and issues, than nonenforcement environmental issues. What is at stake in mediating the enforcement cases may be less about environmental questions and more about financial matters. Even if the environmental stakes are significant, the questions in dispute during enforcement cases tend to be circumscribed: what level of fine is imposed, whether an action violates a permit, what will occur consistent with regulatory requirements. Thus, it would be improper to extrapolate these findings beyond a limited use. However, it can be said that the null hypothesis—that ECR settlement rates are lower than non-ECR processes—was not proved.

Like enforcement disputes, land use conflict is also common. On behalf of the Lincoln Institute for Land Policy, the Consensus Building Institute (CBI) examined one hundred mediated land use cases that occurred between 1985 and 1997 (Susskind and others, 1999a). These cases were chosen from the recommendations of twenty-five land use mediators. CBI built a database of more than one hundred "roughly similar" cases involving natural resource management (twenty-four), infrastructure design (twenty), development and growth (eighteen), comprehensive planning (sixteen), facility siting (sixteen), and environmental cleanup (six). The research is based primarily on interviews of four hundred individuals.

Sixty-one percent of participants stated that their cases settled. Of the participants who indicated that their case was not settled through mediation, 64 percent stated that mediation had helped them make "significant progress" (Susskind and others, 1999a, p. 7). In an interesting affirmation of the complexity and confusion surrounding some types of ECR, 7 percent claimed settlement even though litigation followed. Furthermore, mediators and public officials claimed higher settlement rates than did disputants.

These cases were not compared to a similar set of nonmediated cases; however, 80 percent of participants whose cases settled claimed that no agreement could have been reached without the mediator. Although the authors indicate that they made an effort to include cases that mediators considered failures, there is no way to know how representative these cases are of other such cases. And like enforcement disputes, the key issues involved in land use cases may have little to do with environmental resources. This study also found substantial differences in reported settlement rates by type of environmental issue. For instance, 78 percent of comprehensive planning disputants reported settlement compared to 65 percent for infrastructure design cases, 55 percent for natural resource cases, and 40 percent for environmental cleanup cases.

An ongoing effort at designing compatible program evaluation systems sponsored by the U.S. Institute for Environmental Conflict Resolution (USIECR) coordinated the identification and integration of a multiagency data set of thirty-seven recently evaluated ECR cases that used third-party mediators or facilitators (U.S. Institute for Environmental Conflict Resolution 2004). These cases were screened or assessed by USIECR, the Environmental Protection Agency's Conflict Prevention and Resolution Center, the Federal Energy Regulatory Commission, the Florida Conflict Resolution Consortium, the Office of Collaborative Action and Dispute Resolution at the U.S. Department of the Interior (DOI), and the Oregon Dispute Resolution Commission. Twenty-four of the thirty-seven cases had a sufficient survey response rate (64 percent totaling 191 participants in the aggregate) to be included in their data analysis. These twenty-four cases had as few as two and as many as forty participants. A broad array of cases was included covering upstream (natural resource plans) and downstream (siting of facilities) processes. Issues included air quality, land use, energy, contamination, transportation, urban infrastructure development, and water.

In 75 percent of cases, the respondents reported that they "could not have progressed as far" using any other process. This will have to suffice as an indicator of settlement, however imperfect it may be. Although 75 percent is a substantial figure, there is no way of knowing whether biases inherent in self-reporting (for example, participants who have invested a lot of time in a process may assert more value than is warranted) may have affected that figure.

Evidence of Change in Participants' Relationship, Conflict Management Skills

Common sense might suggest that adversarial processes rarely bring about positive relationship change, although there are exceptions. However, many environmental advocates, citizens, agency personnel, and representatives do become quite skilled at negotiation, coalition building, and other conflict management skills through their advocacy in so-called traditional forums. Unfortunately, there is no published empirical research comparing relationship or conflict management skill changes between ECR and non-ECR processes.

In her thoughtful and thorough review of relationship change in ECR, d'Estrée (2003) observes that measures of relationship change in general are sparse. She cites d'Estrée and Colby's five ways of measuring relationship change in ECR (2003). "Reduction in conflict and hostility" can be measured by actions, rhetoric, or communication tone; "improved relations," or the ways that parties view and relate to one another, can be measured by the parties' discussion of their relationship, their communication tone, how they protect themselves, and trust as indicated by enforcement clauses or other protections; "cognitive and affective shift" is indicated by how parties refer to one another and their behavior; "ability to resolve subsequent disputes" in terms of actions rather than perceptions; and "transformation" as shown by evidence of empowerment and recognition and other major shifts in perception.

Anecdotal evidence from many cases can be found describing powerful relationship changes as a result of ECR processes (see Talbot, 1983; Susskind, McKearnan, and Thomas-Larmer, 1999b; Dukes, 2004b). Although theorists ponder the meaning of such changes (Dukes, 1996), there is limited empirical evidence concerning whether or how often such changes occur, the causes of any such changes, and the impact, if any, of such changes on substantive outcomes. Most studies looking at the question of changes in individual empowerment or capacity building have been single case studies that relied on disputants' reported perceptions (Birkhoff, 2002). But these studies are promising.

Buckle and Thomas-Buckle (1986) found reported value in enhanced negotiating skills even among mediation cases that did not settle. The CBI (Susskind, McKearnan, and Thomas-Larmer, 1999) found that 23 percent of participants in land use mediations that did not settle reported gains in terms such as enhanced relationship. Some of those participants (no proportion is offered) also reported avoiding further disputes or resolving them more easily because of their understanding of how to work things out and because of increased trust. And Innes (1999), whose research will be examined in detail here, does report significant improvements in relationships and trust.

This is the case for O'Leary and Raines (2001, 2003) as well. Their examination of ECR for enforcement actions at the U.S. Environmental Protection Agency found positive results reported for the impact of the process on the long-term relationship between parties. The Environmental Protection Agency (EPA) attorneys offered a mean of 2.13 on a scale of 1 to 5 (1 = highly satisfied with improvements in relationship and 5 = very dissatisfied), while the private parties reported a very high mean of 1.44.

For the USIECR study (2004), 60 percent of participants indicated that they can meet with other participants to discuss issues of concern, 61 percent find it easier to discuss controversial issues, and 64 percent can now work more productively with other participants with whom they have disagreements.

Satisfaction of Participants with Process, the Third Party, and the Outcome

At least as long ago as 1983, researchers cautioned against using satisfaction-based criteria to evaluate ECR. In fact, Talbot (1983) observed that disputants who might misuse mediation to harm other parties could find the process quite satisfactory. Beirle and Cayford (2003) argue that environmental mediation tends to involve less diverse participation than other public participation processes and that participant satisfaction among others with an interest or stake in the issues may differ sharply from those not actually participating in the mediation. Furthermore, many ECR processes are initiated after frustration with other types of processes (see Susskind and others, 1999a).

A study of the EPA compared eight negotiated rule makings (reg-negs) with six conventional rule makings (Langbein and Kerwin, 2000). Within a study population of 101 participants in reg-negs and 51 individuals who filed formal comments during the conventional rule makings, the reg-neg participants were more satisfied with the rule-making process than those who commented on the conventional rule making. However, these results do not control for variations in the intensity of the dispute and the type of issue. In addition, one can easily imagine that some proportion of those filing a formal comment might have an axe to grind, thus prejudicing these results.

In a review of fifty-four waste management mediations in Ontario and Massachusetts, Andrew (2001) found that 61 percent of disputants were satisfied with the mediation process and 61 percent with the outcome. This research did not compare ECR and non-ECR cases, but party satisfaction for parties who have experience with non-ECR processes presumably does reflect an informal comparison with what participants believe may have been achievable elsewhere. "Satisfaction with process" was associated with the efficiency of the process, the ability of the process to identify and resolve key issues, the degree to which parties understood the process, and the degree to which they were able to participate and thereby influence the outcome. "Satisfaction with outcome" was associated with avoiding a conventional adjudicative process and the ability to implement the agreement. Furthermore, satisfaction with process was an accurate predictor of satisfaction with outcome.

The Sipe and Stiftel (1995) research into Florida's enforcement mediation approached this question through participant interviews and does not provide a true comparison for this question with non-ECR cases. They found that 84 percent of the respondents rated the mediator as moderately or very helpful for facilitating group discussion, assisting parties in stating interests, and helping parties establish rules for reaching decisions. The participants found the mediator less helpful (56.2 percent) in ratifying agreements; nevertheless, 89.9 percent of respondents rated the mediator overall as moderately or very helpful.

The respondents from cases that did not reach agreement offered significantly lower evaluations of the mediation process for five of six criteria than did respondents from cases that settled. However, the nonsettlement respondents rated the mediator lower on only two of six criteria. Sipe and Stiftel (1995) speculate that ". . . respondents believed that factors other than the mediator's assistance were responsible for the mediation resulting in impasse" (p. 153).

In their research into one hundred land use mediations, the Consensus Building Institute (Susskind and others, 1999a) reported that 92 percent of participants who claimed that their cases settled during mediation agreed (43 percent) or strongly agreed (49 percent) that their own interests were well served by the settlement. Eighty-six percent of the same participants agreed (51 percent) or strongly agreed (35 percent) that all parties' interests were met. And 88 percent indicated that their settlement was creative and produced the best possible outcome.

In settled cases, 91 percent indicated that the mediator was crucial (67 percent) or important (24 percent), with 80 percent claiming that no agreement could have been reached without the mediator. A total of 75 percent of interviewed participants in unsettled cases described the mediator as crucial (49 percent) or important (26 percent); presumably, they did not mean crucial in blocking agreement.

A survey of 172 environmental lawyers found that 72 percent recommended alternative dispute resolution (ADR) to their clients, and even those who had been unsuccessful at resolving a dispute through ADR remained supportive (O'Leary and Husar, 2002). Interestingly, the most frequently cited challenge to using ADR was access to suitably qualified and skilled third parties.

The USIECR study (2004) found that 79 percent of respondents reported that they were satisfied with the process. A startling 96 percent were very satisfied with the assistance of the third-party mediators or facilitators.

Ninety-five percent reported that their concerns were heard and 96 percent that their concerns were addressed with the assistance of mediators or facilitators.

Transaction Cost Savings

The Sipe and Stiftel (1995) research found 94.9 percent of respondents agreed that mediation was "very" or "moderately" efficient in terms of cost. Just under half of the respondents estimated actual cost savings by avoiding court, with a median estimated savings of $75,000 per party, or $150,000 per case. And 89.8 percent found their mediation "very" or "moderately" efficient in terms of time.

In their comparison of eight regulatory negotiations (reg-negs) with six conventional rule makings, Langbein and Kerwin (2000) found that participants in the reg-negs incurred higher costs. In particular, small businesses found that the costs of participating were greater than in conventional rule making and that the net benefits were not greater than for conventional rule making. However, other participants reported that the value of the benefits of participation exceeded the costs. Manring (1998) found reduced agency or organizational costs but higher costs to the individual participants who participate in the process.

Results also vary in the CBI (Susskind and others, 1999a) study of land use mediation. Ninety-one percent of the interviewees who answered the question (no number is offered) reported that the process cost less than they would have anticipated for other forums, and 85 percent indicated a similar perception that the mediation process took less time. But only 25 percent of regional officials indicated that they thought the process saved both time and money. Fifty percent thought that it cost more and took more time, and some 25 percent indicated time savings but increased costs.

Kloppenberg (2002) reports results from two cases, with one attorney estimating a savings to clients of $200,000 to $400,000 and another attorney for both parties estimating higher costs for mediation. Finally, Andrew's study (2001) of fifty-four cases found that time and cost savings were difficult to identify accurately, although many participants did report that they saved both time and money.

In his evaluation of Hawaii's public disputes mediation pilot program, Lowry (1989) determined that the most valid comparison would be between mediated cases and litigated cases that were settled out of court. He surveyed mediation participants and attorneys who had represented clients in complex litigation cases that had settled out of court. The comparison of seven mediated cases with eleven nonmediated cases found a total elapsed time of twenty-six versus thirty months. The comparison of costs of mediation to litigation costs did not include court administrative costs or mediation program costs. Of the seven mediated cases and seven nonmediated cases for which data were compiled, mediation costs were about one-third less than for litigated cases that settled out of court. However, Lowry cautions that too few cases were evaluated to make valid claims.

What does all of this mean? As Birkhoff (2002) observes, these contradictions cannot be sorted out without additional research. Perhaps the answer will be several answers: cost and time savings vary so widely by the circumstances of each case that comparisons within ECR as a whole are not productive. Clearly, blanket claims that ECR either costs or saves time and money are inappropriate.

Durability of Settlement and Recidivism

Again, there is little empirical research about the durability of settlements within ECR compared to non-ECR cases. Sipe's 1998 study of 150 enforcement cases found no difference in compliance between mediated and nonmediated cases. He concludes that this is due to lack of oversight provided by a mediator. In addition, the likelihood of compliance decreases as the numbers of parties increase; a similar decrease is found when another government entity is a party to the case.

Seventy-five percent of participants in land use mediation cases that settled in the CBI study (Susskind and others, 1999a) reported that their settlement was implemented well (34 percent) or very well (41 percent). Sixty-nine percent indicated a belief that their settlement was more stable than what they may have been able to achieve through another process, with 23 percent indicating that they could not tell.

This question of durability may be less a structural question and more one of best practices. In his reporting of six early mediations, Talbot (1983) found that attention to implementation varied with the mediator. A mediator who is focused on achieving agreement to the exclusion of other goals may not pay sufficient attention to issues of postsettlement activities such as implementation and monitoring.

Agreement-Seeking Processes and Processes That Seek to Meet Other Goals

Buckle and Thomas-Buckle (1986) reviewed eighty-one cases in which environmental mediation was proposed. Of those eighty-one, fifty-seven cases were rejected immediately. Twenty-four proceeded to a first meeting, and of those twenty-four, sixteen proceeded no further. Of the eight cases that went to mediation, two failed to reach agreement, three reached unstable agreements, and three reached stable agreements. From this research, one could easily draw the conclusion that ECR (or at least mediation) is both less and more than is being promised. Certainly a policymaker reading that only three of eighty-one attempted mediations reached a conclusive and stable agreement likely would conclude that the attention being paid to ECR was misplaced, that failure was the norm, and that the potential of ECR was vastly misstated.

And yet that conclusion would be wrong, at least based on this study, for the authors also learned that participants in mediations that do not come to a conclusive agreement nevertheless derive significant benefits from the mediation. Those benefits include identifying for parties themselves their own real interests, generating new ideas for solutions, providing insights for regulators, and improving negotiation skills.

While classic mediation still occurs, much mediation is now more accurately described as mediated consensus building, a descriptor that reflects numerous parties (who may or may not have decision authority), multiple issues, and work that occurs over a longer period of time. But even mediated consensus building may be a lesser part of current ECR work. Much such work blurs the line between mediation and enhanced public involvement. These processes may be primarily exploratory or educational in nature. Some composite processes often do include a facilitator and may precede or accompany efforts more directly tied to reaching and implementing agreements (Dukes, 1996).

Dotson (1993) elaborated on this theme. Using data from over sixty cases handled by the Institute for Environmental Negotiation (IEN) between 1981 and 1993, Dotson found that approximately half the cases actually sought no conclusive agreement. In fact, the ECR field that Dotson described was far broader than mediation. While environmental mediation did make up a significant portion of IEN's caseload, that caseload had expanded to include third-party facilitation of strategic planning, conflict assessment, and dialogue. He suggested, not unreasonably, that such work ought to be evaluated on the participants' own expectations rather than the question of an agreement. Of the thirty IEN cases that met the criteria of an agreement-seeking mediation, fourteen could be identified as conclusive successes by virtue of an agreement, endorsement by authorities, and enactment. That is a much lower rate than that found by Sipe (1998) or Sipe and Stiftel (1995); however, these were not relatively straightforward enforcement disputes but complex, multiparty, multiple issue disputes. Dotson also argued that factors external to negotiations, such as changing political or regulatory environment, provide the strongest explanation for the "failures."

Beierle and Cayford (2003) place consensus-seeking dispute resolution at one end of a continuum of methods for engaging the public in environmental decision making. At the other end are informal consultations. And in the middle would be ranged familiar processes such as public hearings, meetings, workshops, visioning exercises, and design charrettes. What do we know about any differences between and among these processes ranged along this continuum?

Beirle and Cayford (2003) examined 239 cases of environmental decision making on the basis of five key goals of public participation: (1) incorporating public values, (2) improving decision quality, (3) resolving conflict, (4) building institutional trust, and (5) educating the public. They unambiguously declare that dispute resolution has been "clearly more effective in achieving the social goals of public participation" (p. 54). But they offer a large caveat: these goals are achieved ". . . only among the small group of participants" (p. 54). They are "much less effective" in using outreach to spread the benefits of education and trust formation beyond the group.

They conclude that agreement-focused ECR processes "limit whose values are heard, whose conflicts are resolved, and whose priority issues are addressed" (p. 54). The use of ECR invokes a trade-off of "success and significance" (p. 55). Most important for program managers and convenors of such processes, the loss in legitimacy among a wider public sometimes means that agreements are revisited or rejected when other actors get involved.

This finding prompts an important question: How is agreement valued relative to other potential ECR outcomes? This question has prompted scrutiny for many years (see, for example, Susskind and Ozawa, 1983; d'Estrée and Colby, 2000). Moore (1996) developed a rubric for evaluating outcomes directly from participants' views of success. Although derived from a limited database of two case studies involving long-term planning efforts on public lands in Australia and the United States, her analysis reveals the many ways participants themselves define and evaluate success. She introduces the concept of conditional success, where judgment is withheld until there is evidence of implementation or durability. Moore suggests that participants think of success within four dimensions: political, interests, responsibility, and relationship. Politically oriented success refers to acceptance by interested communities such that implementation was politically feasible. Interest-oriented success means protection and enhancement of participant interests. Responsibility-oriented success means the extent that participants feel continuing ownership in the product. The fourth dimension, relationship-oriented success, reflects the quality of relationships among and between factions, public agencies, and the broader community. Participants consider both process and outcome when judging success, and more than half of the sixty-six interviewees in her study referred to more than one dimension when describing success. Like Buckle and Thomas-Buckle (1986), she notes that mediations judged unsuccessful by a mediator may in fact be considered successful by participants.

Innes has published much of her research in planning journals (for example, Innes, 1996; Innes and Booher, 1999). In the most thorough and weightiest tome the field of ECR has yet produced, *The Consensus Building Handbook* (Susskind, McKearnan, and Thomas-Larmer, 1999), Innes, 1999) offers the results of years of studying ECR and in particular long-term collaborative groups addressing environmental issues. She takes what is intimated in Buckle and Thomas-Buckle's study and explains not only why outcomes other than agreement are important but which outcomes are important and how collaborative processes can achieve those outcomes.

I have argued elsewhere (Dukes, 1993, 1996) that an ideology of management—whereby public decision making (whether in law, planning, public administration, or ECR) focuses on improved efficiency, productivity and managerial capability of authorities—competes with a vision of conflict transformation. The most valued outcomes of ECR are not necessarily settlements, however important those may be (and in most circumstances where agreement is sought they are likely to be important). Instead, in many cases, the relational by-products are exactly the outcomes most appreciated by participants. Innes (1999) provides the most comprehensive articulation of how the ECR process can lead to specific transformative outcomes.

Gwartney, Fessenden, and Landt (2002) assessed the impact of a sustained dialogue between business and environmental interests in Eugene, Oregon. They analyzed the content of newsletters from four protagonists from three months before the year-long process began and six months after it ended. Positive interactions, as measured by newsletter contents, increased with the passage of time. Furthermore, the authors claim that the two constituencies engaged in increasing numbers of collaborative enterprises. Although they are careful to caution that timing cannot indicate causality, they also state that they could find no other intervening variable that might explain the change.

ECR Processes That Include Independent Third-Party Assistance and Those That Do Not

Many ECR efforts, particularly place-based initiatives, do not include an independent and impartial third-party mediator or facilitator. For example, in an evaluation of forty-eight community-based collaborative groups described in more detail later (Western Consensus Council and Consensus Building Institute), 61 percent of respondents indicated that they used a facilitator. Of these, only 30 percent indicated that they used a professional facilitator, and 23 percent said that an agency official served as facilitator.

Environmental work is unique in its ability to unearth inherent conflicting interests. Such seemingly innocuous activities as trail development and maintenance bring intense conflict involving property rights advocates, competing trail users, and jurisdictional differences. But an ethos of collaboration and conflict resolution now permeates many public agencies charged with providing environmental protection or managing natural resources, and the language of (if not a commitment to) collaboration is now familiar to environmental advocates, elected officials, and citizens.

Andrew's review of waste management conflicts in Ontario and Massachusetts (2001) found that in many cases, the mediator was a stakeholder. He argues that no empirical evidence supports the claim that neutrality is critical to the success of ECR, with success in his case defined as settlement and participant satisfaction. In a landmark study unprecedented in its scope, Leach, Pelkey, and Sabatier (2002) studied almost 150 watershed collaboratives in California and Washington in terms of their agreement on restoration initiatives, changed working group relationships, and accomplished watershed restoration activities. Their data analysis is not complete but offers some convincing evidence of the accomplishments and challenges of these processes.

Leach and Sabatier (2003) note that a review of thirty-seven studies on multistakeholder watershed partnerships (Leach and Pelkey, 2001) found that effective facilitation and coordination trailed only financial resources as the most cited factor of success. But they criticize the bulk of such studies for factors such as reliance on subjective case studies and surveys biased by insufficient reporting. In this study of fifty watershed partnerships, they found that facilitator traits help explain the level of agreements, whereas coordinator (a person responsible for administrative functions) traits help explain the development of social capital. But factors other than facilitation, such as interpersonal trust and duration of the partnerships, are reported by participants as more important than either facilitation or coordination roles.

Perhaps Leach and Sabatier's most striking finding (2003) is that the use of professional facilitators has a small negative correlation with level of agreement and impacts on the watershed. They speculate that both focus on process and financial costs associated with professional facilitators may cause resentment among participants. A logical explanation might occur to mediators and facilitators: that only the most challenged groups used professional facilitators. However, their analysis demonstrated no such relationship. In addition, the reported effectiveness of facilitators was inversely correlated with level of agreement. They speculate that troubled groups may have some psychological dependency on their facilitators.

Leach and Sabatier's conclusion (2003) is worth noting: ". . . Funding for a professional facilitator or coordinator is justified only if the marginal value of the resulting consensus agreements and improved social capital exceeds the opportunity costs of diverting the funds away from some other type of intervention, such as a tangible restoration project" (pp. 167–168). This conclusion may be hard for mediators, facilitators, and program managers to accept. And it would be inappropriate to generalize from a narrow, if large, set of processes (long-term partnerships addressing watershed issues) to other ECR processes. But their cautions warrant reflection and further research into the third-party role.

Leach and Sabatier (2003) also find that parties with a stake in the issue can be effective facilitators in appropriate circumstances, especially if they are not paid for this role. This question of independent third parties was also examined by O'Leary and Raines (2001, 2003). In their study of ADR for enforcement (usually Superfund) cases at the EPA, they found that both EPA attorneys and private parties subject to enforcement were generally satisfied with mediator quality. This satisfaction is qualified by concern about mediator quality control. A significant proportion of nonagency participants believes that mediator impartiality requires shared funding of mediator costs, although some preferred that EPA pay and others believe that such costs are insignificant. They also suggested that most mediators were not even evaluated on the mediation's completion, which obviously hinders the agency's ability to assess mediator efficacy and systematic efforts to improve mediator practice.

Although the contracting method explicitly prohibits EPA from constraining the contractor's choice of a mediator, a significant number of both agency and nonagency attorneys thought that EPA had in fact chosen the mediator. Fifty-eight percent of the non-EPA participants in these Superfund enforcement cases stated that the mediator's neutrality depends on shared cost (although 21 percent felt it did not matter because the mediator cost is insignificant relative to other costs). While in-house mediators (EPA staff from divisions not engaged in the particular issues under dispute) might seem to be inappropriate and 83 percent of non-EPA participants stated that an in-house mediator would be unacceptable, three respondents had positive experiences with in-house mediators despite initial skepticism. Nonetheless, O'Leary and Raines argue the need for a neutral roster of easily accessible mediators not paid exclusively by EPA.

Public and Private Sponsorship, Interests, and Impacts

ECR advocates have struggled for three decades to gain footing within institutions of governance. Three initiatives provided the strongest boost to the field's efforts at legitimization and institutionalization: (1) the development of state offices of dispute resolution beginning in the mid-1980s (National Institute for Dispute Resolution, 1987), (2) establishment of a dispute resolution and consensus building program at the EPA beginning in the late 1980s, and (3) the formation of the U.S. Institute for Environmental Conflict Resolution in the late 1990s (see www.ecr.gov). These in turn have led to increased use of ECR by promoting infrastructure development, including state and national rosters intended to denote some baseline standard of quality, and programs that facilitate contracting, evaluation, and compilation of best practices (Society of Professionals in Dispute Resolution, 1997).

Anecdotal evidence suggests that ECR that is sponsored by local, state, or federal government now dominates the field's work, but occasional significant work sponsored by private parties or foundations continues. Of forty-eight community-based collaborative groups in the study by the Western Consensus Council and the Consensus Building Institute (2003), 86 percent were sponsored by public agencies. Of one hundred land use mediations analyzed by Susskind and colleagues (1999a), seventy-eight were initiated by government officials. What different implications for ECR practices do public and private sponsorship bring?

This is a significant question. These and other issues remain current (Dukes, 2001): What proportion of ECR work is funded by what types of entities? What influences does this funding have on ECR practice? How has this funding changed over time? Does that dependence shape the ECR field? What funding arrangements are possible that would promote third-party independence and impartiality? One may question sponsorship's impact on case selection (are those cases that administrators choose for ECR the issues and conflict that need addressing?) and on impartiality (do mediators and facilitators dependent on a relatively small set of paying customers show partiality toward outcomes favorable to those customers?).

Unfortunately, there is little research that addresses that comparison directly, although some research that focuses on particular agencies is suggestive of answers. Certainly the largest body of work to date comes from state offices of dispute resolution, several of which include ECR practice.

Lowry's evaluation (1989) of Hawaii's Public Disputes Project program involved thirty-nine cases suggested for mediation. These cases ranged from complex litigation to policy roundtables, with most, but not all, involving environmental matters. Lowry used indirect comparison of ECR by interviewing mediation parties, judges, lawyers in litigated cases comparable to mediated cases, mediators, and program staff.

Of the thirty-nine cases, seventeen reached agreement or partial settlement. Fifteen were still being mediated at the time of the report, and seven cases did not proceed to mediation. Lowry found that mediation respondents reported the mediation process effective in addressing what was actually at stake in the dispute. All of the participants were either satisfied or very satisfied with the mediation process. The evaluation reported high satisfaction with the mediators by participants and judges. It also reported high levels of satisfaction with agreements in terms of addressing major issues, creativity, and implementation. One feature of interest was that mediations were comediated by an attorney and someone who was not an attorney.

The O'Leary and Raines (2001, 2003) study of mediated enforcement cases from the EPA Superfund program tested four assertions common to ADR literature in general: that mediation saves time and money, that it improves working relationships, and that private parties are more likely to resolve disputes among themselves. The research used a combination of telephone interviews of EPA's regional ADR specialists (eighteen or twenty), potentially responsible parties (PRPs—those individuals or corporate bodies whose liability for site cleanup and associated costs is in question) or their attorneys (twenty-five), mediators (twenty-two), and EPA enforcement attorneys (sixty-one); government data; and archival records.

They found that non-EPA participants valued the positive impact on the long-term relationship of the parties, a value that EPA officials shared but at a lower level. The study found that satisfaction with mediators, while generally high, varied widely. Inexperienced mediators drew complaints, and 65 percent of non-EPA parties conditioned their willingness to participate in future mediations on the choice of the mediator. O'Leary and Raines found EPA middle-level managers reluctant to support mediation even when the parties were already engaged in mediation. According to the authors, success depends on further education of EPA attorneys.

White (1998) examined the value of institutionalizing a program of ECR within Michigan. He combined a written survey of public and private environmental stakeholders with more intensive focus group interviews to ascertain business, environmental advocacy, and government support for institutionalizing ECR. He then used the criteria of cost effectiveness, time efficiency, role of champions or adversaries, stakeholder support or opposition to institutionalization of ECR, funding, and availability of skilled mediators. Based on these criteria, he concluded that institutionalization of environmental mediation by the state of Michigan would be appropriate.

Programmatic Processes and Those That Develop Organically

How much influence do ECR participants have on the purpose, goals, and design of the ECR process? This element has barely been examined. Sipe and Stiftel (1995) asked participants in Florida's enforcement mediations to evaluate the level of support provided by the program managers. At least 85 percent found Florida's Conflict Resolution Consortium to be moderately or very helpful in four of six tasks: explaining mediation, arranging mediator selection, setting up a premediation session, and arranging the first mediation session. The tasks of assisting with mediation contractual issues and helping evaluate whether mediation was appropriate received ratings of 62.5 percent and 71.4 percent, respectively.

Upstream and Downstream ECR

Emerson, Nabatchi, O'Leary, and Stephens (2003) suggest that environmental conflict can be classified as upstream, midstream, or downstream. While there is little in the way of comparison between upstream and downstream ECR, one study of place-based efforts bears close examination. The research conducted by the Western Consensus Council and the Consensus Building Institute (2003) is notable for the rich array of findings from its large database of place-based efforts. The study involved a relatively simple two-page "scorecard" for participants in these place-based efforts that included twenty-seven indicators of success grouped by the categories of working relationships, quality of the process, and outcomes.

The researchers found 111 groups that met their criteria: located within the intermountain West, with diverse participation, focused on a local or regional location, in existence for at least one year and maintaining viability, a focus on public lands or resources, and successful in reaching at least one outcome. Forty-eight groups agreed to participate in the study. Highlighted findings include the following:

- Eight-seven percent of participants would recommend a collaborative process to address similar issues in the future, while 7 percent would not.

- Forty-one percent cite "direct pressure on decision makers" as their main alternative to collaboration.

- Seventy percent indicate that their collaborative process resulted in a "more effective and lasting outcome" compared to their next-best alternative.

- Seventy percent believe that collaboration costs less than their alternative, while nearly 30 percent thought that their next alternative would have cost less.

- About 40 percent found that the collaborative process saved time, while an equal number disagreed.

The authors conclude, ". . . People place a high value on breaking down stereotypes, building working relationships, and learning about the interests of other stakeholders" (p. 8).

Impact on Socioenvironmental Systems

Much of environmental ECR addresses environmental, economic, and social issues that affect large ecosystems and include substantial economic and social implications.

The core challenge is understanding ECR's impact on the environment. Perhaps the most challenging question about ECR is: Does ECR actually produce better outcomes than its alternatives? And, more pointedly, does it produce improved environmental outcomes?

Focusing on the latter question is not to ignore questions about other types of outcomes. In fact, attention to the question of environmental outcomes provides an intriguing way to approach economic and social outcomes. Some people have begun to speak of social-ecological systems (B. Aguilar-Gonzalez, personal communication with the author, June 7, 2004) in order to emphasize the reality that humans are an integral part of the environment and reductionist analyses that separate us from our environment risk missing key understandings.

Yet this question of improved environmental outcomes is in many ways an unfair question. Perhaps more fundamental, it is one that is impossible to answer, at least as currently phrased. It is unfair because it holds ECR to different standards than exist for other mechanisms for addressing environmental conflict and assumes a uniformity among ECR processes that does not exist. There is too much variety of subject matter, scale, goals, complexity, and process characteristics to offer any sort of blanket judgment about ECR as a whole.

This question of improved outcomes also suggests an expectation of linear causality and a level of understanding about complex environmental systems that rarely exists, and even then only at a limited level. Furthermore, an ECR process may be only one of innumerable actions with an impact on a particular system, and allocating responsibility among those actions may literally be impossible.

Having declared the question of environmental outcomes unfair and impossible to answer, it nonetheless is critical for anyone who believes that ECR has value to address that question. ECR lacks legitimacy with many critical sectors. Since 2003, three states (Oregon, Massachusetts, and Florida) that had institutionalized public disputes programs with substantial ECR caseloads lost funding or their institutional base in state government. The William and Flora Hewlett Foundation is ending its conflict program, and its environmental program, which used to support many ECR efforts, moved to other priorities in the early 2000s. And many influential environmental advocates remain skeptical about ECR's value. Indeed, as leading federal agencies embrace the language of collaboration, the concern that such language is a cover for allowing environmental protections to lapse grows (Kenney, 2000; McCloskey, 1996).

There is a better question for those who are interested in this issue: How can we respond intelligently and with authority when asked about the impact of ECR on the environment?

Variety of ECR. The answer to that question encompasses several dimensions. First, as should be apparent by now, the reference to "environmental conflict resolution" contains such a variety of elements that generalized conclusions about ECR are virtually meaningless. So the question of outcomes along with any other question posed about ECR needs to be addressed to either a particular ECR effort or a class of ECR processes with similar issues, sponsorship, purposes, funding, structure, and process.

Challenge of Environmental Outcomes. "Environmental outcomes" is too sweeping a term to address without clarification. It *is* possible to ascertain an improved environmental outcome when such outcomes are narrowly defined. Some measurable goals can be tied to participant aspirations and ECR goals. A wolf recovery project that counts numbers of wolves, removal of pest or invasive species, a riparian buffer project that plants trees, an in-stream flow agreement that sets new requirements, a plan that identifies water quality goals, nutrient reduction in a body of water: these are the types of environmental outcomes that may at times be subject to clear, relatively easy, and understandable assessment.

But these actions—"pump" related, using Leopold's term 1949—may not translate into a healthy ecosystem—what he terms "the well." So conclusions of this sort are at best intermediate products that are likely to be inconclusive for the larger question about improving the environment.

Complexity of Environmental Systems. Whatever the scale of the ecological system in question, it functions with such complexity that determining improvement with high confidence levels is very difficult. Understanding current and improved ecosystem health requires a prior understanding of ecological processes and systems interaction particular to a place or system. Such understanding is rare except at a basic level; even simple ecological systems demonstrate all the fascinating but hard-to-pin-down characteristics of complexity, such as fundamental uncertainty and nonlinear dynamics. The idea that anyone can fully describe and model such systems that receive a particular set of inputs, and can then determine the exact impact of those inputs, is inaccurate, if not deceptive. As Brogden (2003) notes in her excellent analysis of this question, what may constitute "the environment" is a moving target.

Linking Environmental and Social Outcomes. We are beginning to value resilience and adaptive capacity as opposed to stability and to speak in terms such as "nature evolving" rather than "maximum sustainable yield" (Holling, Gunderson, and Ludwig, 2002). Exciting work by ecologists, economists, and others examining the interaction between humans and nature is leading to new insights about the links between economic and human development, on the one hand, and ecosystems and institutions, on the other. The standards of resilience and adaptive capacity from ecosystems are being linked to their corollaries in human systems.

Developing Indicators of Improved Environmental Outcomes. Given this emerging way of understanding ecosystems and the incomplete but intuitively appealing link between ecological and social elements, we can posit a new approach to understanding and evaluating outcomes. One way of determining whether any particular ECR process is contributing to improved environmental, economic, and sociocultural outcomes could be to develop ECR function (product) indicators that give us some confidence that improvement is being addressed consistent with our best understanding of what is needed for the particular environmental and social systems at stake. This is not the same as characterizing best practices for group process, although one might anticipate that good process would contribute to good outcomes.

So the question arises: Can we develop indicators that demonstrate an ECR process's likely impact on any complex ecological system? A 2003 workshop convened by the Meridian Institute through support of the Community-Based Collaboratives Research Consortium brought together ecologists, ECR researchers, program managers, and ECR practitioners to examine this question of environmental outcomes (see www.cbcrc.org). New research designs are being developed to further these concepts. Examples of the types of indicators that might be possible follow:

- If understanding of ecosystem functioning requires knowledge of inputs and withdrawals that may not be readily identified by so-called standard science, did the ECR effort provide such knowledge (local, indigenous)? Did participants accept such knowledge?

- If understanding of ecosystem functioning, with all of its complexity and its many values, is considered an important element in making environmental, economic, and social improvements, then did an ECR effort improve collective knowledge and individual understanding of that sort?

- If improvement requires an understanding of the impact of ECR's actions on the conditions under consideration, are conditions being monitored and assessed?

- If improvement requires changes in plans and activities consistent with what is being learned, is an ECR process making those changes (learning from its mistakes)?

- If improvement requires adjustments based on the inherent shifting conditions particular to an environmental system, does the ECR process provide for those adjustments?

- If environmental, economic, and social outcomes are improved when unnecessary (redundant, irrelevant) system-blocking barriers to effective management can be identified, is an ECR process identifying such barriers? Is it contributing to overcoming those barriers?

- If improvement requires an ability to respond quickly, is the ECR process promoting and enacting practices that in fact respond quickly to new information?

- If complex systems contain certain elements or behaviors (nodes) that are most sensitive to inputs and other changes, are ECR processes identifying those key elements and behaviors?

Conclusion

Any synthesis of this sort inevitably has shortcomings, like the inability to incorporate ongoing research that has not yet been published. We can look forward to many such studies. The USIECR work included here is continuing and expanding its scope. Judith Innes and David Booher are conducting ongoing case studies of several collaborative processes in California. Bruce Stiftel and Michael Elliott are exploring research approaches and methods to analyzing long-term institutional and organizational culture changes brought about through years of collaborative processes and projects. Juliana Birkhoff and RESOLVE are developing an ECR database that potentially will allow for substantial cross-case comparisons. Steven Yaffee is documenting how collaborative groups can incorporate evaluation into their planning. Michael Elliott and Greg Bourne are conducting an evaluation for the EPA of several facilitated brownfield redevelopment pilot projects. Andy Rowe and Bonnie Colby are conducting an evaluation that incorporates an assessment of the cost-effectiveness of mediation sponsored by the EPA and the state of Oregon. Paul Sabatier and William Leach continue to extrapolate lessons from their growing database of collaborative watershed projects. And the Community-Based Collaboratives Research Consortium is sponsoring several efforts to get to the question of environmental outcomes for community-based ECR efforts.

A complete catalogue of what is known through "evidenced-based research" (O'Leary, 1995) will never reach the hands (and minds) of other researchers, program managers, and practitioners, much less policymakers and consumers or potential and actual participants. In fact, most of what will inform members of these groups will be their own experience.

Birkhoff (2002) has done the ECR field an enormous favor by examining how mediators and facilitators learn. Her analysis applies to other interested parties as well. The ECR field is fundamentally no different from other professions in how its practitioners learn. As she asserts, individuals working within a knowledge-based profession may not gain that knowledge through academic or empirically derived learning:

> There are other ways of knowing what all of us use to make sense of our world and to pass our understandings on to each other. . . . Whichever way individuals or groups know and learn it is always an approximation, a partial picture, or pictures of reality. Human perceptions are bounded and limited. Since there are many valid ways of knowing and learning, our challenge is to learn how to synthesize learnings from different ways of knowing to enrich our practice and improve the conflict resolution field [p. 3].

We should approach the research presented here and elsewhere as we should approach our own experiences as practitioners, researchers, program managers, funders, or ECR consumers: with an inquiring mind, a tolerance for ambiguity and uncertainty, and an expectation that we will always be hungry for more answers and understanding that allow us to do better work.

References

Amy, D. *The Politics of Environmental Mediation.* New York: Columbia University Press, 1987.

Andrew, J. S. "Examining the Claims of Environmental ADR: Evidence from Waste Management Conflicts in Ontario and Massachusetts." *Journal of Planning Education and Research,* 2001, *21* (2), 166–183.

Bacow, L. S., and Wheeler, M. *Environmental Dispute Resolution.* New York: Plenum Press, 1984.

Beierle, T. C., and Cayford, J. "Dispute Resolution as a Method of Public Participation." In R. O'Leary and L. B. Bingham (eds.), *The Promise and Performance of Environmental Conflict Resolution.* Washington, D.C.: Resources for the Future, 2003.

Bingham, G. *Resolving Environmental Disputes: A Decade of Experience.* Washington, D.C.: Conservation Foundation, 1986.

Bingham, L. B., Fairman, D., Fiorino, D., and O'Leary, R. "Fulfilling the Promise of Environmental Conflict Resolution." In R. O'Leary and L. B. Bingham (eds.), *The Promise and Performance of Environmental Conflict Resolution.* Washington, D.C.: Resources for the Future, 2003.

Birkhoff, J. (2002). "Evaluation and Research." In S. Senecah (ed.), *Critical Issues Papers* (pp. 48–69). Washington, D.C.: Association for Conflict Resolution, 2002.

Brogden, M. "The Assessment of Environmental Outcomes." In R. O'Leary and L. B. Bingham (eds.), *The Promise and Performance of Environmental Conflict Resolution.* Washington, D.C.: Resources for the Future, 2003.

Buckle, L. G., and Thomas-Buckle, S. R. "Placing Environmental Mediation in Context: Lessons from 'Failed' Mediations." *Environmental Impact Assessment Review,* 1986, *6* (1), 55–60.

Conley, A., and Moote, A. *Collaborative Conservation in Theory and Practice: A Literature Review.* Tucson, Ariz.: Udall Center for Studies in Public Policy, University of Arizona, 2001.

Daniels, S. E., and Walker, G. B. *Working Through Environmental Conflict: The Collaborative Learning Approach.* Westport, Conn.: Praeger, 2001.

d'Estrée, T. P. "Achievement of Relationship Change." In R. O'Leary and L. B. Bingham (eds.), *The Promise and Performance of Environmental Conflict Resolution.* Washington, D.C.: Resources for the Future, 2003.

d'Estrée, T. P., and Colby, B. G. *Guidebook for Analyzing Success in Environmental Conflict Resolution.* Fairfax, Va.: Institute for Conflict Analysis and Resolution, George Mason University, 2000.

d'Estrée, T. P., and Colby, B. G. *Braving the Currents: Evaluating Conflict Resolution in the River Basins of the American West.* Norwell, Mass.: Kluwer, 2003.

d'Estrée, T. P., Dukes, E. F., and Navette-Romero, J. "Environmental Conflict and Its Resolution." In B. Bechtel and A. Churchman (eds.), *Handbook of Environmental Psychology.* New York: Wiley, 2002.

Dotson, A. B. *"No Go" Negotiations: Reflections on Practice.* Philadelphia: Association of Collegiate Schools of Planning, 1993.

Dukes, E. F. "Public Conflict Resolution: A Transformative Approach." *Negotiation Journal,* 1993, *9* (1), 45–57.

Dukes, E. F. *Resolving Public Conflict: Transforming Community and Governance.* Manchester: Manchester University Press, 1996.

Dukes, E. F. "Integration in Environmental Conflict." *Conflict Resolution Quarterly,* 2001, *19* (1), 103–115.

Dukes, E. F. "From Enemies, to Higher Ground, to Allies: The Unlikely Partnership Between the Tobacco Farm and Public Health Communities." In W. R. Lovan, M. Murray, and R. Shaffer (eds.), *Participatory Governance: Planning, Conflict Mediation and Public Decision-Making in Civil Society.* London: Ashgate Press, 2004a.

Dukes, E. F. "Why—and Why Not—Dialogue?" In G. Sigurdson (ed.), *The Dialogue Forum Reflections.* Vancouver: Morris J. Wosk Centre for Dialogue, Simon Fraser University, 2004b.

Dukes, E. F., and Firehock, K. *Collaboration: A Guide for Environmental Advocates.* Charlottesville, Va.: Institute for Environmental Negotiation, Wilderness Society, National Audubon Society, 2001.

Emerson, K., Nabatchi, T., O'Leary, R., and Stephens, J. "The Challenges of Environmental Conflict Resolution." In R. O'Leary and L. B. Bingham (eds.), *The Promise and Performance of Environmental Conflict Resolution.* Washington, D.C.: Resources for the Future, 2003.

Glavovic, B., Dukes, E. F., and Lynott, J. "Training and Educating Environmental Mediators: Lessons from Experience in the United States." *Mediation Quarterly,* 1997, *14*(4), 269–292.

Gwartney, P. A., Fessenden, L., and Landt, G. "Measuring the Long-Term Impact of a Community Conflict Resolution Process: A Case Study Using Content Analysis of Public Documents." *Negotiation Journal,* 2002, *18* (1), 51–74.

Holling, C. S., Gunderson, L. H., and Ludwig, D. "In Quest of a Theory of Adaptive Change." In L. H. Gunderson and C. S. Holling (eds.), *Panarchy: Understanding Transformation in Human and Natural Systems.* Washington, D.C.: Island Press, 2002.

Innes, J. "Planning Through Consensus Building: A New View of the Comprehensive Planning Ideal." *Journal of the American Planning Association,* 1996, *62* (4), 460–472.

Innes, J. "Evaluating Consensus Building." In L. Susskind, S. McKearnan, and J. Thomas-Larmer (eds.), *The Consensus Building Handbook: A Comprehensive Guide to Reaching Agreement.* Thousand Oaks, Calif.: Sage, 1999.

Innes, J. E., and Booher, D. E. "Consensus Building and Complex Adaptive Systems: A Framework for Evaluating Collaborative Planning." *Journal of the American Planning Association,* 1999, *65* (4), 412–423.

Kenney, D. S. *Arguing About Consensus: Examining the Case Against Western Watershed Initiatives and Other Collaborative Groups in Natural Resource Management.* Boulder: Natural Resources Law Center, University of Colorado School of Law, 2000.

Kloppenberg, L. A. "Implementation of Court-Annexed Environmental Mediation: The District of Oregon Pilot Project." *Ohio State Journal on Dispute Resolution,* 2002, *17* (3), 559–596.

Langbein, L. I., and Kerwin, C. M. "Regulatory Negotiation Versus Conventional Rule Making: Claims, Counterclaims, and Empirical Evidence." *Journal of Public Administration, Research and Theory,* 2000, *10* (3), 599–632.

Leach, W., Pelkey, N., and Sabatier, P. "Stakeholder Partnerships as Collaborative Policymaking: Evaluation Criteria Applied to Watershed Management in California and Washington." *Journal of Policy Analysis and Management,* 2002, *21* (4), 645–670.

Leach, W., and Sabatier, P. "Facilitators, Coordinators, and Outcomes." In R. O'Leary and L. B. Bingham (eds.), *The Promise and Performance of Environmental Conflict Resolution.* Washington, D.C.: Resources for the Future, 2003.

Leach, W. D., and Pelkey, N. W. "Making Watershed Partnerships Work: A Review of the Empirical Literature." *Journal of Water Resources Planning and Management*, 2001, *127* (6), 378–385.

Leopold, A. *The Land Ethic. A Sand County Almanac.* New York: Oxford University Press, 1949.

Lowry, K. *Mediation of Complex and Public Interest Cases: An Evaluation Report to the Judiciary.* Manoa: Program on Conflict Resolution, University of Hawaii at Manoa, 1989.

Manring, N. J. "Collaborative Resource Management: Organizational Benefits and Individual Costs." *Administration and Society,* 1998, *30,* 274–291.

McCloskey, J. M. "The Skeptic: Collaboration Has Its Limits." *High Country News,* May 13, 1996.

Moore, S. A. "Defining 'Successful' Environmental Dispute Resolution: Case Studies from Public Land Planning in the United States and Australia." *Environmental Impact Assessment Review,* 1996, *16* (3), 151–169.

National Institute for Dispute Resolution. *Statewide Offices of Mediation: Experiments in Public Policy.* Dispute Resolution Forum, Washington, D.C., 1987.

O'Leary, R. "Environmental Mediation: What Do We Know and How Do We Know It?" In J. W. Blackburn and W. M. Bruce (eds.), *Mediating Environmental Conflicts: Theory and Practice.* Westport, Conn.: Quorum Books, 1995.

O'Leary, R. "Dispute Resolution at the U.S. Environmental Protection Agency." In R. O'Leary and L. B. Bingham (eds.), *The Promise and Performance of Environmental Conflict Resolution.* Washington, D.C.: Resources for the Future, 2003.

O'Leary, R., and Bingham, L. B. (eds.), *The Promise and Performance of Environmental Conflict Resolution.* Washington, D.C.: Resources for the Future, 2003.

O'Leary, R., and Husar, M. "What Environmental and Natural Resource Attorneys Really Think About ADR: A National Survey." *Natural Resources and Environment,* 2002, *16* (4), 262–264.

O'Leary, R., and Raines, S. S. "Lessons Learned from Two Decades of Alternative Dispute Resolution Programs and Processes at the United States Environmental Protection Agency." *Public Administration Review,* 2001, *61* (6), 682–711.

O'Leary, R., and Raines, S. S. "Dispute Resolution at the U.S. Environmental Protection Agency." In R. O'Leary and L. Bingham (eds.), *The Promise and Performance of Environmental Conflict Resolution.* Washington D.C.: Resources for the Future, 2003.

Sipe, N. "An Empirical Analysis of Environmental Mediation." *Journal of the American Planning Association,* 1998, *64* (3), 275–285.

Sipe, N., and Stiftel, B., "Mediating Environmental Enforcement Disputes: How Well Does it Work?" *Environmental Impact Assessment Review,* 1995, *15,* 139–156.

Society of Professionals in Dispute Resolution. *Best Practices for Government Agencies: Guidelines for Using Collaborative Agreement-Seeking Processes.* Washington, D.C.: Association for Conflict Resolution, 1997.

Susskind, L., and others. *Using Assisted Negotiation to Settle Land Use Disputes: A Guidebook for Public Officials.* Cambridge, Mass.: Lincoln Institute of Land Policy, 1999a.

Susskind, L., McKearnan, S., and Thomas-Larmer, J. (eds.), *The Consensus Building Handbook: A Comprehensive Guide to Reaching Agreement.* Thousand Oaks, Calif.: Sage, 1999b.

Susskind, L., and Ozawa, C. "Mediated Negotiation in the Public Sector: Mediator Accountability and the Public Interest Problem." *American Behavioral Scientist,* 1983, *27,* 255–279.

Talbot, A. R. *Settling Things: Six Case Studies in Environmental Mediation.* Washington, D.C.: Conservation Foundation, 1983.

U.S. Institute for Environmental Conflict Resolution. *Preliminary Report on ECR Performance: A Multi-Agency Evaluation Study.* Tucson, Az.: U.S. Institute for Environmental Conflict Resolution, 2004.

Western Consensus Council and Consensus Building Institute. *Community-Based Collaboration on Federal Lands and Resources: An Evaluation of Participant Satisfaction.* Presentation at a conference, Evaluating Methods and Outcomes of Community-Based Collaborative Processes, Salt Lake City, Utah, Sept. 14, 2003.

White, N. P. *State Institutionalized Environmental Mediation in Michigan: Appropriate or Inappropriate?* Lansing: Michigan State University, Department of Resource Development, 1998.

E. Franklin Dukes is director of the Institute for Environmental Negotiation (IEN), University of Virginia. Dukes designs dispute resolution and public participation processes, mediates and facilitates, teaches and trains, and conducts research.

Commentary: Comment on Frank Dukes's "What We Know About Environmental Conflict Resolution"

KIRK EMERSON

ROSEMARY O'LEARY

LISA B. BINGHAM

Frank Dukes's summary and analysis of the empirical research concerning environmental conflict resolution (ECR) was a joy to read. Several of his conclusions struck us as exceptionally insightful. Dukes has demonstrated that we have made a lot of progress since the days of earlier critiques of ECR research (O'Leary, 1995), providing an excellent overview of the empirical literature organized around structural questions in the field. What stands out to us, however, is that few of these questions appear to be well settled by the empirical research cited. This appears to be true for such key characteristics as settlement rates, durability of agreements, comparative process efficiency, and apparently even the value of third-party neutrals.

And yet public and private stakeholders continue to turn to ECR and indeed have extended this innovation over the past thirty years beyond its initial application in the litigation context, to other applications upstream—to the enforcement arena, to rule making, and to policy and site-specific plan development. Federal and state laws have been created, including the Administrative Dispute Resolution Act and the Negotiated Rulemaking Act, to clarify and broaden the use of ECR. Administrative programs have been established—among them, the Conflict Prevention and Resolution Center at the U.S. Environmental Protection Agency, the Collaborative Action and Dispute Resolution Center at the U.S. Department of Interior, and the U.S. Institute for Environmental Conflict Resolution at the Morris K. Udall Foundation—to build infrastructure and garner resources to support more ECR. Indeed, the underlying principles of the field are now being drawn on by some federal agencies to overhaul internal management practices and reform individual and programmatic performance measures.

CONFLICT RESOLUTION QUARTERLY, vol. 22, no. 1–2, Fall–Winter 2004 © Wiley Periodicals, Inc., 221
and the Association for Conflict Resolution

This diffusion of innovation in and of itself may demonstrate the power of case studies and anecdotal information (the field's primary research vehicle to date) to influence individual and institutional choices to invest in ECR. It may also demonstrate the extent to which some of the benefits of ECR are reasonably self-evident and transferable. Indeed, we are heartened by the progress to date.

That said, there is much to be gained by broader, more generalizable study, as Dukes observes, and the extent to which this is beginning to occur is also encouraging. We need to do a much better job validating the claims made for ECR, and this can be done only through the collection of considerably larger data sets and the application of more powerful, multivariable analyses. Despite his observation that we may never know all that we would like to know about ECR, Dukes rightly advocates for more systematic analyses of ECR processes and outcomes. Our comments focus on the consequent need for better model specification as well as the challenges and opportunities for collecting data to build knowledge in the field.

Model Specification

One of the chief reasons the ECR research findings are so unclear is that we have not yet perfected the model. One of the most difficult challenges for ECR research is the heterogeneity of the ECR processes themselves (the independent "interventions") as well as the diversity of applications and intended effects (the dependent outcomes). Aside from generally consistent statements on best practices, there has not been agreement in theory or in practice on the essential determinants for "getting to yes" in complex multiparty environmental negotiations. Nor has there been adequate consideration of the full suite of expected outcomes beyond "getting to yes," including short-term and long-term impacts on the ground (the environmental, social, and economic landscape).

Dukes makes a strong case for the need for additional research into several structural questions, and specifically toward a sensible approach to demonstrating such outcomes. Before we can approach the measurement of ECR performance and cost-effectiveness, however, we must be able to specify and reliably measure the antecedent conditions and factors. Recently, with the assistance of program evaluation experts working with state and federal ECR programs (Emerson and Carlson, 2003), several members of the ECR field are beginning to articulate and refine a generally applicable program theory or logic model.

Without going into the specifics of the emerging program theory here, one of its important contributions may be the specification of controllable factors that contribute to ECR outcomes, including optimal prior conditions, the value added by the third-party neutral, access to quality information, and the necessary dynamics among the parties. In the absence of careful specification and measurement of the ECR process inputs and dynamics, researchers will be hard-pressed to adequately predict immediate outcomes, let alone attribute less proximal impacts on the ground to ECR interventions.

The degree to which ECR processes contribute to or cause certain effects to occur is an important question, particularly if we are trying to compare ECR to other problem-solving or dispute resolution approaches. And accordingly, researchers will need to subject the more traditional corresponding approaches to similar scrutiny. That said, one can argue at this point that ECR is not in fact an "alternative process" anymore, but rather an adjunct or enhancement to existing administrative and judicial processes that may be more appropriate and effective under certain circumstances.

ECR does not stand alone. It always operates in the context of policy development or planning or rule making or enforcement or litigation. Indeed, when it is disembodied from more formal or recognized public decision-making forums or channels, anecdotal evidence suggests that it is considerably more difficult to enforce agreements or adopt and implement recommendations. Given this perspective on ECR, the focus of future research programs should not be, "Does ECR do better than the alternative approach?" but rather, "Under what circumstances does ECR optimize desired outcomes?"

Building Knowledge by Building the Database

While the arguments that Dukes and others make concerning the difficulty of demonstrating positive environmental, social, or economic impacts from ECR are compelling, the fact remains that we must continue to examine the outcomes, broadly defined, of ECR. If biophysical scientists such as Charlie Driscoll, a professor of engineering at Syracuse University, can demonstrate that changes in law made by the 1990 Clean Air Act have had a positive effect in lowering acid rain in the Adirondack lakes of upstate New York (despite the plethora of intervening variables found in nature), ECR experts should be able to demonstrate that after some facilitated or mediated ECR agreement, there were optimizing environmental or economic or social or community benefits. We need to do a better job of measuring cost-effectiveness, costs avoided, and benefits, broadly defined. Clearly, ECR is not intended only to produce environmental outcomes. It is intended to address all interests at the table within the legal guidelines established by law, consistent with the provisions in Section 101 of our National Environmental Policy Act (NEPA). We need to consider the metrics for measuring progress toward achieving productive harmony, fulfilling our trustee obligations for future generations, and engaging in practical problem solving with all affected parties and interests. Significantly, these objectives set forth in NEPA 101, our earliest national statement on sustainability, are very much aligned with the principles and practices of ECR and are currently the subject of study by the National Environmental Conflict Resolution Advisory Committee. In 2002, the U.S. Institute for Environmental Conflict Resolution established a federal advisory committee to provide guidance on the U.S. Institute's statutory direction to assist the federal government in implementing Section 101 of NEPA. Now, in its second year, the National Environmental Conflict Resolution Advisory Committee is preparing findings and recommendations to the U.S. Institute on the connection between ECR and NEPA and the potential for optimizing NEPA 101 objectives through collaborative problem solving and ECR processes.

Taking ECR outcomes seriously requires information not only about ECR, but also about the consequences of using traditional mechanisms for policy development and for regulatory enforcement. The entire field of environmental policy and management needs better monitoring tools and systems to measure change. We need to think about how to build and invest in that system, including how ECR and the myriad other mechanisms for resolving disputes and seeking agreements in a conflict-ridden and polarized climate can be assessed.

Researchers and practitioners must begin asking questions that go to the heart of the claims of ECR proponents. For example, in the area of environmental enforcement, what does on-the-ground, in-the-water, or in-the-air testing reveal about the state of the environment and its ecosystems in environmental conflicts before and after ECR activities, or in cases with and without ECR interventions? How do cleanup activities conducted at sites that use ECR compare with those at sites that do not? What is the success of permitting using ECR as compared to permitting under traditional processes? At what rate do different groups of permits generate litigation or enforcement conflict? What are the social and economic costs and benefits, broadly defined, of using ECR?

Questions such as these provide formidable challenges for ECR advocates. Answering them persuasively means that they must collect and analyze data on indicators that go beyond the process, whether settlement occurred, and whether participants report that they are satisfied. They also must collect the best available economic, social, scientific, and technical information about the state of the environmental media, resource, ecosystem, or species that are the subject of the environmental conflict. Research necessary to inform practice in this regard requires interdisciplinary cooperation among social scientists and biophysical scientists to collect and analyze their implications astutely.

Researchers may not be able to draw meaningful conclusions about outcomes for the environment with data from a single case or site. Yet by consistently collecting data at multiple points in time for a number of cases or sites, they can aggregate results and begin to look for patterns. This is especially important and challenging because ECR cases differ widely. It might be possible, however, to examine them for patterns in the proportion of improvement in various social scientific and biophysical scientific indicators over time. Do certain controversial issues leave the agenda of policymakers? By what percentage does a given contaminant decline in the water or soil? Is economic development made possible? By what proportion of the ultimate goal does the environment improve or a species population recover? Are these proportions similar over a given period of time in processes where ECR is embedded and in processes where it is not?

Thus, the future of ECR will depend partially on the extent to which scholars and practitioners can amass data for answering these types of questions. The rub, of course, is that these data are difficult to collect, a challenge compounded by the massive amounts of data required. To truly assess ECR approaches to environmental governance in empirically informed ways, ideally a Bureau of Labor Statistics–equivalent for environmental and public policy conflict resolution processes and programs is needed. Moreover, as ECR programs themselves become institutionalized and funding sources develop higher expectations regarding demonstrated performance, the field needs to build an infrastructure that will support the next generation of research and evaluation. This will require the consistent collection of core information that is electronic, routine, decentralized, and longitudinal and the formation of multidisciplinary research teams.

Consistent Collection of Core Information

Data collection is getting easier. Albeit in fits and spurts, courts and agencies are moving toward consistent, uniform systems that capture every court or agency location and every case. These systems have as a goal the collection of population data and therefore have the potential to assist the field in meeting the need for comprehensive data. Despite this advance, the typical data set produced by an ECR evaluator or researcher contains sample information for a given time period. While they are important, these time-limited studies are less useful for a court or agency than a continuous information management system. At best, they may help answer specific questions at a single point in time. In contrast, universal information guidelines that would encourage the collection of core information that would be gathered consistently at low cost for key underlying contextual variables, process variables, and a few key indicators for future study would be an ongoing management tool—a way for the agency or court to know where it has been, where it stands, and where it is headed. Such a system could become a central instrument for administrators who must make decisions about resources. For this information to be vital, the agency or court must accurately and consistently collect the information. Such a system would be a researcher's treasure trove.

Electronic Data Collection

When data are maintained in electronic format, they are easier to manipulate for empirical analysis. It is easier to transport, alter, and organize the data's format, isolate specific variables, and include additional dimensions for comparison. While most programs have developed paper tools for data collection (such as surveys and tracking forms), it is already possible to use hand-held digital devices for ECR data collection. Facilitators used these new technologies at a recent mass public participation event in New York City in connection with future land use of the site of the former World Trade Center. Over five thousand people assisted by five hundred volunteer mediators and facilitators engaged in deliberations about this critical public policy issue. Similarly, for ECR and other forms of dispute resolution, the originators of the information (disputants, mediators, facilitators, stakeholders, and public officials) can personally input data, which the agency could download directly into the database. This would eliminate labor-intensive data entry. Until such technological advances are implemented, it is important that information be maintained in viable electronic database formats.

Routine Data Collection

Data collection should be a daily, fully integrated part of every public environmental program, not just ECR programs. Government agencies at the national, state, and local levels have made serious efforts to evaluate their performance with various management and benchmarking techniques. New federal laws, such as the Government Performance and Results Act, require federal agencies to set goals and timetables with which they can judge their own performance. Similar mandates are popping up at the state and local levels. These mandates provide a substantial incentive for agencies to integrate information systems into their programs, because they can use the systems to document their performance and identify areas for additional focus and improvement. Adopting routine data-gathering instruments and procedures provides a unique opportunity to integrate new ways of measuring dispute resolution efforts.

In the federal sector, the Paperwork Reduction Act places some limits on data collection from the public. The Office of Management and Budget supervises and enforces these limits. However, the limits do not apply to internal reporting requirements (data the agency's staff collects or enters). In contrast, most administrators of third-party dispute resolution organizations already require neutrals to participate in some form of reporting as a condition of membership on the roster or as a condition of payment for their services. This is true of the Federal Mediation and Conciliation Service (FMCS), the American Arbitration Association (AAA), and the United States Postal Service (USPS) mediation program, REDRESS. Both the FMCS and the AAA mandate the completion of data collection forms at the end of an arbitration case, so that these organizations can summarize and analyze their activities periodically. The USPS mediation program requires mediators to characterize the nature of the dispute and to report how many disputants and representatives were at the table, how long the process took, and whether there was a settlement.

Another common method of routine data collection is the distribution of a survey at the conclusion of a training session or dispute resolution process. The response rate typically is much higher when participants complete the survey immediately on distribution rather than later. While there is often a moment of euphoria immediately after settlement that may inflate results, these methods can be combined with other sources of information and longitudinal checks. If an agency establishes its survey distribution and collection process so that every participant receives one and completes it immediately after the session, the agency can begin to build up a useful body of information. However, this data collection process works only if efforts are routine and seen as part of everyone's job rather than as something sporadic, optional, and mandated by people from outside the organization.

Decentralized Collection

As the number of information gatherers increases, accuracy becomes harder to control. However, if the research goal is to create a picture of an entire system, it is better to have more data that are less rich than to have fewer data that are richer. More data can be collected if more people are collecting them. Providing constrained data entry tools can address some accuracy issues. Properly structured databases can control how data are recorded, and properly maintained databases with decentralized stewardship of information can reduce error rates and provide feedback to researchers, program managers, neutrals, and disputants.

A major issue that will need to be addressed is the dissemination of data, especially to researchers outside of the program or organization. Some visionaries in the field have imagined ideally the construction of a central repository of ECR data, accessible by researchers, evaluators, and the general public. This meta-database could take a form similar to that employed by the Bureau of Labor Statistics, the Department of Justice Juvenile Crime Data, or even the database housed at the University of Michigan that contains hundreds of data sets from researchers across the spectrum of the social sciences.

Longitudinal Collection

One of the challenges researchers and evaluators face in studying the cost-effectiveness of ECR or its comparable value is knowing when to start and when to stop their observations. When did the conflict or controversy begin? When did opportunity costs of delayed environmental protection and forgone investments begin? When did parties get involved and public funds get invested? When did agreements get forged, formalized, and funded? When did implementation begin and conclude? These complex multiparty collaborations or assisted negotiations take time, and their effects evidence themselves over time. Choosing the appropriate study period is a critical research judgment. Measuring outcomes and impacts over time essentially requires longer-term, longitudinal analysis.

Funding constraints impose time limits on all evaluation projects (Hensler, 2002). A time-limited evaluation may provide a very accurate description of what is happening in programs over the course of one year, but it does not account for the fact that all dispute resolution programs are moving targets. Point-in-time data have value, but that value is limited. This type of static data collection and analysis is an intensive and time-consuming process, and a lag always exists between the time period studied and the publication of a report. Longitudinal data collection allows researchers to analyze over time how changes in the court or program affect outcomes. With longitudinal data collection, important changes that affect the agency or the process no longer threaten the efficacy of collected data but merely become additional variables. These types of time-series analyses will become vital and valuable tools for ECR program directors and researchers.

Moreover, the initial and long-term impacts of a program are likely to differ significantly. As Dukes points out, the ECR literature offers some information about programs' initial or short-term impacts, but little or no information is available about long-term effects. As a result, it is difficult to respond to charges that a program's influence is simply a honeymoon effect that will diminish or disappear over time. If the interest is systemic-level data, and the reality is that systems are big, unwieldy, and slow to change direction, then a much longer time frame will be needed than we traditionally have used in our ADR research (Senger, 2000).

How Do We Get There?

If data collection is consistent, electronic, routine, decentralized, and longitudinal, and especially continuous, a world of possible analyses opens up. (The recent formation of a new Research Section at the Association for Conflict Resolution is a positive development for collaboration between researchers and practitioners. See www.acresolution.org.) Researchers could control more meaningfully for the selection bias that afflicts many ADR studies. It is common, for example, to compare mediated cases with litigated ones. This comparison is flawed, because approximately 90 percent of all cases filed in court settle without a trial. How does one know that the case that settled in mediation would have gone to trial without mediation? Moreover, although mediation is voluntary, we cannot just assume that people are more satisfied with it simply because they chose it.

If we step back and look at the system as a whole, we can ask whether the system is functioning better on some dimension after it affords people the choice to use all the various tools appropriately, including ECR, to optimize environmental policy and its applications. A number of studies by the Federal Judicial Center and the Rand Institute of Civil Justice have used multivariate methods to examine important questions. (For searchable databases and annotated bibliographies of ADR evaluation literature, see the following Web sites: www.caadrs.org, www.spea.indiana.edu/icri, and www.crinfo.org.) These must be broadened to include cost-benefit analyses as well as analyses of other social, economic, and community benefits. Imagine how much richer analyses of environmental and public policy conflict resolution processes and programs could be with consistent, electronic, routine, decentralized, longitudinal data collection. Moreover, this quality of data would allow researchers and evaluators to control systematically for context and system design (McEwen, 1999).

Half the battle is envisioning the end point. The default setting for everyone engaged in solving environmental problems needs to be data collection. Researchers and evaluators need to meld data collection with an information system that gives managers and practitioners what they need and something they can routinely use on their own. The ideal would be intense collaboration among managers, records administrators, computer systems technicians, and researchers to attain a well-designed, well-integrated, and well-implemented system. To accomplish this, mind-sets will need to shift at all levels of organizations. Our hope is that in the future with such standardized data collection and analysis, researchers and practitioners alike will be able to step back, look at the system as a whole, and ask under what circumstances ECR optimizes desired outcomes.

References

Emerson, K., and Carlson, C. "An Evaluation System for State and Federal Conflict Resolution Programs: The Policy Consensus Initiative." In R. O'Leary and L. B. Bingham (eds.), *The Promise and Performance of Environmental Conflict Resolution*. Washington D.C.: Resources for the Future Press, 2003.

Hensler, D. R. "ADR Research at the Crossroads." *Journal of Dispute Resolution,* 2002, *2002* (1), 71–78.

McEwen, C. A. "Toward a Program Based Research Agenda." *Negotiation Journal,* 1999, *15* (4), 325–338.

O'Leary, R. "Environmental Mediation: What Do We Know and How Do We Know It?" In J. Walton Blackburn and W. M. Bruce (eds.), *Mediating Environmental Conflicts: Theory and Practice.* Westport, Conn.: Quorum Books, 1995.

Senger, J. M. "Turning the Ship of State." *Journal of Dispute Resolution,* 2000, *2000* (1), 79–95.

Kirk Emerson is the director of the U.S. Institute for Environmental Conflict Resolution (ECR) of the Morris K. Udall Foundation. The institute assists federal agencies in ECR program development, and provides early case consultation, process and system design, and facilitation services, primarily for interagency and intergovernmental conflicts.

Rosemary O'Leary is Distinguished Professor of Public Administration at the Maxwell School of Syracuse University. Previously O'Leary was cofounder and codirector of the Indiana Conflict Resolution Institute. She has won six national awards and one international award for her research.

Lisa B. Bingham is the Keller-Runden Professor of Public Service at the Indiana University School of Public and Environmental Affairs.

Conflict Resolution Education: The Field, the Findings, and the Future

O ver the past two decades, conflict resolution education (CRE) programs have educated children about constructive approaches to managing conflict in their schools and communities. CRE provides critical life skills necessary for building caring communities and establishing constructive relationships (Jones and Compton, 2003). Educators, administrators, and parents advocate CRE as a critical component to the development of safe and drug-free schools (Heerboth, 2000; King, Wagner, and Hedrick, 2001; Oppitz, 2003).

To sustain program development and funding of CRE, questions of efficacy are paramount. This is truer now more than ever before given the emphasis in the No Child Left Behind Act of 2001, which dictates that all instruction in academic and nonacademic areas (including prevention interventions) must be theoretically based and rigorously evaluated.

To what extent does CRE make the differences so hoped for by educators and parents? To what extent are CRE programs meeting the standards set under No Child Left Behind, and therefore worthy of federal support dollars? This article provides an answer within certain parameters. First, CRE is defined and distinguished from related efforts to clarify the nature of program evaluation research that should be included in this review. Second, structural elements that are expected to influence CRE effectiveness are detailed as a framework for the presentation of research. And third, the overall assessment of CRE field research is used as a foundation for discussion of needed future research.

The Field of Conflict Resolution Education

Conflict resolution education "models and teaches, in culturally meaningful ways, a variety of processes, practices and skills that help address individual, interpersonal, and institutional conflicts, and create safe and welcoming communities" (Association for Conflict Resolution, 2002, p. 1). Conflict resolution education programs provide students with a basic understanding of the nature of conflict, the dynamics of power and influence that operate in conflict, and the role of culture in how we see and respond to conflict.

CRE programs are estimated to be in place in fifteen thousand to twenty thousand of our nation's eighty-five thousand public schools. Several states, including Ohio, Oregon, New Mexico, and Indiana, have made significant progress on statewide implementation of conflict resolution education (Batton, 2002; Ford, 2002; Tschannen-Moran, 2001).

Goals of Conflict Resolution Education Programs

Four broad goals are discernable through the CRE literature. Each goal suggests outcomes that may be monitored to evaluate CRE effectiveness.

Create a Safe Learning Environment. In the 1990s, one of the National Education Goals stated, "All schools in America will be free of drugs, violence and the unauthorized presence of firearms and alcohol, and will offer a disciplined environment that is conducive to learning" (U.S. Department of Education, 1998, p. 1). In response to that goal, Congress passed the Safe and Drug-Free Schools and Communities Act of 1994, which funded the Safe and Drug-Free Schools unit in the U.S. Department of Education. Since its inception, that office has sought to develop, implement, and monitor initiatives that can help create safe learning environments in schools. Among those initiatives are conflict resolution education programs (Cuervo, 2003). Programs that emphasize this goal are interested in the following kinds of outcomes:

- Decreased incidents of violence
- Decreased conflicts between groups of students, particularly intergroup conflicts based on racial and ethnic differences
- Decreased suspensions, absenteeism, and dropout rates related to unsafe learning environments

Create a Constructive Learning Environment. Teachers and administrators know that learning cannot take place without a constructive learning environment for students—one with a positive climate, effective classroom management, and a respectful and caring environment where children feel safe to share ideas and feelings (Lieber, 2003). Teachers often wrestle with classroom management and classroom discipline (Girard and Koch, 1996; Kohn, 1996), especially in urban education environments (Feiman-Nemser, 2003; Shann, 1998). For this goal expected outcomes include:

- Improved school climate
- Improved classroom climate
- Increased respectful and caring environment
- Improved classroom management
- Reduced time that teachers spend on disciplinary problems in the classroom
- Increased use of student-centered discipline

Enhance Students' Social and Emotional Development. At the heart of all CRE is the hope of helping children to develop as better people—to be more socially and emotionally competent so that they can lead happier lives and contribute more positively to society (Kessler, 2003). If this is achieved, the logic is that other CRE goals will also be accomplished (Lantieri, 2001).

It is in the pursuit of this goal that CRE programs most often overlap with social and emotional learning programs (Lantieri and Patti, 1996). When CRE is effective in achieving this goal, the benefits include outcomes like these:

- Increased perspective taking
- Improved problem-solving abilities
- Improved emotional awareness and emotional management
- Reduced aggressive orientations and hostile attributions
- Increased use of constructive conflict behaviors in schools and in home and community contexts

Create a Constructive Conflict Community. Creating a constructive conflict community requires developing and advocating for social justice. A constructive conflict community is also one in which there is a shared responsibility for social ills and social accomplishments. In such a community, destructive conflict is seen as something the community needs to address. This is one of the basic assumptions underlying the notion of restorative justice approaches to CRE (Ierley and Claassen-Wilson, 2003).

Success in creating a constructive conflict community would be evident in outcomes including the following:

- Increased parental and community involvement in school affairs
- Increased links between school CRE and community CRE efforts
- Decreased community tension and violence

Conflict Resolution Education and Related Fields

At its inception, CRE was narrowly focused on the application of mediation models to K–12 populations. Yet in the past twenty years, the field has expanded in form and function, an expansion that has increased its potential as much as it has obscured its boundaries. Today CRE overlaps with a number of related fields like peace education, violence prevention, social and emotional learning, and antibias education.

Peace Education. Salomon (2002, p. 7) describes peace education as including ". . . antiracism, conflict resolution, multiculturalism, cross-cultural training and the cultivation of a generally peaceful outlook." According to Sommers (2003), peace education helps develop communication skills of active listening and assertive speech, problem-solving skills of brainstorming or consensus building, and orientation skills of cultural awareness and empathy. CRE and peace education are similar in terms of basic motivations, goals, key skills, and content. Yet CRE is domestically applied and peace education is internationally applied, and peace education has a stronger emphasis on social justice orientations and larger systemic issues of violence than conflict education programs.

Violence Prevention. Violence prevention programs often include a CRE component, but are more likely to include increases in safety and security issues relevant to the prevention of serious violent behaviors that are, luckily, still quite rare in schools (Burstyn and others, 2001). Violence prevention efforts seek to decrease serious risk behavior, including violence toward self and others, risky sexual behavior, and substance abuse (Wilson, Gottfredson, and Najaka, 2001). CRE is focused more on the development of important life skills that help students find nonviolent ways to handle their problems and thereby may decrease violent behavior.

Social and Emotional Learning. CRE and social and emotional learning (SEL) programs help students develop emotional, cognitive, and behavioral competencies (Elias and others, 1997). Conflict resolution educators heartily endorse the following suggested competencies articulated by the

Collaborative for Academic, Social and Emotional Learning. In the emotional domain, students should learn to identify emotions, control anger, manage frustration, and respect others' feelings. In the cognitive domain, students should develop the ability to take the other's role or perspective, problem-solve, set goals, and cooperate. In the behavioral domain, students should build interpersonal skills necessary for positive social interaction, including negotiating disputes, taking responsibility for actions, managing time, respecting others' space, and appreciating social norms. The differences in CRE and SEL are becoming harder to identify as the fields truly integrate.

Antibias Education. Many people have argued convincingly that CRE does and should overlap with antibias education because prejudice is an underlying cause for conflict, and we need to realize the impact of prejudice on schools and communities (Lantieri and Patti, 1996; Oskamp, 2000). Most antibias education efforts fall into one of the following four categories: cross-cultural awareness, prejudice reduction and appreciation for diversity, hate crime prevention, and examining the systemic roots of oppression to dismantle them.

The World of CRE

As Jones and Compton (2003) articulate, CRE encompasses a number of programs and practices. The substantive and developmental foundation of CRE is enhanced social and emotional competencies through SEL (Elias and others, 1997), with particular emphasis on emotional awareness, empathy and perspective taking, strategic expression, and cultural sensitivity. These competencies are often delivered through specific curricula like Second Step in early elementary years. A second foundational tier is the integration of conflict education in ongoing curricula like language arts, social studies, math, and science (Compton, 2002), a development heralded as critical to the institutionalization of CRE (Batton, 2002). Additional content-specific curricula are taught in general or in programmatic areas such as negotiation skills (Druliner and Prichard, 2003). And targeted programs address specific problems like bullying (Title, 2003), peer harassment (Juvonen and Graham, 2001), and bias-related conflicts (Prutzman, 2003; Smith and Fairman, 2004). The processes in which students and adults are educated include peer mediation (Cohen, 2003), dialogue (Johnson, Johnson, and Tjosvold, 2000), use of expressive arts (Conte, 2001), and restorative justice (Ierley and Claassen-Wilson, 2003).

Given the scope of CRE, there are certain parameters that were used in this review. Although CRE initiatives take place in arenas outside schools, like after-school programs (Whittall, 2003) and juvenile justice facilities (Stewart, 2002), this article focuses exclusively on in-school CRE. There are exciting CRE and peace education efforts outside the United States (Harris and Morrison, 2003), but this review concentrates exclusively on CRE practice in the United States. And finally, although the span of CRE is from preschool to higher education and although valuable research has demonstrated the effectiveness of CRE in these age groups (Sandy and Boardman, 2000; Warters, 1995, 2000), this review will focus on K–12 regular and special needs populations.

Research on Conflict Resolution Education

There has been a great deal of research on CRE, making decisions about focus and boundaries in a research review article a challenge. First, previous literature reviews and generic meta-analyses are presented briefly. These resources are helpful and reduce the need to re-report what has already been described, but they have weaknesses. Most of the earlier reviews group studies with very little discussion of how structural elements of the CRE program are related to implementation processes or outcomes. And given the intense interest in reduction of violence, many reviews focus heavily or exclusively on studies that have outcome measures related to violent acts or violent orientations (Wilson, Gottfredson, and Najaka, 2001). The most egregious example is the U.S. Surgeon General's Report on Youth Violence (2001), which identifies peer mediation as ineffective. Since 2001, this report has been cited by CRE critics and uninformed administrators as "proof" that schools should not implement CRE. Yet this conclusion must be understood in terms of the report's focus on looking at "effectiveness" solely in terms of whether the program prevented serious physical violence (such as murder, stabbing, or shooting). In addition, many of the review articles are somewhat outdated, especially given the amount of published and unpublished research on CRE in the past five years.

Second, key structural elements of CRE are detailed: program types or models, educational level, target population, and implementation specifics. These provide the framework for the review of specific research studies.

Third, the review of research is presented. The emphasis is on providing a balance between methodological detail and practical insight based on differences that make a difference.

Earlier Reviews and Meta-Analyses in CRE and SEL

There are solid general reviews of CRE and SEL that readers will find valuable. Johnson and Johnson (1996a) focused primarily on peer mediation programs and conflict education within a cooperative learning context. The review reports positive findings for efficacy of peer mediation and conflict education, particularly on increases in students' conflict knowledge, self-reported prosocial behavior, and negotiation skills and positive impacts on classroom climate.

In 2000, Sandy and Cochran published a review chapter in *The Handbook of Conflict Resolution* that discusses the evidence in support of SEL and conflict education programs for children in preschool through high school. Of the general review pieces, it provides the most detail on preschool interventions and gives an excellent summary of the Peaceful Kids ECSEL (Early Childhood Education Social and Emotional Learning) Program the authors developed and evaluated at Columbia University Teachers College. ECSEL educates teachers and parents to model and teach emotional awareness, cooperative skills, empathy and perspective taking, and problem solving to preschool children. Sandy and her colleagues reported significant increases in children's assertiveness, cooperation, and self-control and significant decreases in aggressive, withdrawn, and moody behaviors. Preschool staff were able to independently integrate the skills in the class, and parents increased in authoritative (as opposed to authoritarian) parenting practices (Sandy and Boardman, 2000).

In the general CRE area, the most comprehensive review is *Does It Work? The Case for CRE in Our Nation's Schools* (Jones and Kmitta, 2000). This book summarizes the results of the CRE research symposia sponsored by the U.S. Department of Education and convened by the Conflict Resolution Education Network in March 2000. Teams of researchers, educators, and CRE practitioners reviewed research on five topic areas: impact on students, impact on educators and teachers, impact on diverse student populations, impact on school climate, and issues of institutionalization. CRE programs increase students' academic achievement, positive attitudes toward school, assertiveness, cooperation, communication skills, healthy interpersonal and intergroup relations, constructive conflict resolution at home and school, and self-control. It decreases students' aggressiveness, discipline referrals, dropout rates, and suspension rates. There is little research on the effects of CRE on teachers. There is substantial evidence that CRE improves school climate (especially for elementary schools) and classroom climate. This book attests to the woeful lack of research on CRE and diverse and nondominant populations. Measures of success do not include diversity-relevant outcomes (impact on intergroup relations or community harmony is largely ignored), and issues of class or socioeconomic status receive very little attention. However, there is evidence that CRE programs that focus on systemic bias or include "contact theory" can improve intergroup relations (see Pettigrew and Tropp, 2000).

Does It Work? has strengths and weaknesses. The multiple perspectives on the research afforded by writing teams of researchers, practitioners, and educators provide insights often unavailable from exclusively researcher-driven reviews. Looking at CRE more broadly than individual outcomes for students or climate outcomes for schools is valuable as much for what it shows is missing as for what it suggests might be found. The weaknesses of the volume include its emphasis on reporting all the research rather than the best research, and the committee-determined format of structuring review chapters around hypotheses that impaired readability.

In the area of SEL, three review articles are noteworthy. Weissberg and Greenberg (1998) provide a comprehensive review of SEL programs and violence prevention programs, arguing for the efficacy of SEL programs on the development of core emotional competencies, especially for younger children. In 2003, Greenberg and colleagues reviewed school-based intervention and youth development initiatives and concluded that programs in this area are most beneficial when they simultaneously enhance students' personal and social assets as well as improve the quality of the environments in which students are educated. They cite a meta-analysis of 161 positive youth development programs (Catalano and others, 2000) that indicates SEL programs make a difference in improvements in interpersonal skills, quality of peer and adult relationships, and academic achievement, as well as reductions in problem behaviors such as school misbehavior and truancy, violence, and aggression. Greenberg and colleagues (2003) argue that skills-building components and environmental change initiatives are critical; optimal delivery of programs is through trained teachers who integrate the concepts into their regular teaching and do so over a longer period of time (six to nine months).

For many educators faced with teach-to-the-test pressures, questions of academic achievement are uppermost. Zins, Weissberg, Wang, and Walberg (2004) provide valuable evidence that programs that enhance students' social-emotional competence foster better academic performance. When students are more self-aware and emotionally connected, they can focus on academics and achieve in a supportive environment.

Structural Elements of Conflict Resolution Education

What structures of CRE initiatives—that is, which programmatic and policy elements—are identifiable as sources of possible variation in impact? This article concentrates on four structural elements, with additional refinement of relevant structural components discussed within these general categories: program model, educational level, target population, and implementation characteristics.

Bodine and Crawford (1998) identified four program models of CRE: the mediation program approach, the process curriculum approach, the peaceable classroom approach, and the peaceable school approach. Although changes in program models are apparent since the creation of this taxonomy, it is still a useful distinction. The mediation program approach includes the use of peer mediation programs, in which students receive training in mediation and mediate disputes among their peers. In the process curriculum approach, students are taught the conflict curriculum as a separate course, a distinct curriculum outside regular class time or as a daily or weekly lesson in a related content curriculum. The peaceable classroom approach is a whole-classroom methodology that incorporates CRE into the core subjects of the curriculum and into classroom management strategies. This model includes what others have termed "curriculum infusion" (Poliner, 2003). The peaceable school approach is a comprehensive whole-school methodology that builds on the peaceable classroom approach by using conflict resolution as a system of operation for managing the school as well as the classroom. Conflict resolution principles and processes are learned and used by all members of the school (including parents). Also called whole-school programs, they often combine peer mediation with additional training and intervention efforts to provide the whole school with information to improve conflict behavior and develop key social and emotional skills.

The second structural factor, which will be treated here as nested within the program model factor, is educational level. CRE efficacy is influenced by use in elementary, middle, or high school contexts. The most obvious reason to distinguish educational level is the social and cognitive development of students (Selman, 1980). Younger students experience conflict differently and have different abilities to process conflict and its management (Jones and Brinkman, 1994). The second reason is the difference in organizational complexity between elementary, middle, and high schools. Elementary schools are smaller in size, more connected in terms of staff relationships, and more accessible to parent and community involvement than secondary schools. Middle schools, often a hotbed of interpersonal conflicts due to students' physical maturation and increasing peer pressures (Crosse and others, 2002), are much larger and shift from a classroom learning structure to a subject-based course learning structure. High schools, often as large as thirty-five hundred students, are extremely complex structures, often divided into smaller internal houses or learning communities to counteract the enforced anonymity and lack of support in the larger, bureaucratic structure (Hoy, Tarter, and Kottkamp, 1991). CRE efforts developed for and successful in one educational level can be dismal failures at another level.

The third structural factor is the target population for the CRE intervention. There are possible dimensions of difference that can be important: ability (in terms of special needs, at-risk, or regular populations), ethnicity, or gender. Of course, target populations may include adult staff and parents, as well as students.

The fourth structural factor is the implementation of CRE. First, there is the question of fidelity: To what extent is the CRE program or practice being implemented as designed? Second is the question of durability: To what extent is the CRE maintained over time? And third is the question of coordination with existing school structures (for example, discipline structures) and other CRE components—the issue of dispute system design.

Research on CRE

The research reviewed met the following criteria (similar to those used in Wilson, Gottfredson, and Najaka, 2001): (1) it evaluated a distinct intervention, program, or practice within the area of CRE as previously defined; (2) the intervention was school based, conducted in a school building, by school staff, or under school auspices; (3) it used a comparison group evaluation methodology, including nonequivalent comparison group research designs, and the comparison group was a no-treatment or minimal-treatment condition; (4) it had adequate sample size; and (5) it measured at least one of the outcomes relevant to CRE goals discussed earlier. In addition, all attempts were made to locate and review research that had not been included in earlier reviews, with special attention to unpublished reports from funded projects and dissertations.

In some program areas there are meta-analyses specific to that type of CRE. Sections reviewing research in that area begin with a brief discussion of those meta-analyses.

Peer Mediation. Peer mediation is the oldest and most common CRE intervention (Cohen, 2003). The National Association for School Principals reports that 75 percent of principals say they have some form of violence prevention or CRE and that peer mediation is the most common form (Cohen, 2003).

Burrell, Zirbel, and Allen (2003) conducted a meta-analysis on forty-three studies published between 1985 and 2003 of peer mediation programs that met the following criteria: (1) focused on K–12 student population, (2) used quantitative methods resulting in numerical measurable effects, and (3) involved at least one variable relating to mediation training or practices in which outcomes of the actual training or practices were measured. The results overwhelmingly support peer mediation effectiveness in terms of increasing students' conflict knowledge and skills, improving school climate, and reducing negative behavior.

When we look at peer mediation research linked to structural factors, can we obtain even more insight about the effectiveness of peer mediation? Specifically, are peer mediation programs equally effective across educational levels? To refine the analysis, it is important to examine the model of peer mediation used as well as the educational levels.

Structurally, peer mediation programs differ in terms of the training delivery and the program implementation, as well as educational level and linkage with other CRE components. These models can be labeled cadre, curriculum or class linked, or mentoring. In cadre peer mediation programs, student mediators are trained outside of classes and mediate disputes in a private area designated for that purpose. In curriculum or class-linked peer mediation, students in a classroom receive training in integrative negotiation and simple mediation process skills, rotate as mediators, and conduct mediations in class when requested by the teacher or peers in dispute. Mentoring peer mediation models involve student mediators' training younger students as peer mediators within the same school or across educational levels. While cadre peer mediation programs exist at all educational levels, curriculum or class-linked models are most common in elementary school, and mentoring models are most common in secondary schools (with middle school or high school mentors serving elementary school mediators).

- *Peer mediation research in elementary schools.* Some early studies do not specify the model of peer mediation used. These studies also tend to focus on program utility outcomes (number of mediations, percentage of agreements reached) or basic knowledge indexes (whether the student learned mediation skills or negotiation skills). In these studies, third- through sixth-grade students trained as mediators demonstrated significant increases in their use of integrative negotiation behaviors after mediation training. In addition, there was a high percentage of mediations reaching agreement (although simplistic agreements were the norm) (Johnson and Johnson, 1996b, 2001a), and there was some initial evidence that mediators may transfer their constructive conflict skills to sibling conflicts at home (Gentry and Benenson, 1992).
- *Cadre models.* Most peer mediation evaluation in elementary schools concerns cadre programs and concentrates on impacts of peer mediation on the mediators. Studies report that compared to nonmediators, mediators demonstrated increased knowledge of constructive conflict resolution (Korn, 1994; Nance, 1996), were able to mediate successfully (Johnson and colleagues, 1995), and demonstrated observable mediation skills (Winston, 1997). Research even suggests effectiveness for special needs students. Meyer's dissertation (1996) research examined the impact of participation in a peer mediation program on self-perceptions and conflict styles of behaviorally at-risk students. The pretest, posttest control group design using fourth- through sixth-grade subjects found no impacts on perception of self-worth or conflict style, but did find reductions in disciplinary referrals for mediators as compared to nonmediators.

Several studies examined the impact of peer mediation experience in the development of social and emotional competencies of mediators. Some research confirms positive impacts of peer mediation on disciplinary referrals, but fails to find differences between mediators and nonmediators on self-concept or social skills as measured by the Social Skills Rating System (Zucca-Brown, 1997). Conversely, Epstein (1996), using the same basic design and the same measure, reported that mediators had a larger increase in social skills than did disputants or control students.

Three studies investigated the impact of peer mediation on perspective taking. In his dissertation, Mankopf (2003) hypothesized that mediators would have better perspective taking, negotiation ability, attitudes toward fighting, and connectedness to school and family than nonmediators and that mediators who mediated more would demonstrate greater developmental gains. He found partial support for these hypotheses: mediators did score higher on perspective taking and negotiation ability, although experience did not play as much of a factor as anticipated. Lane-Garon (1998) studied the impact of peer mediation on cognitive and affective perspective taking of mediators and disputants. A total of 112 students (62 mediators and 50 nonmediators) in grades 4 through 8 were administered perspective-taking measures over the course of an academic year. Both mediators and disputants showed a significant increase in cognitive and affective perspective taking, but mediators' scores were significantly higher than disputants. In a second study, Lane-Garon (2000) examined the impact of peer mediation on cognitive perspective taking, strategy choice, and school climate. Her design compared mediators and nonmediators, by gender and ethnicity, from pretest to posttest. Eighty students in grades 4 through 6 served as subjects. The results show significant increases in mediators' perspective taking and selection of problem-solving conflict strategy. She also found ethnic differences, with African American participants (both mediators and nonmediators) showing the greatest increase in perspective taking and Hispanic participants showing the greatest positive change in conflict strategy choice when compared to Anglo participants.

• *Curriculum or class linked.* Most of the research in class-linked peer mediation comes from the Teaching Students to be Peacemakers Program (TSPP) developed by David and Roger Johnson at the University of Minnesota. TSPP creates a cooperative learning context, instructs students in integrative negotiation and mediation skills and concepts, and uses in-class peer mediation sessions. Teachers are trained to deliver the TSPP lessons (Fitch and Marshall, 1999).

Johnson and Johnson (2001b) conducted a meta-analysis of seventeen evaluation studies examining TSPP effectiveness in eight schools in two countries. Students ranged from kindergarten to grade 9 and were from urban, suburban, and rural schools. The results indicated that students learned the conflict resolution procedures taught, retained their knowledge throughout the school year, applied the knowledge to actual conflicts, transferred skills to nonclassroom and nonschool settings, and used the skills similarly in family and school settings. In addition, some of the studies revealed that exposure to TSPP increased academic achievement and decreased discipline referrals and classroom management problems.

Although not included in the meta-analysis, two earlier TSPP studies (Johnson and Johnson, 1996c; Johnson and others, 1995) showed similar results in terms of students' conflict knowledge and tendency toward integrative negotiation in hypothetical and actual conflicts.

Two other studies investigated class-linked peer mediation using the community boards model and applied in playground mediations. Hart and Gunty (1997) used a nonequivalent control group design to study fourth- through sixth-grade mediators and found that the number of student conflicts and the average time-off-teaching per conflict decreased significantly in the classroom. However, Miller (1995) examined mediators and disputants on self-concept and used teacher and parent ratings of student behavior (Behavior Dimensions Rating Scale) and found no differences on any dependent measures.

• *Mentoring peer mediation.* A relatively recent and exciting approach to peer mediation is the mentoring model in which older students trained as mediators mentor younger students. One of the best programmatic examples is the Winning Against Violent Environments (WAVE) programs developed by Carole Close and institutionalized in the Cleveland Municipal School District. Bickmore (2002) evaluated twenty-eight urban elementary schools in which WAVE high school mediators trained twenty-five to thirty elementary mediators in each school, conducted follow-up visits with schools, presented at school staff meetings, and led workshops for parent groups. Data were collected on the understanding of conflict, attitudes toward conflict, perceptions of school climate (using the Students Attitudes About Conflict survey), attendance rate, number of suspensions, and academic achievement (in terms of Ohio Proficiency Tests of reading and citizenship). The results indicate that peer mediation has significant positive results for mediator and nonmediator attitudes about conflict, understanding of conflict, and perceptions of school climate. The mediators tended to have more significant increases on these measures than nonmediators, but this varied by experience level. In schools where the mediation program was inactive, the mediators did not score higher on these indices than nonmediators. Suspension rates were considerably reduced in the WAVE schools, and academic achievement scores increased in WAVE schools considerably more than the district average.

Lupton-Smith (1996) also examined a mentoring program using high school mentors, but focused on whether the mentoring experience affected the high school mediators' moral reasoning and ego development. The nonequivalent control group design compared mentors with other high school students involved in peer helping activities. The study found no significant differences, a finding perhaps attributable to the selection of a "helping" comparison group.

Lane-Garon and Richardson (2003) report on a cross-age mentoring mediation program in which university students served as mentors to elementary school mediators. Impacts on elementary students' cognitive and affective perspective taking, perceptions of school climate, and academic performance were assessed. The results show strong support for the impact of peer mediation on increases in mediators' cognitive and affective perspective taking and perceptions of school climate (especially in the area of perceived school safety).

Peer Mediation Research in Middle Schools. There is less research on the effectiveness of peer mediation programs in middle or high schools. This makes sense since peer mediation programs are implemented predominantly in K–6 populations. The available research reports on cadre and class-linked programs in middle schools. No evaluations of mentoring programs were found.

- *Cadre models.* The research on these programs reports findings consistent with those in elementary school cadre models, even though middle school students are somewhat more cynical in general about peer mediation (Robinson, Smith, and Daunic, 2000). Mediators in middle school cadre programs, when compared with nonmediators, increase their knowledge of constructive conflict and indicate they will use those approaches (Bell and others, 2000; Stewart, 2000). These students, even very aggressive ones, also increase their self-esteem and self-concept (Fast, Fanelli, and Salen, 2003).
- *Curriculum or class-linked programs.* Once again, and as included in the TSPP meta-analysis, specific research in middle schools using the TSPP program reports that students in sixth through ninth grades benefit from this experience; they gain knowledge about conflict processes, increase their willingness to use integrative negotiation, and have more positive attitudes toward conflict (Dudley, 1995; Dudley, Johnson, and Johnson, 1996; Johnson and Johnson, 1997). However, this research does not demonstrate a positive impact of peer mediation on classroom climate.

Smith, Daunic, Miller, and Robinson (2002) conducted an evaluation of a curriculum-linked peer mediation program in three middle schools over a four-year period. The curriculum was taught schoolwide by teachers, but not all students received mediation training. There was no evidence of improvement in students' or teachers' perceptions of school climate, perhaps due to implementation problems since some teachers did not complete the curriculum in their classes. There were no differences between mediators and nonmediators on any of the dependent measures.

Farrell and his colleagues have found some impressive results from their Responding in Peaceful and Positive Ways (RIPP) program developed for urban middle schools that serve a predominantly African American student population. RIPP is a twenty-five-session social-cognitive conflict education curriculum, with problem solving the major focus of the curriculum; it includes a peer mediation component (Farrell, Meyer, Kung, and Sullivan, 2001). In one evaluation of RIPP with classes of sixth graders at three urban middle schools, students were randomized to intervention ($N = 321$) and control groups ($N = 305$). RIPP participants had fewer disciplinary violations and in-school suspensions than control students, an impact that lasted for twelve months after program implementation (Farrell, Meyer, and White, 2001). In one middle school, RIPP-6 was implemented and outcomes assessed using a battery of measures completed by students at pretest, posttest, and one-year follow-up. Compared with students in the comparison group, students who participated in RIPP-6 reported significantly lower approval of violent behavior, more peer support for nonviolent behaviors, less peer pressure to use drugs, and greater knowledge of the intervention at posttest. They also reported significantly lower posttest frequencies of physical aggression, drug use, and peer provocation (Farrell, Valois, and Meyer, 2002).

Peer Mediation Research in High Schools.   As with middle schools, the peer mediation evaluation research concerns only cadre or curriculum-linked programs.

- *Cadre models.* In general, the research in this area is not supportive of peer mediation. Nelson (1997) studied the impact of mediation on self-esteem, social skills, and frequency of disciplinary referrals, but found no differences between the mediators and the control students, although these findings may be attributable to an inadequate sample size ($N = 51$). Sweeney (1996) was interested in whether mediation affected moral reasoning, orientations to others, and self-esteem; no significant differences were found between mediators and controls.

Potts's dissertation research (2002) shows more promising results. She examined the impact of mediation on interpersonal negotiation strategies (a measure of perspective taking and social problem solving) and coping styles. She compared mediators, disputants, and controls and found that mediators demonstrated higher levels of social competence and that more experienced mediators had the highest levels. Tolson and McDonald (1992) reported that students with high disciplinary referrals sent to mediation had significantly fewer referrals than students sent to traditional disciplinary processes.

- *Curriculum or class-linked models.* Stevahn and her colleagues have contributed the research in this area, although only one study deals with U.S. schools (Stevahn, Johnson, Johnson, and Schultz, 2002). Classes were randomly assigned to receive a five-week conflict curriculum with peer mediation or act as control groups. As in similar studies in elementary and middle schools, the results strongly confirm that training increased student knowledge of conflict and use of integrative negotiation. A very important outcome was that classes with the conflict resolution and peer mediation training also had higher academic achievement, greater long-term retention of academic learning, and greater transfer of academic learning in social studies to language arts.

Comparative Research in Peer Mediation. Only one study has compared different models of peer mediation across educational levels on individual student and school outcomes. The Comprehensive Peer Mediation Evaluation Project (Jones and others, 1997) involved twenty-seven schools in three communities (Philadelphia, Laredo, and Denver). In each community a 3 × 3 field experiment compared program models (peer mediation cadre programs, peer mediation curriculum-linked whole-school programs, and control schools) in each of three educational levels: elementary, middle, and high school. This study was guided by four research questions:

- Does peer mediation have an impact on students' conflict attitudes and behavior in terms of how frequently they are involved in conflict, how frequently they help others who are in conflict, their values about prosocial behavior in general, their conflict styles, their tendency toward aggressive behavior, their development of perspective taking and collaborative conflict orientations, or their ability to demonstrate or enact the skills taught in training?

- Does peer mediation have an impact on teachers' and students' perceptions of school climate?

- Are cadre programs better than whole-school programs (or vice versa)? In terms of impact on students' attitudes and behaviors, school climate, and program utility, is there a difference in the efficacy of these program models?

- Are peer mediation programs equally effective (or ineffective) for elementary, middle, and high schools?

All peer mediation schools (cadre and whole school) received peer mediation training and program implementation at the beginning of fall semester of each year. Schools receiving whole-school programs had curricular infusion training and conflict skills training by the end of fall semester.

Data were collected over two years. The sample consisted of multiple responses from each of the following (approximate numbers used):

- For elementary schools: 140 peer mediators, 1,300 control students, 400 conflict training students, and 275 teachers and administrative staff
- For middle schools: 140 peer mediators, 1,600 control students, 550 conflict training students, and 400 teachers and administrative staff
- For high schools: 150 peer mediators, 2,500 control students, 450 conflict training students, and 550 teachers and administrative staff

Thus, the overall sample consisted of 430 peer mediators, 5,400 control students, 1,400 conflict training students, and 1,225 teachers and administrative staff.

The data from the CPMEP study reveal that peer mediation programs provide significant benefit in developing constructive social and conflict behavior in children at all educational levels. It is clear that exposure to peer mediation programs, whether cadre or whole school, has a significant and lasting impact on students' conflict attitudes and behaviors. Students who are direct recipients of program training have the most impact, although students without direct training also benefit. The data clearly demonstrate that exposure to peer mediation reduces personal conflict and increases the tendency to help others with conflicts, increases prosocial values, decreases aggressiveness, and increases perspective taking and conflict competence. Especially for peer mediators, these impacts are significant, cumulative, and sustained for long periods. Students at all educational levels trained in mediation are able to enact and use the behavioral skills taught in training.

The CPMEP results prove that peer mediation programs can significantly improve school climate at elementary levels, but the impact in middle and high schools is not significant, possibly due to limited diffusion capability in larger organizational environments. Similar results were obtained from a much smaller comparative study in the Dallas Public Schools (Nelson-Haynes, 1996), which found that peer mediation programs have a positive impact on student perceptions of school climate in elementary but not secondary schools.

Process Curricula. Process curricula are reviewed in terms of specific SEL curricula, negotiation and general conflict curricula, and bullying-prevention curricula. No research meeting the review criteria was found for bias awareness programs, dialogue programs, restorative justice, or expressive arts programs in CRE.

- *SEL curricula.* Two SEL curricula have been selected for mention in this section because they have strong overlap with CRE.

The PATHS Program is a classroom-based curriculum implemented by teachers for elementary grades (Kusche and Greenberg, 1995) and is effective for regular and special needs students (learning disabled or emotionally disturbed) (Greenberg and Kusche, 1996). PATHS helps children develop problem-solving, self-control, and emotional regulation skills. The program consists of fifty-seven lessons of twenty- to thirty-minute duration that are taught two to three times per week. A pretest-posttest control group design with random assignment of classrooms from schools in high-risk areas across sites in the United States has been conducted with over sixty-five hundred students from 198 intervention classrooms and 180 matched comparison classrooms (Conduct Problems Prevention Research Group, 1999). The findings reveal PATHS decreased aggression and hyperactive-disruptive behaviors and improved classroom atmosphere. Quality of program implementation (treatment integrity) was significantly related to decreases in teacher reports of classroom aggression and to improved classroom climate. In another investigation, one- and two-year longitudinal findings suggest that the PATHS curriculum may have lasting effects on emotional understanding and interpersonal social problem-solving skills (Greenberg and Kusche, 1996).

The Second Step Program is a classwide social skills program implemented by teachers for all preschool through middle school children (Grossman and others, 1997). The objective of the program is to teach students skills related to empathy, impulse control, and anger management.

The program consists of thirty classroom lessons (each is approximately thirty-five to forty-five minutes in duration) typically taught one to two times per week. A pretest-posttest control group design with random assignment of schools to Second Step training versus control was conducted with 790 second and third graders (see Grossman and others, 1997). Students participating in Second Step were observed to exhibit less physical aggression and more prosocial behaviors than students in the control condition. Observations confirmed that treatment effects were largely maintained over a six-month period.

Additional research suggests that target populations may respond differently to Second Step. Broadbear (2001) found that children of divorce showed more decrease in negative conflict than children from intact marriages. And Washburn (2002) discovered that Second Step was particularly effective with low-income urban, minority students, although Taub's research (2002), which may have been hampered by inadequate sample size, found little positive impact on low-income, rural elementary school students. Finally, some studies fail to show any impact of Second Step (Botzer, 2003; Lillenstein, 2002), although program implementation fidelity is not established in these studies.

One study compared Second Step to a class-linked peer mediation program for third- and fourth-grade students (Harris, 1999). Classes were randomly assigned to treatment and control conditions. Teachers delivered the curricula over a semester. The results indicated no difference in effectiveness of the programs; however, there was a treatment by gender effect: boys performed better in the peer mediation class, and girls performed better in Second Step.

• *Negotiation and general conflict curricula.* Other than research concerning the TSPP program, which some consider to be a conflict curricula more than a peer mediation program, there is very little research on the effectiveness of general negotiation curricula. For example, Program for Young Negotiators (Nakkula and Nikitopoulos, 2001) is a popular program based on interests-based negotiation, but no studies were found that evaluated its effectiveness.

DuRant, Barkin, and Krowchuk (2001) report on a conflict curriculum used with low-income, minority sixth graders in four middle schools; intervention schools had 292 students and the control schools 412 students. The Peaceful Conflict Resolution and Violence Prevention Curriculum, a thirteen-module skills-building curriculum, taught identification of situations that could result in violence; avoidance, confrontation, problem-solving, and communication skills; conflict resolution skills; the conflict cycle; the dynamics of a fight; and how to express anger without fighting. The primary outcome variable was a five-item scale assessing the frequency of fighting and weapon-carrying behaviors and a scale measuring intentions to use violence in eleven hypothetical situations. From pretest to posttest, there was a decrease in the use of violence by students in the intervention group and an increase in the use of violence in the control group.

An innovative approach to delivering a conflict curriculum is through computer-generated lessons. Bosworth and her colleagues (2000) developed SMART talk, a computer-based intervention containing anger management and conflict-resolution modules. The 558 middle school students were randomly assigned to treatment or control groups and were assessed on self-awareness, attitudes toward violence, and intentions to use nonviolent strategies. SMART talk was successful in diminishing students' acceptance of violence and increased their intentions to use nonviolent strategies.

Three studies of conflict education curricula focus on urban minority populations. Heydenberk, Heydenberk, and Bailey (2003) implemented Project Peace, a teacher-delivered CRE program in fourth- and fifth-grade classes and evaluated the impacts on students' moral reasoning and attitudes about conflict (using Students Attitudes About Conflict [SAAC]). All treatment classrooms showed significant increases in moral reasoning ability and constructive conflict orientation. In a two-year study of the impact of a conflict education curriculum in middle and high school special-needs students (in an alternative disciplinary school), researchers found that the conflict curriculum had a significant impact on students' misconduct rates, hostile attribution, and aggressive orientation (Jones and Bodtker, 1999; Bodtker, 2001).

• *Bullying prevention programs.* In the past five years, many states have mandated bullying prevention programs (Title, 2003). School administrators and teachers search for effective curricula to stem the prevalence of bullying behavior (Lumsden, 2002). There is considerable research about bullying behaviors and consequences (Boulton, Trueman, and Flemington, 2002; Espelage and Swearer, 2003; Price, 2003) and teacher orientations to bullying (Craig, Henderson, and Murphy, 2000), but only three studies in the United States examine the efficacy of bullying prevention programs (and one of those is still in progress).

Instead of conducting the necessary research on these programs in U.S. contexts, educators and practitioners continue to refer to research conducted by Olweus in Norway (1991). This large-scale evaluation looked at the efficacy of the bullying program with Norwegian children ages eight to sixteen. The results indicate sustained (at least two years) reductions in school aggression (bullying was reduced by 50 percent), fighting, vandalism, alcohol abuse, and truancy. The effects were more pronounced the longer the program was in place. Other reports of effectiveness of the Bullying Prevention program have been forthcoming from Canada (Pepler, Craig, Ziegler, and Charach, 1994) and England (Whitney, Rivers, Smith, and Sharp, 1994). A study conducted by Melton and others (1998) in the United States was not obtainable. The only other study of an Olweus-based program in the United States was a process evaluation of program implementation (Price, 2003). Cunningham (2001) reports on a study in progress that will evaluate the Healthy Schools bullying prevention program in two urban middle schools, but results are pending.

Orpinas and Horne (2003) studied the application of the Peaceable Place program developed by the Mendez Foundation, a standard conflict education curriculum to teach K–5 students conflict resolution skills, anger management, respect for self and others, and effective communication. There was a 40 percent reduction among younger children (K–2) in mean self-reported aggression and a 19 percent reduction in mean self-reported victimization. Among third through fifth graders there was a 23 percent reduction in mean reported victimization but no significant differences in self-reported aggression.

In her dissertation research, Kaiser-Ulrey (2004) evaluated the BEST (Bullying Eliminated from Schools Together) program developed for middle schools. One hundred twenty-five seventh-grade students were assigned in cohort groups to a treatment or comparison group. Teachers conducted the twelve-week intervention, which consisted of four basic modules including empathy and problem solving. The outcomes measured were bullying incidence, victimization incidence, empathy, prosocial behaviors, global self-esteem, and parental involvement. Results did not support any of the research hypotheses, except for an increase in social skills development of the treatment students.

Peaceable Classroom and Curriculum Integration. One of the most difficult aspects of CRE is finding a way for teachers to incorporate this while they address all the other pressures of mandated curricula and testing (Compton, 2002). Curriculum integration is often done in reading and language arts (Poliner, 2003), but can be done in any subject area.

The National Curriculum Integration Project (NCIP) was a three-year study of curriculum infusion and integration in middle schools in four states (Compton, 2002; Jones and Sanford, 2003; Jones, Sanford, and Bodtker, 2001). A pretest-posttest control group comparison design in each state examined the effect of teaching condition (NCIP experienced teaching, NCIP new teaching, and control teaching) on over a thousand seventh- and eighth-grade students' emotional and conflict competence (conflict orientation, emotional management, perspective taking, and hostile attribution) and classroom climate. Although the NCIP conditions did not significantly influence emotional management, it did have positive impacts on students' perspective taking and use of problem-solving strategies. NCIP has extremely strong positive impacts on classroom climate. As expected, across sites, students in NCIP classes taught by returning, experienced NCIP teachers consistently reported more positive climate (overall and in terms of the dimensions of teacher support, student support, cohesion, safety, and constructive conflict management) than students in classes taught by new NCIP teachers. However, students in either NCIP class perceived a much more positive climate than students in control classes. NCIP impact on classroom climate increased throughout the year, while perceived climate in control classes usually became notably more negative throughout the year.

In terms of the teacher's integration of NCIP concepts into curriculum, when the goals of NCIP are clearly presented, there is strong evidence that teachers are capable of integrating these concepts and practices in their ongoing curricula. There is a learning curve for teachers; it takes sustained effort for a teacher to progress to optimal levels of integration and infusion. However, teachers can effectively mentor other teachers to achieve these levels. Teachers at most sites were able to develop complex and valuable integrated lessons for use in ongoing curricula (mostly English and language arts). While lessons in other disciplines were developed, it was more difficult, especially for the disciplines of math and science.

Peaceable School and Whole-School Programs. Few CRE efforts are truly whole school, and fewer still have been evaluated. One excellent study addresses peaceable school models in elementary schools, and two studies evaluate peaceable school models in middle schools.

At the elementary school level, Responding to Conflict Creatively Program (RCCP) has been the focus of an excellent evaluation (Aber, Brown, and Jones, 2003). RCCP includes teacher training, classroom instruction and staff development, program curriculum, administrators' training, peer mediation, parent training, and a targeted intervention for high-risk youth. RCCP is a complex, multiyear, multilevel CRE program (Selfridge, 2004). Four waves of data on features of children's social and emotional development known to forecast aggression and violence were collected in the fall and spring over two years for a representative sample of 11,160 first to sixth graders from New York City public schools. The results indicate that RCCP, when delivered as designed by the classroom teachers, had a significant impact on reducing attitudes and behaviors predictive of aggression and violence. Positive implications for orientation to academic achievement were also reported. Program fidelity was identified as a critical factor. Students in classes where teachers delivered some RCCP but not the amount or nature prescribed actually performed worse on dependent measures than control students.

The research at the middle school level shows mixed results. Orpinas and colleagues (2000) evaluated a multicomponent violence prevention intervention on reducing aggressive behaviors among students of eight middle schools randomly assigned to intervention or control conditions. The intervention included the formation of a school health promotion council, training of peer mediators and peer helpers, training of teachers in conflict resolution, a violence prevention curriculum, and newsletters for parents. All students were evaluated in the spring of 1994, 1995, and 1996 (approximately nine thousand students per evaluation). Sixth graders in 1994 were followed through seventh grade in 1995 or eighth grade in 1996 or both ($n = 2,246$). Cohort and cross-sectional evaluations indicated little to no intervention effect in reducing aggressive behaviors, fights at school, injuries due to fighting, missing classes because of feeling unsafe at school, or being threatened to be hurt. The Students for Peace experience suggests that interventions should begin prior to middle school, explore social and environmental intervention strategies, and involve parents and community members.

Shapiro and his colleagues (2002) evaluated a middle school CRE intervention (Peacebuilders Program) that trains all school staff to infuse CRE through all aspects of everyday school life. The program was implemented in three middle schools and three elementary schools with one control middle school and one control elementary school. Components of the Peacemakers Program are delivered initially by teachers and remedially by school psychologists and counselors. This study sampled almost two thousand students with pre- and postprogram assessment. There were significant, positive program effects on knowledge of psychosocial skills, self-reported aggression, teacher-reported aggression, a 41 percent decrease in aggression-related disciplinary incidents, and a 67 percent reduction in suspensions for violent behavior.

Assessment and Direction

Not so long ago, when administrators asked, "Does it work?" CRE practitioners had difficulty answering with convincing research evidence. That is no longer the case. This review clearly indicates that although there is more work to be done, the research clearly demonstrates that CRE approaches yield impressive results. The research on peer mediation, especially at elementary levels, confirms that mediators gain social and emotional competency from this experience and that schools can gain from improved classroom and school climate. Those impacts are much less evident with peer mediation in middle and high schools. The research on process curricula is either stunningly good or bad depending on the curricular area. Evidence for the efficacy of basic SEL programs and general conflict education programs is clear. Yet we need much more serious research attention to other curricular areas, especially bullying prevention. The research suggests that general CRE curricula may be effective in preventing bullying, but much more evidence is needed. And some very exciting new practice areas like dialogue, expressive arts, and restorative justice programs have yet to be evaluated rigorously in school settings. Curriculum integration research is solid but not sufficient in quantity or scope. We need replications of the National Curriculum Integration Project to continue to assess this complex process and its benefits. Finally, the whole-school program research, especially on RCCP, proves what many CRE practitioners have known for some time: the need is to address the whole system in a concerted, coordinated, integrated, and sustained effort to yield the most impressive results. It also suggests that a poorly implemented program may be worse than no program at all.

We should concentrate more on longitudinal analyses of CRE. The longest studies we have are three years in duration. But there are students who are potentially affected for life, with only short-term assessments of their experiences.

We need to develop ways of assessing the big questions about attainment of community, social justice, and caring environments. Our attention has been focused on important indicators of larger social objectives, but it is time to attend to the very difficult research tasks of assessing relational and system change.

We must discontinue the emphasis on focusing on segments of CRE in schools that have a variety of potentially synergistic initiatives. We have a program mentality rather than a coordinated-practice mentality. Research goals and designs should be more focused on explaining CRE systems and components and studying their interaction, partial, and cumulative effects.

We should continue to define structural elements that bear on outcomes, enabling practitioners to suggest tailored interventions with reasonable certainty of their effectiveness. And we should attend to structural elements, especially issues of diversity of target population, that have received far too little research attention.

But even with the need for more research, it is clear that CRE programs have a great deal to offer children. The evidence supports Sandy and Cochran's conclusion (2000, p. 340): "Development in conflict resolution education and social-emotional learning skills is so critical to the education of our children that we must actively support infusion of this instruction throughout each child's educational experience, both in school and at home."

References

Aber, J. L., Brown, J. I., and Jones, S. M. "Developmental Trajectories Toward Violence in Middle Childhood: Course, Demographic Differences, and Response to School-Based Intervention." *Developmental Psychology,* 2003, *39,* 324–348.

Association for Conflict Resolution. *School-Based Conflict Resolution Education Program Standards.* Washington, D.C.: Association for Conflict Resolution, 2002.

Batton, J. "Institutionalizing Conflict Resolution Education: The Ohio Model." *Conflict Resolution Quarterly,* 2002, *19* (4), 479–494.

Bell, S. K., and others. "The Effectiveness of Peer Mediation in a Low-SES Rural Elementary School." *Psychology in the Schools,* 2000, *37,* 505–516.

Bickmore, K. "Peer Mediation Training and Program Implementation in Elementary Schools: Research Results." *Conflict Resolution Quarterly,* 2002, *20,* 137–160.

Bodine, R. J., and Crawford, D. K. *The Handbook of Conflict Resolution Education: A Guide to Building Quality Programs in Schools.* San Francisco: Jossey-Bass, 1998.

Bodtker, A. "Conflict Education and Special Needs Students, Part Two: Improving Conflict Competence and Emotional Competence." *Conflict Resolution Quarterly,* 2001, *18,* 377–396.

Bosworth, K., and others. "Preliminary Evaluation of a Multi-Media Violence Prevention Program for Adolescents." *American Journal of Health Behavior,* 2000, *24* (4), 268–280.

Botzer, E. A. "An Evaluation of the Effectiveness of the Second Step Violence Prevention Curriculum for Third Grade Students." *Dissertation Abstracts International Section A: Humanities and Social Sciences,* 2003, *64* (4-A), 1171.

Boulton, M. J., Trueman, M., and Flemington, I. "Associations Between Secondary School Pupils' Definitions of Bullying, Attitudes Towards Bullying, and Tendencies to Engage in Bullying: Age and Sex Differences." *Educational Studies,* 2002, *28,* 133–156.

Broadbear, B. C. "Evaluation of the Second Step Curriculum for Conflict Resolution Skills in Preschool Children from Diverse Parent Households." *Dissertation Abstracts International Section A: Humanities and Social Sciences,* 2001, *61* (11-A), 4300.

Burrell, N. A., Zirbel, C. S., and Allen, M. "Evaluating Peer Mediation Outcomes in Educational Settings: A Meta-Analytic Review." *Conflict Resolution Quarterly,* 2003, *21* (1), 7–26.

Burstyn, J. N., and others. *Preventing Violence in Schools: A Challenge to American Democracy.* Mahwah, N.J.: Erlbaum, 2001.

Catalano, R. F., and others. "Positive Youth Development in the United States: Research Findings on Evaluations of Positive Youth Development Programs." *Prevention and Treatment,* 2000, 5. [http://journals.apa.org/prevention/volume5/pre0050015a.html]. (Aug. 1, 2002).

Cohen, R. "Students Helping Students: Peer Mediation." In T. Jones and R. Compton (eds.), *Kids Working It Out: Stories and Strategies for Making Peace in Our Schools.* San Francisco: Jossey-Bass, 2003.

Compton, R. "Discovering the Promise of Curriculum Integration: The National Curriculum Integration Project." *Conflict Resolution Quarterly,* 2002, *19,* 447–464.

Conduct Problems Prevention Research Group. "Initial Impact of the Fast Track Prevention Trial of Conduct Problems: II. Classroom Effect." *Journal of Consulting and Clinical Psychology,* 1999, *67,* 648–657.

Conte, Z. "The Gift of the Arts." In L. Lantieri (ed.), *Schools with Spirit: Nurturing the Inner Lives of Children and Teachers.* Boston: Beacon Press, 2001.

Craig, W., Henderson, K., and Murphy, J. "Prospective Teachers' Attitudes Toward Bullying and Victimization." *School Psychology International,* 2000, *21* (1), 5–22.

Crosse, S., and others. *Wide Scope: Questionable Quality: Three Reports from the Study on School Violence and Prevention.* Washington, D.C.: Department of Education, 2002.

Cuervo, A. G. "Postscript: The Importance of Supporting Conflict Resolution Education." In T. Jones and R. Compton (eds.), *Kids Working It Out: Stories and Strategies for Making Peace in Our Schools.* San Francisco: Jossey-Bass, 2003.

Cunningham, P. B. "Implementation of an Empirically Based Drug and Violence Prevention and Intervention Program in Public School Settings." *Journal of Clinical Child Psychology,* 2001, *30* (2), 221–233.

Druliner, J. K., and Prichard, H. "'We Can Handle This Ourselves': Learning to Negotiate Conflicts." In T. Jones and R. Compton (eds.), *Kids Working It Out: Stories and Strategies for Making Peace in Our Schools*. San Francisco: Jossey-Bass, 2003.

Dudley, B. S. "Peer Mediation and Negotiation in the Middle School: An Investigation of Training Effects." *Dissertation Abstracts International Section A: Humanities and Social Sciences,* 1995, *56* (1-A), 0142.

Dudley, B. S., Johnson, D. W., and Johnson, R. "Conflict-Resolution Training and Middle School Students' Integrative Negotiation Behavior." *Journal of Applied Social Psychology,* 1996, *26,* 2038–2052.

DuRant, R., Barkin, S., and Krowchuk, D. "Evaluation of a Peaceful Conflict Resolution and Violence Prevention Curriculum for Sixth-Grade Students." *Journal of Adolescent Health,* 2001, *28,* 386–393.

Elias, M. J., and others. *Promoting Social and Emotional Learning: Guidelines for Educators.* Alexandria, Va.: Association for Supervision and Curriculum Development, 1997.

Epstein, E. "Evaluation of an Elementary School Conflict Resolution-Peer Mediation Program." *Dissertation Abstracts International Section A: Humanities and Social Sciences,* 1996, *57* (6-A), 2370.

Espelage, D. L., and Swearer, S. "Research on School Bullying and Victimization: What Have We Learned and Where Do We Go from Here?" *School Psychology Review,* 2003, *32,* 365–384.

Farrell, A. D., Meyer, A., Kung, E., and Sullivan, T. "Development and Evaluation of School-Based Violence Prevention Programs." *Journal of Clinical Child Psychology,* 2001, *30* (2), 207–221.

Farrell, A. D., Meyer, A. L., and White, K. S. "Evaluation of Responding in Peaceful and Positive Ways (RIPP): A School-Based Prevention Program for Reducing Violence Among Urban Adolescents." *Journal of Clinical Child Psychology,* 2001, *30,* 451–464.

Farrell, A. D., Valois, R., and Meyer, A. "Evaluations of the RIPP-6 Violence Prevention at a Rural Middle School." *American Journal of Health Education,* 2002, *33* (3), 167–172.

Fast, J., Fanelli, F., and Salen, L. "How Becoming Mediators Affects Aggressive Students." *Children and Schools,* 2003, *25,* 161–171.

Feiman-Nemser, S. "What New Teachers Need to Learn." *Educational Leadership,* 2003, *60* (8), 25–30.

Fitch, T., and Marshall, J. L. *The Teaching Students to Be Peacemakers Program: Program Overview and Review of the Literature.* 1999. (ED 436 517)

Ford, E. "Oregon's SCRIP Model: Building School Conflict Resolution Education Capacity Through Community Partnerships." *Conflict Resolution Quarterly,* 2002, *19,* 465–477.

Gentry, D. B., and Benenson, W. "School-Age Peer Mediators Transfer Knowledge and Skills to Home Setting." *Mediation Quarterly,* 1992, *10,* 101–109.

Girard, K., and Koch, S. *Conflict Resolution in the Schools: A Manual for Educators.* San Francisco: Jossey-Bass, 1996.

Greenberg, M. T., and Kusche, C. A. *The PATHS Project: Preventive Intervention for Children. Final Report to the National Institute of Health.* Seattle: University of Washington, 1996.

Greenberg, M. T., and others. "Enhancing School-Based Prevention and Youth Development Through Coordinated Social, Emotional and Academic Learning." *American Psychologist,* 2003, *58,* 466–474.

Grossman, D. C., and others. "Effectiveness of a Violence Prevention Curriculum Among Children in Elementary School: A Randomized Controlled Trial." *Journal of the American Medical Association,* 1997, *277,* 1605–1611.

Harris, I. M., and Morrison, M. L. *Peace Education.* (2nd ed.). Jefferson, N.C.: McFarland, 2003.

Harris, P. "Teaching Conflict Resolution Skills to Children: A Comparison Between a Curriculum Based and a Modified Peer Mediation Program." *Dissertation Abstracts International, Section A: Humanities and Social Sciences,* 1999, *59* (9-A), 3397.

Hart, J., and Gunty, M. "The Impact of a Peer Mediation Program on an Elementary School Environment." *Peace and Change,* 1997, *22* (1), 76–92.

Heerboth, J. P. "School Violence Prevention Programs in Southern Illinois High Schools: Factors Related to Principals' and Counselors' Perceptions of Success." *Dissertation Abstracts International, Section A: Humanities and Social Sciences,* 2000, *60* (8-A), 2752.

Heydenberk, W., Heydenberk, R., and Bailey, S. "Conflict Resolution and Moral Reasoning." *Conflict Resolution Quarterly,* 2003, *21* (1), 27–46.

Hoy, W. K., Tarter, C. J., and Kottkamp., R. B. *Open School/Health Schools: Measuring Organizational Climate.* Thousand Oaks, Calif.: Sage, 1991.

Ierley, A., and Claassen-Wilson, D. "Making Things Right: Restorative Justice for School Communities." In T. Jones and R. Compton (eds.), *Kids Working It Out: Stories and Strategies for Making Peace in Our Schools.* San Francisco: Jossey-Bass, 2003.

Johnson, D., and others. "The Impact of Peer Mediation Training on the Management of School and Home Conflicts." *American Educational Research Journal,* 1995, *32,* 829–844.

Johnson, D. W., and Johnson, R. T. "Conflict Resolution and Peer Mediation Programs in Elementary and Secondary Schools: A Review of the Research." *Review of Educational Research,* 1996a, *66,* 459–506.

Johnson, D. W., and Johnson, R. "Effectiveness of Conflict Managers in an Inner-City Elementary School." *Journal of Educational Research,* 1996b, *89,* 280–286.

Johnson, D. W., and Johnson, R. "Training Elementary School Students to Manage Conflict." *Journal of Group Psychotherapy,* 1996c, *49* (1), 24–39.

Johnson, D. W., and Johnson, R. "The Impact of Conflict Resolution Training on Middle School Students." *Journal of Social Psychology,* 1997, *137* (1), 11–22.

Johnson, D. W., and Johnson, R. T. "Teaching Students to Be Peacemakers: A Meta-Analysis." Paper presented at the Annual Meeting of the American Educational Research Association, Seattle, Wash., Apr. 10–14, 2001a.

Johnson, D. W., and Johnson, R. "Peer Mediation in an Inner City School." *Urban Education,* 2001b, *36* (2), 165–179.

Johnson, D. W., Johnson, R. T., and Tjosvold, D. "Constructive Controversy: The Value of Intellectual Opposition." In M. Deutsch and P. Coleman (eds.), *The Handbook of Conflict Resolution.* San Francisco: Jossey-Bass, 2000.

Johnson, D. W., and others. "Using Conflict Managers to Mediate Conflicts in an Inner-City Elementary School." *Mediation Quarterly,* 1995, *12* (4), 379–390.

Jones, T. S., and Bodtker, A. "Conflict Education in a Special Needs Population." *Mediation Quarterly,* 1999, *17,* 109–124.

Jones, T. S., and Brinkman, H. "Teach Your Children Well: Recommendations for Peer Mediation Programs." In J. Folger and T. Jones (eds.), *New Directions in Mediation: Communication Research and Perspectives* (pp. 159–174). Beverly Hills: Sage, 1994.

Jones, T. S., and Compton, R. *Kids Working It Out: Stories and Strategies for Making Peace in Our Schools.* San Francisco: Jossey-Bass, 2003.

Jones, T. S., and Kmitta, D. (eds.). *Does It Work? The Case for Conflict Education in Our Nation's Schools.* Washington, D.C.: Conflict Resolution Education Network, 2000. [www.acresolution.org].

Jones, T. S., and Sanford, R. "Building the Container: Curriculum Infusion and Classroom Climate." *Conflict Resolution Quarterly,* 2003, *21* (1), 115–130.

Jones, T. S., Sanford, R., and Bodtker, A. *The National Curriculum Integration Project: Research Report.* Philadelphia: Temple University, 2001.

Jones, T. S., and others. *Preliminary Final Report of the Comprehensive Peer Mediation Evaluation Project.* Philadelphia: Temple University, College of Allied Health Professions, 1997.

Juvonen, J., and Graham, S. *Peer Harassment in School: The Plight of the Vulnerable and Victimized.* New York: Guilford Press, 2001.

Kaiser-Ulrey, C. L. "Bullying in Middle School: A Study of B.E.S.T.—Bullying Eliminated from Schools Together: An Anti-Bullying Program for Seventh-Grade Students." *Dissertation Abstracts International, Section B: Sciences and Engineering,* 2004, *64* (7-B), 2004.

Kessler, R. "The Heart of the Matter: Social and Emotional Learning as a Foundation for Conflict Resolution Education." In T. Jones and R. Compton (eds.), *Kids Working It Out: Stories and Strategies for Making Peace in Our Schools.* San Francisco: Jossey-Bass, 2003.

King, K. A., Wagner, D. I., and Hedrick, B. "Safe and Drug Free School Coordinators' Perceived Needs to Improve Violence and Drug Prevention Programs." *Journal of School Health,* 2001, *71* (6), 236–242.

Kohn, A. *Beyond Discipline: From Compliance to Community.* Alexandria, Va.: Association for Supervision and Curriculum Development, 1996.

Korn, J. *Increasing Teachers' and Students' Skill Levels of Conflict Resolution and Peer Mediation Strategies through Teacher and Student Training Programs.* 1994. (ED 375 944)

Kusche, C. A., and Greenberg, M. T. *The PATHS Curriculum.* Seattle: Developmental Research and Programs, 1995.

Lane-Garon, P. "Practicing Peace: The Impact of a School-Based Conflict Resolution Program on Elementary Students." *Peace and Change,* 2000, *25,* 467–483.

Lane-Garon, P., and Richardson, T. "Mediator Mentors: Improving School Climate, Nurturing Student Disposition." *Conflict Resolution Quarterly,* 2003, *21* (1), 47–68.

Lane-Garon, P. S. "Developmental Considerations: Encouraging Perspective-Taking in Student Mediators." *Mediation Quarterly,* 1998, *16* (2), 201–217.

Lantieri, L. (ed.). *Schools with Spirit: Nurturing the Inner Lives of Children and Teachers.* Boston: Beacon Press, 2001.

Lantieri, L., and Patti, J. *Waging Peace in Our Schools.* Boston: Beacon Press, 1996.

Lieber, C. M. "The Building Blocks of Conflict Resolution Education: Direct Instruction, Adult Modeling, and Core Practices." In T. Jones and R. Compton (eds.), *Kids Working It Out: Stories and Strategies for Making Peace in Our Schools.* San Francisco: Jossey-Bass, 2003.

Lillenstein, J. A. "Efficacy of a Social Skills Training Curriculum with Early Elementary Students in Four Parochial Schools." *Dissertation Abstracts International Section A: Humanities and Social Sciences,* 2002, *62* (9-A), 29712.

Lumsden, L. *Preventing Bullying.* 2002. (ED D00 036)

Lupton-Smith, H. S. "The Effects of a Peer Mediation Training Program on High School and Elementary School Students." *Dissertation Abstracts International Section A: Humanities and Social Sciences,* 1996, *57* (2-A), 0589.

Mankopf, J. F. "The Effects of Being a Peer Mediator on Adolescents' Perspective-Taking and Connectedness." *Dissertation Abstracts International Section A: Humanities and Social Sciences,* 2003, *63* (11-A), 3866.

Melton, G. B., and others. *Violence Among Rural Youth.* Washington, D.C.: U.S. Department of Justice, 1998.

Meyer, R. H. "The Effect of Participation in a Peer Mediation Program on the Self-Perceptions and Conflict Style of At-Risk Elementary Students." *Dissertation Abstract International Section A: Humanities and Social Sciences,* 1996, *56* (9-A), 3457.

Miller, P. H. "The Relative Effectiveness of Peer Mediation: Children Helping Each Other to Solve Conflicts." *Dissertation Abstracts International Section A: Humanities and Social Sciences,* 1995, *55* (7-A), 1880.

Nakkula, M., and Nikitipoulos, C. "Negotiation Training and Interpersonal Development: An Exploratory Study of Early Adolescents in Argentina." *Adolescence,* 2001, *36* (4), 1–21.

Nance, T. M. "Impact of the Peer Mediation Component of the New Mexico Center for Dispute Resolution Mediation in the Schools Program." *Dissertation Abstracts International Section A: Humanities and Social Sciences,* 1996, *56* (9-A), 3512.

Nelson, K. D. "The Effects of Peer Mediation Training and Practice on Self-Esteem and Social Skills Among Peer Mediators in a Vocational Technical High School." *Dissertation Abstracts International Section A: Humanities and Social Sciences,* 1997, *58* (6-A), 2073.

Nelson-Haynes, L. "The Impact of the Student Conflict Resolution Program in Dallas Public Schools." *Dissertation Abstracts International Section A: Humanities and Social Sciences,* 1996, *56* (9-A), 3458.

Olweus, D. "Bully/Victim Problems Among School Children: Basic Facts and Effects of a School-Based Intervention Program." In D. J. Pepler and K. H. Rubin (eds.), *The Development and Treatment of Childhood Aggression.* Mahwah, N.J.: Erlbaum, 1991.

Oppitz, J. L. "Violence Prevention: Empowering School Counselors—A Study of Strategies Used by Practicing Elementary School Counselors." *Dissertation Abstracts International, Section A: Humanities and Social Sciences,* 2003, *63* (8-A), 2800.

Orpinas, P., and Horne, A. M. "School Bullying: Changing the Problem by Changing the School." *School Psychology Review,* 2003, *32* (3), 431–445.

Orpinas, P., and others. "Outcome Evaluation of a Multi-Component Violence Prevention Program for Middle Schools: The Students for Peace Project." *Health Education Research,* 2000, *15* (1), 45–58.

Oskamp, S. *Reducing Prejudice and Discrimination.* Mahwah, N.J.: Erlbaum, 2000.

Pepler, D. J., Craig, W. M., Ziegler, S., and Charach, A. "An Evaluation of an Anti-Bullying Intervention in Toronto Schools." *Canadian Journal of Community Mental Health,* 1994, *13,* 95–110.

Pettigrew, T. F., and Tropp, L. R. "Does Intergroup Contact Reduce Prejudice? Recent Meta-Analytic Findings." In S. Oskamp (Ed.), *Reducing Prejudice and Discrimination.* Mahwah, N.J.: Erlbaum, 2000.

Poliner, R. "Making Meaningful Connections: Curriculum Infusion." In T. Jones and R. Compton (eds.), *Kids Working It Out: Stories and Strategies for Making Peace in Our Schools.* San Francisco: Jossey-Bass, 2003.

Potts, K. L. "The Relationship Between the Quality and Number of Interpersonal Negotiation Strategies and Coping Styles of High School Students with and Without Peer Mediation Training." *Dissertation Abstracts International Section A: Humanities and Social Sciences,* 2002, *62* (11-A), 3692.

Price, R. H. "Systems Within Systems: Putting Program Implementation in Organizational Context." *Prevention and Treatment,* 2003, *6,* 1–14.

Prutzman, P. "R.E.S.P.E.C.T.: Appreciating and Welcoming Differences." In T. Jones and R. Compton (eds.), *Kids Working It Out: Stories and Strategies for Making Peace in Our Schools.* San Francisco: Jossey-Bass, 2003.

Robinson, T. R., Smith, S. W., and Daunic, A. P. "Middle School Students' Views on the Social Validity of Peer Mediation." *Middle School Journal,* 2000, *31* (5), 23–29.

Salomon, G. "The Nature of Peace Education: Not All Programs Are Created Equal." In G. Salomon and B. Nevo (eds.), *Peace Education: The Concept, Principles and Practices Around the World.* Mahwah, N.J.: Erlbaum, 2002.

Sandy, S. V., and Boardman, S. K. "The Peaceful Kids Conflict Resolution Program." *International Journal of Conflict Management,* 2000, *11,* 337–357.

Sandy, S. V., and Cochran, K. "The Development of Conflict Resolution Skills in Children: Preschool to Adolescence." In M. Deutsch and P. Coleman (eds.), *The Handbook of Conflict Resolution: Theory and Practice.* San Francisco: Jossey-Bass, 2000.

Selfridge, J. "The Resolving Conflict Creatively Program: How We Know It Works." *Theory into Practice,* 2004, *43* (1), 59–68.

Selman, R. *The Growth of Interpersonal Understanding.* New York: Academic Press, 1980.

Shann, M. H. "Professional Commitment and Satisfaction Among Teachers in Urban Middle School." *Journal of Educational Research,* 1998, *92* (2), 67–74.

Shapiro, D. "Editors' Notes." In D. L. Shapiro and B. E. Clayton (eds.), *Negotiation—Interpersonal Approaches to Intergroup Conflict.* New Directions in Youth Development, no. 102. San Francisco: Jossey-Bass, 2004.

Shapiro, J. P., and others. "Evaluation of the Peacemakers Program: School-Based Violence Prevention for Students in Grades Four Through Eight." *Psychology in the Schools,* 2002, *39* (1), 87–100.

Smith, S. N., and Fairman, D. "Normalizing Effective Conflict Management Through Academic Curriculum Integration: The Example of Workable Peace." In D. L. Shapiro and B. E. Clayton (eds.), *Negotiation—Interpersonal Approaches to Intergroup Conflict.* New Directions for Youth Development, no. 102. San Francisco: Jossey-Bass, 2004.

Smith, S. W., Daunic, A., Miller, M., and Robinson, T. "Conflict Resolution and Peer Mediation in Middle Schools: Extending the Process and Outcome Knowledge Base." *Journal of Social Psychology,* 2002, *142,* 567–587.

Sommers, M. "Peace Education: Opportunities and Challenges." Presentation at the Building Bridges to Peace and Prosperity: Education and Training for Action, U.S. Agency for International Development, Washington, D.C., Aug. 11–15, 2003.

Stevahn, L. "Integrating Conflict Resolution Training into the Curriculum." *Theory into Practice,* 2004, *43* (1), 50–63.

Stevahn, L., Johnson, D. W., Johnson, R. T., and Schultz, R. "Effects of Conflict Resolution Training Integrated into a High School Social Studies Curriculum." *Journal of Social Psychology,* 2002, *142* (3), 305–333.

Stewart, J. "A Special Edition on Educational Programs in Juvenile Correctional Facilities." *Journal of Correctional Education,* 2002, *53* (2), 24–35.

Stewart, J. T. "A Formative Evaluation of a Conflict Resolution Program Utilizing Peer Mediation Training on the Knowledge and Attitudes of Middle School Students at a Hillsborough County, Florida, Middle School." *Dissertation Abstracts International Section A: Humanities and Social Sciences,* 2000, *60* (12-A), 4374.

Sweeney, B. C. "Peer Mediation Training: Developmental Effects for High School Mediators." *Dissertation Abstracts International Section A: Humanities and Social Sciences,* 1996, *56* (11-A), 4285.

Taub, J. "Evaluation of the Second Step Violence Prevention Program at a Rural Elementary School." *School Psychology Review,* 2002, *31,* 186–200.

Title, B. B. "School Bullying: Prevention and Intervention." In T. Jones and R. Compton (eds.), *Kids Working It Out: Stories and Strategies for Making Peace in Our Schools.* San Francisco: Jossey-Bass, 2003.

Tolson, E. R., and McDonald, S. "Peer Mediation Among High School Students: A Test of Effectiveness." *Social Work in Education,* 1992, *14* (2), 86–94.

Tschannen-Moran, M. "The Effects of a State-Wide Conflict Management Initiative in Schools." *American Secondary Education,* 2001, *29* (3), 2–32.

U.S. Department of Education. *Violence and Discipline Problems in U.S. Public Schools 1996–1997.* Washington, D.C.: U.S. Department of Education, 1998.

U.S. Office of the Surgeon General. *Youth Violence: A Report of the Surgeon General.* Washington, D.C.: U.S. Department of Health and Human Services, 2001.

Warters, W. C. "Conflict Management in Higher Education: A Review of Current Approaches." In S. A. Holton (ed.), *Conflict Management in Higher Education.* New Directions for Higher Education, no. 92. San Francisco: Jossey-Bass, 1995.

Warters, W. C. *Mediation in the Campus Community: Designing and Managing Effective Programs.* San Francisco: Jossey-Bass, 2000.

Washburn, J. J. "Evaluation of a Violence Prevention Program with Low-Income, Urban, African-American Youth." *Dissertation Abstracts International Section B: Sciences and Engineering,* 2002, *62* (9-B), 4242.

Weissberg, R. P., and Greenberg, M. T. "School and Community Competence Enhancement and Prevention Programs." In I. E. Siegel and K. A. Renninger (eds.), *Handbook of Child Psychology, Vol. 4: Child Psychology in Practice.* (5th ed.) New York: Wiley, 1998.

Whitney, I., Rivers, I., Smith, P. K., and Sharp, S. "The Sheffield Project: Methodology and Findings." In P. K. Smith and S. Sharp (eds.), *School Bullying: Insights and Perspectives.* London: Routledge, 1994.

Whittall, S. T. "School's Out: Time for Fun, Relaxation, and Peaceful Conflict Resolution Education." In T. Jones and R. Compton (eds.), *Kids Working It Out: Stories and Strategies for Making Peace in Our Schools.* San Francisco: Jossey-Bass, 2003.

Wilson, D. B., Gottfredson, D. C., and Najaka, S. S. "School-Based Prevention of Problem Behaviors: A Meta-Analysis." *Journal of Quantitative Criminology,* 2001, *17,* 247–276.

Winston, M. L. "Assessing the Effects of a Peer Mediation Training Program on Skills Acquisition, Maintenance, and Generalization." *Dissertation Abstracts International Section A: Humanities and Social Sciences,* 1997, 57(7-A), 2863.

Zins, J. E., Weissberg, R. P., Wang, M. C., and Walberg, H. J. (eds.). *Building School Success Through Social and Emotional Learning.* New York: Teachers College Press, 2004.

Zucca-Brown, S. "An Elementary School Mediation Program: Its Effect on Student Mediators and School Violence." *Dissertation Abstracts International Section A: Humanities and Social Sciences,* 1997, *58* (6-A), 2077.

Tricia S. Jones is a professor in the Department of Psychological Studies in the College of Education, Temple University in Philadelphia. Jones is the past president (1996–1997) of the International Association of Conflict Management. She currently serves as the editor-in-chief of *Conflict Resolution Quarterly.*

Commentary: Considering Conflict Resolution Education: Next Steps for Institutionalization

O ver the past two decades, conflict education programs have educated children about constructive approaches to managing conflict in their schools and communities. For many, conflict resolution education (CRE) provides an answer to an increasingly troubling incidence of violence.

As Tricia Jones's review of CRE research confirms, these programs are effective in a variety of ways. Fortunately, this research has helped convince policymakers at the federal level that CRE is legitimate and deserving of support. The U.S. Department of Education's *Creating Safe and Drug Free Schools Action Guide* (1996) provides the following conclusion:

> The effective conflict resolution education programs highlighted . . . have helped to improve the climate in school, community, and juvenile justice settings by reducing the number of disruptive and violent acts in these settings, by decreasing the number of chronic school absences due to a fear of violence, by reducing the manner of disciplinary referrals and suspensions, by increasing academic instruction during the school day, and by increasing the self-esteem, and self-respect, as well as the personal responsibility and self-discipline of the young people involved in these programs.

In 2001, the Safe and Drug-Free Schools Office in the Department of Education published a list of promising and exemplary programs. This list was generated by an expert review of evidence regarding the effectiveness for various programs. The resulting list contained nine exemplary and thirty-three promising programs—many of them conflict education programs.

As Jones notes in her article, even with an impressive body of proven benefits, there is more research that needs to be done, and her suggestions for fruitful directions in research are a critical foundation for institutionalization. There are many questions remaining to be answered about

CONFLICT RESOLUTION QUARTERLY, vol. 22, no. 1–2, Fall–Winter 2004 © Wiley Periodicals, Inc., 269
and the Association for Conflict Resolution

children's individual benefits from CRE. Perhaps the most critical pertain to the long-term effects of participation in CRE. We have the opportunity to study how CRE can positively alter the direction of a child's life and the choices they make from their early years through high school and even into higher education. To see improvements in this work, we must also focus our research on what enables a teacher to better convey these skills to students, both for K–12 faculty and in higher education. Standards covering particular skill areas, topical content, and training amounts in each area have yet to be devised for the fields of CRE and SEL.

What is the difference in the academic performance and social skills of a child provided with CRE and one denied CRE? We have indicators that CRE and SEL can have profound impacts on the adults that children become and the lives they lead in terms of successful personal and professional relationships (Elias and others, 1997). Our research should follow these children into their lives and look at their abilities to work well with others in professional contexts, to form and maintain lasting and loving relationships, to partner and parent well, to connect with community. If CRE is about life skills, as many scholars and practitioners believe, how skilled are the lives led by those who have had the opportunity to participate in CRE when compared to those who have not?

These questions highlight the need for consideration of the institutionalization of CRE. If we accept that these programs are beneficial when used in the right contexts and implemented with fidelity, our attention should be on how best to provide CRE opportunities not only to the children in all schools, but also to classroom educators and adults that are a part of the school community. What is necessary to have CRE become a norm in the way that school communities operate? This is where I will focus the remainder of my comments.

What We Need to Succeed: Institutionalization Issues for CRE

Eiseman, Fleming, and Roody (1990) define institutionalization as the process by which an innovation becomes embedded in operating procedures of a system. They list six indicators of the institutionalization of an innovation: (1) acceptance by relevant actors; (2) stable, routinized implementation; (3) widespread use of the innovation; (4) firm expectations that the practice will continue within the organization; (5) continuation of the program that is dependent on features of the organizational culture, structure, and procedures rather than the actions of specific individuals; and

(6) routine allocations of time and money. Relatively few CRE efforts have met all of these operational criteria. Many observers may conclude that CRE has begun to meet the first indicators in some regions in the United States but falls far short on the last five.

While CRE and SEL programs have been in existence for decades in the United States and are accepted as legitimate, as exemplified by legislation regarding CRE and SEL in almost every state, CRE implementation is still primarily stand-alone programming, such as peer mediation, rather than a comprehensive approach for all students and staff. CRE has usually been introduced into schools through external channels and treated as add-on programs rather than integrated into ongoing curricula, classroom activity, and everyday operation of the school. There are several reasons that CRE has yet to be fully institutionalized and seen as a necessary component of all education levels and incorporated as such.

First, it has been only in the past ten years or so that we have amassed evidence of the efficacy of these programs, thus justifying their institutionalization. And the critical support for these programs was not provided by the U.S. Department of Education and organizations like CASEL until 2000. It was essential that research demonstrate that CRE and SEL deliver promised benefits before integration into the larger education system was a possibility.

Second, CRE and SEL programs started as a means to provide students with specific knowledge and skills. As a result, the program models used were often stand-alone programs like peer mediation or intensive, short-term curricula like Program for Young Negotiators. The basic service delivery system was developed around CRE and SEL as add-on programming. This works fairly well when resources are plentiful. When resources dwindle and pressures to focus on academic content standards or state proficiency tests increase, these programs are often cut, reduced in size, or underresourced. CRE and SEL educators have learned that the best means of institutionalizing these programs is to make them a part of the daily life of the school through the daily work of its teachers. It maximizes their impact and their staying power (Elias and others, 2003).

Third, recent efforts at curriculum integration, like the National Curriculum Integration Project (NCIP) (Compton, 2002), focused on in-service teacher education in CRE and social and emotional learning (SEL). The assumption of these efforts was that the learning process was optimized if seasoned teachers were selected for training and implementation. While the NCIP program yielded hypothesized benefits (Jones and

Sanford, 2003), the evaluation of NCIP identified a number of resource and administrative challenges to securing adequate support for teachers involved (Jones, Sanford, and Bodtker, 2001). Unless a school had adequate resources to pay for external training, consultation, and coaching, the teachers did not have insufficient time to develop these skills and apply them in their classes. Basically, the in-service route seemed effective only for relatively well-funded and stable schools.

The culmination of these factors is that we have CRE programs that work but have been implemented in ways that reduce their centrality and diminish the probability of their long-term survival. To overcome this, we need to focus efforts in four areas: developing preservice teacher education in CRE and SEL, developing more flexible models for best practice implementation that build internal capacity within the school district, forming better partnerships with other organizations, and forming international networks.

Preservice

While there are few preservice programs in conflict education or SEL offered by colleges of education, some are beginning to offer courses in this or integrate some CRE into their course content. The lack of preservice CRE may be attributed to general lack of specific skills training in CRE and knowledge of its benefits, lack of CRE curriculum that fits easily into conventional preservice course work, and connections of CRE to the national content standards and statewide exams for first-year educators.

While not widespread in teacher preparation, colleges of education are beginning to integrate CRE at graduate levels. Examples are American University's M.A. in teaching and M.A. in international peace and conflict resolution, a dual graduate degree program in which students must take fifteen credit hours of course work in peace and conflict resolution; Lesley University's M.Ed. in curriculum and instruction with an emphasis in conflict resolution and peaceable schools, which prepares adults for leadership of programs that address social, emotional, and ethical development of children; Teachers College Columbia University's International Center for Cooperation and Conflict Resolution, which offers courses for graduate students in organizational and social psychology and in education related to conflict resolution; and Wilmington College's requirement that all graduate education students complete a course in CRE before graduation.

Motivation to incorporate CRE and SEL is increased when state standards change. For example, the state of Wisconsin requires that an applicant for an initial regular teaching license must demonstrate competency as verified by a professional education program or school district supervisor in resolving conflicts between pupils and between pupils and school staff and assisting pupils in learning methods of resolving conflicts. As a result, the University of Wisconsin's School of Education, Teacher Certification Program, has a conflict resolution requirement (six hours of course work or equivalent in outside training).

Preservice CRE may affect the national challenge of teacher attrition. Educators agree that the level of teacher attrition in the first few years of teaching is unacceptably high (Darling-Hammond, 2003). The National Center for Education Statistics (1997) reports that about one-third of new teachers leave the profession within five years. And this problem is especially significant in urban education environments. Teacher turnover is 50 percent higher in high-poverty than in low-poverty schools (Ingersoll, 2001), and new teachers in urban districts exit or transfer more often than their suburban counterparts (Hanushek, Kain, and Rivkin, 1999).

The research on teacher attrition reveals that a key factor is the new teacher's inadequate preparation for dealing with the realities of managing the classroom. Unable to handle conflict among students and deal with disruptive behavior, teachers become frustrated and are more likely to leave the profession (National Center for Education Statistics, 1997; Norton and Kelly, 1997; Tapper, 1995; Taylor, 1998). Undoubtedly, the adequacy of teacher preparation is instrumental in its effect on teacher attrition rates (Henke, Chen, and Geis, 2000).

New teachers complain that their education departments are not properly preparing them in conflict education and classroom management. Trube and Leighfield (2004) completed a survey of faculty in two-year and four-year teaching institutions in Ohio during spring 2003 and report that 89 percent report being completely or seriously underprepared in their teacher preparation programs in the areas of CRE and SEL. Ninety-two percent of the respondents indicated that "it is important that teacher candidates in my licensure area have knowledge and skills in conflict management."

Nancy Carlsson-Paige, professor of education at Lesley University, states, "If we are going to make progress in teaching conflict resolution to young people, we have to begin working more systematically with college faculty and pre-service teachers" (personal communication, September 2003). James A. McLoughlin, dean of the College of Education at Cleveland State University, affirms, ". . . We realize that teaching and learning do not occur in isolation. Context as a conceptual framework includes the range of influences surrounding and infusing the teaching-learning process. In this connection, the idea of conflict resolution, diversity, and social-emotional learning are of central significance, particularly in urban settings where issues surrounding race, multiculturalism, socioeconomic status and exceptionality are in higher focus than in the larger society" (personal communication, October 2003).

Recently, the George Gund Foundation funded the Conflict Resolution Education in Teacher Education project (CRETE). CRETE is designed to educate teacher candidates about CRE and SEL so they can develop these competencies through their course work, student teaching, and initial professional practice. CRETE is designed to work with mentoring and induction processes to heighten new teachers' abilities to apply the skills and knowledge acquired through the project. And CRETE is designed to evaluate, refine, and prepare project protocols and instructional materials for dissemination to other colleges of education throughout the nation.

The CRETE project builds on a history in higher education initiatives by the Ohio Commission for Dispute Resolution and Conflict Management. The commission has held Conflict Resolution Education Institutes for Higher Education Professional Preparation Faculty over the past five years. The goal of the institute is to assist faculty in providing future educators with the conflict resolution skills they will need to be leaders in creating safer, more supportive learning environments. The institute prepares faculty to examine personal conflict resolution skills, illustrate successful integration of conflict resolution content and skills into higher education courses, and develop strategies for institutionalizing conflict resolution in the professional preparation curricula of Ohio colleges and universities. Through this project, Ohio has also begun to make linkages between CRE and the National Council for Accreditation of Teacher Education (NCATE) review that the majority of education departments undergo, and PRAXIS, a professional assessment for beginning teachers, which thirty-five of forty-three states use for teacher licensure. These types of linkages encourage and assist the faculty in legitimizing time spent on integrating this into their current syllabi and operations, as well as helping them to persuade other faculty to do the same.

In-School Capacity

While there is currently a long list of best practice curriculum and programs for CRE and SEL, a vast majority of schools implementing them do not adhere to the best practice training guidelines for implementation and thus tend to not achieve the optimal results possible. This lack of adherence to "proper" implementation is due in part to the need for a more flexible model of best practice that includes addressing the challenge of limited resources for "proper" training. One way to address this is to include in the initial training a focus on preparing a core group of educator-trainers within the school district that will be prepared to continue the ongoing staff development and technical assistance needed in order to help enhance institutionalization. This will assist with challenges such as staff turnover and dwindling resources for outside trainers. This and the work in higher education would benefit from the development of a core group of standards for training adults in CRE, enabling them to optimally deliver the services and train their colleagues and the parents and students who work in the school community.

Partnerships

Forming partnerships with organizations and institutions will be key to successful institutionalization. Fortunately, several of these partnerships have already been formed with organizations like CASEL, Educators for Social Responsibility, and the Association for Conflict Resolution, to name a few. At a minimum, there should be a network of professional associations and university as well as independent consortia.

In addition, there should be a stronger partnership between government, statewide education organizations, and CRE organizations. All states have legislation that requires the provision of CRE in some form (teacher preservice, in-service, continuing education, and others). But, those agencies responsible for implementing the legislation do not always have the CRE expertise to effectively implement the legislation. There is little information available on the support mechanisms that states assume will enable compliance with existing law. It would be valuable to find out about these support mechanisms and the nature of their use.

International Clearinghouse

Work in CRE is becoming more prevalent around the world, with particular strongholds in European countries such as Norway, the Netherlands,

United Kingdom, France, Germany, and Ireland (Harris and Morrison, 2003). There is considerable interest in CRE from South America, Africa, Asia, and the Middle East. There is a need for some international network to link these efforts to accomplish the following:

- Development of a clearinghouse of current information on CRE programs
- Creation of research and evaluation agendas
- Development of an international youth network
- Promotion of teacher and professional educator preparation in CRE
- Clarification of culturally and contextually sensitive implementation processes to enable application of CRE efforts to fit the cultural and social-political conditions of the community of use

Suggestions for Future Research

This section suggests specific research that is critical to accomplish CRE institutionalization:

- *Survey colleges of education for CRE graduate, undergraduate, and continuing education readiness.* A critical component of institutionalization lies in the ability of colleges of education to promote CRE courses and curricula at graduate levels, with elective and continuing education components, and preservice initiatives. A nationwide survey would provide valuable information. First, it would yield an accurate picture of the current state of effort in this area. Second, the survey would clearly identify colleges of education and their programs that may serve as models for other colleges of education to follow. Third, this survey would allow us to compare our progress with related fields like character education, a comparison that may enlighten us on best practices for moving forward.

- *Conduct case studies on social-political factors with an impact on institutionalization in a specific school or district.* Understanding influences on program institutionalization is important. For example, Ritter and Boruch (1999) reported on Tennessee's STAR project, which sought to reduce class size. Similar case study research on CRE innovation and institutionalization, for example, in the Cleveland District, may help us better understand and attend to the social, political, and economic forces that affect the field. Case studies should be encouraged, especially on schools and districts where one or more of the following characteristics exists: there is a specific staff member or program coordinator (at the district level or a full-time position at the school level); there has been a planning process in which the institutionalization of the CRE program has been a goal from the beginning; there is a clearly articulated K–12 coordinated effort in place and operating; or there is a communication infrastructure within the school or district that has been established and supported specifically to maximize the success of the CRE program.

• *Investigate large-scale institutionalization efforts in terms of political process and influence in related fields.* We understand relatively little about the process used to build a political initiative for a field like CRE. Examining the process used for character education or collaborative learning will contribute to identifying the machinery and process that helps make collaborative efforts and implementation happen.

• *Research what strategies, content areas, and minimum amounts of training of educators must be done in order for them to be able to not only model the skills of CRE, but also convey these skills to their university students and K–12 students.* While there are general guidelines for CRE content areas in which educators should be competent, the knowledge regarding the amount of training and optimal strategies for training them have not been developed or researched.

While significant strides toward institutionalization of CRE have been made since 1995, there is still much work to be done in order to see CRE institutionalized not only into the daily operations of our schools, but also in teacher preparation and educational policies and procedures nationally and internationally.

References

Compton, R. "Discovering the Promise of Curriculum Integration: The National Curriculum Integration Project." *Conflict Resolution Quarterly,* 2002, *19,* 447–464.

Darling-Hammond, L. "Keeping Good Teachers." *Educational Leadership,* 2003, *60* (8), 6–14.

Eiseman, J., Fleming, D., and Roody, D. *Making Sure It Sticks: The School Improvement Leader's Role in Institutionalizing Change. The School Improvement Leader: Four Perspectives on Change in Schools.* 1990. (ED 326 965)

Elias, M. J., and others. *Promoting Social and Emotional Learning: Guidelines for Educators.* Alexandria, Va.: Association for Supervision and Curriculum Development, 1997.

Elias, M. J., and others. "Implementation, Sustainability, and Scaling Up of Social-Emotional and Academic Innovation in Public Schools." *School Psychology Review,* 2003, *32,* 303–320.

Hanushek, E. A., Kain, J. F., and Rivkin, S. G. *Do Higher Salaries Buy Better Teachers?* Cambridge, Mass.: National Bureau of Economic Research, 1999.

Harris, I. M., and Morrison, M. L. *Peace Education.* (2nd ed.) Jefferson, N.C.: McFarland, 2003.

Henke, R., Chen, X., and Geis, S. *Progress Through the Teacher Pipeline: 1992–93 College Graduates and Elementary/Secondary School Teaching as of 1997.* Washington, D.C.: National Center for Education Statistics, U.S. Department of Education, 2000.

Ingersoll, R. M. "Teacher Turnover and Teacher Shortages: An Organizational Analysis." *American Educational Research Journal,* 2001, *38,* 499–534.

Jones, T. S., and Sanford, R. "Building the Container: Curriculum Infusion and Classroom Climate." *Conflict Resolution Quarterly,* 2003, *21,* 115–130.

Jones, T. S., Sanford, R., and Bodtker, A. *The National Curriculum Integration Project: Research Report.* Philadelphia: Temple University, 2001.

National Center for Education Statistics. *Job Satisfaction Among America's Teachers: Effects of Workplace Conditions, Background, Characteristics, and Teacher Compensation.* 1997 (Oct. 2002). [www.nces.org].

Norton, M. S., and Kelly, L. K. *Resource Allocation: Managing Money and People.* Larchmont, N.Y.: Eye on Education, 1997.

Ritter, G. W., and Boruch, R. F. "The Political and Institutional Origins of a Randomized Controlled Trial on Elementary School Class Size: Tennessee's Project STAR." *Educational Evaluation and Policy Analysis,* 1999, *21,* 111–125.

Tapper, D. "Swimming Upstream: The First-Year Experiences of Teachers Working in New York City Public Schools." Paper presented at the American Education Research Association conference, 1995.

Taylor, A. W. "Factors Affecting Retention of Teachers in the Teaching Profession." *Dissertation Abstracts International Section A: Humanities and Social Sciences,* 1998, *58* (8-A), 2950.

Trube, B., and Leighfield, K. "Knowledge, Skills and Dispositions in Conflict Management Education: The Role of Teacher Preparation Programs in Ohio." Unpublished manuscript. Chilicothe: Ohio University–Chilicothe, 2004.

U.S. Department of Education. *Creating Safe and Drug Free Schools: An Action Guide.* Sept. 1996. [http:// ww/ed/gov/offices/oese/sdfs/actguid/conflict.html].

U.S. Department of Education. "Safe, Disciplined and Drug Free Schools Exemplary and Promising Programs List." 2002. [http://www.ed.gov/offices/oeri/orad/kad/expert-panel/drug-free.tml].

Jennifer Batton is the current director of Education Programs for the state of Ohio's Commission on Dispute Resolution and Conflict Management. As such, she works to provide grants, free professional development, publications, technical assistance, and research to all of Ohio's public preschools, Head Starts, primary and secondary schools, colleges, and universities.

Victim-Offender Mediation: Three Decades of Practice and Research

MARK S. UMBREIT
ROBERT B. COATES
BETTY VOS

Crime victims meeting face-to-face with the offender stretches the very concept of mediation, yet it has strong empirical grounding and is being widely practiced in courts and communities throughout the world. Its focus on promotion of offender accountability, victim assistance, and making of amends appears to address many unmet needs of individuals, families, and communities affected by criminal behavior.

Victim-offender mediation is a process that provides interested victims of primarily property crimes and minor assaults the opportunity to meet the juvenile or adult offender, in a safe and structured setting, with the goal of holding the offender directly accountable for his or her behavior while providing importance assistance and compensation to the victim (Umbreit, 2001). With the assistance of a trained mediator, the victim is able to let the offender know how the crime affected him or her, to receive answers to questions, and to be directly involved in developing a restitution plan for the offender to be accountable for the losses he or she incurred. The offender is able to take direct responsibility for his or her behavior, to learn of the full impact of what he or she did, and to develop a plan for making amends to the person he or she violated.

Victim-offender mediation programs were initially referred to as victim-offender reconciliation programs (VORP) in the mid-1970s and 1980s. Some programs still go by the name of VORP. Today, most programs throughout the world identify themselves as victim-offender mediation (VOM). In the United States, some programs are also called "victim-offender meetings" or "victim-offender conferences." In recent years, an increasing number of VOM programs have been periodically working with cases involving severe violence, including homicide. This requires advanced training and far more preparation of the parties over many months prior to ever meeting face-to-face (Umbreit, Vos, Coates, and Brown, 2003; Umbreit and Vos, 2000). This article, however, focuses on by far the most widespread application of VOM, in property crimes and minor assaults, in thousands of cases in numerous countries throughout the world. For those interested in learning more about the relatively small but growing practice and impact of victim-offender dialogue in severely violent crime, the book *Facing Violence: The Path of Restorative Justice and Dialogue* (Umbreit, Vos, Coates, and Brown, 2003) reports on a five-year study of the development, implementation, and impact of the first two states (Texas and Ohio) to offer victim-offender dialogue services in cases of severe violence, on a statewide basis.

While many other types of mediation are largely settlement driven, victim-offender mediation is primarily dialogue driven, with the emphasis on victim healing, offender accountability, and restoration of losses. Contrary to many other applications of mediation in which the mediator first meets the parties during the joint mediation session, a very different process is used in most victim-offender mediation programs, based on a humanistic model of mediation (Umbreit, 1995b, 1997, 2001). A humanistic model of mediation involves reframing the role of the mediator from being settlement driven to facilitating dialogue and mutual aid; scheduling separate premediation sessions with each party; connecting with the parties through building rapport and trust while not taking sides; identifying the strengths of each party; using a nondirective style of mediation that creates a safe space for dialogue and accessing the strengths of participants; and recognizing and using the power of silence.

Most victim-offender mediation sessions do in fact result in a signed restitution agreement. This agreement, however, is secondary to the importance of the initial dialogue between the parties that addresses emotional and informational needs of victims that are central to their healing and to development of victim empathy in the offender, which can lead to less criminal behavior in the future. Several studies (Coates and Gehm, 1989; Umbreit and Coates, 1993; Umbreit, 1995a) have consistently found that the restitution agreement is less important to crime victims than the opportunity to talk directly with the offender about how he or she felt about the crime.

From its inception in Kitchener, Ontario, when the first victim-offender mediation program was established in 1974, many criminal justice officials have been quite skeptical about victim interest in meeting the offender. Victim-offender mediation is clearly not appropriate for all crime victims. Practitioners are trained to present it as a voluntary choice to the victim and as voluntary as possible for the offender. With more than twenty years of mediating many thousands of cases throughout North America and Europe, experience has shown that the majority of victims presented with the option of mediation choose to enter the process. A statewide public opinion poll in Minnesota (Pranis and Umbreit, 1992) found that 82 percent of a random sample of citizens from throughout the state would consider participating in a victim-offender program if they were the victim of a property crime. A multistate study (Umbreit, 1994a) found that of 280 victims who participated in victim-offender mediation programs in four states, 91 percent felt their participation was totally voluntary.

As the oldest and most widely developed expression of restorative justice (Bazemore and Umbreit, 1995; Van Ness and Heetderks, 2002; Zehr, 1990, 2002), with a quarter of a century of experience and more than fifty empirical studies (Umbreit, Coates, and Vos, 2001b, 2002) in North America and Europe, victim-offender mediation and dialogue programs currently work with thousands of cases annually through more than three hundred programs throughout the United States and more than twelve hundred in primarily Europe but also Canada (where it all began), Israel, Japan, Russia, South Korea, South Africa, South America, and the South Pacific. A recent national survey that examined to what degree victim-offender mediation was supported by formal public policy found a considerable amount of legislative backing (Lightfoot and Umbreit, forthcoming). Twenty-nine states had legislation, in one form or another, that addressed victim-offender mediation. Of these, fourteen states had quite specific legislation that spoke to various issues related to the use and development of victim-offender mediation and fifteen states had a briefer reference to victim-offender mediation.

Today, restorative justice policies and programs, including victim-offender mediation, are developing in nearly every state and range from small and quite marginal programs in many communities to a growing number of state and county justice systems that are undergoing major systemic change. Examples of such systemic change initiatives are occurring in Arizona, California, Colorado, Illinois, Iowa, Minnesota, New York, Ohio, Oregon, Pennsylvania, Texas, Vermont, and Wisconsin.

The American Bar Association (1994) has addressed restorative justice through the practice of victim-offender mediation, its most widely used and empirically validated practice. The ABA has played a leadership role over many years in promoting the use of mediation and other forms of alternative dispute resolution (ADR) in civil court–related conflicts, yet for most of that time, it remained skeptical and often critical of mediation in criminal court settings. That changed in 1994 after a year-long study, when the ABA fully endorsed the practice of victim-offender mediation and dialogue. The association recommended its use in courts throughout the country and also provided guidelines for its use and development.

Restorative justice policies and practices, including VOM, have recently been endorsed by two important international bodies: the United Nations and the Council of Europe. Meeting in 2000, the United Nations Congress on Crime Prevention considered restorative justice in its plenary sessions and developed a draft proposal, "UN Basic Principles on the Use of Restorative Justice Programs in Criminal Matters" (United Nations, 2000). The proposed principles encourage the use of restorative justice programming by member states at all stages of the criminal justice process, underscore the voluntary nature of participation in restorative justice procedures, and recommend beginning to establish standards and safeguards for the practice of restorative justice. This proposal was adopted by the United Nations in 2002. The Council of Europe was more specifically focused on the restorative use of mediation procedures in criminal matters and adopted a set of recommendations in 1999 to guide member states in using mediation in criminal cases (Council of Europe Committee of Ministers, 1999).

Another clear expression of the growing support for restorative justice in America is seen in the National Organization for Victim Assistance's endorsement of restorative community justice. During the early years of this movement, most victim advocacy groups were quite skeptical. Some still are; however, a growing number of victim support organizations now actively participate in the restorative justice movement.

Considerable empirical work has been done over the past twenty-five years or so to document the impact of victim-offender mediation programs. Here, we look at how this ongoing experiment with restorative justice through victim-offender mediation is doing. Fifty studies of victim-offender mediation in five countries were reviewed for this article. In addition, we reference a meta-analysis of eight conferencing and twenty-seven VOM programs (Latimer, Dowden, and Muise, 2001).

In terms of program structure, all the VOM programs under study in this review share in common the process of facilitating some form of dialogue between crime victims and the offenders who have harmed them. In most programs, this dialogue takes place in person, though there has been some experimentation with shuttle mediation, in which a third party carries information back and forth between the involved parties.

The major structural variations across the programs under review are related to the justice system processing of the cases being handled. Programs may take cases after an offender has been apprehended but prior to any court referral, after court referral but before adjudication or conviction, after adjudication or conviction but before disposition or sentencing, or after disposition or sentencing. In some programs, restitution amounts are set by a judge before any dialogue meeting; in most others, the restitution agreement is an outcome of the meeting.

There are additional variations in the auspices under which programs operate, including governmental, private nonprofit, and church related. Differences among such programs are difficult to ascertain, in particular because nearly all VOM programs seek and receive some governmental funding for portions of their operations and must therefore adhere to many of the same regulations required in governmentally operated programs. To date, no studies are known to have assessed differences in outcome along any of these structural variations, with the exception of shuttle mediation.

The outcome variables assessed in the studies under review include participants' satisfaction, variously reported as satisfaction with their meeting, with the program, with the agreement, with their preparation for the meeting, or with the justice system handling of their case, as well as whether they would recommend participation to others in similar circumstances; participants' assessment of the fairness of the mediator, the process, and the outcome; the amounts and types of restitution agreed on and offender compliance with the restitution agreements; diversion; recidivism; and costs.

Characteristics of Victim-Offender Mediation

A national survey of VOM programs in the United States (Umbreit and Greenwood, 1999) provides an overview of the types of cases typically brought to mediation. Juvenile offenders are more likely to be the primary focus of U.S. VOM programs, with 45 percent of programs offering services solely to juveniles and an additional 46 percent serving both juveniles and adults. Only 9 percent of VOM programs nationwide are focused on adults alone. Among the reports reviewed for this chapter, 49 percent studied only juvenile programs, 29 percent studied programs serving both, and 22 percent studied programs serving only adults.

VOM programs across the United States are most often offered by private, nonprofit community-based agencies (43 percent of programs). Various elements of the justice system are responsible for another 33 percent of VOM programs, including probation (16 percent), correctional facilities (8 percent), prosecuting attorney offices (4 percent), victim services (3 percent), and police departments (2 percent). The remaining 23 percent are offered by churches or church-related agencies.

In the U.S. survey, fully two-thirds of the cases referred to VOM are misdemeanors; the remaining third are felony cases. The four most common offenses referred, in order of frequency, were vandalism, minor assaults, theft, and burglary. Together, these four offenses accounted for the vast majority of referrals. The primary referral sources were probation officers, judges, and prosecutors.

Not surprisingly, the participating programs reported a wide range of points in the justice system process at which VOM occurs. Slightly over a third (34 percent) are true diversion, occurring after an offender has been apprehended but prior to any formal finding of guilt. Just under a third (28 percent each) occur postadjudication but predisposition, and postdisposition. A small number of programs (7 percent) reported that their mediations could occur at any point in the process, and the remaining 3 percent reported working with cases prior to any court involvement.

All of the programs in the 1999 survey reported that participation was completely voluntary for crime victims. Voluntary offender participation was reported by 79 percent of the surveyed programs. Not all victims, however, have felt they had a choice. A 1996 study of VOM programs in England (Umbreit and Roberts, 1996) found that victims who participated in face-to-face mediation were more likely than victims who participated in a form of shuttle mediation to feel that they participated voluntarily. In studying juvenile VOM programs in six Oregon counties, Umbreit, Coates, and Vos (2001a) found that 91 percent of the victims experienced their participation as voluntary. Offenders are even more likely than victims to report that they did not see their participation as voluntary. In the same Oregon study, nearly half of the juvenile offenders felt they had no choice.

Careful preparation of participants has been one of the hallmarks of the VOM movement. In the national survey (Umbreit and Greenwood, 1999), 78 percent of the programs reported that participants received at least one preparation meeting. In general, preparation meetings are understood to consist of personal, face-to-face contact with the participants by either the actual mediator or some other worker from the VOM program. In fact, such meetings sometimes are carried out by telephone. In some programs, the offenders are more likely than the victims to have received their preparation in face-to-face meetings (Umbreit, Coates and Vos, 2001a).

In spite of such variation, preparation usually gets high marks from both offenders and victims in studies that have evaluated participant satisfaction with their preparation. Across six empirical studies reporting percentages (Collins, 1984; Fercello and Umbreit, 1999; Roberts, 1998; Strode, 1997; Umbreit, Coates and Vos, 2001a), the proportion of victims feeling adequately prepared to meet the offender ranged from 68 to 98 percent. Only three studies reported offender opinions of their preparation for mediation (Fercello and Umbreit, 1999; Roberts, 1998; Umbreit, Coates, and Vos, 2001a). Offender satisfaction with preparation ranged from 89 to 93 percent.

An additional study (Roberts, 1995) reported on a Canadian program working with violent crimes. This program developed an unusual and more intensive preparation component: offenders and victims were videotaped in conversation about the offense with program staff, and these videos were then shared with their counterparts. Although no percentages were given, the study reported that parties were strongly satisfied. Similarly, in his exploratory study of seven violent cases that came to mediation, Flaten (1996) noted that preparation was cited as the single most important factor contributing to the success of mediation.

Who Participates and Why

Across a range of programs, participation rates by victims who have been referred to victim-offender mediation vary from about 40 to 60 percent. A few studies have addressed the characteristics that are predictive of referred cases coming to mediation. Three studies in the United States (Coates, Burns and Umbreit, 2002; Gehm, 1990; Wyrick and Costanzo, 1999) found that individuals representing a business or an institution that had been victimized by a crime were more likely to participate in VOM than individuals who were simply personally victimized; a British study (Marshall, 1990), however, found the opposite.

Two studies in the United States examined offender race/ethnicity as a potential factor in the likelihood of a case's coming to mediation.

Gehm (1990), in a study of programs in Indiana, Wisconsin, and Oregon, found that victims were more likely to mediate if the offender was white. Wyrick and Costanzo (1999), however, found in California that white offenders were no more likely to reach mediation than Hispanic offenders, although they were significantly more likely to do so than offenders of other minority groups.

Seriousness of offense has yet to demonstrate any consistent pattern as a predictor of participation rates. Its impact may vary greatly by program type and focus. Gehm (1990) found that victims were more likely to participate if the offense was a misdemeanor rather than a felony. In their California sample, Wyrick and Costanzo (1999) found that property offense cases were significantly more likely to be mediated than personal offense cases. They also found that the time lapse between the crime and the referral was correlated differently with participation rates by type of offense. Longer time lapses for property cases resulted in fewer mediations, while longer time lapses in personal offenses resulted in more mediations.

Several studies noted that victim willingness to participate was driven by a desire to receive restitution, hold the offender accountable, learn more about why the offender committed the crime and share their pain with the offender, avoid court processing, help the offender change behavior, or see that the offender was adequately punished (Coates and Gehm, 1985; Perry, Lajeunesse, and Woods, 1987; Roberts, 1995; Niemeyer and Shichor, 1996; Strode, 1997). In two of these studies (Coates, Burns, and Umbreit, 2002; Umbreit, Coates, and Vos, 2001a), the top-ranking victim reason for choosing to participate was to help the offender. Offenders choosing to participate often wanted to take direct responsibility for their own actions, pay back the victim, apologize for the harm they caused, and get the whole experience behind them.

Less is known about why some persons who are referred to VOM elect not to participate. Only a handful of studies have interviewed such persons to examine their choosing not to participate. Among victims, refusals typically come from persons who believed the crime to be too trivial to merit the time required, feared meeting the offender, wanted the offender to have a harsher punishment, or felt that too much time had elapsed since the crime (Coates and Gehm, 1985; Umbreit, 1995a). Additional concerns expressed by occasional victims in a recent Minnesota study (Coates, Burns, and Umbreit, 2002) included feeling the meeting would not be safe, pressure from family or friends not to participate, and not wanting to help the offender. A mitigating factor in some programs is that restitution may already be established by a judge before a referral is made to mediation; victims may perceive they have less to gain in such situations.

Even less attention has been given to offender reasons for nonparticipation. In one study, offenders reported that they were sometimes advised by lawyers not to participate (Schneider, 1986). And some simply did not want "to be bothered" (Coates and Gehm, 1985).

Participant Satisfaction

Victim-offender mediation proponents often speak of their efforts as ways of humanizing the justice system. Traditionally, victims were left out of the justice process. Neither victims nor offenders had opportunities to tell their stories and to be heard. The state somehow stood in for the victim, and the offender seldom noticed that his or her actions had an impact on real, live people. In addition, victims were left with stereotypes to fill their thoughts about offenders. VOM, reformers believed, offered opportunities for both parties to come together in a controlled setting to share the pain of being victimized and to answer questions of why and how this occurred. This personalizing of the consequences of crime, it was thought, would enhance satisfaction levels with the entire justice process.

The vast majority of studies reviewed reported in some way on satisfaction of victims and offenders with victim-offender mediation and its outcomes. Across program sites, types of offenders, types of victims, and cultures, high levels of participant satisfaction were found.

Before exploring the nature of this satisfaction further, it must be remembered that 40 to 60 percent of persons offered the opportunity to participate in VOM refused. The voluntary nature of participating in VOM is a self-selection factor overlaying the findings reported here. The high levels of satisfaction may have something to do with the opportunity to choose. Perhaps those who are able to choose among justice options are more satisfied with their experiences.

Expression of satisfaction with VOM is consistently high for both victims and offenders across sites, cultures, and seriousness of offenses. Typically, eight or nine out of ten participants report being satisfied with the process and with the resulting agreement (Davis, Tichane, and Grayson, 1980; Coates and Gehm, 1985; Perry, Lajeunesse, and Woods, 1987; Marshall, 1990; Umbreit, 1991, 1993, 1994a, 1994b, 1998, 1999; Umbreit and Coates, 1993; Warner, 1992; T. Roberts, 1995; Carr, 1998; L. Roberts, 1998; Evje and Cushman, 2000).

Even in an England-based study (Umbreit and Roberts, 1996), which yielded some of the lowest satisfaction scores among the studies reviewed, 84 percent of the victims engaged in face-to-face mediation were satisfied with the mediation outcome. For individuals involved with indirect mediation, depending on shuttle mediation between parties without face-to-face meetings, 74 percent were satisfied with their experience. These findings were consistent with an earlier study based in Kettering where a small subsample of participants were interviewed indicating that 62 percent of individual victims and 71 percent of corporate victims were satisfied (Dignan, 1990). About half of the offenders responding reported being satisfied. Participants involved in face-to-face mediation were more satisfied than those who worked with a go-between.

Victims often reported being satisfied with the opportunity to share their stories and their pain resulting from the crime. A victim stated she had wanted to "let the kid know he hurt me personally, not just the money. . . . I felt raped" (Umbreit, 1988, p. 988). Some pointed to their role in the process with satisfaction. One victim said: "We were both allowed to speak. . . . he [the mediator] didn't put words into anybody's mouth" (Umbreit, 1988, p. 988). A female victim indicated she felt better having a stake in punishment (Coates and Gehm, 1985). Another indicated that "it was important to find out what happened, to hear his story, and why he did it and how" (Umbreit and Coates, 1992b, p. 106). Numerous victims were consumed with the need for closure. A victim of violent crime indicated that prior to mediation, "I was consumed with hate and rage and was worried what I would do when he got out" (Flaten, 1996, p. 398).

Of course, not all victims were so enamored with the process. A male victim complained, "It's like being hit by a car and having to get out and help the other driver when all you were doing was minding your own business" (Coates and Gehm, 1985, p. 254). A Canadian stated, "Mediation process was not satisfactory, especially the outcome. I was not repaid for damages or given compensation one year later. Offender has not been adequately dealt with. I don't feel I was properly compensated" (Umbreit, 1995a, p. 162).

Offenders generally report surprise about having positive experiences. As one youth said, "He understood the mistake I made, and I really did appreciate him for it" (Umbreit, 1991, p. 195). Some reported changes: "After meeting the victim I now realize that I hurt them a lot. . . . To understand how the victim feels makes me different" (Umbreit and Coates,

1992a, p. 18). One Canadian offender stated his pleasure quite succinctly: "Without mediation I would have been convicted" (Umbreit, 1995a, p. 144).

The following comment reflects the feelings of some offenders that victims occasionally abused the process: "We didn't take half the stuff she said we did; she either didn't have the stuff or someone else broke in too" (Coates and Gehm, 1985, p. 12).

Secondary analysis of satisfaction data from a U.S. study and a Canadian study yielded remarkably similar results (Bradshaw and Umbreit, 1998; Umbreit and Bradshaw, 2003). Using step-wise multiple regression procedures to determine those variables most associated with victim satisfaction, we discovered that three variables emerged to explain over 40 percent of the variance. In each study, the key variables associated with victim satisfaction were that (1) the victim felt good about the mediator, (2) the victim perceived the resulting restitution agreement as fair, and (3) the victim, for whatever reason, had a strong initial desire to meet the offender. The last variable supports the notion that self-selection and choice are involved in longer-run satisfaction. These findings also underscore the important role of the mediator, and the actual outcome or agreement resulting from mediation.

These high levels of satisfaction with victim-offender mediation also translated into relatively high levels of satisfaction with the criminal justice system. Where comparison groups were studied, those victims and offenders going through mediation indicated being more satisfied with the criminal justice system than those going through traditional court prosecution (Davis, Tichane, and Grayson, 1980).

Fairness

Related to satisfaction is the question of fairness. Many studies of victim-offender mediation asked participants about the fairness of the mediation process and the resulting agreement (Davis, Tichane, and Grayson, 1980; Collins, 1984; Coates and Gehm, 1985; Strode, 1997; Umbreit, 1988, 1991, 1994a; Umbreit and Roberts, 1996; Evje and Cushman, 2000).

Not surprising, given the high levels of satisfaction, the vast majority of VOM participants (typically over 80 percent) across settings, cultures, and types of offenses reported believing that the process was fair to both sides and that the resulting agreement was fair. Again, these experiences led to feelings that the overall criminal justice system was fair. Where comparison groups were employed, those individuals exposed to mediation came away more likely to feel that they had been treated fairly than those going through the traditional court proceedings. In a study of burglary victims in Minneapolis, Umbreit (1989a) found that 80 percent who went through VOM indicated that they experienced the criminal justice system as fair compared with only 37 percent of burglary victims who did not participate in VOM.

These positive satisfaction and fairness experiences have generated support for VOM as a criminal justice option. When asked, typically nine out of ten participants would recommend a VOM program to others (Coates and Gehm, 1985; Umbreit, 1991; Evje and Cushman, 2000).

Restitution

Early on, restitution was regarded by many VOM program advocates as an important by-product of bringing offender and victim together in a face-to-face meeting. Restitution was considered somewhat secondary to the actual meeting, where each party had the opportunity to talk about what happened. The form of restitution, or what is called reparation in some jurisdictions, is quite varied, including direct compensation to victim, community service, work for victim, and sometimes unusual paybacks devised between victim and offender. Today, some jurisdictions see VOM as a promising major vehicle for achieving restitution for the victim. The meeting is necessary to establish appropriate restitution amounts and garner the commitment of the offender to honor a contract. Victims frequently report that while restitution was the primary motivator for them to participate in VOM, what they appreciated most about the program was the opportunity to talk with the offender (Coates and Gehm, 1985).

In many settings, restitution is inextricably linked with victim-offender mediation. About half the studies under review looked at restitution as an outcome of mediation (Collins, 1984; Coates and Gehm, 1985, Perry, Lajeunesse, and Woods, 1987; Umbreit, 1988, 1991; Galaway, 1989; Warner, 1992; Roy, 1993; Evje and Cushman, 2000). Of those cases that reached a meeting, typically 90 percent or more generated agreements. Restitution of one form or another (monetary, community service, or direct service to the victim) was part of the vast majority of these agreements. Looking across the studies reviewed here, it appears that approximately 80 to 90 percent of the contracts are reported as completed. In some instances, the length of contract exceeded the length of study.

One study was able to compare restitution completion between those youth participating in VOM with a matched group who did not (Umbreit and Coates, 1992b). In that instance, 81 percent of participating youth completed their contracts contrasted with 57 percent of those not in the VOM program. In another study comparing an Indiana county whose restitution was integrated into victim-offender mediation with a Michigan county with court-imposed restitution, no difference in completion rates were found (Roy, 1993). Each was just shy of 80 percent completion.

A study of juvenile VORP in six California counties showed a staggering increase in average obligated restitution paid. In comparison to restitution paid by youths who did not participate in VOM, the increases ranged from more than 95 percent in Sonoma to more than 1,000 percent in Los Angeles County (Evje and Cushman, 2000).

Diversion

Many VOM programs are nominally established to divert offenders into less costly, less time-consuming, and often less severe options. Although diversion was a goal lauded by many, others expressed concern about the unintended consequence of widening the net, that is, ushering in youth and adults to experience a sanction more severe than they would have if VOM did not exist. While much talk continues on this topic, there is a dearth of study devoted to it. Only a handful of the studies reviewed here address this question.

One of the broadest studies considering the diversion question was that conducted over a three-year period in Kettering, Northamptonshire, England (Dignan, 1990). Offenders participating in the VOM program were matched with similar nonparticipating offenders from a neighboring jurisdiction. The author concludes that at least 60 percent of the offenders participating in the Kettering program were true diversions from court prosecution. Jurisdictional comparisons also led him to conclude that there was a 13 percent widening of the net effect—much less than local observers would have predicted.

In a Glasgow, Scotland, agency where numbers were sufficiently large to allow random assignment of individuals between the VOM program and a comparison group going through the traditional process, it was discovered that forty-three percent of the latter group were not prosecuted (Warner, 1992). However, most of these pled guilty and were fined. This would suggest that VOM in this instance was a more severe sanction and indeed widened the net of government control.

In a very large three-county study of mediation in North Carolina, results on diversion were mixed (Clarke, Valente, and Mace, 1992). In two counties, mediation had no impact on diverting offenders from court. In the third county, the program may have reduced trials by as much as two-thirds.

Mediation impact on incarceration was explored in an Indiana-Ohio study by comparing consequences for seventy-three youth and adults going through VOM programs with those for a matched sample of individuals who were processed in the traditional manner (Coates and Gehm, 1985). VOM offenders spent less time incarcerated than did their counterparts. And when incarcerated, they did county jail time rather than state time. The length and place of incarceration also had substantial implications for costs.

Recidivism

While recidivism may be best regarded as an indicator of society's overall response to juvenile and adult offenders, it is often also a traditional measure used to evaluate the long-term impact of justice programs. Accordingly, a number of studies designed to assess VOM have incorporated measures of recidivism.

Some simply report rearrest or reconviction rates for offenders going through the VOM program under study (Carr, 1998; Roberts, 1998). Since no comparison group or before-and-after outcomes are reported, these recidivism reports have local value, but offer very little meaning for readers unfamiliar with typical rates for that particular region.

One of the first comparative studies to report recidivism on VOM was part of a much larger research project regarding restitution programs (Schneider, 1986). Youth randomly assigned to a Washington, D.C., VOM program were less likely to have subsequent offenses resulting in referral to a juvenile or adult court than youth in a comparison probation group. These youth were tracked for over thirty months. The results were 53 percent and 63 percent, respectively, and the difference was statistically significant. A third group, those who were referred to mediation but refused to participate, also did better than the probation group. This group's recidivism prevalence was 55 percent.

The study based in Kettering, England (Dignan, 1990), compared recidivism data on the VOM offenders who went through face-to-face mediation with those who were exposed only to shuttle mediation. The former group did somewhat better than the latter: 15.4 percent compared to 21.6 percent. As with satisfaction measures reported earlier, face-to-face mediation seems to generate better results in both the short run and longer run than the less personal indirect mediation.

In a study of youth participating in VOM programs in four states, youth in mediation had lower recidivism rates after a year than did a matched comparison group of youth who did not go through mediation (Umbreit and Coates, 1992a). Overall, across sites, 18 percent of the program youth reoffended compared to 27 percent for the comparison youth. Program youth also tended to reappear in court for less serious charges than did their comparison counterparts.

The Elkhart and Kalamazoo county study (Roy, 1993) found little difference in recidivism between youth going through the VOM program and the court-imposed restitution program. VOM youth recidivated at a slightly higher rate: 29 to 27 percent. The author noted that the VOM cohort included more felons than did the court-imposed restitution cohort.

A study of 125 youth in a Tennessee VOM program (Nugent and Paddock, 1995) reported that these youth were less likely to reoffend (19.8 versus 33.1 percent) than a randomly selected comparison group. The VOM youth who did reoffend did so with less serious charges than did their comparison counterparts.

A sizable cohort of nearly eight hundred youth going through mediation in Cobb County, Georgia, between 1993 and 1996 was followed along with a comparison group from an earlier period (Stone, Helms, and Edgeworth (1998). No significant difference in recidivism rates was found: 34.2 percent mediated to 36.7 percent nonmediated. However, the study also reported that three-quarters of the mediated youth who returned to court did so because of violation of the conditions of mediation agreements.

Wynne and Brown (1998) report on a longstanding study of the Leeds Victim Offender Unit, which began in 1985. Of the ninety offenders who met in face-to-face mediation from 1985 to 1987, 87 percent had had previous convictions before mediation. Sixty-eight percent had no convictions during a two-year follow-up after mediation.

In another English study focused on seven varying restorative justice schemes across England, Miers and others (2001) contend that "the only scheme that routinely involved victims (West Yorkshire) was for the most part both lower cost and more effective than the other schemes."

And this same program had a "significant impact on reoffending, both in terms of the offence frequency and offence seriousness" (p. x).

Stone (2000) compared youth going through Resolutions Northwest's Victim Offender Mediation Program in Multnomah County, Oregon, with a comparison group. Eighty percent of the youth processed through VOM did not recidivate during a one-year follow-up period, while 58 percent of the comparison group did not reoffend during a year of follow-up.

In a Lane County, Oregon, study, Nelson (2000) took a different tack. One hundred and fifty youth referred to VOM from July 1996 to November 1998 in that county were also followed for a year after referral. Comparing their referral frequencies the year prior to the referral to VOM with the year after, all referred youth had 65 percent fewer referrals to the system in the subsequent year. Juveniles referred to VOM but refusing to participate had 32 percent fewer referrals; youth who met with their victims had 81 percent fewer referrals than the preceding year; and juveniles who fully completed their agreements had 76 percent fewer referrals compared with 54 percent fewer referrals for youth who did not complete any part of the agreement.

Recidivism data were gathered on VOM programs in two additional Oregon counties in the study conducted by Umbreit, Coates, and Vos (2001a). These data reflect one-year-before-intervention comparisons of number of offenses with one year after. For the group of youth in the Deschutes County program, there was a 77 percent overall reduction in reoffending. Similarly, for the group of juveniles going through the victim-offender program in Jackson County, there was an overall 68 percent reduction in recidivism.

In a six-county VORP study in California conducted by Evje and Cushman (2000), one of the VORPs experienced a 46 percent higher rate of recidivism than its comparison group. In the other five counties, the VORP groups ranged from 21 to 105 percent less recidivism than their comparison groups.

Nugent, Umbreit, Wiinamaki, and Paddock (1999) conducted a rigorous reanalysis of recidivism data reported in four studies involving 488 VOM youth and 527 non-VOM youth. Using ordinal logistical regression procedures, the authors determined that VOM youth recidivated at a statistically significant lower rate than non-VOM youth, and when they did reoffend, they did so for less serious offenses than the non-VOM youth.

Costs

The relative cost of correctional programs is difficult to assess. A handful of the studies reviewed here have addressed the question of the costs of handling cases in VOM programs, but as yet there is no broad agreement on how such costs should be ascertained. Some studies simply reported the costs of VOM programs in terms of the dollars spent per case handled. Even these data are difficult to interpret, since many programs rely heavily on volunteer hours donated by community members who serve as mediators, and the value of their labor does not show up in the reported costs. Similarly, the returned value to the community from hours spent by offenders in community service restitution efforts through VOM programs is not reflected in such data.

Cost per unit case is obviously influenced by the number of cases handled and the amount of time devoted to each case. The results of a detailed cost analysis in a Scottish study were mixed (Warner, 1992). In some instances, mediation was less costly than other options and in others more. The author notes that given the "marginal scope" of these programs, it remains difficult to evaluate their cost if implemented on a scale large enough to have an impact on overall program administration.

Evaluation of a large-scale VOM program in California led the authors to conclude that the cost per case was reduced dramatically as the program went from being a fledgling to being a viable option (Niemeyer and Shichor, 1996). The cost per case was $250.

An alternative way of considering the cost impact of VOM is to consider broader system impact. Reduction of incarceration time served can yield considerable savings to a state or county (Coates and Gehm, 1985). Reduction of trials, such as in Henderson County, North Carolina, where trials were reduced by two-thirds, would have tremendous impact at the county level (Clarke, Valente, and Mace (1992). And researchers evaluating a VOM program in Cobb County, Georgia, point out that although they did not do a cost analysis, time is money (Stone, Helms, and Edgeworth, 1998). The time required to process mediated cases was only a third of that needed for nonmediated cases.

The potential cost savings of VOM programs when they are truly employed as alternatives rather than as showcase add-ons is significant. Yet a cautionary note must continue to be heard. Like any other program option, these programs can be swamped with cases to the point that quality is compromised. And in the quest for savings, there is the temptation to expand the eligibility criteria to include individuals who would not otherwise penetrate the system or take on serious cases that the particular program staff are ill equipped to manage. Staff and administrators must be prepared to ask, "Cost savings at what cost?"

Meta-Analysis

Increasingly the field of social science is witnessing the emergence of meta-analyses, that is, methods of research synthesis across a set of empirical studies. Meta-analysis typically involves reviewing the relevant literature, including published journal articles, books, and perhaps less well-known research monographs. Data are extracted from these studies and aggregated for further statistical analysis. Three such studies are reported on here.

Nugent, Umbreit, Wiinamaki, and Paddock (1999) conducted a rigorous reanalysis of recidivism data reported in four previous studies involving a total sample of 1,298 juvenile offenders: 619 who participated in VOM and 679 who did not. Using ordinal logistical regression procedures, the authors determined that VOM youth recidivated at a statistically significant 32 percent lower rate than non-VOM youth, and when they did reoffend, they did so for less serious offenses than the non-VOM youth.

Nugent, Williams, and Umbreit (2003) have expanded their effort to include fourteen studies to compare the prevalence rate of subsequent delinquent behavior of VOM participants with that of adolescent offenders who did not participate in VOM. This analysis relied on a combined sample of 9,037 juveniles. The results "suggested that VOM participants tended to commit fewer reoffenses . . . [and] tended to commit less serious reoffenses" (Nugent, Williams and Umbreit, 2003).

In another large meta-study, the Canadian Department of Justice (Latimer, Dowden, and Muise, 2001) reviewed eight conferencing and twenty-seven victim-offender mediation programs. In order to qualify for inclusion in this analysis the study had to have (1) evaluated a restorative justice program, defined as follows: "restorative justice is a voluntary, community-based response to criminal behavior that attempts to bring together the victim, the offender and the community in an effort to address the harm caused by the criminal behavior"; (2) used a control group or comparison group that did not participate in the restorative justice program; (3) reported on at least one of the four outcomes—victim satisfaction, offender satisfaction, restitution compliance, or recidivism; and (4) provided sufficient statistical information to calculate an effect size.

Some of the major results of this analysis are:

Victim satisfaction. In all but one of the thirteen restorative programs studied, victims were more satisfied than those in traditional approaches. The authors indicate that "VOM models tended to yield higher levels of victim satisfaction rates than conferencing models when compared to the non-restorative approaches" (p. 10). They suggest that this result may be explained by the conferences' typically having more participants, and thus it may be more difficult to find as much satisfaction with an agreement.

Offender satisfaction. Initial analysis shows "no discernible impact" on offender satisfaction. However when an outlier program is removed, "moderate to weak positive impact on offender satisfaction" is noted (p. 11).

Restitution. "Offenders who participated in restorative justice programs tended to have substantially higher compliance rates than offenders exposed to other arrangements" (p. 12).

Recidivism. "Restorative justice programs, on average, yielded reductions in recidivism compared to non-restorative approaches to criminal behavior" (p. 14).

The authors discuss and consider the issue of self-selection bias, that is, victims and offenders choose to participate in these programs. They note that McCold and Wachtel (1998) attributed apparent differences in recidivism to the effect of self-selection bias. Latimer, Dowden, and Muise (2001) conclude: "Notwithstanding the issue of self-selection bias, the results of this meta-analysis, at present, represent the best indicator of the effectiveness of restorative justice practices, i.e. those individuals who choose to participate in restorative justice programs find the process satisfying, tend to display lower recidivism rates and are more likely to adhere to restitution agreements" (p. 17).

Future Research Recommendations

It is clear from this review that VOM is usually effective in meeting the felt needs of the victims and offenders who participate, that it tends to have a positive impact on restitution and recidivism, that it can serve as a diversion from court proceedings, and that it may show potential for reducing the costs of handling some juvenile and criminal cases. There are not yet sufficient data to begin to address the question of whether these outcomes are affected by structural variations in program auspices, nature and type of service delivered, or point in the justice system process at which the service is offered.

The next wave of research and evaluation of VOM programs needs to set the stage for addressing these unanswered questions. In part, this can be accomplished by ever larger sample sizes, through which both individual program evaluations and subsequent meta-analysis can sort outcomes into meaningful categories and examine variation. It will be important for such studies to preserve and report the relevant categories along which variation has been measured.

The need for longitudinal studies to test the strength and durability of victim and offender satisfaction, perceptions of fairness, and recidivism is obvious. Also, there is a need to go much deeper on the issues of satisfaction and fairness. What are the contributing variables that cause this, and how can programs continue to refine their procedures to maximize the possibility of high levels of fairness and satisfaction? Finally, there is a clear need for more rigorous designs to be employed, including random assignment into different treatment groups.

An overarching research issue derives from the nature of restorative justice initiatives in general. As VOM increasingly moves into the mainstream of justice system offerings and VOM programs receive ever more funds from governmental auspices, there is the potential for overemphasizing the offender-related outcome variables at the expense of the value of the program as perceived by participating victims and community members. VOM-related research needs to continue to insist that victims and communities have a voice in decisions about how harm is to be repaired and how programs are to be evaluated and that the impact of the program on the involved offenders is not the only important outcome criterion.

Conclusion

Just as interest in victim-offender mediation is growing within the justice arena, so is the body of empirical knowledge collected to evaluate, shape, and refine it. Involving victims, offenders, and community members in sorting out possible solutions to conflicts is yielding, for the most part, positive responses from participants. The vast majority of participants find the experience satisfactory, fair, and helpful. In a number of jurisdictions, rates of restitution completion have climbed. And offenders going through mediation approaches often have lower levels of offending than they did before or than compared with a similar group of offenders who did not meet with their victims.

Studies reviewed here range in rigor from exploratory to experimental random assignment designs. More questions need to be pursued and broadened, but given the empirical evidence generated over the past twenty-five years or so and across many countries, it seems reasonable to say that victim-offender mediation does contribute to increased victim involvement and healing, to offenders' taking responsibility for their behaviors and learning from this experience, and to community members' participating in shaping a just response to law violation.

References

American Bar Association. *Criminal Justice Policy on Victim-Offender Mediation/ Dialogue.* Chicago: American Bar Association, 1994.

Bazemore, G., and Umbreit, M. S. "Rethinking the Sanctioning Function in Juvenile Court: Retributive or Restorative Responses to Youth Crime." *Crime and Delinquency,* 1995, *41,* 296–316.

Bradshaw, W., and Umbreit, M. "Crime Victims Meet Juvenile Offenders: Contributing Factors to Victim Satisfaction with Mediated Dialogue." *Juvenile and Family Court Journal,* 1998, *49* (3), 17–25.

Carr, C. *VORS Program Evaluation Report.* Inglewood, Calif.: Centenela Valley Juvenile Diversion Project, 1998.

Clarke, S., Valente, E., and Mace, R. *Mediation of Interpersonal Disputes: An Evaluation of North Carolina's Programs.* Chapel Hill: Institute of Government, University of North Carolina, 1992.

Coates, R., Burns, H., and Umbreit, M. *Victim Participation in Victim Offender Conferencing: Washington County, Minnesota Community Justice Program.* St. Paul, Minn.: Center for Restorative Justice and Peacemaking, 2002.

Coates, R., and Gehm, J. *Victim Meets Offender: An Evaluation of Victim-Offender Reconciliation Programs.* Valparaiso, Ind.: PACT Institute of Justice, 1985.

Coates, R., and Gehm, J., "An Empirical Assessment." In M. Wright and B. Galaway (eds.), *Mediation and Criminal Justice.* Thousand Oaks, Calif.: Sage, 1989.

Collins, J. P. *Final Evaluation Report on the Grande Prairie Community Reconciliation Project For Young Offenders.* Ottawa: Ministry of the Solicitor General of Canada, Consultation Centre (Prairies), 1984.

Council of Europe Committee of Ministers. *Mediation in Penal Matters.* Council of Europe, Strasbourg, France, Sept. 1999.

Davis, R., Tichane, M., and Grayson, D. *Mediation and Arbitration as Alternatives to Prosecution in Felony Arrest Cases: An Evaluation of the Brooklyn Dispute Resolution Center.* New York: VERA Institute of Justice, 1980.

Dignan, J. *Repairing the Damage: An Evaluation of an Experimental Adult Reparation Scheme in Kettering, Northamptonshire.* Sheffield: Centre for Criminological Legal Research, Faculty of Law, University of Sheffield, 1990.

Evje, A., and Cushman, R. *A Summary of the Evaluations of Six California Victim Offender Reconciliation Programs.* San Francisco: Judicial Council of California, Administrative Office of the Courts, 2000.

Fercello, C., and Umbreit, M. *Client Satisfaction with Victim Offender Conferences in Dakota County, Minnesota.* St. Paul, Minn.: Center for Restorative Justice and Peacemaking, 1999.

Flaten, C. "Victim Offender Mediation: Application with Serious Offences Committed by Juveniles." In B. Galaway and J. Hudson (eds.), *Restorative Justice: International Perspectives.* Monsey, N.Y.: Criminal Justice Press, 1996.

Galaway, B. "Informal Justice: Mediation Between Offenders and Victims." In P. Albrecht and O. Backes (eds.), *Crime Prevention and Intervention: Legal and Ethical Problems.* New York: Walter de Gruyter, 1989.

Galaway, B. "Victim-Offender Mediation by New Zealand Probation Officers: The Possibilities and the Reality." *Mediation Quarterly,* 1995, *12,* 249–262.

Gehm, J. "Mediated Victim-Offender Restitution Agreements: An Exploratory Analysis of Factors Related to Victim Participation." In B. Galaway and J. Hudson (eds.), *Criminal Justice, Restitution, and Reconciliation.* Monsey, N.Y.: Criminal Justice Press, 1990.

Latimer, J., Dowden, C., and Muise, D. *The Effectiveness of Restorative Practice: A Meta-Analysis.* Ottawa: Department of Justice, Canada, Research and Statistics Division Methodological Series, 2001.

Lightfoot, E., and Umbreit, M. S. "An Analysis of Statutory Provisions for Victim-Offender Mediation." *Criminal Justice Policy Review,* forthcoming.

Marshall, T. "Results of Research from British Experiments in Restorative Justice." In B. Galaway and J. Hudson (eds.), *Criminal Justice, Restitution, and Reconciliation.* Monsey, N.Y.: Criminal Justice Press, 1990.

McCold, P., and Wachtel, B. *Restorative Policing Experiment: The Bethlehem Pennsylvania Police Family Group Conferencing Project.* Pipersville, Penn.: Community Service Foundation, 1998.

Miers, D., and others. *An Exploratory Evaluation of Restorative Justice Schemes.* London: Home Office, 2001.

Nelson, S. *Evaluation of the Restorative Justice Program.* Eugene, Ore.: Lane County Department of Youth Services, 2000.

Niemeyer, M., and Shichor, D. "A Preliminary Study of a Large Victim/Offender Reconciliation Program." *Federal Probation,* 1996, *60* (3), 30–34.

Nugent, W., and Paddock, J. B. "The Effect of Victim-Offender Mediation on Severity of Reoffense." *Mediation Quarterly,* 1995, *12,* 353–367.

Nugent, W., Williams, M., and Umbreit, M. "Participation in Victim-Offender Mediation and the Prevalence and Severity of Subsequent Behavior." *Utah Law Review,* 2003, (1), 137–165.

Nugent, W. R., Umbreit, M., Wiinamaki, L., and Paddock, J. "Participation in Victim-Offender Mediation and Severity of Subsequent Delinquent Behavior: Successful Replications?" *Journal of Research in Social Work Practice,* 1999, *11* (1), 5–23.

Perry, L., Lajeunesse, T., and Woods, A. *Mediation Services: An Evaluation.* Manitoba: Attorney General: Research, Planning and Evaluation, 1987.

Pranis, K., and Umbreit, M. S. *Public Opinion Research Challenges Perception of Widespread Public Demand for Harsher Punishment.* Minneapolis: Citizens Council, 1992.

Roberts, L. "Victim Offender Mediation: An Evaluation of the Pima County Juvenile Court Center's Victim Offender Mediation Program (VOMP)." Unpublished master's thesis, University of Arizona, 1998.

Roberts, T. *Evaluation of the Victim Offender Mediation Project, Langley, BC: Final Report.* Victoria, B.C.: Focus Consultants, 1995.

Roy, S. "Two Types of Juvenile Restitution Programs in Two Midwestern Counties: A Comparative Study." *Federal Probation,* 1993, *57* (4), 48–53.

Schneider, A. "Restitution and Recidivism Rates of Juvenile Offenders: Results from Four Experimental Studies." *Criminology,* 1986, *24,* 533–552.

Stone, K. "An Evaluation of Recidivism Rates for Resolutions Northwest's Victim-Offender Mediation Program." Unpublished master's thesis, Portland State University, 2000.

Stone, S., Helms, W., and Edgeworth, P. *Cobb County [Georgia] Juvenile Court Mediation Program Evaluation.* Carrolton: State University of West Georgia, 1998.

Strode, E. "Victims of Property Crime Meet Their Juvenile Offenders: Victim Participants' Evaluation of the Dakota County (Minn.) Community Corrections Victim Offender Meeting Program." Unpublished master's thesis, Smith College of Social Work, 1997.

Umbreit, M. "Mediation of Victim Offender Conflict." *Journal of Dispute Resolution,* 1988, *1988,* 85–105.

Umbreit, M. "Crime Victims Seeking Fairness, Not Revenge: Toward Restorative Justice." *Federal Probation,* 1989a, *53* (3), 52–57.

Umbreit, M. "Violent Offenders and Their Victims." In M. Wright and B. Galaway (eds.), *Mediation and Criminal Justice.* Thousand Oaks, Calif.: Sage, 1989b.

Umbreit, M. "Minnesota Mediation Center Produces Positive Results." *Corrections Today,* Aug. 1991, pp. 194–197.

Umbreit, M. "Juvenile Offenders Meet Their Victims: The Impact of Mediation in Albuquerque, New Mexico." *Family and Conciliation Courts Review,* 1993, *31,* 90–100.

Umbreit, M. *Victim Meets Offender.* Monsey, N.Y.: Criminal Justice Press, 1994a.

Umbreit, M. "Crime Victims Confront Their Offenders: The Impact of a Minneapolis Mediation Program." *Research on Social Work Practice,* 1994b, *4,* 436–447.

Umbreit, M. "Restorative Justice Through Mediation: The Impact of Offenders Facing Their Victims in Oakland." *Journal of Law and Social Work,* 1995a, *5,* 1–13.

Umbreit, M. *Mediation of Criminal Conflict: An Assessment of Programs in Four Canadian Provinces.* St. Paul, Minn.: Center for Restorative Justice and Peacemaking, 1995b.

Umbreit, M. "Restorative Justice Through Mediation: The Impact of Programs in Four Canadian Provinces." In B. Galaway and J. Hudson, (eds.), *Restorative Justice: International Perspectives,* Monsey, N.Y.: Criminal Justice Press, 1996.

Umbreit, M. "Restorative Justice Through Victim-Offender Mediation: A Multi-Site Assessment." *Western Criminology Review,* 1998, *1,* 1–29.

Umbreit, M. "Victim Offender Mediation in Canada: The Impact of an Emerging Social Work Intervention." *International Social Work,* 1999, *42* (2), 215–227.

Umbreit, M., and Bradshaw, W. "Factors That Contribute to Victim Satisfaction with Mediated Offender Dialogue in Winnipeg: An Emerging Area of Social Work Practice." *Journal of Law and Social Work,* 2003, *9* (2), 35–51.

Umbreit, M., and Coates, R. *Victim Offender Mediation: An Analysis of Programs in Four States of the US.* St. Paul, Minn.: Center for Restorative Justice and Peacemaking, 1992a.

Umbreit, M., and Coates, R. "The Impact of Mediating Victim Offender Conflict: An Analysis of Programs in Three States." *Juvenile and Family Court Journal,* 1992b, *43* (3), 21–28.

Umbreit, M., and Coates, R. "Cross-Site Analysis of Victim-Offender Mediation in Four States." *Crime and Delinquency,* 1993, *39,* 565–585.

Umbreit, M., Coates, R., and Vos, B. *Juvenile Victim Offender Mediation in Six Oregon Counties.* Salem: Oregon Dispute Resolution Commission, 2001a.

Umbreit, M., Coates, R., and Vos, V. "The Impact of Victim Offender Mediation: Two Decades of Research." *Federal Probation,* 2001b, *65* (3), 29–35.

Umbreit, M., and Fercello, C. "Family Group Conferencing Program Results in Client Satisfaction." *Juvenile Justice Update,* Dec.–Jan. 1998, *3* (6), 3–13.

Umbreit, M., and Greenwood, J. "National Survey of Victim Offender Mediation Programs in the U.S." *Mediation Quarterly,* 1999, *16,* 235–251.

Umbreit, M., and Roberts, A. W. *Mediation of Criminal Conflict in England: An Assessment of Services in Coventry and Leeds.* St. Paul, Minn.: Center for Restorative Justice and Peacemaking, 1996.

Umbreit, M. S. "Humanistic Mediation: A Transformative Journey of Peacemaking." *Mediation Quarterly,* 1997, *14,* 201–213.

Umbreit, M. S. *The Handbook of Victim Offender Mediation: An Essential Guide to Practice and Research.* San Francisco: Jossey-Bass, 2001.

Umbreit, M. S., Coates, R. B., and Vos, B. "The Impact of Restorative Justice Conferencing: A Multi-National Perspective." *British Journal of Community Justice,* 2002, *1* (2), 21–48.

Umbreit, M. S., and Vos, B. "Homicide Survivors Meet the Offender Prior to Execution: Restorative Justice Through Dialogue." *Homicide Studies,* 2000, *4* (1), 63–87.

Umbreit, M. S., Vos, B., Coates, R. B., and Brown, K. *Facing Violence: The Path of Restorative Justice and Dialogue.* Monsey, N.Y.: Criminal Justice Press, 2003.

United Nations. *Basic Principles on the Use of Restorative Justice Programmes in Criminal Matters.* New York: United Nations, July 2000.

Van Ness, D., and Heetderks, K. *Restoring Justice.* (2nd ed.) Cincinnati, Ohio: Anderson Publishing Company, 2002.

Warner, S. *Making Amends: Justice for Victims and Offenders.* Aldershot, England: Avebury, 1992.

Wynne, J., and Brown, I. "Can Mediation Cut Reoffending?" *Probation Journal,* 1996, *45,* 21–26.

Wyrick, P., and Costanzo, M. "Predictors of Client Participation in Victim-Offender Mediation." *Mediation Quarterly,* 1999, *16,* 253–257.

Zehr, H. *Changing Lenses: A New Focus for Crime and Justice.* Scottsdale, Pa.: Herald Press, 1990.

Zehr, H. *The Little Book of Restorative Justice.* Intercourse, Pa.: Good Books, 2002.

Mark S. Umbreit is a professor and founding director of the Center for Restorative Justice & Peacemaking at the University of Minnesota, School of Social Work. Umbreit is a fellow at the International Centre for Healing and the Law in Kalamazoo, Michigan, and he has been a consultant-trainer for the U.S. Department of Justice for twenty-three years. He is the author of six books and numerous articles and book chapters.

Robert B. Coates has been involved in justice research since the later 1960s and is currently senior research associate at the Center for Restorative Justice & Peacemaking at the University of Minnesota, School of Social Work.

Betty Vos practiced and taught social work at the University of Utah before joining the Center for Restorative Justice & Peacemaking at the University of Minnesota as a senior research associate.

Commentary: Restorative Justice: Beyond Victim-Offender Mediation

HOWARD ZEHR

This is an appropriate time to be taking stock of victim-offender mediation and the restorative justice field in which it is situated: the spring of 2004 marked the thirtieth anniversary of the first case of what was then called the Victim Offender Reconciliation Program (VORP), the case that is widely credited with initiating the contemporary restorative justice movement. This first case, in Elmira, Ontario, did not grow out of the conflict resolution movement directly. In fact, Dave Worth, one of the two men who facilitated that first case (it involved twenty-two property offenses), once told me that as they took these offenders to meet their victims, their role as facilitators was to say, "You knock on the door and say you are the offenders. We'll be right behind you." In spite of the crude approach, this first case was so successful that the movement was born, serving perhaps as a testimony to the power of encounter in itself. Shortly after this, the other facilitator, Mark Yantzi, wrote a master's thesis on the role of the third party in the victim-offender conflict, and the fields of conflict resolution and victim-offender reconciliation began to connect.

The first such program in the United States seems to have grown more directly out of the mediation field. Apparently my colleague Ron Kraybill, then a seminary student in Elkhart, Indiana, wrote a paper in the mid-1970s suggesting the use of mediation in the justice arena. This served as a catalyst for the beginning of the first program in the United States. From early on, then, the fields of conflict resolution and restorative justice have intersected.

In their article, Mark S. Umbreit, Robert B. Coates, and Betty Vos have provided a helpful overview of victim-offender mediation (VOM). Here, I situate VOM within the larger field of restorative justice, explore some of the intersections between restorative justice and conflict resolution or transformation (Lederach, 2003), and suggest some of the critical issues ahead for restorative justice as well as conflict transformation.

It is important to note that VOM is only one of a number of victim-offender encounter models being used in the restorative justice field today. Family group conferences (FGCs) originated in New Zealand in 1989, responding in part to the concerns and values of the indigenous Maori tradition. Like VOM, these are facilitated encounters but with a significantly larger circle of participants, including not only victims and offenders but family members, police, and others. In New Zealand, FGCs form the hub of the entire juvenile justice system, with courts serving as a backup instead of the norm. (MacRae and Zehr, 2004). Various forms of FGCs have been implemented in many communities in North America, England, South Africa, Australia, and elsewhere.

An even larger circle of participants is included in peacemaking circles; of the various encounter models, circles most consciously include community members. Circles are usually facilitated by a "circle keeper," who uses a talking piece and a circular process to guide the interchange. Unlike most other mediation processes, circles often explicitly name and draw on core values of the participants. Initially entering the restorative justice field from Canadian First Nation indigenous roots, circles have been widely adapted not only in cases involving crime but also within schools, religious institutions, and the workplace and for facilitating community dialogues or problem solving (Pranis, Stuart, and Wedge, 2003).

While programs are often designed around one of these approaches, increasingly these models are being blended, blurring the lines between them. Also, programs often see these models as options to be employed depending on the nature of the specific case. In addition, there is considerable discomfort with the term *mediation* in the justice arena. Unlike civil mediations, there is often a clear case of wrongdoing in criminal cases, and victims are often uncomfortable with the moral neutrality implied by the term *mediation*. Some use the term *victim-offender conferencing,* further blurring the distinction between models.

Whatever its form, victim-offender conferencing is today situated within a larger framework of restorative justice. As a conceptual framework, restorative justice seeks to reframe the way we conventionally think about wrongdoing and justice: away from our preoccupation with law-breaking, guilt, and punishment toward a focus on harms, needs, and obligations. Restorative justice especially emphasizes the importance of the engagement and empowerment of those most affected by wrongdoing and the use of problem-solving approaches. Some have termed it a needs-based understanding of justice, in contrast to the desserts-based approach of the Western legal model (Sullivan and Tift, 2001).

Although a notable consensus is evident on the basic elements or outlines of restorative justice, there is no clear agreement on a specific definition or list of principles. However, the general idea is suggested by the following definition (Zehr, 2002a): "Restorative justice is a process to involve, to the extent possible, those who have a stake in a specific offense and to collectively identify and address harms, needs and obligations, in order to heal and put things as right as possible" (p. 37).

Elsewhere I have argued that restorative justice reflects three basic assumptions: (1) crime is a violation of people and relationships, (2) violations create obligations, and (3) the central obligation is to put right the wrongs (Zehr, 2002a). Translated into a set of principles, restorative justice calls one to:

- Focus on the harms and consequent needs of the victims, as well as those of the communities and the offenders.

- Address the obligations that result from those harms (the obligations of offenders as well as of communities and society).

- Use inclusive, collaborative processes to the extent possible.

- Involve those with a legitimate stake in the situation, including victims, offenders, community members, and society.

- Seek to put right the wrongs.

In the past three decades, the conceptual framework as well as the practices of restorative framework have received wide currency internationally. Restorative justice was used to help provide a conceptual framework for the mission of the Truth and Reconciliation Commission in South Africa, for example, and is being advocated or implemented in many countries in a variety of arenas. The European Economic Community has called on its members to begin implementing restorative measures by the year 2006 and governments in the United Kingdom, Canada, and elsewhere are actively promoting restorative measures. A survey published in 2000 (O'Brien, 2000) found that twenty-three U.S. states had implemented restorative justice programs and that the majority of states have used restorative justice language in law or policy documents.

With its focus on interpersonal relationships, human need, and collaborative, problem-solving processes, restorative justice might be viewed as a peacemaking or conflict-resolution approach to justice. Indeed, after working in the restorative justice field for many years, I now teach in an international graduate-level conflict transformation program in which most of my colleagues have come from the conflict resolution field. This has encouraged all of us to explore the links and overlaps between our fields. In addition, our work in the aftermath of the Oklahoma City and Nairobi embassy bombings, as well as the events of September 11, 2001, have increasingly drawn us into trauma work. This has been a fruitful interaction, and we have found that the three fields—conflict transformation, trauma healing, and restorative justice—are highly interrelated and have much to learn from one another. While space does not allow full exploration of these intersections, the following suggest some of the lessons that we have learned:

1. An experience of victimization and even trauma is involved in most situations of conflict and wrongdoing. Both restorative justice and conflict transformation must acknowledge and address this sense of victimization and the resulting needs—often for everyone involved, including those who have offended. (Indeed, it can be argued that much offending—perhaps most or all violence—grows out of a sense of victimization or an experience of trauma.)

2. Most, if not all, situations of conflicts and harm involve questions of justice and injustice, and situations of injustice frequently involve trauma. James Gilligan (1996) has argued that "all violence is an effort to do justice, or undo injustice" (pp. 11–12). Both conflict and justice processes therefore must find ways to address these issues of justice and injustice. The conflict resolution and transformation field has not often acknowledged or provided a language to do this, but restorative justice does provide such a framework that is consistent with the values and principles of conflict transformation. Indeed, restorative justice might be viewed as a peacebuilding or conflict transformation approach to justice.

3. Processes to resolve harm or conflict often must find ways to explicitly address both needs and responsibilities. Too often, resolution processes focus on the former and downplay the latter.

4. Personal and communal narratives (referred to as story and "restorying") play critical roles in conflict resolution, trauma recovery, and restorative justice. Opportunities for storytelling must be incorporated into our processes.

5. Successful resolution and transformation often turns on the creation of empathy for one another by the participants. The dynamics that impede or encourage empathy need conscious attention by practitioners. They also merit further research.

6. Humiliation or shame plays a role in most conflicts, traumas, and harms. Conflict resolution and justice processes need to acknowledge and address this dynamic in some way. At a minimum, these processes require sensitivity to the way shame and humiliation affect participants. To be successful, they often require proactive steps to remove or transform shame.

7. Both restorative justice and conflict transformation reflect a common set of underlying values, and both need to make these more explicit. If these are not made explicit, practices are highly susceptible to misuse. These values, which include respect, humility, empowerment, and engagement, can be seen as reflecting an underlying worldview based on a sense of interconnectedness.

8. Structural injustices and problems play a role in many crimes, conflicts, and traumas. Both fields are in danger of overlooking or even perpetuating such injustices by individualizing conflicts and harms.

9. Both fields are susceptible to unconscious biases—of gender or culture, for example. Both need to more consciously incorporate the voices of women, people of color, and indigenous people.

10. Like all other social interventions, both conflict transformation and restorative justice have unintended consequences of which we must be aware. Both fields are susceptible to forces of co-optation and diversion that can sidetrack them from their intent. Indeed, these processes are inevitable and require conscious vigilance on the part of practitioners and advocates.

The role of trauma in conflict transformation, restorative justice, and peace building has emerged as an especially important focus of our work at Eastern Mennonite University. After September 11, our program was funded by Church World Service to conduct an ongoing series of seminars for religious leaders and caregivers from around the world. Termed STAR (Seminars and Trauma Awareness and Recovery), these seminars explore the intersection of trauma, conflict, and justice and brought those of us working in various related fields into the same teaching and practice arenas. This has helped us to understand that trauma is pervasive and multidimensional. It affects individuals not only emotionally and psychologically but spiritually and physically as well; indeed, the cognitive processing of the brain is often altered (Levine and Frederick, 1997). However, trauma also has a profound impact on communities and societies. Trauma shapes overall behavior, including patterns of wrongdoing and conflict, as well as processes of recovery, resolution, or transformation. The social as well as the individual dimensions of trauma must be addressed as part of peace building and restorative justice processes.

Through STAR, our faculty and staff have begun to explore how trauma affects both victim and offender and especially the ways that victimization and trauma, if not adequately addressed, can cause people to get stuck in a victim identity and can lead to offending behavior. More recently an awareness has come of perpetrator-induced trauma and its role in perpetuating the cycle of victimization and offending; severe offending can itself cause trauma in offenders (MacNair, 2002). This is an arena that deserves much more research: how trauma arises, how it affects social as well as individual well-being, how it plays into victimization and into offending behavior, what approaches and strategies can be used to address trauma not just on the individual level but with communities and even larger societies. Within that larger research agenda are important questions about the role of shame and humiliation in trauma, victimization and offending behavior, and processes of recovery or transformation (Zehr, 2002b). (For more on this topic, see the work of Evelin Linder and her colleagues at www.humiliationstudies.org.)

Figure 1, which is part of a larger analysis used in the STAR seminars, suggests some of the ways trauma plays itself out in victim and offender experiences and thus has an impact on the search for peace and justice.

Questions 8, 9, and 10 above suggest an area of special importance for further research. Where are these fields going wrong? What are the dangers, and how can we address them? In the field of restorative justice, this suggests questions such as these (Zehr and Toews, 2004):

• Will restorative justice truly be as victim oriented as it claims given the offender-centered nature of Western justice systems?

• Can we move beyond the focus on offender accountability and address their needs more holistically? Can we better understand and incorporate the dynamics of transformation, including the role of honor and humiliation and of "restorying" in offenders' journeys? When we talk about shame in these processes, can we avoid the wrong lesson being learned? Already there are examples of practitioners seeking to impose shame rather than emphasizing the removal or transformation of shame.

• Can restorative justice become a way to truly empower communities, encouraging not only involvement but also responsibility? Can we do this without sidetracking victims and while forging new partnerships between government and community?

Figure 1. Trauma in Victim and Offender Experiences

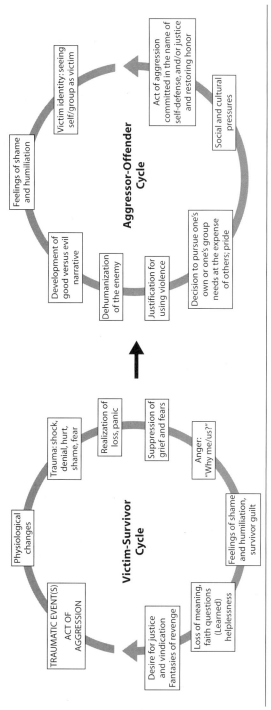

Victim-Survivor Cycle

Physiological changes

TRAUMATIC EVENT(S) ACT OF AGGRESSION

Desire for justice and vindication Fantasies of revenge

Loss of meaning, faith questions (Learned) helplessness

Feelings of shame and humiliation, survivor guilt

Anger: "Why me/us?"

Suppression of grief and fears

Realization of loss, panic

Trauma: shock, denial, hurt, shame, fear

Aggressor-Offender Cycle

Act of aggression committed in the name of self-defense, and/or justice and restoring honor

Social and cultural pressures

Decision to pursue one's own or one's group needs at the expense of others; pride

Justification for using violence

Dehumanization of the enemy

Development of good versus evil narrative

Feelings of shame and humiliation

Victim identity: seeing self/group as victim

Source: © Conflict Transformation Program, 2002. These diagrams were developed by Howard Zehr, Carolyn Yoder, Nancy Good Sider, Barry Hart, Lisa Schirch, and Jayne Docherty. The victim cycle is based on the work of Botcharova (2001).

- Can we learn to genuinely listen to and incorporate the perspectives of indigenous communities and people of color without expropriating their traditions or recolonizing them?
- Can we move beyond the individualization of wrongdoing to address social causes?
- Can we learn from our mistakes and avoid "butterfly collecting"? That is, can we truly open ourselves to self-reflection and evaluation and openly share the bad as well as the good?

One significant difference between restorative justice and conflict transformation is that restorative justice is usually applied in situations where there is a legitimate structure, such as a legal or disciplinary system, to name wrongdoing. Thus, even where there may be some shared blame, restorative processes often begin with a clearly identified wrong and "offender." This is one reason for discomfort with the term *mediation* in the restorative justice field. Yet most conflicts involve a sense of both wrongdoing and harm, perhaps on the part of all parties, and these often must be explicitly addressed in any resolution process. Conflict resolution processes often have not done this well.

However, if restorative justice is thought of as a set of guiding questions, it may help to address such issues in conflict transformation processes. What if we found ways to address the following questions not only in restorative processes but in conflict transformation processes as well?

- Who has been hurt in this situation, and what are their needs?
- What obligations result from these hurts and needs, and whose obligations are they?
- What are the causes of these hurts and needs, and what can be done to address them?
- Who has a stake in this situation?
- What is the appropriate process to involve these stakeholders in an effort to put things right and resolve the conflicts?

While preparing to write this commentary, I watched a role play in the United Kingdom by high school students and their principal. In the first role play, they showed the way a fight between two girls had been handled in the past: the principal behind his desk interrogating participants and meting out judgment. In the second, they illustrated a conference or circle process in which the principal took part as one of the participants, without dominating the process, led by a facilitator. Each party told his or her story and expressed a sense of harm and wrongdoing and then began to acknowledge his or her responsibilities. A consensus was achieved that acknowledged some mutual harm as well as shared blame and allowed the disputants to leave as friends.

"Why," I asked myself, "is this called *restorative justice* rather than *mediation*? Why did it specifically emerge from the restorative justice field rather than the mediation field?" After all, the process itself looked much like a form of mediation. Perhaps the reason it emerged from the restorative justice field is that restorative justice, unlike mediation, provided a context and language for specifically naming and dealing with wrongdoing and injustice. It specifically allowed space for concepts of right and wrong, of justice and injustice, to be named and explored, and provided a conflict-resolving concept of justice to facilitate that process. Restorative justice, then, provides a conflict transformation approach that allows wrongdoing to be named and addressed and provides a concept of justice appropriate for this interaction.

Recently my colleague Lisa Schirch has argued that there is a larger umbrella field that she calls "strategic peacebuilding" (Schirch, 2004). Many fields that we often see as somewhat separate or even competing—justice work, conflict resolution, human rights advocacy, trauma healing, and so on—might actually be conceived as part of and contributing to the overall work of building a peaceful and just world. That, perhaps, is the most important agenda ahead for those of us in the conflict transformation and restorative justice fields.

To pursue that agenda, we will have to surmount some substantial personal, institutional, and cultural barriers. A major obstacle is the tendency to divide up the world into separate fields of study and practice, each with its own traditions, definitions of professionalism, and language. The last is especially significant: the interrelated fields of conflict "resolution" and conflict "transformation" themselves use somewhat different terminology and frameworks, and the differences are even more significant between them and the fields of restorative justice or trauma healing. To learn from each other, we will have to develop a common language or at least find ways to understand one another's language.

The competitive nature of our disciplines, and indeed our culture, provides another challenge. To learn from each other, we will have to begin to ask first, "What can I learn from the other?" rather than, "How can I critique the other?" Competition for resources and attention is also an issue. For example, restorative justice is sometimes seen as threatening the hard-won gains of other fields, such as victim services.

To overcome these obstacles, we will need to see each other as coworkers instead of rivals. We will need to come together to learn from each other and to develop joint, coordinated strategies for study and practice. Most important, perhaps, we must together explore our common values and understandings. "Building a just and sustainable peace requires coordination of action and a coherent overall framework," Schirch argues, and calls for us to develop a common vision of "justpeace" (Schirch, 2004).

References

Botcharova, O. "Implementation of Track Two Diplomacy: Developing a Model of Forgiveness." In R. G. Helmick and R. L. Petersen (eds.), *Forgiveness and Reconciliation*. Philadelphia: Templeton Foundation Press, 2001.

Gilligan, J. *Violence: Reflections on a National Epidemic.* New York: Random House, 1996.

Lederach, J. P. *The Little Book of Conflict Transformation.* Intercourse, Pa.: Good Books, 2003.

Levine, P., and Frederick, A. *Waking the Tiger: Healing Trauma: The Innate Capacity to Transform Overwhelming Experiences.* Berkeley, Calif.: North Atlantic Books, 1997.

MacNair, R. *Perpetration-Induced Traumatic Stress: The Psychological Consequences of Killing.* Westport, Conn.: Praeger, 2002.

MacRae, A., and Zehr, H. *The Little Book of Family Group Conferencing, New Zealand Style.* Intercourse, Pa.: Good Books, 2004.

O'Brien, S. P. *Restorative Justice in the States: A National Assessment of Policy Development and Implementation.* Fort Lauderdale, Fla.: Florida Atlantic University, Balanced and Restorative Justice Project, Oct. 2000.

Pranis, K., Stuart, B., and Wedge, M. *Peacemaking Circles: From Crime to Community.* St Paul, Minn.: Living Justice Press, 2003.

Schirch, L. *The Little Book of Strategic Peacebuilding.* Intercourse, Pa.: Good Books, 2004.

Sullivan, D., and Tift, L. *Restorative Justice: Healing the Foundations of Our Everyday Lives.* Monsey, N.Y.: Willow Tree Press, 2001.

Zehr, H. *The Little Book of Restorative Justice.* Intercourse, Pa.: Good Books, 2002a.

Zehr, H. "Journey to Belonging." In E. Weitekamp and H.-J. Kerner (eds.), *Restorative Justice: International Foundations*. Devon, U.K.: Willan Publishing, 2002b.

Zehr, H., and Toews, B. (eds.). *Critical Issues in Restorative Justice*. Monsey, N.Y.: Criminal Justice Press, 2004.

Howard Zehr joined the graduate Conflict Transformation Program (CTP) at Eastern Mennonite University in 1996 as professor of Sociology and Restorative Justice. Prior to this he served for nineteen years as director of the Mennonite Central Committee, U.S. Office on Crime and Justice. He now serves as codirector of CTP.

From the Funder's Perspective

TERRY AMSLER

This special issue of *Conflict Resolution Quarterly* devoted to a survey of the field and applied conflict resolution research is especially welcome and timely. There is an increasing call from many quarters for knowledge about the appropriate applications and demonstrable outcomes of conflict resolution–related practices. At the same time, "industry-like" forces in the field tend to focus our attention more narrowly on specialization within the field. In response, the authors of this issue provide an important compilation of field research and evaluation literature across a broad sweep of the conflict resolution landscape.

This is a very useful piece of work. The similar format of each review article encourages the comparison of findings across sectors. The commentaries help to place the knowledge gained in a more dynamic framework that is particularly useful as the William and Flora Hewlett Foundation makes its exit from a nearly two-decades-long role as a field builder and supporter. The foundation hopes that the collective work presented here will aid practitioners, field-related organizations, researchers, users of these processes, foundations, and others to better understand what we know about the utility, quality, and impacts of conflict resolution practice, as well as provide a base on which further knowledge-building efforts can be considered and pursued.

The review articles are impressive for several reasons, not the least of which is the sheer volume and breadth of material covered. There are rich sources of information across all of the reviewed topic areas, not only about techniques, processes, and satisfaction-related indicators of success but about substantive design and impact studies that support the claim that the conflict resolution field has added considerable and measurable value to our society's ability to address disputes and controversies successfully. There may indeed be fewer studies that adequately document the systemic impacts of conflict resolution programs and processes, as suggested by

Robert Baruch Bush's survey (forthcoming) of conflict resolution scholars asking what intellectual work remains unfinished in the field, and knowledge gaps certainly exist throughout all the practice areas. Yet the assembled literature suggests that we may know more, and may prudently make more claims, than at least some observers of the field may have anticipated. With regard to another concern raised by Bush's survey—that actors in the conflict resolution field have done an inadequate job of advancing policymakers' and parties' receptivity to conflict resolution options—the authors of this issue suggest there is a wealth of information to bring to bear on this continuing challenge.

It is particularly important that these reviews and commentaries appear in a journal such as *CRQ,* which has a broad practitioner readership. The accumulating knowledge about these various communities of practice has direct application to the design of programs and the strategies and tools of practitioners. Individual practitioners have an ethical responsibility to become and remain acquainted with the collective learning that will allow them to more accurately represent their practice to relevant constituencies and potential clients and to continue to improve their own work. It is also fitting for the Association for Conflict Resolution to maintain such a journal for its members and the field and to seek ways to move relevant learning into the minds, models, materials, and skill sets of its members. This "translation" into usable knowledge is another sort of ethical responsibility and can be supported in many ways, including association publications, the Web site, section and chapter work, and section and association meetings. Perhaps the ACR Research section, as well as other groups, may help to complete the circle by encouraging a better integration of the knowledge-building needs of practitioners with the capacities of the academic and research community.

The very soon to be post–Hewlett Conflict Resolution Program world will require that additional leadership and stewardship be demonstrated by the leading conflict resolution organizations. By some measures, the Hewlett Foundation has played only a small part in the full activities of a very broad, diverse, and many-membered field. At the same time, the foundation's role in the creation and support of leading practitioner and support organizations, academic programs, and innovative knowledge-building and field-building initiatives has been substantial and in some cases perhaps critical to the field's development. One might reasonably argue that in some cases, what Hewlett funded helped to define the contours and parameters of the field itself. In the areas of knowledge building, the Hewlett Foundation's role has been unique, with a significant number of academic programs, theory centers, and other institutions and organizations receiving support.

It may therefore be of some benefit to use this issue as a jumping-off point for a discussion about whether there is some slack to be picked up—and by what entities—relating to the ongoing and strategic agenda of building and using knowledge related to the conflict resolution field. There are questions about how knowledge gets transferred effectively, in various directions and for various purposes, among scholars, practitioners, parties in conflict, and the general public. How can the research included here, for instance, be packaged and made more available to policymakers? How can such research be expanded with better data sets, sample sizes, and, where appropriate, experimental or quasi-experimental designs? How can actors in the conflict resolution field, including academics and practitioners, establish more effective means of communicating and collaborating with one another in general and in specific endeavors? How does the specialization of practitioners, and the fact of scholars spread across a variety of disciplines, affect the field's ability to learn and to grow wisely and well?

In general, how do we continue to advance the state of the field's knowledge? And whose job is this, especially with the Hewlett Foundation's departure from its lengthy field-building and stewardship role? The conflict resolution world is fundamentally different in its accomplishments and its challenges than it was even a few years ago. It is probable that the way we think about the nature of the field itself, organize and support its institutional forms, identify and address important areas of inquiry, and craft and implement supportive communication strategies all need revision. There are tremendous opportunities for creative work by existing and new scholars, for thoughtful (and at times courageous) new collaboratives of researchers and practitioners, and for the development of a broader contingent of funders, to address these questions. For this to occur, it is important that individuals, organizations, and institutions in the field step up to take an active role in the considered reflection on these issues and to ensure that investments in the intellectual capital of the field continue. This will require less defensive practitioners, and practitioner organizations with their heads out of the sand and a broader view of their responsibilities. It will also require an academic community working more proactively against the isolation and specialization that can often result in ignorance of work in other sectors and disciplines, and of practice generally.

Practitioners and scholars alike will read, refer to, and, most importantly, use this issue of *CRQ* for some time to come. I thank *Conflict Resolution Quarterly,* the Association for Conflict Resolution, the Indiana Conflict Resolution Institute, and each review and commentary author for their respective contributions to this issue. I extend a special note of appreciation to Lisa Bingham, director of the Indiana Conflict Resolution Institute, and Tricia Jones, *CRQ* editor, for having the vision and leadership to create and bring this idea to fruition. The William and Flora Hewlett Foundation, and its Conflict Resolution program area in particular, are very pleased to be associated with such an important issue of *CRQ.*

Reference

Bush, R. B. The *Knowledge Gaps Project: Unfinished Work, Open Questions.* Forthcoming.

Terry Amsler is the program director for the Hewlett Foundation's Conflict Resolution program area, having served previously as a program officer with responsibilities for the foundation's domestic (U.S.) conflict resolution portfolio. Amsler previously directed the U.S.–based work for Partners for Democratic Change, an international conflict and change management organization, and has also served as the executive director of both the Oregon Dispute Resolution Commission and San Francisco's Community Board Program.

INFORMATION FOR CONTRIBUTORS

Conflict Resolution Quarterly publishes scholarship on relationships between theory, research, and practice in the conflict management and dispute resolution field to promote more effective professional applications. *Conflict Resolution Quarterly* is sponsored by the Association for Conflict Resolution (formerly the Academy of Family Mediators, the Society for Professionals in Dispute Resolution and the Conflict Resolution Education Network).

Articles may focus on any aspect of the conflict resolution process or context, but a primary focus is the behavior, role, and impact of third parties in effectively handling conflict. All theoretical and methodological orientations are welcome. Submission of scholarship with the following emphases is encouraged:

- Discussion of a variety of third-party conflict resolution practices, including dialogue, facilitation, facilitated negotiation, mediation, fact-finding, and arbitration
- Analyses of disputant and third-party behavior, preference, and reaction to conflict situations and conflict management processes
- Consideration of conflict processes in a variety of conflict contexts, including family, organizational, community, court, health care, commercial, international, and educational contexts
- Sensitivity to relational, social, and cultural contexts that define and impact conflict
- Interdisciplinary analyses of conflict resolution and scholarship providing insights applicable across conflict resolution contexts
- Discussion of conflict resolution training and education processes, program development, and program evaluation and impact for programs focusing on the development of more competent conflict resolution in educational, organizational, community, or professional contexts

A defining focus of the journal is the relationships among theory, research, and practice. All articles should specifically address the implications of theory for practice and research directions, how research can better inform practice, or how research can contribute to theory development with important implications for practice.

Conflict Resolution Quarterly publishes conventional articles and other features, including the following:

- *State-of-the-art articles:* Articles providing a comprehensive reporting of current literature on a specific topic and a critique of that theory and research in terms of how well it informs conflict practice.
- *Implications-for-practice commentary:* Readers' comments on the implications for practice of previously published articles, discussing how the articles have informed them in terms of practice.
- *Book reviews:* Reviews of current books on conflict management and dispute resolution. Preference is given to book review essays that review three or more books in a related topic area in light of current scholarship in that area.
- *Training and education notes:* Short articles focusing on the practice of dispute resolution training, studies of dispute resolution training, or reviews of curricula or software programs for dispute resolution training.

Manuscript Preparation

All submissions should be prepared according to the *Chicago Manual of Style* (15th edition, University of Chicago Press). Double-space everything in the manuscript, including quotes and references. Indent the first line of each paragraph and leave no extra space between paragraphs. Margins should be at least one inch wide, and there should be no more than 250 words per manuscript page. Use 8 ½-inch × 11-inch nonerasable bond paper and type or print on one side only. The printed copy from word processors must be in regular typewriter face, not dot matrix type.

The text should be directed to a multidisciplinary audience and be as readable and practical as possible. Illustrate theoretical ideas with specific examples, explain technical terms in nontechnical language, and keep the style clear. Do not include graphs or statistical tables unless necessary for clarity. Spell out such abbreviations as *e.g., etc., i.e., et al.,* and *vs.* in their English equivalents—in other words, use *for example, and so on, that is, and others,* and *versus* (except in legal cases, where *v.* is used).

Conventional Articles and State-of-the-Art Articles. These papers should be no longer than thirty double-spaced pages of text (or 7,500 words). Submissions should include a cover page providing title and author name(s) and contact information (address, telephone number, and e-mail address). Submissions should also include a short abstract of the article (no more than 100 words). Hard-copy paper submissions should include three copies of the paper with a detachable cover page.

Practitioner Responses, Implications-for-Practice, Commentary, Book Reviews, and Training and Education Notes. These features should be no more than ten double-spaced pages of text (or 2,500 words). Submissions should contain a cover page clearly indicating the nature of the submission and providing author name(s) and contact information. Papers can be submitted via e-mail if sent as a file attachment prepared in Word 6.0 or 7.0 or in rich text format. Hard-copy paper submissions should include three copies of the paper with a detachable cover page.

Citations and References. Cite all sources of quotations or attributed ideas in the text, including the original page number of each direct quotation and statistic, according to the following examples:

> Knight (1983) argues cogently that references are a pain in the neck.
> As one authority states, "References are a pain in the neck" (Knight, 1983, p. 35).

Do not use footnotes. Incorporate all footnote material into the text proper, perhaps within parentheses. (Brief *endnotes,* if used sparingly, are acceptable and should be double-spaced in numerical order and placed before the reference section. Endnotes must not contain bibliographical data.)

Use the following examples in typing references:

Single-author book or pamphlet
Hunter, J. E. *Meta-Analysis: Cumulating Research Findings Across Studies.* Newbury Park, Calif.: Sage, 1982.

Multiple-author book or pamphlet
Hammond, D. C., Hepworth, D. H., and Smith, V. G. *Improving Therapeutic Communication: A Guide for Developing Effective Techniques.* San Francisco: Jossey-Bass, 1977.

Edited book/multiple edition
Brakel, S. J., and Rock, R. S. (eds.). *The Mentally Disabled and the Law.* (2nd ed.) Chicago: University of Chicago Press, 1971.

Chapter in an edited book
Patterson, G. R. "Beyond Technology: The Next Stage in the Development of Parent Training." In L. L'Abate (ed.), *Handbook of Family Psychology and Therapy.* Vol. 2. Homewood, Ill.: Dorsey Press, 1985.

Journal or magazine article
Aussieker, B., and Garabino, J. W. "Measuring Faculty Unionism: Quantity and Quality." *Industrial Relations,* 1973, *12* (1), 117–124.

Paper read at a meeting
Sherman, L. W., Gartin, P. R., Doi, D., and Miler, S. "The Effects of Jail Time on Drunk Drivers." Paper presented at the American Society of Criminology, Atlanta, Nov. 6, 1986.

Unpublished report
Keim, S. T., and Carney, M. K. "A Cost-Benefit Study of Selected Clinical Education Programs for Professional and Allied Health Personnel." Arlington, Va.: Bureau of Business and Economic Research, University of Texas, 1975.

Government report
Florida Advisory Council on Intergovernmental Relations. *Impact Fees in Florida.* Tallahassee: Florida Advisory Council on Intergovernmental Relations, 1986.

Unpublished dissertation
Johnson, W. P. "A Study of the Acceptance of Management Performance Evaluation Recommendations by Federal Agencies: Lessons from GAO Reports Issued in FY 1983." Unpublished doctoral dissertation, Department of Business Administration, George Mason University, Washington, D.C., 1986.

Figures, Tables, and Exhibits.
Clean copies of figures should accompany the manuscript. Upon an article's acceptance, authors must provide camera-ready artwork. Tables, figures, and exhibits should be double-spaced on separate pages, and table notes should be keyed to the body of the table with letters rather than with numbers or asterisks. Exhibits (used in place of appendixes) should also be typed double-spaced on separate pages. All figures, tables, and exhibits should have short, descriptive titles and must be called out in the text.

Publication Process

When a manuscript is accepted for publication, authors are asked to sign a letter of agreement granting the publisher the right to copyedit, publish, and copyright the material. Manuscripts under review for possible publication in *Conflict Resolution Quarterly* should not be submitted for review elsewhere or have been previously published elsewhere.

Article submissions and questions regarding editorial matters should be sent to:

Tricia S. Jones, Editor
Conflict Resolution Quarterly
Department of Psychological Studies
College of Education
Temple University
Philadelphia, PA 19122
tsjones@astro.temple.edu

ORDERING INFORMATION

MAIL ORDERS TO:
Jossey-Bass
989 Market Street
San Francisco, CA 94103-1741

PHONE subscription or single-copy orders toll free to (888) 378-2537 or to (415) 433-1767 (toll call).

FAX orders toll free to (888) 481-2665.

SUBSCRIPTIONS cost $80.00 for individuals in the United States, Canada, and Mexico; $205.00 for institutions, agencies, and libraries in the United States; $245.00 for institutions, agencies, and libraries in Canada and Mexico; and $104.00 for individuals and $279.00 for institutions, agencies, and libraries in the rest of the world. Standing orders are accepted. New York residents, add local sales tax. (For subscriptions outside the United States, orders must be prepaid in U.S. dollars by check drawn on a U.S. bank or charged to VISA, MasterCard, or American Express.)

SINGLE COPIES cost $40.00 plus shipping (see below) when payment accompanies order. California, New Jersey, New York, and Washington, D.C., residents, please include appropriate sales tax. Canadian residents, add GST and any local taxes. Billed orders will be charged shipping and handling. No billed shipments to Post Office boxes. (Orders from outside the United States must be prepaid in U.S. dollars by check drawn on a U.S. bank or charged to VISA, MasterCard, or American Express.)

SHIPPING (single copies only): $5.00 for first item, $3.00 for each additional item. Call for information on overnight delivery or shipments outside the United States.

ALL ORDERS must include either the name of an individual or an official purchase order number. Please submit your orders as follows:
Subscriptions: specify issue (for example, CRQ19:1) with which you would like subscription to begin.
Single copies: specify volume and issue number.

MICROFILM available from University Microfilms, 300 North Zeeb Road, Ann Arbor, MI 48106.

DISCOUNTS FOR QUANTITY ORDERS are available. For information, please write to Jossey-Bass, 989 Market Street, San Francisco, CA 94103-1741.

LIBRARIANS are encouraged to write to Jossey-Bass for a free sample issue.

VISIT THE JOSSEY-BASS HOME PAGE at http://www.josseybass.com on the World Wide Web for an order form or information about other titles of interest.